BATTLES OVER FREE TRADE

CONTENTS OF THE EDITION

VOLUME 1
General Introduction
By Mark Duckenfield

The Advent of Free Trade, 1776–1846
Edited by Gordon Bannerman and Cheryl Schonhardt-Bailey

VOLUME 2
The Consolidation of Free Trade, 1847–1878
Edited by Gordon Bannerman and Anthony Howe

VOLUME 3
The Challenge of Economic Nationalism, 1879–1939
Edited by Anthony Howe and Mark Duckenfield

VOLUME 4
The Emergence of Multilateral Trade, 1940–2006
Edited by Mark Duckenfield

Index

BATTLES OVER FREE TRADE

General Editor: Mark Duckenfield

Volume 3
The Challenge of Economic Nationalism, 1879–1939

Edited by
Anthony Howe and Mark Duckenfield

LONDON AND NEW YORK

First published 2008 by Pickering & Chatto (Publishers) Limited

Published 2016 by Routledge
2 Park Square, Milton Park, Abingdon, Oxfordshire OX14 4RN
711 Third Avenue, New York, NY 10017, USA

First issued in paperback 2015

Routledge is an imprint of the Taylor & Francis Group, an informa business

Copyright © Taylor & Francis 2008
Copyright © Editorial material Anthony Howe and Mark Duckenfield

All rights reserved, including those of translation into foreign languages. No part of this book may be reprinted or reproduced or utilised in any form or by any electronic, mechanical, or other means, now known or hereafter invented, including photocopying and recording, or in any information storage or retrieval system, without permission in writing from the publishers.

Notice:
Product or corporate names may be trademarks or registered trademarks, and are used only for identification and explanation without intent to infringe.

BRITISH LIBRARY CATALOGUING IN PUBLICATION DATA

Battles over free trade: Anglo-American experiences with international trade, 1776–2006
1. Free trade – History
I. Duckenfield, Mark
382.7'1'09

ISBN-13: 978-1-138-66051-9 (pbk)
ISBN-13: 978-1-1387-5034-0 (hbk)
ISBN-13: 978-1-85196-935-7 (set)

Typeset by Pickering & Chatto (Publishers) Limited

CONTENTS

Introduction   xi

The Rise and Fall of Fair Trade, 1879–92   1

'The Past and the Future. A Historical Sketch of Fair Trade, and Commercial Policy since "the Settlement of 1846"', *Fair-Trade* (1885)   7

'The Story of the Movement', *Fair Trade* (1888)   10

Robert Andrew Macfie, Letter to the Shipping and Mercantile Gazette, 25 November 1880, in R. A. Macfie, *Cries in a Crisis* (1881)   13

G. W. Medley, 'England under Free Trade' (1881), in *Pamphlets and Addresses* (1899)   15

Annie Besant, 'What is Really Free Trade', in *Free Trade v. Fair Trade* (1881)   17

Sampson Lloyd, *The Fair Trade Policy: A Reply to the Charge of 'taxing the Poor Man's Loaf'* (1882)   23

'The Fair-Trade Party'; Correspondence of J. B. Barkworth, 'Protection for Home Agriculture', and R. A. Macfie 'Protection for Manufacturing Industries', *Fair-Trade* (1886)   30

Manchester Chamber of Commerce, 'Manchester and the Manchesterians: Storming the Citadel', *Fair-Trade* (1886)   34

'Causes of Trade Depression', *Fair-Trade* (1886)   36

Royal Commission on Depression in Trade and Industry, 'Minority "Fair Trade" Report', *Parliamentary Papers* (1886)   40

Robert Andrew Macfie, 'The Fair-Trade Policy', *Fair Trade* (1888)   44

Tariffs and Empire, 1880–1902   45

G. Smith, 'The Canadian Tariff', *Contemporary Review* (1881)   49

G. Baden Powell, 'Protection in Young Communities', *Fortnightly Review* (1882)   51

S. Bourne, 'Imperial Federation in its Commercial Aspect', *Imperial Federation* (1886)   56

'Imperial Federation', *Fair-Trade* (1886)   59

'The Fair Trade Scheme of Commercial Federation', *Imperial Federation* (1887)	62
R. Giffen, 'Commercial Union between the UK and its Colonies' (1891)	64
Howard Vincent, *Commercial Union of the Empire* (1891)	67
British Empire League, *Report of Inaugural Meeting of the League* ([1896])	72
British Empire League, *Report of Speech of the Right Hon. Joseph Chamberlain* ([1896])	74

Tariff Wars in Europe, 1880–1914   77

'Protection in Germany', *Economist* (1881)	83
Trade and Treaties Committee, First Report, 24 January 1891, *Parliamentary Papers* (1890–1)	84
R. Giffen, 'The Relative Growth of Free Trade and Protection', 25 May 1892	88
Memo on Terminating the Belgian and German Commercial Treaties, 10 June 1897	90
Tariff Wars between European States: Report on the Franco-Italian Tariff War, 1888–99; Reports on the Tariff War between Germany and Russia; Summary of the Franco-Swiss Tariff War, 1893–5, *Parliamentary Papers* (1904)	96
'Commercial Diplomacy 1860–1902'	106

Free Trade versus Tariff Reform: The Edwardian Battleground   115

R. D. Denman, 'The City and the Tariff Question', *Westminster Gazette*, 23 June 1903	119
Philip Snowden, *The Chamberlain Bubble* (1903)	121
Editorial on Labour Representatives and the Tariff Commission, *Morning Post*, 16 January 1904	124
'What Co-Operative Women Think', *Free Trader*, 23 October 1903	127
C. Booth, 'Fiscal Reform', *National Review*, January 1904	129
B. R. Wise, *Free Trade and Imperial Preference* (1905)	133
Tariff Commission Memo, 'Colonial Preference and Imperial Reciprocity', 22 July 1908	138
F. W. Hirst, 'The City and Tariff Reform', *Free Trader*, May 1910	142

Tariff Battles in North America, 1880–1914   145

W. E. Gladstone, 'Free Trade', *North American Review* (1890)	149
Editorial, *The Times*, 9 October 1890	152
A. K. McClure, *The McKinley Tariff Robbery and Fraud* (1892)	154

Edward Atkinson, 'Arguments in Favor of such Discrimination in Framing the Tariff as shall Best Promote Domestic Industry', in *Arguments against the Dingley Bill* (1897) 157
J. A. Hobson, *The Fruits of American Protection* (1907) 160
'Tariff Reform in Canada', *Nation*, 20 August 1910 165
Canadian National League, *Reciprocity with the United States* (1911) 168
'Canada's Answer', *The Standard of Empire*, 29 September 1911 170
'The New American Tariff', *Economist* (1913) 173
Swire Smith, *The New American Tariff (Simmons-Underwood) and the Wool Industry of Bradford* (1914) 175

The Paris Economic Conference, 1916 183
Foreign Office Note of Invitation from the French Ambassador for the British Government to Participate in an Economic Conference in Paris, 10 February 1916 187
Foreign Minister Edward Grey's Memorandum on British Participation in Paris Economic Conference, 11 February 1916 188
Confidential Correspondence between Edward Grey and Sir Francis Villiers, British Ambassador to Belgium, 6 March 1916 and 5 April 1916 189
J. A. Hobson, 'The New Protectionism', *War and Peace* (1916) 192
'The End of the War and After', *Economist* (1916) 197
'Who Were Our Best Customers?', *Economist* (1916) 201
'The Paris Economic Conference and After', *New Statesman* (1916) 206
Commercial Correspondence between Edward Grey and Sir Francis Villiers, British Ambassador to Belgium, 27 June 1916 209
Report on the American Press's Response to the Paris Conference, June 1916 210
'The Economic War', *War and Peace* (1916) 212
'The Allies' Economic Combine', *New Republic* (1916) 215
Considered Views of Interdepartmental Committee to Consider Dependence of the British Empire on the United States, October 1916 218
Confidential Cabinet Report of the Foreign Office on the Interdepartmental Committee to Consider the Dependence of the British Empire on the United States, 31 October 1916 219
Confidential Telegram from Sir Conyngham Greene (British Ambassador to Japan) to Edward Grey (Foreign Minister) regarding Japanese Participation in the Paris Economic Conference, 27 June 1916 229
Recommendations of the Economic Conference of the Allies Held at Paris on June 14, 15, 16 and 17, 1916, *Parliamentary Papers* (1916) 237

A. Stanley, 'Economic Desiderata in the Terms of Peace', February 1917 — 243
Secret Report on Economic and Non-Territorial Desiderata, Committee on Terms of Peace, Imperial War Cabinet, April 1917 — 247
Memorandum by the Board of Trade on Economic Considerations Affecting the Terms of Peace, November 1918 — 252

The Smoot-Hawley Tariff Act, 1930 — 261
Republican Party Platform of 1928, 12 June 1928 — 265
'Hoover Promises to Call Congress to Act on Farm Aid if December Session Fails', *The New York Times*, 28 October 1928 — 267
Herbert Hoover, State of the Union Address, 3 December 1929 — 269
'1028 Economists Ask Hoover to Veto Pending Tariff Bill', *The New York Times*, 5 May 1930 — 272
Official Protests about Tariff Bill 1930 from Foreign Governments, *Congressional Record*, 9 June 1930 — 275
Herbert Hoover, Statement Upon Signing the Tariff Bill 1930 into Law, 15 June 1930 — 290
'The New American Tariff', *Economist* (1930) — 294
'The United States Tariff and Swiss Trade', *Economist* (1930) — 295
Cordell Hull, 'Economic Policies of the Government', *Congressional Record*, 16 February 1931 — 296
Reed Smoot, 'Our Tariff and the Depression', *Current History* (1931) — 300
Franklin D. Roosevelt, National Radio Address, 'Forgotten Man', 8 April 1932 — 311
Herbert Hoover, Campaign Speech at Butler University, Indianapolis, Indiana, 28 October 1932 — 314
'Trade Agreements or Free Trade?', *Review of the River Plate*, 29 July 1934, translated by UK Embassy, Buenos Aires — 322

The Ottawa Imperial Economic Conference, 1931–2 — 325
Report of the Committee on the Proposed Imperial Economic Conference at Ottawa, 23 November 1931 — 329
'Dominion Industries', *The Times*, 18 December 1931 — 337
'Memorandum of a Conversation with the [Canadian] Prime Minister on Friday, March 11th, Concerning Agenda for the Imperial Conference', 14 March 1931 — 340
Letter from the High Commissioner for the United Kingdom in Ottawa to Sir Edward Harding (Under Secretary of State for Dominions), 17 March 1932 — 344

Minutes of the Fourth Meeting at the Board of Trade with Industrial Advisors [Motor Trade Representatives] Prior to the Ottawa Imperial Economic Conference, 3 June 1932	346
'Imperial Preference', *Economist* (1932)	349
Notes on the Cotton Delegation in a Letter from the High Commissioner for the United Kingdom in Ottawa to G. G. Whiskard (Dominions Office), 15 June 1932	353
Secret Note by the United Kingdom Delegation on the Canadian Tariff Proposals, 8 August 1932	356
Memorandum by Industrial Advisors Representing the British Trades Union Congress on the Imperial Economic Conference, 8 August 1932	360
J. G. Coates (Leader of the New Zealand Reform Party) to Stanley Baldwin, 8 August 1932	362
Most Secret Report of a (UK) Delegation Meeting at Ottawa on the Australian and New Zealand Negotiation and a Duty on Meat, 15 August 1932	364
Selections from the Ottawa Agreement, August 1932	370
'Textile Industry Reserves Opinion', *Montreal Gazette*, 23 August 1932	379
'Premier Disappointed: Taschereau Says Little Done For Lumber Industry', *Montreal Gazette*, 23 August 1932	381
'Ottawa Reactions', *Sydney Morning Herald*, 24 August 1932	382
'The Riddle of Ottawa', *Adelaide Advertiser*, 24 August 1932	384
'The Harvest of Ottawa', *Economist* (1932)	386
'An Ottawa Impression', *Economist* (1932)	389
Copyrights and Permissions	393

INTRODUCTION

As previous volumes have shown, while the making of trade policy has rarely been simply the product of abstract economic reasoning, it has rarely escaped from the intellectual climate of the times. Evangelical religion and classical political economy were therefore both vital conditioning forces in the rise of free trade, and in the same degree the challenge of economic nationalism after 1879 was informed and reinforced by a widespread reaction against classical political economy and laissez-faire which took the forms of neo-mercantilism and historical economics. This intellectual challenge was at its sharpest in Germany, where the 'Socialists of the Chair' had spearheaded the attack on what they constructed as 'Manchesterism'; against the classical emphasis on the individual in the market, impelled by self-interest, they now valorized the importance of the historical forces shaping economies, and the priority of the interest of the state as a good greater than the sum of the self-interests of the individual.[1] In this reaction, an important part was played by the neo-Listians (arguably Listian ideas of self-sufficiency were of greater influence in the 1880s than they had been in the 1840s), reinforced by economists such as Adolf Wagner and Gustav Schmoller, and many of the members of the influential Verein für Sozialpolitik.[2] Significantly, besides the republication of Friedrich List's works in the 1880s (including the first complete English edition of *The National System of Political Economy* in 1885), Schmoller, author of many works on trade policy, had produced a major re-evaluation of mercantilism, which epitomized the historical economists' rejection of Smithian economics, and inspired similar reassessments in other countries, for example by William Ashley and W. A. S. Hewins in Britain.[3] Similarly in Italy, the Venetian school of 'Socialists of the Chair', led by Luigi Luzzatti, stressed the need for the state to use tariffs as part of its regulation of society; significantly Luzzatti himself was later in charge of renegotiating Italy's commercial treaties. But arguably it was the Listian model, itself based on a high external tariff and protection for infant industries, which now became the leading nostrum of statesmen seeking to add tariffs to the armoury of the state. List himself had borrowed his model from the Americans Alexander Hamilton and Henry Clay, and possibly the growing economic success of the United States now added to the prestige of this model, replacing that of British free trade. That List's influence was widespread from the 1880s can be found especially in states with burgeoning nationalist movements such as Hungary, Catalonia, Bulgaria, India and China (where his works were translated in the 1920s). In Ireland, the intellectual progenitor of Sinn Fein, Arthur Griffiths, adopted List's 'National System' as his gospel and viewed Bismarckian Germany as an example of its practical success.

Despite these trends, however, one might still argue that there was no widespread repudiation of the pure theory of free trade. In Britain, for example, this was restated effectively against the tariff reformers by Alfred Marshall and others; likewise in Germany, the intellectual basis of protectionist policies was repudiated by both left Liberals such as Lujo Brentano and by revisionist Socialists, such as Eduard Bernstein. During the First World War, the historical economists' case that tariffs should become an instrument of the state naturally gained a greater hearing in all belligerent powers, but it did not replace the view stated by J. A. Hobson and others that the international division of labour should be restored as fully as possible. Even in 1916 – in the midst of the war – the Allied Economic Conference in Paris which advocated the creation of a preferential system of trade among the Allies with discrimination against neutral and outright punitive measures against Germany was met with scepticism among Liberals in Britain and scorn in the then neutral United States. After the First World War, there is little doubt that among academic economists, classical political economy held sway. This had probably always been true even in the United States, where the leading university-based economists were most often proponents of free trade. This advocacy was most powerfully voiced in the famous protest of over 1,000 members of the American Economic Association against the Smoot-Hawley tariff in 1930.

The interwar Great Depression undermined the standing of classical economists as laissez-faire policies were widely blamed for the collapse in industrial output, depressed farm prices and the surge in unemployment throughout the industrialized world. Among many new and old democracies, public opinion no longer tolerated a passive state in the face of economic calamity. Traditional calls from distressed industries and their workers for tariff protection were accompanied by growing pressure for radical interventions in the market and for state regulation and supervision of the economy. This environment proved fertile ground for a return to protectionist policies, autarky and national self-sufficiency.

II

The intellectual breach with classical political economy from the 1870s is in itself insufficient to explain the depth of the reaction towards economic nationalism. Nevertheless, the widespread resort to 'national' policies directly related to List's concerns and those of the historical economists, whereby statesmen rejected the British model of a revenue-only tariff, in favour of using tariffs to shape economies in relation to resources and non-economic goals. However, while the British model had sought to limit the power of rent-seeking interests, the new model arguably encouraged the mobilization of economic interests in search of state favours. One of the key aspects therefore of the challenge to free trade was the degree to which states now favoured coalitions of interests who promised to bargain their political support in exchange for 'rents'. The classic example of this mode of political economy occurred in Germany, where the 'marriage of iron and rye' emerged as the basis of the Bismarckian regime after 1879.[4] In the United States, the Republicans forged more of a marriage of 'wheat and tin' with their 1860 campaign slogan of 'Vote Yourself a Farm, Vote Yourself a Tariff'. Farmers desiring homesteads and industrializing cities in the American north-east all found this an enticing appeal, only the southern plantation states favoured free trade – but the southern economy, of course, was dependent on extravagant state intervention to prop up their system of slave labour, a system which created vast rents for the slavocracy until its destruction in the American Civil War.

The so-called 'Great Depression', 1873–96, has often been considered crucial in the mobilization of such interests. The slowdown, as it seemed to many contemporaries, in the European economy, encouraged disillusionment with free trade, while encouraging interest groups hit by falling prices and falling profits to seek state support. The influx of cheap American grain imports not only threatened the agrarian sector, but the 'production profiles' of economies all revealed exposed sectors which readily sought state support, whether textiles in Germany or steel and tinplate in America. Not only were producers mobilized but increasingly unemployment (or fear of it) made possible cross-class coalitions, whereby employers drew workers away from nascent socialism to the employment benefits of tariffs which kept out 'unfair' foreign competition.[5]

Some historians have therefore argued that democratization in the 1880s increased the demand for protection, but it is the evidence of economic pressure group activity which is the more powerful.[6] For example the part played in Germany by the Central Association of German Manufacturers by campaigning, before its implementation, against the free trade tariff of 1877, set a pattern in which a variety of industrial and agrarian organizations sought to shape tariff policy. France also provides an instructive example, for here the failure to renew the lynchpin of the free trade era, the Anglo-French commercial treaty of 1860, had initially led not to a return to full-scale protection but to a regime of modified free trade.[7] This was to change decisively with the Méline tariff of 1892. France had only belatedly felt the effects of falling world prices, but her rural producers had become increasingly well organized, with membership of the Society of French Agriculturalists growing from 1,782 in 1863 to some 10,000 in 1890. Although avowedly non-party, it was central to protectionist politics in France. The French countryside also saw the flourishing of *syndicats agricoles*, growing from 93 in 1886 to 863 in 1896, with over 300,000 members. Their weekly paper, *La Democratic Rurale*, was the leading organ of Jules Méline's campaign for higher tariffs. However, Méline also effectively allied with industrial protectionists, so that by 1890 the majority in the French Chamber of Deputies favoured protection. With the successful passage of the Méline tariff in 1892, France acquired the highest levels of tariffs on foodstuffs in Europe, helping to ensure France remained 'a land of peasants' but also in effect slowing down economic modernization and encouraging the French retreat into self-sufficiency which lasted well into the twentieth century.[8]

Well-organized producers have therefore been readily identified as the central force behind the return to protection in Europe after 1879, just as they have been seen as crucial to the coalition of interests which supported high protection in the United States. There the tariff had been a crucial revenue instrument for the government during the Civil War but had later become a key means of integrating diverse economic interests in support of a growing tariff wall.[9] Nevertheless, the interests of such producers were also commonly linked with the interests of working men, where tariffs were identified with employment prospects, while the revenue from tariffs contributed to the funds available for state welfare benefits. American tariffs were therefore often part of a form of welfare politics which sought to undercut the appeal of free trade and socialism. In France the theme of rural democracy was distinctly anti-socialist, linking the defence of agriculture with the rapprochement of classes and the national interest.[10] In Germany, too, Otto von Bismarck put tariffs at the centre of an avowedly national policy, relegating free traders to the ranks of nihilists and enemies of the Reich. More widely, neo-mercantilism, which stressed the nation-state as the key unit, came to focus on the division of labour within the nation rather than within the unfettered world market.

In this context, therefore, it is plausible to suggest that the return to protection in Europe was fuelled by economic interest groups which were either threatened by free imports or which required state support to compete successfully in the world market. For example it was widely held that Continental sugar-beet producers won markets only with the support of state subsidies and likewise that German carriage rates were set at unfairly low levels to assist exporters. But the converse is also plausible, that liberal free trade policies had reflected the interests of export producers, classically cotton masters in England, or later car manufacturers in the United States. It is also clear that in the debate over the reintroduction of tariffs in Britain in the early twentieth century, many producers dependent on exports (or free imports of raw materials) continued to support free trade. One can also argue that in the case of Britain, the surviving free trade power, the economy was increasingly based on the service sector, with the City of London dominating the world's shipping, insurance and banking sectors. Britain it seemed therefore had the most to gain from the free flow of commodities and services in an increasingly global economic system. But while in theory free trade benefited the City of London, paradoxically City financiers and rentiers increasingly drifted politically to support for tariffs.[11]

Arguably in Britain, the keenest free traders were to be found not in the City of London but in the working-class electorate. In part, this reflected the importance of employment in export industries but more deeply it was the product of a deeply-rooted political culture in which free trade was identified with working-class welfare through opposition to food taxes, and fear of a return to the 'Hungry Forties'. Tariffs in Britain tended to be identified through the lens of consumption, rather than that of production, and in the early twentieth century the electorate, and non-electors, especially women, were galvanized as consumers.[12] Interestingly with respect to Britain, the leading Treasury official Edward Hamilton wrote, 'In the days of Protection, producers were more powerful than consumers. Nowadays consumers are the more powerful and will remain so.'[13] In addition, whereas in the 1840s the rent-seekers were identified as self-interested aristocrats, it was now the growing number of large companies and trusts that were identified with tariffs, which threatened not only consumers but small shopkeepers and small producers. In Germany cartels had supposedly emerged as the leading beneficiaries of tariffs, while in the United States the revolt against the tariff, which some discerned by 1913, was fuelled by the threat which rent-seeking trusts posed to democracy and political morality. Even in Britain, the increasing tendency of industrialists to combine effectively, whether in trusts, cartels or employers' associations, also posed a long-term threat to free trade. Such bodies were often linked to 'trade warriors' such as Dudley Docker and the Federation of British Industries, while the Empire Industries Association also became a powerful lobbying group for tariffs in the 1920s.[14]

III

The demand for tariffs in Europe after 1879 offered to politicians the opportunity to build up broad-based coalitions of producers, whose interests would be satisfied by the construction of intricate tariffs as world customs schedules lengthened in the years after 1879. In the United States too the Republican

Party had in effect emerged as such a coalition during and after the Civil War. In this way political life itself was restructured along relatively 'consensual' economic lines rather than divisive constitutional and religious ones. For example, in Germany, tariffs were central to Bismarck's 'Second Founding' of the Reich; for decades, while pursuing free trade policies, Bismarck had relied on Liberal and Protestant support in the unification of Germany and in the Kulturkampf; in 1878–9, he abandoned these domestic allies and used tariffs to help cement a new anti-socialist alliance based on the landed, clerical and conservative parties. Nevertheless, the state itself also stood to gain in direct ways from the widespread resort to tariffs in Europe after 1879 for, so long as tariffs did not become prohibitive, they offered to states a source of revenue which was more easily tapped and less visible and politically contentious than direct taxation. It is therefore significant that Britain, the only country with an efficient system of direct taxation, was the only country not to reintroduce tariffs after 1879.

The fiscal advantages of tariffs were uppermost in Germany. Within the federal structure of the empire, where direct taxation was local, arguably the most attractive feature of tariffs to Bismarck was as a form of revenue that was imperial, and which even permitted a reduction of demands on local taxes. J. M. Hobson has calculated that Germany's customs revenue yield grew as a proportion of net revenue from 29 per cent in 1875–9 to 52 per cent after the tariff acts of 1885 and 1887.[15] This additional revenue could be devoted to state goals, which included welfare benefits but which were primarily geared to the military requirements of the state, and which came in a form that avoided the extensive parliamentary battles over expenditure that Bismarck had faced in the 1870s. Likewise in Russia, it can be plausibly argued that tariffs were primarily designed for their fiscal yield, and that they were used mainly to finance the military ambitions of the tsarist state. In Italy, British politicians observed a clear link between protection and militarism, lamenting the link between 'national vanity' and 'bloated armaments'. All states faced growing demands for revenue in the later nineteenth century, but tariffs in most cases were the least contentious way to raise such revenue. Only Britain remained the exception, and here those growing demands were met by increased direct taxation, signified by the People's Budget of 1909. Interestingly, in the United States, the possibility of liberalizing the tariff was closely linked to the introduction of income tax, for the first federal income tax was part and parcel of the Underwood tariff of 1913.[16] Income tax and freer trade were presented as the best means to free the American people from the rapacity of the 'trusts'. For the Democratic Party, long in opposition at the federal level, the income tax provided the means of liberating the central government from the fiscal demands of a revenue-based tariff, allowing them to generate revenue while simultaneously enabling them to make good on their free trade promises. In time, it opened up an avenue for funding the creation of the New Deal and America's welfare state.

The German and American federal models remained an important part of European debate on free trade. In the creation of both states, the emergence of the nation had been in part based on its economic success as a customs union, integrating states which had formerly had very different external tariffs. The idea of the customs' union remained at the forefront too of British colonial debate, with the slow evolution towards intra-colonial free trade and Australian federation in 1901, the most serious obstacle to which had been the conflict between 'free trade' New South Wales and 'protectionist' Victoria. This remained a key battlefield in Australian politics after the federation was created, with a tariff much closer to that of Victoria than New South Wales. In the next few years the tariff battle remained at the heart of Australian politics until Alfred Deakin successfully reshaped a ministerial and electoral consensus in favour of imperial preference and 'new protection', supported by former free traders such as B. R. Wise who now advocated 'democratic imperialism' against 'colourless cosmopolitanism'.[17]

But the 'Zollverein' model appealed most of all to those who wished to unify not simply the Australian or South African colonies but the British empire as a whole. The notion of an imperial Zollverein had occasionally surfaced in British politics in the 1840s but it only became an important political platform with the fair trade movement of the 1880s. This movement was in part a reaction to the breakdown of the Cobden treaty system, inspired by the belief that Britain should not offer free trade to those who did not reciprocate, but it also was inspired by the desire to link together the British empire, whose tariff politics had become increasingly fragmented as many self-governing parts of the empire had resorted to protectionist tariffs. An imperial Zollverein – a customs union with a common external tariff – therefore grew in appeal, as a means of greater imperial economic unity and a means to meet the growing economic challenge of the rising industrial powers of Europe and the United States. Fair trade failed, but the desire for some form of imperial Zollverein remained a paramount theme in imperial politics, and in the early twentieth century it was brought to the heart of British politics by the tariff reformers, although their Zollverein was to be based on protection and imperial preference rather than free intra-imperial trade. The tariff reformers looked directly to the inspiration of the German historical economists, seeking a 'national policy' for the British empire which would better serve its interests than the 'curse of Cobdenism', Britain's attachment to unilateral cosmopolitan free trade, which they believed undermined Britain's long-term economic power.[18] The leading geographer Halford Mackinder now abandoned free trade in favour of a model of the world divided into tariffs blocs as a necessity in a new international order. Britain, the tariff reformers believed, needed a constructive imperial strategy in order to survive in a new age of global economic closure, signalled not only by tariff wars in Europe but by the re-emergence of the idea of Mitteleuropa, and the consolidation of land-based territorial states in Europe.[19] Some economists sympathetic to tariffs now reinterpreted Adam Smith as a prophet of empire, rather than of its dissolution.[20]

In Britain, the challenge to over half a century of free trade consensus emerged with Joseph Chamberlain's call for 'tariff reform' in the aftermath of the Boer War.[21] Chamberlain saw tariff reform as a solution to the many foreign and domestic challenges facing British policymakers in the early years of the twentieth century. The economic threats to Britain's industry of American and German producers could be stymied by depriving them of markets throughout the British Empire. In international relations, Britain's eroding position could be shored up through a consolidation of the Empire with imperial preference on tariffs, making the Empire a single economic entity. Finally, the domestic discontent evidenced by the increasingly strident demands of Britain's working classes could be resolved through welfare programmes paid for by the expanded tariff list. All of these, but especially the last, would enhance the electoral prospects of the Conservative Party, which was in danger of being eclipsed in an age of mass democracy. An influential minority of the Conservative Party remained committed to free trade and Chamberlain's public campaign brought about not only his own resignation from the Cabinet, but also those of prominent free traders, including Chancellor of the Exchequer Charles Ritchie. This deep political split fatally weakened the Conservatives in the run-up to the 1906 general election, in which they were comprehensively defeated by the Liberal Party rallying around its traditional support for free trade. Deprived of influence over government, supporters of the newly-created Tariff Reform League championed imperial preference and organized rallies, recruited speakers and distributed pamphlets throughout the country. By 1908, the Tariff Reform League was annually sending out 120,000 copies of its journal, *Monthly Notes*, to its members and it had over 600 local branches – most with hundreds of members – by 1910, with a budget of over £42,000 in 1908 alone.[22]

The explanation for the pre-war defeat of tariff reform also lay in the battle of ideas and interests. The free trade case was sustained by the vitality of the economist's belief that the international division of labour would ensure the welfare of the working classes at home and the progressive development of the extra-European world. Within this vision, Britain's attachment to free trade continued to provide not simply a benefit to Britain but a public good for the world as a whole, keeping open the maximum extent of free trade. The directly-governed British empire continued to provide the world's largest free trade zone, with 300 million consumers, while the domestic British market continued to absorb huge amounts of foreign goods, especially from Germany and the United States.[23] In so far as recent commentators have argued that the period 1890–1914 approximated one comparable to the late twentieth century in terms of economic globalization, this rested to a large extent upon Britain's readiness to forego tariffs, retaliation and trade wars. Arguably, Britain's attachment to free trade was, as her critics claimed, part of her own 'national policy', merely disguised in a philanthropic garb. The French economic nationalist Jules Méline thus claimed he would have been a free trader had he been English. However, the hegemony based on free trade also spawned the economic competitors which would come to undermine that very hegemony.[24] As John Maynard Keynes was to argue, the period before 1914 had seen the emergence of the economic 'serpents' in the shape of bounties, cartels, preferential and protectionist tariffs which would destroy the antebellum economic 'paradise' nurtured by British free trade.[25]

After three successive electoral defeats – once in 1906 and twice in 1910 – the challenge to Britain's tradition of free trade only began to make headway under the pressures of the First World War. Wartime finance included a variety of import duties, first on luxuries, then on a much broader range of consumables. Allied efforts to engage in total economic warfare against the Central Powers and their desire to rebuild their economies and shackle Germany's after the war led the Paris Economic Conference (1916) not only to encourage further wartime restrictions on neutral trade with the Continent and closer Allied economic cooperation, but to call for trade preferences among the Allied powers to continue after the war. In the eyes of wartime geostrategists, what had been imperial preference before the war became Allied preference during the war.

Despite the proclamation of Allied solidarity during the war, the economic climate after 1918 was extremely harsh. The post-war reconstruction of the world financial system proved a fragile edifice in all its manifestations. The restored gold standard – a pale reflection of its former glory in any event – lasted a mere six years and the international trading system was never fully restored. In the United States, the Republican Party, having won the presidency and control of both houses of Congress, passed the 1922 Fordney-McCumber tariff. Designed to protect American industry from resurgent European competition and to reduce income tax rates, it raised import duties by almost 50 per cent over the levels in the Underwood Act. French tariffs were quickly reinstated after the war to assist in the rebuilding of French industry. Australia remained a high tariff country with substantial protection for industry subsidizing less efficient agricultural producers – indeed, the 1929 Brigden Report provided an intellectual justification for Australia's high tariffs, arguing that the international market power in wool and wheat enjoyed by Australia allowed tariffs to be imposed to safeguard industry without serious disadvantages.[26] Even Canadian tariffs, while decreasing in the 1920s, remained well above British levels.

The Smoot-Hawley tariff had a series of international consequences, as dozens of countries rushed to retaliate against the United States with higher tariffs of their own. Among the British Dominions, Canada was especially hard-hit as the United States was its dominant trading partner. In an election in which they laboured under the economic burden of the Great Depression, MacKenzie Smith's Liberals – usually proponents of free trade – found themselves no match for Richard Bennett's protectionist Conservatives either in promising the highest level of retaliation against the Smoot-Hawley Act or in intervening in the economy. Bennett won a landslide and promptly implemented a sharp increase in import duties. Australia, which had already been raising its tariffs throughout the 1920s, pushed its tariffs upwards, more than quadrupling the number of goods on the high tariff list.

Britain's abandonment of the gold standard in 1931 and the Conservative dominance of the National government led to the repudiation of free trade and opened the door for imperial preference. Canada and Australia were now potential allies in a movement to consolidate trade within the empire. The pro-empire, pro-protection Conservatives under Bennett in Canada faced rejection by their major trading partner, the United States, and sought to develop deeper ties with the mother country. Imperial preference fitted quite closely with Australia's existing policy preferences – high tariffs plus privileged access for Australian agricultural products to the British market. Both were open to the opportunity of advantageous treatment vis-à-vis third parties that differential tariffs within the British Empire promised. The Imperial Economic Conference held in Ottawa in 1932 sought to make these potential gains concrete. As such, it was a unique attempt at a multilateral trade solution within the existing imperial framework. The disparity of national and economic interests revealed the limits both of the imperial ideology and that of trade cooperation within the Empire. Individual Dominions – particularly Canada – would reach bilateral agreements with the Americans based on their own, not imperial, economic interests. A multilateral trade agreement and the return of the free traders would have to wait until after the Second World War.

IV

The texts in this volume were selected for inclusion to highlight debates over different conceptions of free versus 'fair' trade, the role of interest groups and how political conflicts over trade were intermediated by representative governing institutions. The texts are drawn from a wide variety of public and private sources and are supplemented by contemporary accounts published in periodicals. Articles from journals such as *Fair Trade*, the journal of the Fair Trade League, and the responses of free trade supporters like the stock jobber George

Webb Medley, a member of the Cobden Club who funded and wrote several pro-free trade tracts, highlight the nuances of arguments between competing advocates of free and fair trade. Likewise, different intellectuals' positions on contentious trade issues are presented. For example, J. A. Hobson's attacks on the 1916 Paris Economic Conference serve to provide a taste of the intellectual turmoil during both the Great War and the Great Depression. Finally, other famous, but scarce, documents are also included – the letter from 1,028 American economists calling on President Hoover to veto the Smoot-Hawley tariff is often mentioned in academic accounts of American tariff debates and the Great Depression. Unfortunately, it is rarely, if ever, quoted, and it is reproduced here in its entirety to give readers a view into the manner in which public economists sought to influence policy in this earlier era. We also include the arguments of proponents of protection, such as Senator Reed Smoot, who are often portrayed as either economic ignoramuses or political log-rollers par excellence. Smoot's analysis of the world economic situation and the role of protection as a desirable policy goes some way towards remedying this popular simplification.

Government records of Royal Commission inquiries, internal Cabinet deliberations, trade negotiation strategies, Tariff Commission reports and confidential Foreign Office telegrams are used to develop a picture of official activities relating to trade policy and negotiations in the later nineteenth and early twentieth centuries. The minority report of the 'fair traders' who dissented from the 1886 Report of the Royal Commission on Depression in Trade and Industry is included to supplement the positions and arguments presented by fair trade pamphleteers. Secret Foreign Office and Colonial Office telegrams prior to both the Paris Economic Conference and the Imperial Economic Conference in Ottawa impart the views – as presented to British diplomats – of foreign politicians and diplomats on foreign economic policy. These supplement the direct accounts of British policymakers themselves in their correspondence with each other, and also the press accounts from countries such as Australia and Canada.

Notes
1. E. Grimmer-Solem, *The Rise of Historical Economics and Social Reform in Germany 1864–1894* (Oxford: Clarendon Press, 2003); see also K. Tribe, *Strategies of Economic Order. German Economic Discourse, 1750–1950* (Cambridge: Cambridge University Press, 2007), pp. 66–94.
2. From 1892 the Verein published a highly important and still useful series of monographs on trade policy in different states, *Die Handelspolitik der wichtigeren Kulturstaaten in den letzten Jahrzehnten*. This included C. J. Fuchs, *The Trade Policy of Great Britain and her Colonies since 1860* (Berlin, 1893), trans. C. H. M. Arnold (London: MacMillan, 1905), with an introduction by the tariff reform MP James Parker Smith.

3. G. Schmoller, *The Mercantile System and its Historical Significance, Illustrated Chiefly from Prussian History: Being a Chapter from the Studien ueber die wirhschaftliche Politik Friedrichs des Grossen: 1884* (1895), trans. W. J. Ashley (New York: Macmillan, 1910).
4. C. Schonhardt-Bailey, 'Parties and Interests in the "Marriage of Iron and Rye"', *British Journal of Political Science*, 28 (1998), pp. 291–330.
5. H. Rosenberg, 'The Great Depression in Central Europe, 1873–96', *Journal of Economic History*, 13:1–2 (1943), pp. 58–73; S. B. Saul, *The Myth of the Great Depression* (London: Macmillan, 1985); P. A. Gourevitch, *Politics in Hard Times* (Ithaca, NY: Cornell University Press, 1986).
6. A. S. Milward, 'Tariffs as Constitutions', in S. Strange and R. Tooze (eds), *The International Politics of Surplus Capacity: Competition for Market Shares in the World Recession* (London: Allen & Unwin, 1981), pp. 57–66.
7. A. L. Dunham, *The Anglo-French Commercial Treaty of 1860* (Ann Arbor, MI: University of Michigan Press, 1930); M. S. Smith, *Tariff Reform in France, 1860–1900* (Ithaca, NY: Cornell University Press, 1980).
8. E. O. Golob, *The Méline Tariff* (New York: Columbia University Press, 1944); T. Zeldin, *France, 1848–1945, Vol. 1: Ambition, Love and Politics* (Oxford: Clarendon Press, 1973), pp. 649–54.
9. A. E. Eckes, *Opening America's Market: U.S. Foreign Trade Policy since 1776* (Chapel Hill, NC: University of North Carolina Press, 1995); J. Goldstein, *Ideas, Interests, and American Trade Policy* (Ithaca, NY: Cornell University Press, 1993); A. Howe, 'Free Trade and the International Order: The Anglo-American Tradition, 1846–1946', in F. M. Leventhal and R. Quinault (eds), *Anglo-American Attitudes* (Alderahot: Ashgate, 2000), pp. 142–67.
10. H. Lebovics, *The Alliance of Iron and Wheat: The Third French Republic, 1860–1914* (Baton Rouge, LA: Louisiana State University Press, 1988).
11. A. Howe, 'The Liberals and the City of London, 1900–1931', in R. Michie and P. Williamson (eds), *The British Government and the City of London in the Twentieth Century* (Cambridge: Cambridge Unviersity Press, 2004), pp. 135–52.
12. F. Trentmann, 'National Identity and Consumer Politics: Free Trade and Tariff Reform', in D. Winch and P. K. O'Brien (eds), *The Political Economy of British Historical Experience, 1688–1914* (Oxford: Oxford University Press, 2002), pp. 215–40.
13. Hamilton Diary, 20 April 1902, BL, Add. MS 48679.
14. A. J. Marrison, *British Business and Protection, 1903–1932* (Oxford: Clarendon Press, 1996); R. P. T. Davenport-Hines, *Dudley Docker: The Life and Times of a Trade Warrior* (Cambridge: Cambridge University Press, 1984).
15. J. M. Hobson, *The Wealth of States* (Cambridge: Cambridge University Press, 1997), p. 62.
16. M. Daunton, *Trusting Leviathan* (Cambridge: Cambridge University Press, 2001); W. E. Brownlee, 'Economists and the Formation of the Modern Tax System in the United States: The World War I Crisis', in M. Furner and B. Supple (eds), *The State and Economic Knowledge* (Cambridge: Cambridge University Press, 1990), pp. 401–35.
17. B. R. Wise to Alfred Deakin, 6 April 1906, Deakin Papers, National Library of Australia.
18. P. J. Cain, 'Wealth, Power and Empire: The Protectionist Movement in Britain, 1880–1914', in P. K. O'Brien and A. Clesse (eds), Two Hegemonies: Britain 1846–1914 and the United States 1941–2000 (Aldershot: Ashgate, 2002), pp. 106–15; P. J. Cain, 'The Economic Philosophy of Constructive Imperialism', in C. Navari (ed.), British Politics

and the Spirit of the Age (Edinburgh: Edinbugrh University Press, 1996), pp. 41–65; E. H. H. Green, *The Crisis of Conservatism* (London: Routledge, 1995).
19. Interestingly, F. Naumann, *Central Europe* (*Mitteleuropa*, 1915; London: King, 1916) was introduced in its English translation by the leading tariff reformer and historical economist W. J. Ashley.
20. J. S. Nicholson, *A Project of Empire* (London: Macmillan, 1909).
21. F. Trentmann, 'The Strange Death of Free Trade: The Erosion of "Liberal Consensus" in Great Britain, c. 1903–1932', in E. F. Biagini (ed.), *Citizenship and Community: Liberals, Radicals and Collective Identities in the British Isles, 1865–1931* (Cambridge: Cambridge University Press, 1996), pp. 219–50.
22. A. S. Thompson, 'Tariff Reform: An Imperial Strategy, 1903–1913', *Historical Journal*, 40:4 (1997), pp. 1033–54. The £42,000 is equivalent to approximately £4 million in 2007 currency.
23. Hence the turn of the century appearance of works on the 'American invasion' of England, just as the 1890s had seen a 'Made in Germany' scare. See, for example, B. H. Thwaite, *The American Invasion, or England's Commercial Danger and the Triumphal Progress of the United States, with Remedies Proposed to Enable England to Preserve her Industrial Position* (London: Swan Sonnenschein & Co., 1902).
24. See especially O'Brien and Clesse, *Two Hegemonies*.
25. J. M. Keynes, *Economic Consequences of the Peace* (London: Macmillan, 1919), p. 10.
26. J. B. Brigden, D. B. Copeland, E. C. Dyason, J. F. Giblin and C. H. Wickens, *The Australian Tariff: An Economic Enquiry* (Melbourne: Melbourne University Press, 1929).

THE RISE AND FALL OF FAIR TRADE IN BRITAIN, 1879–92

The fair trade movement in Britain was a reaction against the protectionism of European industrial powers, and a perceived diminution in Britain's 'Great Power' status. The movement attempted to arrest this decline, by organizing the economic base of Britain on a new footing, and reorienting British commercial policy away from unilateral free trade. The proposals of the National Fair Trade League comprised protection of domestic industries and, more contentiously, agriculture, accompanied by preferential duties for the British colonies, effectively creating an imperial trading zone or Zollverein. Raw materials were to be admitted duty free, and no commercial treaties made unless terminable at one year's notice.[1] Countervailing duties were to be levied on products of foreign countries offering export bounties. The latter measure, particularly the concern of the sugar industry, was justified on the basis of re-establishing competitively 'fair' trading conditions by offsetting 'artificial conditions of production'.[2] These measures aimed at recovering Britain's commercial liberty, free from compromising treaties. Denying that they sought to re-establish the pre-1846 mode of protectionism, fair traders justified protective measures on the basis of 'fair' trade.[3]

Fair trade was an important influence in Joseph Chamberlain's later tariff reform campaign, not least in challenging Chamberlain's personal assumptions as to the validity of free trade.[4] The failure of fair trade was not inevitable. Indeed, the movement worried many senior political figures, and represented a more serious threat to free trade than earlier reciprocity movements.[5] Although the movement was unlucky in becoming embroiled in the vicissitudes of party politics and parliamentary calculations, the fundamental cause of its failure lay in failing to secure sufficient working-class support or the official backing of a major political party. In both areas, opposition mounted by free traders, in the Liberal Party, Cobden Club and the press, was vitally important. The multi-faceted popularity of free trade, and more pointedly the obloquy attached to protectionism, posed an insuperable hurdle to mass support even amidst a depression in trade and industry.[6]

In terms of national economic composition, or 'production profile', support for fair trade was most marked in industries adversely affected by foreign tariffs and foreign competition, but this was by no means the majority of British industry.[7] In their critique of 'one-sided' free trade, fair traders argued that Britain's unilateralism was a grotesque distortion of free trade principles, and highly damaging to British industries.[8] As other countries had failed to follow Britain's example, was it not logical to follow suit and impose tariffs on the products of foreign countries? For many, retaliation, in presenting Britain with the necessary bargaining power to negotiate tariff reductions, meant a return to reciprocal commercial agreements as the guiding principle of British commercial policy. The danger of reciprocity and retaliation was that it could descend into a zero-sum game, with the closure of the international trading system, and the emergence of autarkic, neo-mercantilist states. This was a risk fair traders were willing to take.[9]

The fair trade movement began as a result of Anglo-French negotiations for renewing the 1860 commercial treaty. The French government renounced the 1873 treaty, itself a temporary prolongation of the 1860 treaty, on 31 December 1878. With that treaty then due to expire on 1 January 1880, the interim period allowed the emergent protectionist movement in Britain to agitate the question. A major concern for the Liberal government was the likely reaction to a 'retrograde' treaty, defined as making concessions to French protectionism, as this would only contribute to the popularity of fair trade.[10] However, France was under similar pressure, and refused to make any further concessions. With French protectionism in the ascendancy, and Britain insistent on at least the terms of 1860, there was no basis for renewal, but in 1882 merely a simple most-favoured-nation treaty which would expire in 1892.[11] The main argument against any new treaty was that the 1860 treaty had failed in its objective of converting France to free trade. Favours bestowed upon France had merely led to French competition in the British market, and the continuation of protective duties, alongside the escalation of objectionable practices such as export bounties. Significantly, in the early meetings preceding the formation of the Fair Trade League, the members resolved themselves into a 'French Treaty Committee'.[12] Renewal would end the possibility of reforming commercial policy. Benjamin Disraeli had argued reciprocity was no longer possible, for even if Britain recovered commercial freedom, there were no longer a sufficient number of customs duties to bargain with.[13] The fair trade position was underpinned by a more positive notion of commercial freedom, and for this reason Anglo-French negotiations must be defeated, or 'the country would again have been in the condition described by Lord Beaconsfield'.[14]

The fair traders appear to have had a reasonable case. With Continental states increasingly protectionist, British industries suffering from foreign competition were frustrated that government had divested itself of its negotiating power.[15] The industries most affected by French tariffs and imports were textiles industries such as woollens, worsteds and silk, although sugar refiners were also prominent. Industrialists played a formative role in founding the movement and agriculture played a subsidiary, though divisive and damaging, part in dictating its course.[16] A rise in food imports in the 1870s, particularly American and Russian grain, and a delayed result of Corn Law repeal, raised calls for protection, with foreign competition identified as the cause of agricultural depression.[17] Such calls risked identifying fair trade with the 'dear loaf' and food taxes, and were electorally unpopular.[18] The official organ of the movement reiterated it was 'only for the sake of carrying the commercial federation of the Empire' that import duties on food products were contemplated.[19] As with those who advocated countervailing duties on sugar, the movement, as a vehicle for tariff reform, was highly conscious of being hijacked by particularist interest groups.[20]

The food issue was important in inhibiting support, not least amongst those sympathetic to the movement.[21] It was politically sensitive to raise the question of protection, and fair traders, in their emphasis on the modernity of the movement, and the moderation of their proposals, sought to distance themselves from protectionists of the Corn Law era.[22] Yet, whilst many Conservatives were sympathetic, political difficulties were particularly acute, especially after the Second Reform Act of 1867.[23] Lord Salisbury, Conservative leader from 1881, would not endorse food taxes but held out the prospect of retaliation as a device for lowering foreign tariffs, and acceded to a long-standing demand of fair traders in appointing a Royal Commission into the Depression of Trade and Industry.[24] The Committee issued two reports, both of which declared foreign tariffs and bounties as injurious to British trade, but the minority 'Fair Trade' report contained a closely argued statement of the fair trade case for imperial preference and duties on foreign manufactures.[25] Fifty-two Chambers of Commerce also condemned foreign competition and tariffs, leading to calls for government action to alleviate distress.[26] Working-class support was vital if fair trade was to be successful. Whilst many workers in affected industries joined their employers in supporting fair trade, most workers, imbued with notions of popular political economy, remained attached to free trade.[27] Political conditions and the reconfiguration of parties in the wake of the Home Rule crisis of 1886 also damaged fair trade. Constrained from raising the question in Parliament, agitation turned towards the country, but a trade recovery led to steady decline, and in 1892 the League was disbanded.[28]

The fair trade movement was important, not least in demonstrating that free trade was not quite as secure as its protagonists claimed. A British protectionist tradition clearly survived, and proved adaptable to modern conditions of an expanding industrial economy.[29] It was a tradition which claimed to understand foreign protectionism, but which sought national measures to combat it. Building upon Alexander Alison's theory of 'young' and 'old' states, the English historical economist William Cunningham saw the adoption of free trade by Britain in historical terms, and argued that it was logical for other nations to adopt protection, as this was to 'imitate the steps by which England attained to greatness'.[30] The failure of fair trade largely emanated from an unjustified association with the discredited agricultural protectionism of the 1840s. Yet it seems clear that fair trade represented a departure from the predominantly rural protectionism of the past, and more accurate to view it as the forerunner of tariff reform. Most notably, prominent figures in this movement later assumed the lead in founding the United Empire Trade League.[31]

Gordon Bannerman

Notes
1. 'National Fair-Trade League', *Times*, 3 August 1881, p. 12a
2. C. J. Fuchs, *The Trade Policy of Great Britain and her Colonies since 1860*, trans. C. H. M. Archibald (London: Macmillan, 1905), p. 191.
3. See 'The Past and the Future', *Fair-Trade* (1885), below, pp. 7–9.
4. 'Mr. Chamberlain on Preferential Trade', *Times*, 9 July 1904 p. 9a.
5. B. H. Brown, *The Tariff Reform Movement in Great Britain, 1881–1895* (New York: Columbia University Press, 1943), pp. 5–7.
6. A. Howe, *Free Trade and Liberal England, 1846–1946* (Oxford: Clarendon Press, 1997), pp. 129–36; 'The Cobden Club', *Times*, 23 July 1881, p. 9e.
7. That is 'the situation of the nation's economic actors in the international economy' related to policy preferences, P. Gourevitch, *Politics in Hard Times: Comparative Responses to International Economic Crises* (Ithaca, NY, and London: Cornell University Press, 1986), p. 76; Brown, *The Tariff Reform Movement*, pp. 64, 130.
8. W. F. Ecroyd, 'British Trade', *The Times*, 18 July 1881, p. 11d.
9. Fuchs, *The Trade Policy of Great Britain*, pp. 192–4; Howe, *Free Trade and Liberal England*, p. 155.
10. Brown, *The Tariff Reform Movement*, pp. 23–4; to the extent that many free traders preferred no treaty to one which would enhance fair trade's popularity, see Howe, *Free Trade and Liberal England*, p. 179, nn. 163, 169.
11. Howe, *Free Trade and Liberal England*, pp. 177–80.
12. See 'The Story of the Movement', *Fair Trade* (1888), below, pp. 10–12.
13. W. F. Monypenny and G. E. Buckle, *The Life of Benjamin Disraeli, Earl of Beaconsfield*, 6 vols (London: John Murray, 1910–20), vol. 6, pp. 496–7.
14. See Robert Andrew Macfie, Letter to the Shipping and Mercantile Gazette, 25 November 1880, below, pp. 13–14.
15. See 'Causes of Trade Depression', *Fair-Trade* (1886), below, pp. 36–9.
16. Brown, *The Tariff Reform Movement*, p. 139
17. 'Business in 1884', *The Times*, 1 January 1885, p. 8a; 'American Competition', *The Times*, 28 July 1885, p. 13d.
18. See Sampson Lloyd, *The Fair Trade Policy* (1882), below, pp. 23–9.

19. *Fair-Trade*, 1:109 (11 November 1887); cf. earlier illustrations of free trade and fair trade loaves, in *Fair-Trade*, 1:2 and 1:4 (30 October and 6 November 1885).
20. See the attack on those preaching a 'mutilated creed', in *Fair-Trade*, 1:24 (26 March 1886).
21. See Macfie, 'The Fair-Trade Policy', *Fair Trade* (1888), below, p. 44.
22. Pro-Corn Law MPs C. N. Newdegate and W. S. J. Wheelhouse were described as 'Old World Protectionists' with 'extreme views', in *Fair-Trade*, 1:211 (25 October 1889).
23. Lord Randolph Churchill stated his belief 'that low prices in the necessaries of life and political stability in a democratic Constitution are practically inseparable', cited in Brown, *The Tariff Reform Movement*, p. 68.
24. Ibid., p. 60.
25. See Royal Commission on Depression in Trade and Industry, *Parliamentary Papers* (1886), below, pp. 40–3.
26. H. Vincent, 'Conservatives and the Defence of British Industry', *Times*, 29 November 1887, p. 8c; A. Marrison, *British Business and Protection, 1903–1932* (Oxford: Clarendon Press, 1996), pp. 106–8.
27. See Annie Besant, 'What is Really Free Trade', in *Free Trade v. Fair Trade* (1881), below, pp. 17–22; Fuchs, *The Trade Policy of Great Britain*, p. 203
28. Brown, *The Tariff Reform Movement*, pp. 65–73
29. The Conservative MP and fair trader Sampson Lloyd translated the first English version of Friedrich List, in 1885, S. H. Zebel, 'Fair Trade: An English Reaction to the Breakdown of the Cobden Treaty System', *Journal of Modern History*, 12 (1940), pp. 161–85, on p. 170, n. 40.
30. For Alison, see Alexander Alison, *Universal Free Trade* (1852), in Volume 2 of this edition, pp. 48–52; W. Cunningham, *The Growth of English Industry and Commerce in Modern Times: Laissez Faire*, 6th edn (Cambridge: Cambridge University Press, 1925), p. 869.
31. Zebel, 'Fair Trade', pp. 182–3.

THE RISE AND FALL OF FAIR TRADE, 1879–92

'The Past and the Future. A Historical Sketch of Fair Trade, and Commercial Policy since "the Settlement of 1846"', *Fair-Trade. A Weekly Journal Devoted to Industry and Commerce*, 1:1 (16 October 1885), pp. 4–5.

THE PAST AND THE FUTURE.

It was therefore not until 1881 that the actual effects of the work of individual propagandists became more self-evident. In that year the Anglo-French Treaty was expiring. That Treaty had been Mr. Cobden's work, and, though in many respects eminently unfair to England, was in itself an eloquent tribute to the value of the principle of Reciprocity. When the idea of some such Treaty was conceived in 1860 its necessity had become apparent. The prophecies so freely made, that all the nations of the world would in a very few years follow us in our Free-Trade policy, had been utterly falsified. Even at that early period there was imminent danger that the instalment already secured would prove a failure. It was, at any rate, impossible to proceed with the further abolition of import duties, without first using what bargaining power was left us – and it was then considerable – to procure even the shadow of Reciprocity. Political events in France favoured such negotiations. The new Empire sought alliance with England, and was pliable to overtures for at least a modification of the old prohibitive tariffs. In the negotiations which followed Mr. Cobden undoubtedly secured important remissions of import taxation against our goods. But even this result was only possible (1) by reason of our remaining bargaining power, and (2) at the cost of treating Spain unfairly in respect to home duties; and in all probability it would have been impossible, had we not then been in full possession of our manufacturing power, with practical command of the markets of the world. It is matter of history now that the Anglo-French Treaty lasted, with one renewal, twenty years. But in 1881 the position of affairs was altered. The Treaty of 1861 [*sic*] had been notoriously tentative in character, and was assumed, or at least hoped, to be but the precursor of a still greater advance on the part of other States, in the direction of free exchange of commodities. Instead, however, of this hope being realised, the French Republic was not sufficiently satisfied with the trial to follow in the steps of the Empire. How far political prejudice on the part of France again operated need not be discussed here. Enough for us to know that in the later years the English people themselves were also indisposed to a renewal of conditions, in respect to which a sense of general unfairness was felt throughout the commercial community.

It was the agitation against the conclusion of a third Treaty with France for another ten years which precipitated the formation of the Fair-Trade party. Early in the spring of 1881 the Gladstone Cabinet made active overtures to the French Government to secure a renewal of the Treaty which would expire at Midsummer. If personal considerations could have prevailed, everything seemed favourable to the success of such proposals. Both Lord Granville and Sir Charles Dilke were *personæ gratæ* in Paris, and each was eminently qualified to discuss details with French diplomatists without the usual difficulties attending personal negotiations with aliens. But not merely was France ill-disposed to treat, saying frankly that we had now nothing to offer, but the commercial community of the United Kingdom was absolutely sick of these one-sided arrangements. The consideration of this question brought together several leading men of both political parties, practically versed in our more prominent industries, who, as individuals, had for some time agitated for a reconsideration of our general fiscal policy. A special committee was formed in May of that year, which sat at the Westminster Palace Hotel, to watch the Treaty negotiations. The leading towns, in unison with local Chambers of Commerce, sent up petitions to Parliament praying that there should be no renewal, excepting under more favourable terms, and with liberty to terminate it at twelve months' notice. The result of that temporary agitation is well known. In the end the negotiations collapsed, and England was therefore once more free to consider her policy. The great danger had been the renewal of such a treaty for ten years, for no other tariff treaty then existed – nor exists to-day – which we have not power to rescind by giving a year's notice. The circumstances under which Lord Beaconsfield declared reciprocity to be dead were therefore at once changed.

Hence, those who had been for the moment associated saw their opportunity to lead public thought into a still wider direction, to inquire into the disabilities under which British industry was avowedly suffering, and to propound a policy by which the future well-being of the nation might be secured. Out of their deliberations the cause known as 'Fair-Trade' has grown. Its development has been slow and gradual – far too slow in the minds of many ardent adherents – but it has been sure. Its views have been distorted and misrepresented on all sides, but they have nevertheless made their way in four short years, and are to-day recognised as an important factor in the politics of the hour. It has been slain over and over again, and is now more alive than ever. Other subjects may meet with but slender response at political meetings, but when the trade question is broached, each man's attention is rivetted. Whilst many even yet are afraid to avow Fair-Trade boldly in all its bearings, it is no longer spoken of with bated breath, and treated as something outside the pale of open discussion. And why? Simply because the belief in the virtues of one-sided Free-Trade has been destroyed by the logic of events, as well as by argument. Simply because the prophecies of the Fair-Traders have come true, and those of the Cobden Club school have come untrue. Simply because the people at large are beginning to see practically that the very things which they have been taught to believe would bring them good times, have brought nothing but bad times. Simply because the nation is beginning to feel that the theorists have had their way too long, and that it is time that practical business men should arrange for themselves the conditions, under which both home industries and commerce may be profitably developed.

But, while congratulating ourselves so far, we may not boast as they that put off their armour. The battle is really only beginning. Hitherto a very inconsiderable force has laid siege to the fortress, and has had to wait for public opinion to reinforce it. The enemy's fortifications have, indeed, been undermined, but the struggle for possession lies with the many. The course of our trade, the signs of industrial prosperity and adversity, the progress of other nations as well as our own, have all to be carefully watched. Opponents have still to be answered, and their oft-repeated arguments must be over and over again refuted. Timid followers have to be reassured, and foes converted into friends. What has been done is not a tithe of what has to be done; and those who have first put their shoulders to the wheel will probably not be those who will complete the task. It is to the more speedy furtherance of these ends that this journal has been founded; and in the hope that it may be instrumental in uniting Fair-Traders to common action, as well as affording a medium for the regular publication of facts and statistics needful to a thorough understanding of the question. Nor is it founded without trusting that in some measure, though, doubtless, at a distance, it may be useful in directing attention to, if not affording direct information on, some of the many and varied topics which must engage the attention of the Royal Commission on Trade.

'The Story of the Movement', *Fair Trade. A Weekly Journal Devoted to Industry and Commerce*, 1:138 (1 June 1888), p. 489.

THE STORY OF THE MOVEMENT.

IT is now a little more than ten years since anything like serious reaction set in against the one-sided Free Trade, which has resulted from the 'settlement of 1846,' and all the events which succeeded that period; and yesterday (Thursday, May 31st) the National Fair-Trade League celebrated its seventh anniversary by the annual general meeting of its members at Birmingham, followed in the evening by a banquet at the Masonic Hall in that town. It is, therefore, an appropriate time to recall very briefly the leading episodes which have occurred during such ten years.

It was really in 1877 that men's minds first began to awaken to the great increase of our excess imports. The question how these were being paid for was the dawn of the revolution against the fixed opinion, which for a generation had dominated Englishmen. During the whole of that time, indeed, there had been many who had clung faithfully to the principles of the older policy, under which the English nation had waxed great and powerful, as the first commercial people of the world. But these voices had been hushed amidst the general applause which had acclaimed the prosperous era when the force of science and invention had had its full play in our midst, and of which Englishmen by their trading pre-eminence gained in the past, were in the early stages alone able to take full advantage. But when those conditions no longer existed, and other nations were able to take their place in the race of competition, then the first doubts arose as to the reality and permanence of the marvellous progress which had signalised the years of 'leaps and bounds.'

Among the first public signs of the awakening, as though from a dream, may be noted the series of letters which the late Mr. Rathbone, then M.P. for Liverpool, contributed to the *Economist*, on the question of 'our excess imports.' Needless to say that he, like others at that period, never for one moment doubted the wisdom of Free Trade. Nay, as yet it was not even generally seen that no such thing as Free Trade existed. About the same time also the first keynote of a practical scheme that should replace the one-sided policy which far-sighted men then saw was on its trial, and more than likely to break down, was sounded by Mr. W. Farrer Ecroyd, afterwards M.P. for Preston, and one of the Commissioners on the recent Royal Commission on the Depression of Trade and Industry. In his pamphlet entitled 'Self-help,' which has since run through so many editions, Mr. Ecroyd first propounded in print the proposals on which the Fair-Trade policy, as subsequently promulgated, was practically founded. To Mr. Ecroyd, therefore, belongs the palm of having first suggested the practical plan of solving the great difficulties attending the provision of the surplus food stuffs needed by our population in excess of our home supplies, together with securing improved markets for our great labour industries, threatened with extinction by the continuous contraction of foreign markets shut off by hostile tariffs, and the reduced purchase power at home.

During the years 1877–80 all agitation on the question was carried on by a species of guerilla warfare, waged by individuals, and without any attempt at corporate cohesion. To Mr. David MacIver, at that time M.P. for Birkenhead, belongs the great merit of having kept the question alive in the House of Commons in those years. In fact, Mr. MacIver, in entire neglect of the usual precautions of wary politicians, who take care only to attach themselves to a movement when it is sufficiently strong and popular, became by his persistent action a political martyr to the cause of 'Reciprocity;' although many in Parliament at that time doubtless approved his action, and did at times support him by their votes. In the House of Lords, during that period, the question was raised by Lord Bateman in the spring of 1879, in which debate Lord Beaconsfield intervened, saying that so long as our hands were tied and bound by long-term commercial treaties, the principle of Reciprocity was practically dead. But the general election of 1880 scattered many who, in the lower House, had been united on this question, Mr. David MacIver being happily among the few on our side who retained his seat for Birkenhead. It is to Mr. MacIver that the foundation of the League is mainly due. In February of 1881 he first broached the idea, in a letter to a London correspondent, that the time had come for an organisation to be formed. He was speedily joined in his plans by a few who had already given proofs, either in public or in private, of their earnestness in the cause, including Mr. S. Cunliffe Lister, the League's president; Mr. Sampson S. Lloyd, its first chairman of Executive Committee; Mr. Edward Charles Healey, its first treasurer; Sir Henry Mitchell, of Bradford; Sir Frederick Young, the active promoter of the Royal Colonial Institute; and Mr. R. A. Macfie, of Edinburgh, ex-member for the Leith Boroughs. These six gentlemen signed the circular which summoned the first meeting, at the Westminster Palace Hotel, for the 17th May, 1881, a meeting which was attended also by Mr. David MacIver, Mr. W. J. Harris, afterwards member for Poole, Sir A. Galt, and others. This meeting, after fully discussing various points, adjourned for a fortnight, and on the 31st inst. re-assembled in increased numbers. At the later meeting the name of the National Fair-Trade League was decided on; and it was agreed to raise a preliminary fund, towards which £800 was subscribed at the table.

No haste was shown, however, to come before the public. It was felt that before the League opened its doors a carefully devised policy should be framed, and in doing this the members of the first committee had the careful and thoughtful guidance of those who had already, in their personal and individual capacities, ventilated views to be known thereafter under the name of Fair-Trade. It was not, indeed, until the month of August that the programme of policy, resulting from these consultations, was fully prepared and laid before the country, by means of lengthy advertisements in the *Times* and other newspapers. This, however, was done in the first days of August of that year, and at once the League received support of adherents in all parts of the kingdom, thereby laying the foundation for an organisation which now possesses branches, lodges, and official correspondents in over 400 centres of the United Kingdom.

Meantime, however, pending such action, immediate work was needful in reference to the negotiations then in progress for the renewal of the Anglo-French Treaty. Sir Charles Dilke was at that moment strenuously urging on such renewal in Paris, with, however, no other weapon than 'persuasion.' It was in the interests of Fair-Trade to defeat these negotiations, as had a new ten years' treaty been signed with France, the country would again have been in the condition described by Lord Beaconsfield in the year 1879 (already referred to). Thereupon the members of the League's first Committee resolved themselves into a 'French Treaty Committee,' which sat permanently for several weeks at the Westminster Palace Hotel, and whence several demonstrations, as well as petitions from all parts of the country, were organised. Happily, in this, its first work, the League was well supported by the Chambers of Commerce, and in the result the Government of the day abandoned the negotiations.

Such was the origin of the movement which has grown by degrees, and often most painfully, to its present position. It would be, of course, impossible to detail in a brief article of this kind the various steps that have been taken, or of the many events which have tended to mar or facilitate its progress. In the main its work has been well before the public, and probably no movement of the kind has ever made such solid progress – certainly none with so slight an expenditure of money. A year ago it was reported in these columns that the whole expenditure of the central office, which included money spent on country demonstrations and meetings, as well as printing and ordinary clerical work, had for the first five and a half years, from May 31st, 1881, to December 31st, 1886, only amounted to £7799. 2s. 1d., or an average of something like £1400 a year.

As time has rolled on, the very healthy sign of the formation of other organisations has come to the front. New men have naturally come forward to take the place of some who have dropped off, partly through death, partly through illness or business requirements, but none from apathy or want of good will. A few, indeed, who originally joined the League have objected to the prominence it has given to its food proposals; whilst, on the other hand, sections of the agricultural community have given practical proof of their belief that the League does not go far enough in that direction by the formation of independent societies, formed to place the needs of agriculture in the front. But the middle path has been steadily maintained by those who have had the official conduct of the movement, and when eventually the record of the League and its work comes to be written, the names of S. Cunliffe Lister, W. Farrer Ecroyd, David MacIver, Sampson S. Lloyd, and Ed. Ch. Healey will go down to posterity as the chiefs of those who had the foresight to see the distress that was coming on the land, and the courage and penetration to divine the remedy. J. E.

Robert Andrew Macfie, 'Letter to the Shipping and Mercantile Gazette, 25 November 1880', in R.A. Macfie, *Cries in a Crisis for Statesmanship Popular and Patriotic to Test and Contest Free-Trade in our Manufactures*, 2nd edn (London: Edward Stanford, 1881), p. 109.

FRENCH SHIPPING BOUNTIES.

To the Editor of the 'Shipping and Mercantile Gazette.'

'Sir, – When such bodies as the Edinburgh and Glasgow Chambers of Commerce denounce in the strongest terms the threatened French shipping bounties as a proceeding fraught with consequences in the extremest degree injurious to the shipping interests of our country, there is no occasion to multiply testimonies and warnings, although that I might do, – (especially in your columns). Let me, in a few words, adduce some considerations which may well be present in the minds of the deputations who, I am glad to learn, will be received to-morrow by the patriotic Secretary of State for Foreign Affairs. The aim of our good neighbour across the channel is to make France, by the transference hence of as much as she can obtain of our commerce, our manufactures, our shipbuilding, our shipping, our packet lines, and our warehousing business, greater commercially, and to make her more powerful politically as well as stronger in ways too familiar to require mention here. Why should Britons help her in this? Its intention and effect obviously are not such as British statesmanship should go an inch out of its way to facilitate. If the Treaty of Commerce which French statesmen wish our nation to enter into is at all like the Treaty which is now in force, we shall most unnecessarily, and, I do not doubt, also most decidedly hamper our own action, and be helping France to carry out her bold and not fully developed designs. We do not know what arrows she, who is very astute, as we now find, may have in her quiver. These may be very awkward ones I fear. Surely at a time when Germany and the United States and Russia, and probably other Powers, are contemplating legislation similar to that of France in favour of their shipping and navigation, it would be most unwise – because in ways that we cannot foresee hazardous – to tie our hands and to put ourselves into a position from which we cannot, till ten long years elapse, extricate ourselves and recover that liberty of action, the value and necessity for which bitter experience will have taught us. Let us therefore avoid new treaties, and retain the power of discriminating, or, if your readers prefer the word, of retaliation – a word which I do not like, – by not binding ourselves through any instrument to admit the produce and manufactures of other countries free of duty. Let us avoid the obligation to supply other countries with coal free of export duty; let us, above all, regain the power of filling our exchequer by import duties, if ever circumstances shall make it expedient to spend money largely. If the French know that the Chancellor of the Exchequer has this very large source of income to draw upon, and that at the same time he, by differential duties, can mark dissatisfaction with Powers who do not respond in a friendly manner to our liberal admission of their goods, they deriving, as they do, truly vast advantages from admission on favourable terms to the British market, will certainly be much more careful not to endanger the inestimable privilege, for such it is, and will, beyond a doubt, be much more conciliatory and amiably responsive. I, for my part, have not the smallest doubt that the present Treaty engagements are very pernicious. They have justly been pronounced objectionable, or inconsistent with sound principles of commercial policy, by such ardent free-traders as Messrs. Hugh Mason and John Slagg, members of Parliament, in their 1872 report regarding the French Treaty, presented to the Manchester Chamber of Commerce, and, I presume, adopted by that very influential Chamber. To go no further for evidence than the distasteful twistings in respect to wine duties which the unfortunate French Treaty has necessitated, surely the troubles that are accumulating upon our negotiators, even in that single and secondary matter, are enough to sicken and arouse shrewd statesmen. All I can say is, after looking at the Blue-Book on French industry and commercial Treaty questions, and with the knowledge that reaches me from different quarters of what practical men think on the subject, the Foreign Secretary need not apprehend that his ceasing to treat with the French will cause regrets in commercial circles. – Yours, etc.,

AN EX-MEMBER OF PARLIAMENT.
EDINBURGH, *Nov.* 24.

G. W. Medley, 'England under Free Trade' (1881), in *Pamphlets and Addresses* (London: Cassell, 1899), pp. 60, 63.

The ruling idea of the Fair Trader is, apparently, to accomplish one of two things. If the foreigner taxes our manufactures, we are to tax his; if he admits our goods free, we are to admit his goods free. He contends that if we are compelled, in the first case, to keep out foreign goods, our workmen will step into the place thus left vacant, and supply our home market with these or similar goods. But there are goods with which we cannot be supplied at home owing to disabilities of soil and climate, to say nothing of race, but which it is of actual necessity, or prime convenience, for us to obtain. After what I have said, it must be clear that by taxing these, so far from helping the British workman, we should only impoverish him. There are other commodities, however, which the Fair Trader thinks would be supplied by the home workman instead of the foreigner. But, to be of any advantage to the British manufacturer, the British workman, and the British consumer, the following impossible state of things must occur. In addition to the goods which we now make for the foreigner, we must be ready to supply our home market with much of what the foreigner now supplies us, and of which we are in future to cut him out. He is to sit down quietly under this, and buy of you just as much as he did before, although you have taken away so much of his purchasing power by cutting him out! At present, the foreigner makes certain goods better and cheaper than we can. When he is cut out, our consumers will consent, cheerfully as a matter of course, to pay higher prices for these same goods! Then, on account of the new home business which is to spring up, there is to be no fresh capital required, no fresh plant, no additional workers; or if there are, there is to be no increased cost in these respects, there is to be no change in any respect whatever, except that our manufacturers will have cut out the foreigner and got the home market in addition to the foreign market!

But, gentlemen, this is all most absurd, and I am sure I need say nothing more respecting it. I would rather proceed to inquire how it is our own people cannot supply us with certain things which now come to us from abroad; for instance, French silks and French woollens. The simple fact is, of course, that from a variety of causes our manufacturers and workmen either cannot or will not supply us with these things. Whatever be the cause, I am not here to-night to point out the remedy, but, whatever that may ultimately turn out to be, no Free Trader will allow that it is to be found in taxing the foreign product. If, for instance, foreign silks and foreign woollens were to be driven out of this country by hostile tariffs, it is certain that, over and above the actual loss to us as traders, which, as I have shown, would be involved by these trades being killed, our consumers – that is, the bulk of this nation – would be driven to adopt and use fabrics of a kind and quality which they do not want. There is not much fear of such an eventuality, however, for I do not believe the people of this country would put up with such intolerable tyranny.

As you know, complaints have been heard of the woollen manufactures of Bradford having passed away to their French rivals. But what are the facts? As I gather them they stand thus. We find that British alpaca or lustre has been superseded by French merino. Some years ago alpaca was in high favour. Now it is neglected, and the soft woollen worsteds of France have superseded it. How was this? As I read it, it was because, when alpaca was formerly made of pure fine lustrous wools only, it was in favour; but when manufacturers, aiming at cheap production and high profits, mixed the new wool with cotton, they produced nothing but a shoddy, which soon lost favour. Our French competitors, it appears, saw their opportunity; they bought their wools in our own market in London, they took it to France, adopted for it new machinery and every process which promised improvement, sought for and found new dyes, inventing soft half-tints and subdued shades of colour, and then brought it back to us made up into those fabrics which are now so much in vogue, and which are known by the name of French merinos and cashmeres. Now, I wish to ask whether this is creditable to us as manufacturers? There can be no question that, from some cause or other, our manufacturers have allowed the French to steal a march on them. Let them meet the modern demand by doing as the French have done; let them adapt their machinery, and study new processes, and, depend upon it, we shall then hear very little about French competition in this department.

Now, having thus disposed of the Fair Trader's argument for taxing foreign manufactures, let me say a few words respecting his assertion that our excess of imports is to be considered the measure of our national loss. We now, on the average, import more than we export – considerably over 100 millions' worth of commodities annually. We Free Traders say that instead of this being a loss to us, it is a profit to us, and that if we did not get in this excess of value we should be doing a very bad business indeed. I want to know, in the first place, why the shipowners of Great Britain, who possess one-half of the world's effective ocean tonnage, are not to receive what is due to them for the freights they carry, and if so, how they are to be paid. I want to know, in the second place, why those among us who hold foreign bonds, shares and investments of every kind, are not to be paid the interest which is due to them, and if so, how they are to be paid. I want to know, in the third place, why our shipbuilders, who last year built 90 iron, and 160 wooden ships for the foreigner, are not to receive the price of those ships, and if so, how they are to be paid. I want to know, in the fourth place, why our merchants and bankers, who advance the capital by which our 700 millions of foreign commerce is put in motion, are not to receive the interest on their capital, and if so, how they are to be paid. And in the fifth place, I want to know if our merchants and brokers, who carry on this 700 millions of foreign trade, are to earn any commission thereon, and if so, how they are to be paid.

Annie Besant, 'What is Really Free Trade', in *Free Trade v. Fair Trade* (London: Freethought Publishing Company, 1881), pp. 1–8.

WHAT IS REALLY FREE TRADE?

It has now become necessary to lay clearly down the economic principles on which the doctrine of Free Trade is founded, and to show that the results of Free Trade, so far as it has been tried, have been beneficial to the community as a whole. Foolish people have depreciated the teaching of political economy, and have sneered at it as 'cold,' 'dry,' and 'hard.' If the masses of the people were not ignorant of political economy, the absurd fallacies promulgated by landlords' agents would be laughed out of England. Euclid's theorems may be cold, dry, and hard, but they are true; and political economy is a science as much as mathematics, and disregard of, or ignorance of its teachings, does not alter the facts on which it is based.

The first point to grasp firmly is the meaning of 'wealth.' Wealth is all that is useful to man, produced by labor from the raw material supplied by nature. To produce wealth is to extract 'the instruments of human subsistence and enjoyment from the materials of the globe' (Mill). Gold and silver are not necessarily wealth, although they are convenient symbols of it. A nation might have a superfluity of the necessities and luxuries of life, and might be very wealthy, while a very small stock of coin might be circulating through it. If the stock of useful things were very large, and the stock of coin were very small, the nominal value of the coin would change, but there would be no alteration in the amount of wealth in the nation. If twelve loaves of bread are to be exchanged for twelve pennies, the value of a penny will equal that of a loaf; if there are twelve loaves of bread to be exchanged for twelve shillings, the value of a shilling will equal that of a loaf. The country is neither the richer nor the poorer by the fact that in the one case the loaf costs a penny and in the other a shilling. The wealth depends on the number of loaves, and not on the number of the symbols exchanged for them. Money, in itself, is valueless; it is only valuable so far as it is recognised as a convenient medium of exchange. Suppose that bullion were continually flowing into a country in exchange for manufactures, and that the country imported nothing save gold, that country would be growing continually poorer, while its stock of money grew larger and larger. *Prices* would rise, but wealth would not increase. The laborer would, perhaps, receive 30s. for work previously paid for by 10s., but he would pay 3s. for every 1s. worth of goods he bought. He would be neither richer nor poorer for this apparent rise; and as the drain of manufactures and the influx of bullion continued, he would receive more and more coin, but would find that he grew really poorer, because every 1s. of wage would buy less and less, as time went on, of the necessaries and the comforts of life, and the decrease of purchasing power would be swifter than the increase of coin. Or suppose that 1 ton of coals can be exchanged against 20 lbs. of beef, it may be more convenient to pay 26s. in coin for the coal, and 26s. in coin for the beef, than for the collier to carry his coals to the butcher and exchange the coal for the 20 lbs. of beef; but the exchangeable value of these commodities remains the same if prices rise side by side, and the ton of coal is 'worth' 50s. and the 20 lbs. of beef sell for 50s. also. Still 1 ton of coal balances 20 lbs. of beef; and whether this real wealth be reckoned against 26, 50, or 100 pieces of coin is not of the smallest real importance.

A limited supply of bullion in a country will mean nominally high prices, while a large supply will mean nominally low prices. Either of these conditions may be perfectly healthy, but rapid changes from one condition to the other cause distress and poverty. If prices are calculated on a small supply of bullion, a sudden influx of bullion means ruin to the traders, because they are compelled to part with their goods at a price which, in the changed condition, is not their fair equivalent; on the other hand, if prices are calculated on a superfluity of bullion, a sudden drain will impoverish the buyers, who no longer find their diminished number of coins capable of supplying their needs. Sudden fluctuations in the purchasing power of money are injurious both to producers and consumers.

Now the utility of ordinary commodities is a tolerably constant quantity. In order to live man must eat, must be clothed, must have shelter. All man's material needs imperiously demand supply, and the producers of these various necessities must, if they are to be comfortable, exchange their productions amongst themselves. If a man grow wheat he needs cloth, and the one commodity can be exchanged against the other. The exchangeable value of commodities, however, varies, and this value must rest ultimately on the cost of production. If a man in Lapland wanted to exchange reindeer for tobacco, the man who had to bring tobacco over hundreds of miles to Lapland would require much reindeer-flesh raised on the spot in exchange for his toilsomely acquired goods. But if a man in Havana wanted reindeer, he would have to hand over much tobacco raised on the spot for the reindeer brought from afar. The cost of production, including in 'production' all that is necessary to place the commodity within reach of the buyer, controls the exchangeable value of commodities.

Now, since a man's enjoyment depends on the amount of the necessaries and the comforts of life which he can obtain in exchange for his labor, it is manifest that if the Havana man wants reindeer and cannot raise it without ruinous expense at home, it is better for him that his reindeer should be imported from Lapland as cheaply as possible; while if the Laplander desires tobacco, it is no advantage to him to pay a heavy duty upon it as well as to pay the carriage from abroad; he might possibly grow tobacco in Lapland, but if home-grown tobacco cost 15s. per 1b. and Havana tobacco 8s., the Laplander would obtain more comfort by buying Havana tobacco than by buying that raised in Lapland.

We have here the fundamental reason for Free Trade. Things required for man's life and comfort should be produced wherever the circumstances are on the whole most favorable to production. This is thoroughly recognised within the bounds of a single nationality. A Middlesex man would not be insane enough to persist in sinking mines in order that he may possibly discover and then raise his own coal at vast expense, and tax heavily all coal coming from the Forest of Dean or from Durham, where circumstances are favorable to the production. Yet the same man, who would think himself an idiot if he acted in this way within his own country, would make his wife pay more dearly for her ribbons, by taxing all those which come from France, where circumstances favor the production, in order to bolster up the trade at Coventry, where it is forced and not natural. All that raises the exchangeable value of any useful article is clearly detrimental to the person who desires to possess it. Now if the exchangeable value be controlled by the cost of production, everything which raises that cost must clearly be mischievous to the consumer. Any excise duties on home-made articles, any tolls, are so much added to the cost of production. There is no reason why this argument should be restricted to commodities produced in our own country; it applies equally to all duties levied on imports, since without these duties the article could be sold more cheaply, being produced in the place most favorable to its production. Again, to encourage by bounties the production of an article in places where the production is more costly, is merely to burden the taxpayer for the temporary benefit of the manufacturer. Capitalists in each country should invest their capital in the classes of manufactures most suitable to the climate, the soil, and the genius of the people; they should not be encouraged to start naturally unremunerative industries by bounties, or by import duties on foreigners; such protection puts money into the pockets of the capitalists for a time, but it taxes the community for their benefit, and ultimately injures even themselves by drawing them away from occupations wherein the same amount of labor would produce more wealth.

I do not deny that duties levied on foreign goods may temporarily enrich the capitalists employed in the home-manufacture of the particular goods taxed. But the real value of the commerce of a nation is not in the vast fortunes accumulated by merchant princes; commerce is valuable for the comfort it spreads among the masses of the people. A very high duty on tea might turn a few tea-merchants into millionaires, but it would rob hundreds of thousands of homes of a luxury that adds much to the comfort of daily life. The cry for import duties is a cry to tax the comforts of the poor for the enrichment of the wealthy speculators. Every attempt to encourage home-production or to check importation by prohibitory or retaliatory duties, must necessarily result in increased price to the consumer.

You will now be in a position to fairly estimate the absurdity of the alarm-cry raised as to the excess of imports over exports. What are imports? Additions to the wealth of the country. Imports are spoken of as though they drained the country, instead of increasing its wealth. The reason of the blunder is, of course, in the confusion between 'wealth' and 'money;' 'money is going out of the country,' sob the alarmists. So long as we keep sufficient bullion to serve as the medium of exchange – and failing this if we have the wealth itself we can very easily make the negotiable symbol of the wealth – what does it matter if imports exceed exports? We are so much the richer by the excess, since in exchange for our smaller quantity the world's wealth pours into our laps. Import duties would check this flow, and so check the increase of wealth. This excess of imports over exports, estimated during the last twenty-seven years at no less than £1,742,737,010, is really the profit made by our merchants on their trading; if the goods exported were as valuable to us as those imported, how would merchants carry on their business? A return of the Board of Trade quoted by Mr. Cross in the House of Commons, in August last, showed that in 1880 we exported to India 587,000 tons of coal, valued at £265,000 in the table of exports. The price paid in India for this coal bought 60,000 tons of jute, valued in our import tables at £1,080,000. In this transaction there was an excess of import over export of no less than £735,000, but the £735,000 were profit, not loss, and the same explanation applies to the general figures. The excess of imports means excess of profits. Some of the alarmists, on the other hand, cry out that the excess is 'paid out of our capital, and we are living upon that.' If this were true, the aggregate wealth of the country would be diminishing; but it is doing nothing of the kind. Income Tax was levied in 1861 on £335,654,211; in 1879 it was levied on £578,046,297. If a man who had paid Income Tax on £500 ten years ago, paid Income Tax on £1,000 last year, and yet complained that he was growing poorer and living on his capital, he would be laughed at for his pains. The Savings' Banks' returns show a similar increase; in 1861, £41,000,000 were invested in these banks; in 1879 the invested capital amounted to £75,000,000. One other word of comfort for those who think that wealth consists in actual bullion. During the last eleven years we have imported £35,666,830 more gold and silver than we have exported. So that while our imports of material wealth have so enormously exceeded our exports, the value of property, of capital in the Savings' Banks, and of the amount of gold and silver in the country have all increased. This is perfectly natural if, as I contend, excess of imports means increase of national wealth; it is perfectly incomprehensible if the excess means impoverishment. Let me, however, point out to you that while the returns affecting foreign *trade* – and on these depend the arguments of those who would impose duties on foreign goods – are satisfactory, those on agriculture are not. During the last three years the amount of agricultural produce has diminished to the extent of at least £150,000,000 worth. This diminution of production really does affect the national prosperity, for we are that much the poorer in actual wealth. If the agriculturists produce less, they have clearly less to exchange for manufactured commodities, and the home market is thereby depressed. The argument as to imports and exports failing, the great *raison d'être* of Protectionists vanishes; but we will none the less consider their desire for Retaliation and Reciprocity.

It is urged that if other nations will not admit our goods duty free we should not admit theirs. In the name of common sense, why not? If they are so stupid as to prefer to pay more than they need, is that any reason why we should imitate their folly? Mr. Jones elects to pay 3s. 6d. for a saucepan sold by Mr. Smith which, admitted to his house without a commission to the cook, would cost only 3s. Is this ridiculous behavior of his any reason why Mr. Smith should 'retaliate' by levying a commission on a teapot sold by Mr. Jones, before his wife is permitted to buy it and make a cup of tea? If Mr. Jones chooses to pay 6d. more than he need for his saucepan, the more fool he. Mr. Smith may well laugh at his silliness, but need surely not emulate it.

It is sometimes answered that countries which cling to protection are the better for it, and America is cited as the stock example. Let me say first that America is a continent rather than a nation, and secondly that America is prospering as far as she adopts Free Trade, and suffering as far as she rejects it. The Hon. D. Wells pointed out in 1873 that Free Trade was thoroughly practised between the forty-seven states of the union; America has all varieties of soil and climate within her own borders; she can raise cotton and sugar in the South, dig coal and iron in the North, raise corn in the West, cattle in the South-West; it is as though Free Trade extended all over Europe, and no fair argument can be drawn from such a continent and applied to a small country; if Virginian goods found prohibitory duties on Massachusetts borders we should soon hear of trouble, and this is the difficulty we have in Europe. Further, America does suffer from Protection just in the very few things she cannot raise or make. To quote once more from Mr. Wells: when it was necessary to lay a railroad out of Chicago Bessemer steel was needed for the rails, and 2,000,000 dollars over the selling value of the rails were paid owing to the duties. This railroad is used chiefly for the transport of agricultural produce, and the freight on this is raised to pay interest on the surplus cost due to Protection. Thus every Western farmer suffers, and must suffer in perpetuity, for that money sunk in paying unnecessary duties. Feather-pated sprigs of nobility like Lord Randolph Churchill ask us to tax imports on the plea that we shall thus tax the foreigner; perhaps Lord Randolph Churchill will explain how that 2,000,000 dollars was paid by the foreigner; the English seller got his price for the rails; the American Company paid 2,000,000 dollars more than the price; the American farmers pay heavier freight to make up the yearly interest on the Company's outlay. It appears to me that the whole 'tax' is levied on Americans and not on us, yet in this case we are 'the foreigners.'

The best answer to those who say that Protection benefits the American workers, is some very dry figures, showing the cost of twelve necessaries of life for a family of two adults and two children in the city of New York. The rise of price of these commodities in 1873 over the price in 1880 is 92 per cent.; the price of beef has doubled; mutton has risen from 9 cents to 15 cents per lb.; butter from 18 cents to 30 cents. Rent has risen from 5 dollars a month to 12. In 1873, 347 dollars pay for the same house, fire, and food as were bought in 1860 for 181 dollars, 87 ½ cents. We have seen, however, that the mere price of things may mislead us; and, comparing the wages of eight leading handicrafts in 1860 and 1873, we find that they have also increased to the amount of a fraction over 60 per cent. Lastly, let us compare the really important figures as to *the amount of labor necessary to buy the necessaries of life* in 1868 and 1873, for this, and this only, can tell us whether a man's condition has really improved or deteriorated; in 1860, taking the same eight handicrafts, it is found that the number of full days' work, necessary to obtain the same twelve necessaries of life varies from 103 to 121 days; in 1873, the number varies from 115 to 147. Taking them all together, the results of 859 days' work in 1860 equal the results of 1027 days' work in 1873, the increase of labor being 167 days, or 19 ½ per cent. (These figures are taken from a report of the Cobden Club, June, 1873.) Harder toil or lessened comfort, such is the dilemma offered to the American workers by Protection.

The question may fairly be put to me: If, as you show, the national wealth is increasing, how do you account for the lower rate of wage now earned by the workers, and how do you reconcile this increase of national wealth with the burdens on labor which you last week admitted needed lightening? My answer is: I have here spoken only of trade, and have shown that prohibitory, retaliatory, and reciprocal duties are not needed for its protection. But while the absolute wealth of the country is increasing the share of the wealth falling to the producers is diminishing, and hence the distress. We want a more equal distribution of wealth, a fairer share of the profits to go to the producer. Protective duties will not help us in this trouble. They would only intensify it by making life yet more costly. Protective duties are claimed in the name of diminishing trade and national impoverishment. I have proved that these do not exist, and that the remedies are therefore not needed. Next week I shall deal with the real reasons and the real remedies for the pressure felt by our workers.

Sampson Lloyd, *The Fair Trade Policy: A Reply to the Charge of 'Taxing the Poor Man's Loaf'. A Letter to the Earl of Derby, as Chairman of the Cobden Club Banquet, 1882, from the Executive Committee of the National Fair-Trade League* (London: National Fair-Trade League, 1882), pp. 8–16.

THE FAIR-TRADE POLICY.
A REPLY TO THE CHARGE
OF
'TAXING THE POOR MAN'S LOAF.'

A Letter to

THE RIGHT HON. THE EARL OF DERBY,

Indeed, we need not seek for a more convincing proof of the fact that the whole conditions of the world's trading in relation to our wants are altered, than in this very question of our bread supplies. Our annual consumption of wheat is in round numbers 24,000,000 quarters. Of these we may rely in average years upon 11,000,000 quarters being grown at home. We are at present receiving about 4,000,000 quarters from our own Colonies and Dependencies, thus leaving a balance of 9,000,000 quarters which we need to import from foreign States. And this balance comes to us almost entirely from two hostile tariff nations, Russia and the United States, the latter supplying us with by far the larger portion. But according to the most reliable reports from all the grain-producing countries of the world, excluding India and our Colonies, the surplus stocks of the East and West, after supplying all home wants, amount to no less than 30,500,000 quarters per annum, of which 20,000,000 quarters are grown in the United States alone. This brings us to the consideration of the requirements of all importing countries, excluding Great Britain, and judging by the experience of past years, other nations are certainly not likely to need more than 10,500,000 quarters annually at the most. Hence we have 20,000,000 quarters left to supply the demand in this country, amounting only to 9,000,000 quarters; a supply which, to use the words of a recent writer and a well-known expert on this question,[1] is simply 'knocking at our doors' seeking for admission. And these cases – the bullock and our bread supplies – are fair examples of all food products now pouring into our ports, and likely to continue to do so. A market is wanted and must be had.

---

1 See 'Answer to the Cobden Club and England's Power of Retaliation,' by W. J. Harris. (William Ridgway, London.)

With such a change then in the conditions on which our markets are supplied, is it conceivable that there would be any appreciable increase in the price of the working man's food, or decrease in the size of his loaf, by the imposition of any moderate duties, raised, be it always understood – as your lordship has laid down should be the rule in the taxing of imports – for revenue purposes only and not for protection? For I think I need scarcely point out, that a more equitable incidence of taxation, by which the 9,000,000 quarters of foreign wheat should bear their fair share of that taxation which is now all paid by agricultural produce raised at home, would not add to our taxes. Nor would it necessarily operate by increasing prices to consumers. To reduce this reasoning to figures, for the sake of argument, I will assume that a 5s. duty on foreign wheat is levied, though I should here mention that the Fair-Trade party has never officially put forward any figure of this kind, it being manifestly the work of legislation to fix such a detail according to the need of the moment. But, assuming a 5s. duty were imposed, a sum of £2,250,000 would thereby accrue to the exchequer, and I will here also assume – though I am far from admitting it – that the whole of this £2,250,000 is borne by British consumers. But if it were, it is manifest that a like deduction of £2,250,000 could be made from the burden of internal taxation. Such a sum would permit the reduction of agricultural burdens, which press on the 'food of the people' produced at home. Or it would allow the remission of part of the duties on tea and coffee, or on tobacco, which are necessaries as well as luxuries to the working man. It would not add one penny to our national taxation, though this is a common assumption among opponents. And in effect it would compel hostile tariff States, in their own interest, to give us that fair play they now deny. For have I not shown the great probability, that in the conditions of the world's wheat trade the foreign producer would in the end pay his due share of our taxation, as toll or duty for the market-place he finds on our shores? Nor, as far as the Western farmer is concerned, would such a charge on his profits militate against his sending us those surplus stocks *for which he has no market elsewhere*, since the recent Commission has elicited the fact that his wheat can be laid down in Liverpool, and yet yield him a handsome profit, at 35s. per quarter, if not indeed at much less, while 45s. per quarter may be at present reckoned on as a nominal average price in our markets.

Neither is this argument at all confined to the grain productions of the world. Wherever we look, the anxiety to find markets for surplus food productions is greater even than the desire to receive them, especially when unaccompanied by that return trade which can alone in the end sustain our power of purchase. Whether this is the result of our free import system, or – as Fair-Traders are more inclined to think – of the many circumstances that have combined to make the free import era so extraordinary in the annals of the world, it would serve no practical end to enquire. Sufficient that the position exists; and that it is for us to make a proper use of it. Nor must we forget that the conditions of society itself have greatly changed, since – to use your lordship's own words – there was a question 'in which a small section of the rich found themselves in antagonism at once to the mercantile manufacturing plutocracy, and to the main body of the working classes.' May we not fairly say that these words might be again employed to describe the position to-day – but with one most important difference? The small section of the rich now in antagonism to the working classes is no longer that of landowners. They are the capitalists and the investors, who have become rich in the remarkable epoch through which we have passed, whose interests are now especially antagonistic to those of labour. By the virtue of foreign investments, by the power of utilising capital to equal, if not greater advantage, in the employment of labour on foreign soil, monied interests thrive and flourish, and home industry is handicapped by the very sources of their prosperity. Hence, while your lordship speaks well when you say that forty years ago the English democracy said, *'Here are laws which make our food dear; let us get rid of them'* – beware of the possibility that the same democracy of to-day may not say, *'Here are laws by which the mere capitalist waxes rich by the very means that deprives us of employment at home; let us get rid of them.'* And it will be fortunate if such revulsion of feeling stops at the getting rid of the laws which encourage the protection of foreign labour, and deny the reality of freedom to our own. There is more reason to believe in the spirit of Communism being roused by the creation of a few large capitalists at the expense of the working classes, than to admit Sir Charles Dilke's strange theory that Socialism is the result of Protection.

With regard to your lordship's criticism on the Home and Colonial policy, which is so integral a portion of the Fair-Trade policy, I can only write with considerable brevity. It is, indeed, a subject so vast and so many sided, that to treat it with any development would require a treatise of itself. Your lordship is struck, as all the world has been, with some very remarkable facts. You find that, in the face of all the Free-Trade propaganda that England has waged, not only have foreign nations continued protectionist – or if they have occasionally relaxed their tariffs they have eventually retraced such step – but even the English Colonies and Dependencies have, as a rule, refused to accept the Cobdenite faith. But it seems to your mind a still stranger thing that any body of Englishmen, with such an experience before them, should propose to deal differently with protectionist Dependencies, than with independent States which are also protectionist. On the ground that our Colonies will not accord us Free-Trade in return, any more than nations like Russia or the United States will, you treat the idea of the commercial Federation of the Empire as an absurdity. It is not my purpose here to defend that idea at any great length. Your lordship has singularly enough produced one of the greatest arguments in its defence when congratulating the Cobdenites on the only speck of brightness that appears in their horizon.

'Light,' you said, 'comes to us from the East.' The approximation to Free-Trade established in India is that little Star in the East, which you hold up to the eye of the faithful at this latest of the Cobden Club banquets. What a satire upon the vanity of human wishes and prophecies! After forty years of propaganda in the wilderness of the world, the only 'Light that comes to us,' the only bit of blue cloud in the distance, is the 'bold step' which your lordship vaunts the British Finance Minister of India has taken. In other words, and to put the matter quite plainly, the free imports of British manufactures have been imposed upon nearly two hundred millions of people by the force of arms and the might of a Power that rules by conquest. Your lordship, as Chairman of the Cobden Club festival, cites this as the 'one quarter' where 'there is a prospect of better things!' Surely does the brightness of this star pale when we approach it more nearly.

But if it be so great a matter of congratulation thus to inculcate the principle of free interchange of goods between the Mother Country and one portion of her Dependencies – though force has to be used to accomplish it – why is it so unreasonable, why so ridiculous, to attempt in a more peaceable fashion, and by the ordinary operations of mutual self-interest, to strengthen the bonds between England and her Colonies generally? Your lordship rightly contends that our Colonists are moved by that first law of nature which individuals should suppress, but which in nations is the highest patriotism – the spirit of selfishness. You are equally right in saying that the slightest dictation from Downing-street is likely to be resented, *i.e.,* when there are no bayonets – as in India – to compel compliance. It is a sign of their growing strength, and the natural result of the 'let alone' policy, which England, for good or for evil, has adopted as regards the distant parts of her Empire. Therefore the ties of mutual interest can alone be relied on to weld together once more a strong commercial feeling between all who hail Queen Victoria as their monarch. Is it so wonderful, my Lord, that these ties have not been strengthened during a period when we have never treated our Colonial dependencies as anything nearer or dearer to us than the most estranged foreign State? Can we complain; nay, can we blame our distant children for looking after themselves, and themselves alone, when we, their parents, have thought so little about them? In the era of Commercial Treaties, extended over a long terms of years with the honest intention, I doubt not, of accomplishing real Free-Trade in the end, the 'favoured nation clause' has prevented us from even treating with our Colonies in trade as the circumstances of each case dictated. As long as this era lasted we never had a concession or a commercial privilege to offer our Colonists, that we were not also bound by Treaty to give to the foreigner. This was not the way to prove that the ties of kindred had claims, or that blood was thicker than water. With the lapse of the French Treaty, however, that era is practically at an end. England is now free to extend the hand of kinship in trade, as in Imperial interests, to her Colonies and Dependencies. She has no right, in the first instance, to regard one colony with different feelings than another. She cannot, for example, say to Victoria: 'You are Protectionist, and therefore I will only deal with New South Wales, which is Free-Trading.' Fair-Traders, especially, are not so unreasonable or chimerical as to believe in the possibility of an immediate Zolverein [*sic*], 'with absolute Free-Trade the rule within it, and Protection against all outside.' These are your own words, and it does not require the strength of your lordship's voice to expose its present absurdity in practice, whatever the distant future may have in store, when all who are now working and projecting shall have long disappeared from the scene. But what they do believe as possible, and deem right at least to attempt, is, that if England, not merely as an act of justice, but simply in the welfare of her own interests, says to every Dependency alike, 'We will give you a preference in our markets for your food stuffs, relying that you in return will give us a preference in your markets for the products of British industry,' that this right-hand of fellowship will not be rejected. No Fair-Trader imagines for a moment that protective Victoria will relax all her tariff, and only impose on British manufactures what it may suit New South Wales to impose. Each Colony will naturally stand on its own bottom, and deal with us according to its separate interest, until the day may come – not yet to be foreseen – when absolute Free-Trade throughout will be possible. At the most a differential treatment is all that can be expected in the beginning, in exchange for that differential treatment which Fair-Trade offers, when it proposes a moderate duty on *foreign* food only, and free imports from all parts of the Empire. And if, after a fair trial, either of our Colonies or Dependencies proves intractable, and is either not alive to the benefits attaching to such reciprocal trading, or even regard it as contrary to their interests, it would become a question for the legislators of that day to determine whether such a Colony or Dependency were not cut off *ipso facto* from the commercial ties with which we had endeavoured to bind her, and how far she should continue to share in her general privileges as part of the British Empire. But that portion of this great subject is more purely political, and is apart from those commercial questions with which Fair-Trade only deals.

And speaking of those Colonies which now adopt a different fiscal policy, I know not whether it was intended as a main portion of your argument, or merely incidental thereto, to introduce a comparison between Victoria and New South Wales. Your lordship says, 'as if on purpose that the experiment [a Free-Trade or Protectionist policy] should be fairly tried, the two most important Australian Colonies have adopted an opposite policy: Victoria goes for Protection; New South Wales for Free-Trade. They are very similarly circumstanced in other respects, so that it is a perfectly fair fight, and we, at least, are not likely to feel any doubt as to the result.'

I have quoted this passage at length, so that there should be no question as to your lordship's meaning. The prosperity of New South Wales as the result of a free-trading community, compared with Protectionist Victoria, is always thrown in the teeth of those who decry Free-Trade in itself. In any case, indeed, this can never be an answer to those whose aim is to promote the reality of Free-Trade, and who only differ as to the means most likely to attain it. But, is your lordship altogether right in regarding the comparison as just, or saying that 'it is a perfectly fair fight?' I doubt if it is – nay, I am sure it is not. In the first place, New South Wales is generally much better adapted than Victoria for agricultural and pastoral pursuits. There are also far greater facilities in New South Wales for obtaining land, and instead of Free-Trade there causing an emigration of the labour classes, as is the case at home, there is an immense immigration into the Colony, both of squatters and of farmers, even from her sister Victoria. Nor can this immigration be regarded as the operation of a policy of comparative Free-Trade, but as the result of the greater internal advantages which New South Wales offers. Moreover, whilst her Government (though professedly free-trading) is rigid enough in the taxation of Chinese labour, it has for a long time past spent many thousand pounds annually in promoting free or partially free passages for immigrants from Europe. And added to all these material and substantial advantages, the possession of coal-fields in New South Wales gives her an enormous superiority over Victoria. But, my Lord, supposing the comparison were as you say, that the fight were perfectly fair, and that the conditions of the two Colonies were on 'all fours,' of what value is your argument when we reflect that head for head South Australia is far outstripping both her sister Colonies in her commercial supremacy? Had New South Wales stood first in this respect in the group of our Australian Colonies, then *prima facie* your argument might have been reasonable; but since South Australia, whose import taxation is practically protective, is, in the proportion of her foreign trade as compared with her population, far ahead of either of these and other Colonies, it cannot be that New South Wales is prosperous merely because, as far as her revenue permits, she is Free-Trade. It is more practical to admit, as is the case, that very different factors than either Protection or Free-Trade, taken by itself, have contributed and are still contributing to the comparative welfare of each Colony.

Finally, my Lord, I would urge that it is not by post-prandial speeches, however thoughtfully considered, and however temperately delivered, that whatever there is of a good in the reality of Free-Trade can be secured. Nor, say Fair-Traders, is it ever likely to result so long as we stand ostentatiously before the world, declining to adopt any other methods than mere example and persuasion. So long as nations, imposing hostile tariffs on the products of British labour, feel assured that in no case are we likely to withdraw from them the free markets they find here, those hostile tariffs will not be reduced. But if they once feel that there is such a thing as even tiring out the patience of John Bull, we may hope for the dawn of better things. The proof of this lies in the opinions already expressed by thinkers and politicians in the United States, as to what would ensue were the Fair-Trade policy to be adopted in England. Many of these opinions are cited in the Annual Report of the National Fair-Trade League,[1] should your lordship care to investigate the subject further. Nor does it seem to me other than commercially suicidal for any sensible people to shrink from such a policy, simply because a name – may I say, my Lord, the shadow of a name – has gained possession of their ears and their minds for a generation. Especially need they not shrink on the score of that political 'bogey' – the 'taxing the poor man's loaf' – when we remember the vast resources of our own Empire, and how in any eventuality, we contain within ourselves the strength and the power of self-sustenance, even in the impossible event of our food supplies from foreign States being diminished. The events of the last year have released us from the bonds which for so, long have crippled our Statesmen, in the shape of Treaty engagements. Those ties are now happily broken. We have regained our lost bargaining power, as far as international law is concerned, if we will only use it. Nothing but the voice of the people is needed to say that, as business men, we will employ as a nation the same means that we would use as private traders, to enforce a reasonable interchange of transactions on the principles of fair-play.

I am, my Lord,

Your most obedient Servant,

(By direction of the Executive Committee of the National Fair-Trade League)

SAMPSON S. LLOYD,

Chairman.

National Fair-Trade League,
23, Cockspur Street, S.W.,
July 14th, 1882.

---

1 See Advertisement, next page. [Ed.: Not included here.]

'The Fair-Trade Party'; Correspondence of J. B. Barkworth, 'Protection for Home Agriculture', and R. A. Macfie, 'Protection for Manufacturing Industries', *Fair-Trade. A Weekly Journal Devoted to Industry and Commerce*, 1:16 (29 January 1886), pp. 124–5, 126–7.

THE FAIR-TRADE PARTY.

Our correspondence columns to-day indicate some marked, but not singular, diversity of thought among Fair-Traders. By a coincidence, unsought by us, we have been favoured with communications from gentlemen representing phases of thought, varying from those who look upon agriculture as the first thing to be protected, to those who would omit cereals altogether from any share in the application of the principle of Fair-Trade. We are not sorry to be able to present all these views at a glance to our readers. One, at least, of our correspondents, Mr. Macfie, formerly member for Liverpool, in the Liberal interest, was one of the early founders of the National Fair-Trade League, but honourably retired when he found that that body proposed the imposition of moderate duties on all foreign food, while importing it free from our own Empire. Another of our correspondents, Mr. Barkworth, was an early subscriber to the League, but he too retired – though for a precisely opposite reason, namely, that the League's Colonial policy was unfair to the producers of the United Kingdom, and that it mattered nothing to the British farmer whether he be ruined by American food stuffs or by Indian and Canadian corn. Mr. Turner, on the other hand, as an active member of, and representative of the agricultural interest on the League's General Council, as well as president of one of its branches, has always vigorously combatted that, however just and fair may be the cry for equal taxation on everything that comes into our markets, even though from our own Empire, it was wise and expedient, under all the circumstances of the hour, and as much as agriculturists could fairly expect, to promote the colonial food policy of the League. Doubtless that food policy is in some measure of the nature of a compromise between two schools of thought. It enables those who approach the consideration of the question from the Protectionist point of view, and who, in short, regard home production as the first source of real wealth, to apply their principles to the Empire instead of to the United Kingdom only, and to be, in fact, Imperial Protectionists. And it equally enables those who have sympathy with the cause from the Free Traders' point of view, to seek by such means to attain the highest possible maximum of Free Trade, or a policy of commercial interchange over an area sufficiently large and productive to be self-subsisting.

Mr. Haggard, to whose letter we also call attention, brings in his turn to the controversy the keen arithmetical power of the financier, who, having discarded the prejudice surrounding the phrase of 'taxed food,' is able to see the sophistry involved in the word cheapness, without regard to other factors. These letters will, we think, do much to clear up many points that may have puzzled sympathisers with Fair-Trade, and will explain some of the difficulties the cause has had to encounter.

There is little doubt that in many minds some of the results of the late general election have created for a time despondency as to the possibility of ever carrying even such moderate proposals, in respect to the taxation of foreign food, as have been propounded by the Fair-Trade League. The rejection of the more prominent names connected with the movement has created a feeling that, as far as the present Parliament is concerned, the cause has not advanced. The 'big loaf' cry is credited with their defeat at the poll, and doubtless it is with that impression that Mr. Macfie – and it is only just to say that there are many who agree with him – suggests that the popularly obnoxious part of the League's programme of policy should be eliminated. It is noticeable, by the way, that Mr. Macfie produces no argument in support of his contention. His only reason is that it is unpopular, and that the organisation which hitherto has mainly, though not entirely, promoted the cause, would increase in numbers and in strength, as well as in public favour, were it to sink the corn question, or to go in for 'Fair-Trade' only for manufactures. We are prepared to agree with Mr. Macfie that, if present or immediate popularity be essential, his would be a politic and desirable plan. But we confess we think that a somewhat stronger reason is needed to justify a departure from a policy which has been carefully thought out, and strenuously maintained for nearly five years in the teeth of much obloquy and opposition, and which, moreover, Sir Thomas Farrer, the best mouthpiece which the Cobden Club has yet found, has declared to be the only defensible part of the Fair-Trade scheme. Mr. Macfie himself would appear almost to admit the wisdom of such policy, for he too speaks of the products of our Empire in a strain that might suit the Imperial Protectionist. At the same time, however, he distinctly proposes there shall be no question of any duties whatever on cereals – he does not say *food stuffs* – though it is difficult to understand that he can defend such conclusion on any other ground than pandering to prejudice. Mr. Barkworth is distinctly more logical in his reasoning, though he, we venture to think, scarcely realises the exact effect of his consistency. The great argument against our giving a preferentially free market to the products of our Empire, is that our Colonies and Dependencies will not reciprocate. We confess that even if the difficulty be real it has little weight. In the first place, we can certainly not expect our Possessions, which we have practically treated as aliens in commerce, ever since the favoured-nation clause became part of our commercial system, to say at once that they will join us in an inter-free trading policy, or indeed until we lead the way. And in the next place, the possibility of rebuff is infinitesimally small. The greater part of our empire is under our absolute control. Were the Fair-Trade policy to be inaugurated to-morrow, we should as easily, and with greater justice, incorporate India in such 'Bund,' as we have already forced free imports on her at the point of the British bayonet. Of our Crown Colonies we are sure. Of Canada we have also every moral assurance that the Dominion would cordially adopt a policy, which would divert British custom from the United States to the products of her North-West territories. With the Australias only is there any doubt of such policy being accepted in its entirety, and even if they did refuse to come in, the dissension of a population of three millions out of nearly three hundred millions of people would scarcely invalidate its practical success. To condemn such imperial policy as a device in favour of manufactures, and opposed to agriculture, is surely to underrate the importance of finding an outlet for the surplus capital and overcrowded population of the Mother Country within the borders of her own empire; and to overlook the importance, economically and politically, of regarding Greater Britain as one kingdom.

As to what the present Parliament may do in the direction of Fair-Trade, or the reverse, we anticipate little, and shall, therefore, not be disappointed. The elements of which it is composed are so new to the trade of legislation that it were idle to look forward to any actual or solid steps being taken to grapple seriously with questions involving statesmanship of a high order. We must await with a little patience until the surface politicians have had time to settle down. The best of the new men are not likely to come to the fore at once, and time must be given to many who are now almost unexpectedly compelled to bring forward the wild schemes which, as irresponsible agitators, they have been in the habit of airing from platform to platform. But none the less are we well content to know that, in spite of the loss of more tried Fair-Traders, we are not without a solid phalanx of men who, when the time arrives, will not be found wanting. From careful examination of the various election addresses, coupled with personal communication with new members, we are satisfied that those who have publicly expressed their disapproval of our present fiscal policy, number at least a third of the present House of Commons, and this is a much larger proportion than we had in the last Parliament. Among these we find exactly the same divergence of thought, as we do in the letters of our correspondents this week. We have the few who are out-and-out Protectionists, who would tax imports of everything that interfere with the products of the United Kingdom, avowedly to raise prices and make home production more profitable. And there are some, more politic, if less bold, who would raise the cry of taxing manufactured imports only, on the ground that it is like beating the head against a stone wall to touch 'food,' though these in their turn are after all but Protectionists of a worse form than those who would merely legislate for the United Kingdom, since they seek the good of one class at the expense of the other. Others there are again who prefer to be looked on as Retaliationists, and simply sigh for Reciprocity, not thinking of the only means possible to secure it; whilst the considerable majority of such 'third' is composed of members willing either to accept the Fair-Trade policy in its entirety, or pledged to abide by the results of the Royal Commission. Nor is it by any means an unhealthy sign that there should be these differences in degree. All are at least agreed upon one thing. Each is a foe to the present one-sided system, the singular outcome of theories, every one of which has been falsified in practice. It may be urged in all probability, that whilst all may be opposed to one enemy, it is a pity that they do not fight under one banner. Neither, however, do we think this a misfortune, but rather a boon. The greater the liberty the greater the activity. The chief danger, if any, lies in the desire among those who are saturated with their own convictions, to dominate the rest. The greater the earnestness the greater the bigotry. And there will be doubtless some, especially among the more recent converts, who would gladly step into the boat that has been launched, and steer it their own way. The more there are of these, also, the better for the cause. The stronger the latter must become, the greater will be the multitude of counsellors, and the more powerful will be the combined onslaught upon those prejudices which have too long ruled our people. The stream itself is broad, and the current is now happily strong enough, to carry many boats in the same direction. Whilst, therefore, firmly adhering to the principle that all *foreign* imports of things which displace home production, whether they be of the nature of food or of manufactures, should contribute to our national revenue equally with the taxation our own producers pay, we yet hail as friends those whose courage stops short of 'food.' And whilst convinced that the wiser policy for our crowded population is to treat the whole Empire as one kingdom, and not the United Kingdom only, we can yet respect the motives of those who see only the first and immediate interests of these islands – although we confess we hardly see on what principle they extend their views as far as the *three* kingdoms, and do not contend that Ireland and Scotland should be protected against England, or even county against county. In these days of rapid intercourse there is almost as much difference between parts of the British Isles as there is between our distant Possessions. But for ourselves, our aim is to promulgate a definite and national policy suitable to the present needs of our Empire and her ever growing population, regardless as to whether it may be popular or unpopular in all its parts. And to those who differ from us in detail, whether they be those who go further than we do, or who dare not go so far, all we ask is that we may march together as far as our common roads lead us. For whether it be this school of thought or another, or this body of men or that, which may eventually carry the day, is matter of supreme indifference, provided the battle be only fought and won.

Manchester Chamber of Commerce, 'Manchester and the Manchesterians: Storming the Citadel', *Fair-Trade. A Weekly Journal Devoted to Industry and Commerce*, 1:56 (5 November 1886), pp. 37–40.

FAIR – TRADE.

A Weekly Journal Devoted to Industry and Commerce.

LONDON, NOVEMBER 5, 1886.

MANCHESTER AND THE MANCHESTERIANS.

Storming the Citadel.

It naturally behoves Mr. Jacob Bright to speak up on behalf of the policy with which his family name is so closely connected. But we certainly hardly expected to find such arguments as those he offered to the Manchester Athenæum Lecture and Debating Society, last week, gravely put forward in these days when our increasing dependence upon external food supplies is daily attracting more and more attention as an element of national danger. Mr. Jacob Bright, however, almost seems to regard this in the light of a public benefit. In his inaugural address at the opening of the Athenæum session he said:–

'In 1846, thanks to Manchester and associated towns, Corn Laws were repealed, and the period of Free Trade began. Perhaps he could give no fact which would put in stronger light the enormous benefit that we had obtained by the change than that in the present year some 26,000,000 quarters of wheat were required for the food of the United Kingdom, and only 8,000,000 out of that quantity were grown at home.'

Now, what Mr. Jacob Bright means, no doubt – for we do not for an instant distrust his absolute sincerity – is, that being now compelled to consume so much corn grown outside the country, it is satisfactory to know we can get at it. But is not this very much like putting the cart before the horse? Is it not self-evident that the need for such supplies is, in the first place, a peril to be considered? We are not, indeed, prepared to lay all the blame, or indeed any great part of the blame, for this position on the repeal of the Corn Laws. That science and invention, in preparing new modes for the migration of persons and the distribution of commodities throughout the world, has had more to do with the new food supplies at our command than any fiscal question, is, in our view, only historical truth. But whatever the causes, to contend that such dependence of itself, and by consequence the ruin of so much of our productive power and internal wealth which food imports displace, is a national boon and sign of 'enormous benefit' to the country, is surely the most stupendous and falsest paradox that was ever offered for the consideration of an intelligent audience.

In the face of such assertions, which cannot claim even the merit of ingenious casuistry, the assumption that national progress in other respects is the result of the 'legislation of 1846,' is comparatively mild. Mr. Jacob Bright may be pardoned, of course, on account of family reasons when he follows his illustrious brother's example, and claims everything that has taken place since 1846 even down to the School Board itself, as the direct result of the abolition of the old Corn Laws. But surely he might have had the modesty not to have claimed, as he did at the Manchester Athenæum, the 'great diminution of the hours of labour' as also a result! Who were the most bitter opponents against the restriction of the hours of labour but the Anti-Corn Law League 'economists,' led by Mr. Jacob Bright's own brother? Nor can we easily understand how any gentleman, who presumably understands the history of his own times, could recapitulate, as Mr. Jacob Bright did, the circumstances of Ireland, without drawing a moral wholly opposed to the theory the benefits of '1846' have secured us. He said, and said truly –

'While painting that somewhat roseate picture, it was impossible for him to pass over in absolute silence a circumstance of a very different, and indeed of the most painful character that it was possible to conceive – he meant the history of Ireland during that period. At about the time of the establishment of Free Trade, Ireland had a population of 8,000,000. That population had come down to 5,000,000. How had that come about? Largely by emigration, but in a larger degree by starvation and famine; in fact, the course of depopulation in Ireland had been attended, there could be no doubt, by suffering of the deepest and broadest character.'

But what is it that has mainly incited this calamitous state of affairs? What else but the fact that Irish industries have been simply exterminated by the famous Free Trade theory, and that her prosperity has been knocked on the head primarily in consequence of the so-called 'enormous benefits?' Is it because the Bright family are defective in logical capacity, that we find such strangely absurd conclusions drawn from facts which speak exactly the contrary? or is it that the halo of platform brilliancy has so completely blinded their vision as to prevent them seeing clearly? But happily such blindness, however infectious, is not incurable in others, and when we find that in Manchester itself – in the very heart of the whilom free trading citadel – the Chamber of Commerce has, by the narrowest of majorities, just escaped censuring the continuance of the policy through which 'Bright's benefits' have been conferred, we may justly indulge in hopes that the old superstitions are passing away.

'Causes of Trade Depression. A Letter to Iddesleigh, Chairman of the Royal Commission on Depression in Trade', *Fair-Trade. A Weekly Journal Devoted to Industry and Commerce*, 1:14 (15 January 1886) pp. 105–6.

FAIR – TRADE.

A Weekly Journal Devoted to Industry and Commerce.

Vol. I. – No. 14. pp. 105–6

15 JANUARY, 1886.

CAUSES OF TRADE DEPRESSION.

GENERAL AND SPECIAL. – A LETTER.

To the Right Hon. the Earl of Iddesleigh, *Chairman of the Royal Commission on the Depression in Trade.*

My Lord, – There are those amongst us who regard with fear and dislike the inquiry by Royal Commission into the causes of the prevalent industrial depression, feeling instinctively that, if the inquiry be successful in arriving at sound conclusions, an economic policy, in which they have (or believe themselves to have) a vested interest, and of which they have made themselves the advocates, will be brought into great jeopardy; because its condemnation by a public, whose eyes have been opened to the false and mischievous character of the notions upon which the system actually rests, may be expected to speedily follow their detection and exposure. There are many others who, in common with myself, having heartily welcomed the appointment of the Commission, are watching its progress with great interest, not unmingled, however, with anxiety, lest the prevalent idolatory [sic] of mere opinion, supported by plausible sophistry, and deference to prejudices advocated by the superficial thinkers and writers of the hour, should lead the Commission to stultify itself through want of due regard for fundamental facts, and cause it to end ignominiously as a mere Babel of conflicting opinions [...].

Reserving for the present some remarks on a remedy for the *general* depression, I will now proceed to the consideration of the *particular* depression under which this country is also suffering.

Not having reliable statistics at hand to furnish the numbers of labourers employed in agricultural work at the present and at former times, I will take supposititious quantities, which may be considered as mere guesses in round numbers. Whether or not these quantities are near approximations to the actual numbers is of very little moment, because they are given merely to illustrate the principle, and the correctness of the principle is not dependent upon that of the numbers. So, then, let us say that at the time (be it more or less than fifteen years since) when the agricultural industry of this country was in its most flourishing condition, the number of labourers employed by it (taking the whole United Kingdom) exceeded the number employed at the present time by five hundred thousand, and that these labourers were earning, on the average, 15s. a week. Then they were earning £375,000 a week and £19,500,000 a year.

What, my lord, would be the effect, or kind of effect, on the existing state of industrial depression peculiar to this country, supposing an annual sum of about £20,000,000 were to be divided in weekly payments of £375,000, amongst 500,000 of those members of the labouring class at the present time in a half-famishing condition, barely able, with the benevolent help of their fellow-subjects, to keep body and soul together, enabling them, as, of course, it would do, to become forthwith customers of the tradesman – purchasers of clothing, food, and furniture?

This, however, is by no means a sufficient, or even just, presentation of the full case; for our agricultural industry has been for about the last forty years, by that economic policy which has made our country the laughing-stock of the civilised world, so heavily handicapped, that it is not too much to say it has been perforce prevented (even in the most prosperous period preceding the depression) from developing itself to anything like the extent it would have done under a wise and judicious policy. The fair question, my Lord, is, How many labourers would the agriculture of the United Kingdom be now employing if, fairly and justly protected against unrestricted competition in its own market with foreign producers, a moiety (or even a small part) of the enormous profits earned by the labour of this country, which have been sent abroad during the last thirty or forty years to promote the industrial development of other nations, had been applied in this – our own country – to the enlightened development of its agricultural resources; in bringing all land capable of being advantageously cultivated under cultivation; in applying to it the increased knowledge gained by the progress of agricultural chemistry and of scientific farming; and, above all, in substituting the vigour and energy belonging to a prosperous and profitable industry, well supported by capital, for that half-hearted and spiritless lassitude which inevitably attaches itself to a profitless and failing industry, ungratefully discarded and most unjustly oppressed by the insensate nation to which it belongs. 'Taxing the food of the people.' That is the way the *people* (save the mark!) has been beguiled and persuaded into regarding an import duty sufficient to protect and promote the great agricultural interests of this country. The statement is virtually and really as false as it has been mischievous. It is now, however, firmly lodged in the uncultured brain of the Demos, and, as he has been recently hoisted up into the throne, and told to consider himself monarch of all he surveys, it may there constitute a practical and serious difficulty in the way of immediately dealing with the urgent necessities of the case by means of import duty. Happily there is an alternative method to which this prejudice cannot be applied, and by which the necessary result may be attained. It is to give a bonus or bounty to the home-producer, sufficient to enable him to realise a reasonable profit whatever the price of imported produce may be. So much[1] per 100 bushels of wheat, or other grain, certified as grown on the farm; so much per head for cattle, sheep, pigs, &c., raised on the land; so much for dairy produce of certified good quality. A considerable number of duly qualified Revenue officers would have to be employed, and the system possibly might be (and just at first most probably would be) more troublesome, and, perhaps, more expensive, than the system of import duties. It may, however, be adopted and carried into effect easily. Some degree of ability and skill in efficiently organising the requisite arrangements would be called for; but nothing that can properly be called difficulty stands in the way of adopting and applying the specified system. It would allow the foreign producer and the British capitalist, who has invested his profits in other countries, to bring in their foreign produce at as low a price as they pleased, just the same as at present, so that it could not be called, even by the most rampant sophist, 'taxing the food of the people.' And, at the same time, it would enable our own farmers to undersell the foreign produce, in the home market, however low the price.

'But,' someone may inquire, 'do you propose to pay this bonus out of the public treasury?' Certainly; by all means. 'Oh! would not that be equivalent to taxing other classes for the benefit of the farmer and agricultural labourer?' Not at all; it would be taxing them for *their own* benefit. It is a matter that concerns you, me, and everyone else in the kingdom, and would benefit each of us just as much as the farmer. We should be all taxed alike and benefitted alike. What more legitimate and proper use of a national treasury can there be than to make payments for national purposes imperatively required to satisfy the necessities and promote the well-being of the entire community? It is for the self-protection of the nation against further injury and ultimate ruin it is called for, and from the nature of the case this can only be primarily effected by the protection of the farmer.[2]

1   The amount of the Bonus would be on a sliding-scale; determined semi-annually; differentiated and regulated according to the price of imported produce at the time.
2   Those who feel a deep-rooted aversion to the word 'Protection' may call this alternative system, 'The Politic Promotion of Home Industry'.

Agriculture, although by far the most extensive and important of our national industries herein concerned, does not stand alone. There are others which are in the same category, and to which the same considerations apply. To mention only one other, as a portentous example of what the persistence in an unjust and unwise policy has done and is doing, there is (or was) our valuable silk weaving industry, already exterminated, or very nearly so, by the same baneful influence which has blighted the prosperity of our agriculture. In my letter replying to Mr. Royston's inquiry, published in FAIR-TRADE of January the 8th, the circumstance is pointed out that unrestricted competition in the home market with the foreign producers of all parts of the world is not the sole cause of the whole, nor even of the most injurious part, of that destructive excess of importation now blasting the prosperity and threatening the very existence of our native industries. It is shown therein that the interest on the immense capital, invested by British capitalists in foreign countries during the period of great commercial prosperity (and probably also a part of that capital itself) is now being brought to this country, year by year, in the form of foreign produce and manufactured goods, at such low prices as to force the market. It is useless to deny or doubt the *circumstance*, because there are the reliable official data – the Board of Trade returns – to demonstrate it. There may, however, very likely be persons who will argue, 'Ah, well: if, as far as the public is concerned, we are now getting all this food and all these goods for nothing – i.e., without giving anything in exchange for them, *that* cannot surely be a cause for lamentation.' But it *is* a cause for lamentation, because, if the food and manufactured goods were produced in our own country, we should get it all for *nothing*, just as much; with this difference, that our labourers would then be employed and our industries thriving, instead of our labourers being deprived of their employments and our industries of their prosperity.

Having now indicated, in rough outline, the whole case, distinguishing between that particular depression from which our country alone is suffering, and that general depression from which all civilised nations (including our own) are, proportionately to their commercial and industrial development, suffering in common, I will conclude by expressing the hope that the exposition may be found of utility to members of the Royal Commission, and also to others who have the subject under consideration, by putting before them, with some degree of comprehensiveness and clearness, the full conditions of that great economic problem with which they are called upon to deal. – I have the honour to be, my Lord, very respectfully yours,

KUKLOS.

Royal Commission on Depression in Trade and Industry, 'Minority "Fair Trade" Report', *Parliamentary Papers*, XXIII (1886), Cmnd 4893, paras 132–45.

132. For it must be remembered that the adoption of the system of protection by all foreign countries has not merely left our producers, alone amongst all others, destitute of an artificial stimulus; that they might well have endured without complaint. But it has at last brought upon them an unnatural, and practically subsidised competition. From this they have none the less right to be defended, because, in the presence of general or even partially prevailing free trade, they would be the last to desire protection of any kind.

133. The measures we have indicated would counterwork the effects of protection, and strengthen the position of our producers, directly in the home market, and indirectly, though substantially, in neutral markets. It is, of course, out of our power to obtain more free access to the protected markets of countries like the United States, France, and Germany themselves. In past years we had little occasion to regret this, or to trouble ourselves about it. Their course of action did not harm us so long as we were able, in spite of it, to obtain full employment for all our available labour. To buy everything in the cheapest market – though not permitted to sell in the dearest – may be the best policy, so long as we can find other full and equally remunerative employment for the home enterprize and industry which we displace in so doing. But no longer; for, from the moment in which the combined effect of protective tariffs abroad and foreign competition at home limits our market so as to cramp the free and full exercise of our industries, it begins to choke the living fountain of our wealth, our social well-being, and our national strength. We think the evidence is conclusive that during the past ten or twelve years this point has been reached, and that the adoption of a national policy suited to the changed conditions is imperatively demanded.

134. For though we may be unable to alter the protectionist policy of other nations, we can do much to free ourselves from its injurious effects. The more we can draw our supplies of imported food from countries which will largely, and under moderate tariff rates, accept the products of our industries in exchange, the fuller and the steadier will be the employment of our population.

135. Our command of the fiscal arrangements of India has saved the industry of Lancashire from the calamity which must have overwhelmed it, had that great empire come under the control of a commercial policy like that of Russia or the United States. And the growth of our Colonies, with their very large consumption per head of British manufactures, has helped all our industries to endure with less suffering the stifling pressure of foreign tariffs.

136. But these aids, though welcome, are insufficient. It is a striking fact that during the past 20 years 67 per cent. of our emigrants have gone to the United States, and only 27½ per cent to our own Colonies. The more extreme protectionist policy of the United States, so far from repelling immigrants, has operated as an effectual bribe to both capital and labour, by holding out the inducement of higher prices and higher wages.

137. It would be an act of suicidal folly on our part to attempt to counterwork these influences by a like system of enormous import duties, designed to raise the price of commodities for the advantage of home producers. We have a far better and more effectual remedy at command. A slightly preferential treatment of the food products of India and the Colonies over those of foreign nations would, if adopted as a permanent system, gradually but certainly direct the flow of food-growing capital and labour more towards our own dependencies and less towards the United States than heretofore.

138. When it is noted that in the year 1884 the Australian colonies, with only 3,100,000 inhabitants, purchased 23,895,858*l*. worth of our manufactures, whilst the United States, with about 55,000,000 inhabitants, purchased only 24,424,636*l*. worth, it will be apparent how great would be the effect of a policy which should lead to the more rapid peopling of the Australian colonies in giving fuller employment to our working classes at home, and thus increasing the healthful activity of the home trade, as well as the import of raw materials for our various industries to operate upon. On the other hand, it must be pointed out that the growth of our Colonies in population, wealth, and the other requisites of successful manufacturing enterprise, and the necessity felt by them of counterbidding to some extent the bribe which the high tariff of the United States offers to capital and labour, must operate to convert gradually the revenue duties of the Colonies, which now permit so large an import of British manufactures, into protective duties which will seriously restrict that import.

This has already happened in the case of the Dominion of Canada, and it is an influence which may act with increasing and disastrous force upon the most valuable portion of our export trade, unless a fiscal policy be adopted which will enable the various portions of the Empire to co-operate more effectually for mutual aid and defence in commercial matters.

139. We believe that specific duties, equal to about 10 per cent. on a low range of values, imposed upon the import from foreign countries of those articles of food which India and the Colonies are well able to produce, would sufficiently effect this purpose. Their adoption would, of course, involve the abolition of the heavy duties on tea, coffee, cocoa, and dried fruits, which are now levied on Indian and colonial, equally with foreign produce. It would widen the basis of our revenue, and render us less dependent upon the sustained productiveness of the income tax and the duties upon intoxicating liquors. And, what is even more

important, it could not fail to draw closer all portions of the empire in the bond of mutual interests, and thus pave the way towards a more effective union for great common objects.

140. Here again, as explained in para. 129, in regard to import duties on manufactures, we ought only to aim at countervailing legislative interference with natural conditions.

The fiscal legislation of foreign countries has (1) narrowed our markets artificially and unendurably; and has (2) deflected the movement of capital and emigration from our own Colonies, where they would have contributed largely to the employment of our industries, towards the United States, where they are artificially prevented by high tariffs from so doing. The measure proposed in para. 139 is, we are convinced, the only instrument at our disposal for neutralising this interference, and is so strictly limited as to prevent its general and permanent effect reaching beyond the fulfilment of that legitimate purpose.

For there would be no exclusion of foreign food products; they would come in on payment of the duty named; and we are convinced that if any effect were produced upon the prices of the articles in question it would be very slight indeed, and limited in duration to the time required, under the stimulus of preferential treatment, to increase the production of them in India and the Colonies; for so vast and varied are the resources of the empire, that competition within its limits would inevitably keep down prices at the lowest remunerative level just as effectually as in the outer world.

141. As already stated (paras. 57, 58) the circumstances of the world have rapidly changed, and the fear is no longer of the want of a sufficiency of commodities at low money prices, but of a sufficiency of employment. We are indeed convinced that, were it possible that the adoption of such a policy as we have just indicated should raise the price of the articles in question by the whole amount of the duty, the increased employment afforded by the larger demand for commodities, arising from the improved position of the producers at home and in our dependencies, would far more than repay our labouring population for the slightly increased cost of their food. And this view is corroborated by the fact that during the past 15 years the periods of greatest industrial prosperity have not been those in which agriculturists were impoverished by low prices, but those in which they realised fair rates for their produce, and were able to contribute largely to the demand for the productions of all other industries.

142. If any existing commercial treaties or conventions contain provisions which would impede the complete adoption of such fiscal measures as have been here suggested, we are of opinion that the earliest opportunities ought to be taken of recovering our freedom in this respect.

143. We fear that neither these nor any other measures which could be proposed would effectually relieve the very serious depression of agriculture, the position of which is, under existing circumstances, inherently weaker than that

of other leading industries. Under universal free trade our great manufactures of metals and textiles would at once, in the face of all rivalry, expand to the utmost limits of the available labour, whilst our agriculture would still have to meet foreign competition based on superior natural advantages. Again, under a system of free trade within the empire and moderate duties on the import of foreign food and manufactures, our manufacturers would have little to fear from Indian or colonial competition, which to our agriculturists would be real and formidable.

To some slight extent, however, the proposed duties on foreign food products might operate to check the rapid decline of arable cultivation, and the consequent diminution of agricultural employment, whilst the increased activity of other industries would operate still more beneficially by augmenting the preferential demand for home-grown articles of food.

144. We cannot pass from this subject without expressing our conviction that the continuous decline of agricultural production and employment, considered in regard to its present and future effect on the physical health and moral and social condition of the people, and on the wealth and strength of the nation, constitutes a danger so grave as to demand the anxious consideration of the country and the legislature.

145. In conclusion, we desire to express our sense of the ready assistance which we have received in the course of our inquiry from the several bodies and individual witnesses whom we have consulted; and we would also commend to the careful attention of all classes of Your Majesty's subjects the valuable and complete collection of information as to the economical condition and prospects of the country which will be found in the appendices to our several Reports, and a list of which is annexed to this document. We think that, while the information which we have been able to collect will tend to diffuse clearer views on the subject of our commercial position, it will also show that it can only be strengthened by using all the means at our command to restore to our industries that position of equal advantage, in relation to foreign competitors, which the fiscal legislation of other countries has done so much to destroy. It is only by the persistent exercise, on the part of the nation as well as of individuals, of the same energy, courage, watchfulness, and readiness of resource by which our great industries and world-wide commerce were originally built up, that we can ensure their continued prosperity and growth, and look forward with well-grounded confidence to the full and profitable employment of our population. If our labours should tend in any degree to the promotion of this result, we venture to think that they will not have been entirely thrown away.

Dunraven[1]
W.Farrer Ecroyd
P.Albert Muntz
Nevile Lubbock

22 December 1886

---

1 Subject to the reservation and remarks which follow.

Robert Andrew Macfie, Letter 'The Fair-Trade Policy', *Fair-Trade. A Weekly Journal Devoted to Industry and Commerce*, 1:139 (8 June 1888), p. 510.

Fair-Trade, 8 June 1888

THE FAIR-TRADE POLICY

SIR, – In a prominent article you yesterday say, 'It is to Mr. MacIver that the foundation of the League is mainly due ... He was speedily joined in his plans by ... Mr. R. A. Macfie, of Edinburgh, ex-member for the Leith burghs. These six gentlemen signed the circular which summoned the first meeting.'

As I am thus honourably mentioned, will you allow me space to express my great regret that I have not been able to become or continue a member of the League, and to tell why? Entirely and only, and to my great disappointment, the question of *duties on cereal food* was not left an open one. I saw no objection whatever to the favourers of such duties being leaders in the movements at first contemplated, but I could not join in an endeavour to bring their distinctive aims about, whether in the light of principle or of mere expediency. Probably it is now seen that my views, plainly stated at the time of origination, should have been acted on. Is it too late to mend?

May I avail myself of the present opportunity, to urge, *first*, that our great object as Fair-Traders should be to impress statesmen, and the people, with the fact that, and the reason why, the *consumer* should be much less thought of than the producer – who must needs be also a consumer, but is actually and potentially much more and much better as a citizen than the other; and *secondly*, that statists [*sic*] should be set to work to ascertain, calculate, and demonstrate how vastly more fruitful in pecuniary and defensive national good the one is beyond the other; and making wares at home is, compared with importing them in the employment it gives, the population it rears. I don't think a thorough-going investigation has ever been made on these lines and followed out in its wide benefit-revealing ramifications. I am sure the result of solving the problem and exhibiting the superiority (all involved in our tenets) would surprise even the foremost and most ardent among ourselves. It would bring many useful recruits to our ranks.

R. A. Macfie, Dreghorn, Colinton, Midlothian
2 June 1888

TARIFFS AND EMPIRE, 1880–1902

As the first section has shown, at the centre of the fair trade challenge to free trade in later Victorian Britain lay an alternative vision whose essence was an imperial Zollverein, whereby trade within the British Empire would be consolidated, allowing the strengthening of the British imperial state. In this way, Britain, whose trade with Europe and the United States was increasingly restricted by rising tariffs, would find freer markets in her colonies, which in return would be given preference within the British market; Britain in particular would receive secure supplies of grain, so removing the potential threat to her food supply in time of war. In this way the economic grievances of the fair traders harmonized with a growing mood in which imperial federation was seen an essential to Britain's survival as a 'Great Power', the only way in which she could match the power of the rising empires based on land masses. These themes therefore became an insistent part of British politics in the 1880s, articulated by the highly influential Imperial Federation League, with power bases within the intelligentsia as well as the Liberal and Conservative parties.[1]

This theme of imperial consolidation was also one which found a good deal of support in the self-governing colonies. Yet since the 1850s at least the tariff history of the colonies had been at odds with that of Britain itself. Tariff autonomy declared by Britain in 1846 had led to local battles over free trade within the components of the Empire, most of which resulted in victories for those who promoted the defence of local industries against British competition. As a result, Canada by 1879 had formulated her 'National Policy', while in the Australian colony of Victoria the McCulloch tariff of 1866 had begun a trend towards a strongly protectionist policy.[2] The tariff map of the British empire by the 1880s, as the federationists found, was itself extremely complex, and completely at odds with the expectations of the free traders of the 1840s, as the reactions of men as diverse as William Gladstone and the third Earl Grey reveal.[3] Many now debated the merits of tariffs in young countries: for some, a desirable means of building up a balanced economy, able to generate employment for a growing population; but for others, tariffs forfeited the comparative advantages of the colonies, whilst building up political corruption.[4]

The extent of tariff-making in the empire by the 1880s therefore set clear limits to the potential success of any scheme for imperial economic unity. On the one hand, for free traders, any scheme which reopened the possibility of imperial preference, as did all the schemes of the fair traders, was anathema. On the other hand, the idea of free trade within the empire was one which offered the possibility of harmonizing free trade and imperial sentiment. Yet by the 1880s, the extent of colonial protectionism rendered a free trade empire a political impossibility. In this context, the federationists were ready to debate a series of proposals which were regularly brought before imperial conferences, while the *Statist* held an open competition for the best Zollverein scheme. For the most part in the 1880s and 1890s, an imperial Zollverein implied free trade (in the sense of revenue-only tariffs) within the empire combined with protective duties against foreign countries in the form of a common external tariff. This model was favoured by fair traders and received the support of many Chambers of Commerce and Conservative MPs. It was canvassed extensively, not only by the Fair Trade League but also by the United Empire Trade League and the British Empire League; it was the model which the future tariff reformer Joseph Chamberlain first supported. The idea of an imperial Zollverein therefore engendered a genuinely Empire-wide debate among interested politicians, economic interest groups, a host of pressure groups in metropole and periphery, and an increasingly influential and imperially-minded press, while a series of budding imperial businessmen and statesmen, such as Howard Vincent and John Lough, traversed the empire in praise of the imperial economic ideals satirized by Max O'Rell (the London-based Frenchman Blouet), in *John Bull & Co. The Great Colonial Branches of the Firm: Canada, Australia, New Zealand and South Africa* (1894). Several attempts were made to turn the Zollverein into reality, for example, when it was debated at the Colonial Conference of 1887. But these efforts all stumbled on two rocks; from the imperial side, the fiscal needs of the colonies made a common tariff difficult, while a revenue-only tariff was politically unacceptable to autonomous colonies that wished to build up their own industries and were not content to become agrarian appendages of industrial Britain. From the metropolitan perspective, the weight of free-trade sentiment in Britain remained preponderant: as the Earl of Derby informed Lady Jersey, the wife of the governor of New South Wales, 'public opinion here will not stand differential duties against foreign countries for the benefit of colonists who are much better off than the average Englishman and it seems that without such duties no Imperial Zollverein is possible'.[5]

Economic disharmony within the Empire was also made obvious by two further issues, those of sugar bounties and the Indian cotton duties. Since the 1870s the rise, and free importation, of bounty-fed continental sugar beet had aroused the opposition of the West India interest, with the support at times of free traders, who opposed bounties as artificial interference with trade, although other free traders argued that no obstacles should be placed in the way of the cheapest possible imports. Ultimately this led to an important policy innovation when, after much canvassing in several conferences, the European powers agreed to what was in effect the first multinational trade convention in 1902. This gave power to a supranational authority in Brussels to enforce equality in the market, but it gave rise to constitutional opposition (the transfer of sovereignty to Brussels!) and economic opposition among sugar-users and consumers.[6] Britain therefore withdrew from the Convention in 1912, and it withered as a tool of international market regulation. Sugar highlighted tension between metropolitan consumers and imperial producers; the Indian cotton duties by contrast divided two groups of producers, as British cotton manufacturers organized to oppose the cotton duties whereby the Indian government sought to limit British imports, and to protect the growing Indian cotton industry, albeit an industry in which British investment was prominent. Unlike the self-governing colonies, India lacked tariff autonomy, so that pressure from Lancashire, uniting employers and working men, was successful both in the 1870s and 1890s in enforcing the abolition of the protective element in such duties.[7]

Nevertheless the empire remained for many the key to Britain's future prosperity and, despite these conflicts and the failure of the Zollverein, a new generation of statesmen, led by Chamberlain, sought in the early twentieth century to redesign the Empire fit to revivify the 'weary Titan'. In doing so they now had to take account of the permanence of colonial protectionism and also the readiness of the colonies, led by Canada in 1897, to offer preference to Great Britain. The offer of preference contained its own dangers, for example Germany now instituted a tariff war against Canada for its infraction of 'British free trade', but it also offered a potential means of harmonizing the aspiration of the colonies and Britain. Imperial economic unity would now be based on an acceptance of colonial protection, but protectionist tariffs would be lowered in respect of British goods. At the same tine Britain would abandon free imports by imposing tariffs against foreign goods, and offering preference to imperial ones.[8] This was the imperial ideal which Chamberlain would bring back into the Edwardian debate on empire which is considered in the section on Free Trade versus Tariff Reform, below.

Notes
1. D. Bell, *The Idea of Greater Britain* (Princeton, NJ: Princeton University Press, 2007); E. H. H. Green, 'The Political Economy of Empire, 1880–1914', in A. Porter (ed.), *The Oxford History of the British Empire: The Nineteenth Century* (Oxford: Oxford University Press, 1999), pp. 346–68.

2. B. Forster, *A Conjunction of Interests: Business, Politics, and Tariffs, 1825–1879* (Toronto: University of Toronto Press, 1986); C. Goodwin, *Economic Enquiry in Australia* (Durham, NC: Duke University Press, 1966); G. D. Patterson, *The Tariff in the Australian Colonies, 1856–1900* (Melbourne: R. W. Cheshire, 1968); J. A. La Nauze, *Political Economy in Australia: Historical Studies* (Melbourne: Melbourne University Press, 1949).
3. R. W. Rawson, *Synopsis of the Tariffs and Trade of the British Empire* (London: Imperial Federation League, 1888), *Sequel to Synopsis of the Tariffs and Trade of the British Empire* (London: Imperial Federation League, 1889); for Gladstone and Grey, see A. Howe, *Free Trade and Liberal England, 1846–1946* (Oxford: Clarendon Press, 1997), pp. 189, 215.
4. See especially George Baden Powell, 'Protection in Young Communities', *Fortnightly Review* (1882), below, pp. 51–5.
5. 15 August 1891, cited in Howe, *Free Trade and Liberal England*, p. 217.
6. Ibid., pp. 204–13, 277; G. A. Pigman, 'Hegemony and Trade Liberalization: The Brussels Sugar Convention of 1902', *Review of International Studies*, 23 (1997), pp. 185–210; R. Munting, 'Contrasts in Political Economy: Britain, Germany and the International Sugar Economy before 1914', in C. Dipper, A. Gestrich and L. Raphael (eds), *Krieg, Frieden und Demockratie* (Frankfurt am Main and Oxford: Peter Lang, 2001), pp. 103–16.
7. P. Harnetty, 'The Indian Cotton Duties Controversy, 1894–1896', *English Historical Review*, 77:305 (1962), pp. 684–702; I. Klein, 'English Free Traders and Indian Tariffs, 1874–96', *Modern Asian Studies*, 5 (1971), pp. 251–71.
8. For the imperial genesis of tariff reform, see especially J. Amery, *The Life of Joseph Chamberlain, Volume 5: 1901–1903* (London: Macmillan, 1969).

TARIFFS AND EMPIRE, 1880-1902

G. Smith, 'The Canadian Tariff', *Contemporary Review*, 40 (1881), pp. 378-80.

THE CANADIAN TARIFF.

ENGLAND is angry with Canada about the new Canadian tariff; and angry she would have a right to be if the tariff were, as she seems to suppose, Protectionist and directed against the mother country.

Directed against the mother country with any unkind intention it is impossible that the Canadian tariff, or any other measure adopted by Canada, should be. The feeling of British Canadians towards England is as warm as any reasonable Englishman can desire. The French are French, and their hearts turn to their own mother country. The Irish are Irish, though less Fenian than their compatriots in the United States, as their conduct with regard to the Land League has shown. But the British of all parties retain their affection for England. The gradual relaxation of the political tie has only strengthened the natural bond.

Nor is the Canadian tariff Protectionist, except in relation to the coal tax, which is imposed avowedly for the purpose of compelling Western Canada to burn Nova Scotia coal, but does not concern England. It is not Protectionist, at least in its main object or in its direct intention, though it may be said to have a Protectionist or quasi-Protectionist aspect to which reference shall presently be made. It is the offspring of sheer fiscal necessity. There was a large and growing deficit, which it was imperative to fill. There were only three ways of filling it: further borrowing, direct taxation, and an increase of the import duties. Further borrowing would have been profligate; it would of course have impaired our credit, and would only have staved off the need; the English creditors of Canada, at all events, would not have desired that we should take this course. From direct taxation all statesmen in communities like Canada shrink on political and social, as well as on financial grounds. An increase of the import duties alone remained. The effect has been an addition to the revenue, which has not only filled the deficit, but produced a surplus, though of what amount it would not be safe to say before next winter, when the Finance Minister will make his statement. The character of the tariff as a revenue tariff is thus vindicated by the result. The writer of this paper has been assured by leading commercial men in Canada, who are in principle Free Traders, and who are unconnected with politics, that the measure on the whole was as well framed as the circumstances would permit; and the Opposition, while as a matter of course it has denounced the Government plan, has as yet propounded no counter plan of its own. The object, announced from the Throne, was not the protection of native industry, but the equalization of revenue with expenditure, and the framers are men who have always professed Free Trade sentiments, besides being the heads of the Conservative and Imperialist Party.

The tariff is directed, if against anybody, against the people of the United States, who were excluding Canada from their markets, and at the same time throwing their surplus goods, whenever there was a glut, at very low prices into the markets of Canada, not perhaps in large quantities, but in such a way as to derange the calculations of Canadian manufacturers, and prevent, so it was alleged, the free growth of Canadian enterprise. There is a rider to the tariff providing that if the United States will lower their duties, Canada will lower hers. Sir John Macdonald and his colleagues are, in fact, able to boast that the result of their policy has been a diminished importation of American, and an increased importation of British goods, though it would be unsafe to join in their exultation without knowing the statistics of smuggling, which, on that long and perfectly open frontier, always goes on to a large extent, and has no doubt increased since the raising of the duties on American goods, being in fact the irregular protest of Nature against an artificial line.

The Canadian tariff, we repeat, is the offspring of sheer fiscal necessity. And how was the fiscal necessity produced? How comes it to pass that, though Canada has had no Civil War, and her defence is mainly undertaken by England, her financial condition is now actually worse than that of the United States, – that her public debt is heavier in proportion to her population, and much heavier in proportion to her wealth than theirs, – that while their debt is being rapidly reduced, hers is still increasing, – and that her most experienced financier, Sir Francis Hincks, finds it his duty to warn her, in the *Montreal Journal of Commerce*, that her liabilities are being piled up at a most dangerous rate, and that the reckoning day is at hand? The answer will show that Imperialism, though it may be a magnificent policy, is a policy for which you pay, and that for the increased duties laid by her North-American Colonists on her goods, England has mainly herself to thank.

Of the public debt of Canada, half, at least, may be set down to the account of public works, undertaken not so much for the commercial objects of the Colony, as for the political objects of the Empire, and especially to the account of a vast system of political and military railways, destined to carry into effect a policy of British antagonism to the United States.

G. Baden Powell, 'Protection in Young Communities', *Fortnightly Review*, 31 (1882), pp. 375–9.

General Prosperity and Growth. – I have said that Victoria and New South Wales each imports twice as much per head of population as we do in these islands. It is obvious that any policy which affects their imports must affect their general life and well-being to a degree unknown even in these commercial islands. And I pass to compare the two colonies in regard to general prosperity and growth. The signs of this are external and internal; the signs are to be seen in their dealings with the outside world and also in their domestic condition.

Firstly, then, as regards their dealings with the outside world. This is a most significant index of their actual welfare, seeing that their external trade is double in value per head of population to what it is even in England. This trade is a sure indicator of prosperity, inasmuch as it is a sure indicator of any increase or decrease in consumption and production, the two visible factors of prosperity. Ten years ago New South Wales was doing an external trade of the annual value of £19,000,000. A decade of steady increase brought this total up to £29,500,000 in 1880. Ten years ago Victoria was doing an annual external trade of £27,600,000. In the succeeding decade a wavering line of rise and fall brings us to an annual total of £30,500,000 for 1880. Under the high tariff external trade increased during the decade by one-ninth only. Under the low tariff external trade increased by more than one-half of its previous annual total. The full significance of this is seen when we find New South Wales, at the end of the decade, doing £10,000,000 more annual trade than at the beginning, while Victoria was only doing some £3,000,000 more. Ten per cent. profit on such trade would mean an addition to the annual national income of New South Wales of £1,000,000, and to that of Victoria only some £300,000.

Incidentally it is worthy of note that the German Government, perhaps the best informed Government at present in existence, has chosen for the headquarters of its Consul-General for Australasia the capital of the low tariff colony; although the high tariff colony is at the present moment ahead in number of population and in value of external trade. The Germans evidently judge of the certain future by means of the recorded past.

Further instruction follows on further analysis of this external trade. If we turn to the exports we find that ten years ago the value of articles, the produce or manufacture of the colony itself, was exactly 77 per cent. of the total value exported from each colony. At the end of the decade we find the amount of this native produce exported had *risen* to 83 per cent. in New South Wales, but had *fallen* to 68 per cent. in Victoria. In other words, under the low tariff there had been increase, and under the high tariff decrease in the exportable surplus of native products, a most important sign of prosperity and growth.

If we turn to the imports we find that ten years ago there entered New South Wales goods to the value of £9,000,000. At the end of the decade this annual value had mounted to £14,000,000, an increase of 60 per cent. Ten years ago the imports into Victoria were of the value of £12,500,000. At the end of the decade this annual value had mounted to £14,600,000, an increase of 20 per cent. only. In other words, not only the power but the using of the power to purchase foreign produce (and there was profit accruing to each purchase made) increased by about three times the speed under the low tariff to what it did under the high tariff.

There is another point in this external trade of much significance. In New South Wales there has been an increase in the tonnage of the shipping visiting the colony during the decade, from 1,500,000 to 2,600,000 tons. In Victoria the increase has been from 1,300,000 to 2,200,000. It may be said that this difference in growth is inevitable under a low as opposed to a high tariff, but it none the less represents a fountain of popular well-being, drawn upon in the one case to a much more profitable extent than in the other.

In connection with this shipping there are the very important records of ballast. There came to New South Wales during the decade 3,000,000 tons of shipping in ballast. There left New South Wales during the decade 117,000 tons of shipping in ballast. There came to Victoria during the decade 113,000 tons in ballast. There left Victoria 2,500,000 tons, the greater proportion of which proceeded to New South Wales. Empty ships *arriving* in New South Wales have increased from an annual tonnage of 220,000 in 1870 to a tonnage of 320,000 in 1880. Empty ships *leaving* Victoria have increased from an annual tonnage of 198,000 tons in 1870 to a tonnage of 250,000 in 1880. It will be observed that the conditions are exactly reversed in favour of the growth of the low tariff colony.

The domestic or internal condition and growth of these two colonies will complete the illustrations we would give of their growth and prosperity.

In the first place, in regard to population, we find that that of New South Wales has increased from 520,000 in 1870 to 740,000 in 1880, an increase of 48 per cent. The population of Victoria has increased from 730,000 in 1870 to 860,000 in 1880, an increase of only 17 per cent. In the second place, in regard to *wealth*, already we have seen in every point we have touched upon the far greater rapidity with which wealth-producing developments have been proceeding in New South Wales than in Victoria. From this we infer the fact that wealth is being produced in similar ratio. And when we read that the value of rateable property has doubled in New South Wales in the decade, and only increased by one-half in Victoria, we have our inference signally verified by recorded facts.

Singular evidence is afforded, also, by the statistics of the Savings Banks. In New South Wales the deposits have increased from £930,000 to £1,500,000;

and the number of the depositors from 21,000 to 32,000. In Victoria the deposits have increased from £1,100,000 to £1,600,000; but the depositors have increased in number from 38,000 to 76,000. In other words, the average amount deposited has risen in New South Wales steadily from £44 per head to £47. In Victoria the average deposited per head has fallen from £29 to £15. This is evidence corroborating the fact so commonly asserted that in democratic Victoria wealth is accumulating in the hands of the few. This is a result generally associated with a high tariff by all writers on political economy. It is a result which in its direct antagonism to the wholesome principle of equable distribution of wealth stamps it as one of the most injurious results of a high tariff.

Illustrative of this tendency is the fact that the average wages of skilled labour grew in New South Wales, during the decade, from being lower to being higher than similar wages in Victoria. That wages should have risen under a low tariff faster than under a high tariff is a fact of great importance, especially to countries wherein manhood suffrage gives to the wage-earner so much political power and responsibility. But it is a fact of which most people are ignorant.

It is well also to notice that the prices of the necessaries of life – of wheat, tea, and provisions and tools and implements – are generally lower in New South Wales than in Victoria. This, of course, adds much force to the before-recorded results in the nominal rates of wages, for it adds the essential element of greater relative purchasing power under the low tariff.

In order to form an exact estimate of social well-being we must build a general judgment on numerous details; and among these details marriages afford apposite information. In New South Wales during the decade the annual number of marriages has steadily increased from 3,800 to 5,100; an increase of one-third. In Victoria the increase in annual number has been from 4,700 to 5,100; an increase of one-eighth only. While in New South Wales marriages are in the proportion of 7 to every 1,000 of population, in Victoria they are but 6. And this is the more remarkable when we remember that in New South Wales there are 80 women to every 100 men, whereas in Victoria there are 90 women to every 100 men.

Ample details have thus accumulated during the past decade to show that in regard to all outward signs of prosperity and growth – social, industrial, commercial – the colony with the low tariff has progressed with far greater rapidity than the colony with the high tariff. This exhibits the great practical use of statistics. They are thus brought to substantiate, by the cold logic of recorded acts and facts, the reports and rumours that have been rife in these two colonies. The newspapers, it is true, had provided from day to day pictures of New South Wales altogether devoid of the sombre economical colouring that had become the salient feature in the accounts of Victoria. Nor has there been in New South Wales that general outspoken discontent among capitalists as well as among working men which has from time to time manifested itself in Victoria. Under the high tariff each industrial class in Victoria has in its turn bitterly complained of the duties that specially weigh upon it. The latest information carries on the tale to deputations of miners demanding of Government a lowering of duties on imported mining machinery and tools. The farmers have been for some time threatening to give up their farming because of the high prices they are forced to pay for their implements and materials – high prices unknown over the border in the low tariff colony of New South Wales. Multitudes of labourers, the very men who by their votes supported the policy of 'Protection' to native labour, have had from time to time to stave off starvation at relief work wages. It has been for some time more than suspected that capital had set in a strong current towards other colonies; it was not, however, known that the current of labour, far less easily transferable, had set in the same direction. The skilful and conscientious estimates of population made from year to year by the Victorian Statistical Department, under the guidance of that very able statist Mr. Hayter, proved, when the actual records of the census of this year came to be taken, to be no less than 76,000 of people over the mark in a population of 850,000. Mistaken popular opinion refused to recognise the enormous emigration of labouring men *and their families* that had been proceeding all the while. But by this official recording of facts this popular error has now been set straight.

It is well, in conclusion, to summarise the general lessons of these recorded results. In his address to the Economic Section at the jubilee meeting of the British Association Mr. Grant Duff put forward as a text the sentence, 'Methods that answer follow thoughts that are true.' This idea may be profitably amplified into the corollary, 'Thoughts that are true follow knowledge of methods that answer.' In this article the object has been to afford knowledge of methods that answer and of methods that do not answer; and this knowledge has been sought in the recorded results of rival methods. This knowledge, when acquired, must be followed by thoughts that are true. In Victoria itself it is hoped this record of what has already taken place will give fresh impulse to the reactionary movement in favour of a lower tariff. Signs of this movement are already apparent. The new Premier, Sir Bryan O'Loghlan, has issued a Royal Commission to inquire into the working of the tariff, and he apologetically promises the people of Victoria 'a free breakfast table.' These are thoughts that are true, and they seem to be following on the knowledge of methods that do not answer.

In the wider sphere of the British Empire these recorded results may stimulate local parliaments to maintain low tariffs. We must look to the spread of sound knowledge and to the honest subordination of class interests to the common national good rather than to fostering duties on foreign wheat, if we would successfully set the great and growing commerce of the empire on sound and profitable economic foundations. Until the Canadian Dominion, for political rather than economic purposes, not long ago swerved from the right path, there was not one colony, and that one the unfortunate colony of Victoria, among the eight great self-governing colonies enjoying independence of fiscal action, that had burdened itself with a high tariff. It would seem that Victoria has paid the penalty of its backsliding. That the others did not follow suit is plain evidence of the great practical common sense and public loyalty of the majority of British colonists. To this and to the spread of knowledge of recorded results we may look for a continuance of this tendency towards low tariffs throughout the British Empire. This tendency, if persevered in, will enable every Englishman, no matter where he may be domiciled over the wide empire, to thrive on the fact which has done England itself such unbounded material good, that whatever he uses or consumes is obtained by him at the lowest possible cost. Such action is urgently recommended by economic science, for it must contribute to the material prosperity of every industrial worker throughout the whole British Empire.

GEORGE BADEN-POWELL.

S. Bourne, 'Imperial Federation in its Commercial Aspect', *Imperial Federation*, 1:1 (January 1886), pp. 8–10.

IMPERIAL FEDERATION IN ITS COMMERCIAL ASPECT.

AMONGST the many aspects in which 'Imperial Federation' is viewed, the one which is presented less frequently than others is that of the commercial intercourse it would promote between the several Colonies, as well as with the mother-country. [...]

Leaving out of the question at present all existing or prospective relations with other countries, it may be safely affirmed that, as between every portion of the Empire, there ought to be

NO RESTRICTIONS UPON PERFECT FREEDOM OF TRADE.

It is no infringement of this principle to except from its operation the manufacture or the trading in anything which is forbidden by the highest consideration of morality, or public safety. As, for instance, the supply of intoxicating liquors to untutored tribes, or restrictions where there is a certainty of their being misused. In like manner, the sale of arms, or instruments of offence, which are to be used in the promotion of fratricidal warfare, or destruction of constituted authority, and injurious to the public weal. In all these cases the higher claims of religion and justice must be held supreme, because whatever is for the good of the several members of the one body, and not inconsistent with the restraints which society rightly puts upon the liberty of individuals, must override the right of every man to do what he wills with his own. Subject to such limitations, it is clearly for the general benefit that whatever advantages, whether natural or acquired, exist in any one place, should be equally at the service of those in other localities, unhampered by protective duties. If these advantages, notwithstanding the extra cost of transport, which must always be borne by the more distant consumer, are so great as to outweigh those of rivals on the spot, it is false economy to subject one member of the Empire to an unnecessary charge, for the purpose of fostering a more costly manufacture nearer home. The mother-country has fully recognised this in dealing with her home and Colonial subjects alike; and if federation is to take place, it would seem but just that all the federates should follow her leading. Even admitting that Canada is justified in creating Custom-house barriers on her line of contact with the United States, the same justification cannot be accepted from Victoria, for a like maintenance on the border line which separates her from New South Wales. No real parental or fraternal union can exist under such circumstances.

It is an utter mistake to allege that the exigencies of the Colonial chest, which may possibly require

THE IMPOSITION OF CUSTOMS DUTIES

for revenue purposes, sanction the unfriendly act of levying duties which protect the local producer against those of other Colonies. The home Government has solved this supposed difficulty by imposing an Excise duty on all goods manufactured within its own borders, exactly equivalent to the Customs duties which she levies on those goods when brought in from outside; and she makes no difference at all between English, Scotch, Irish, Indian, or Colonial suppliers. The products of the soil, and the industry devoted to manufacture, should be open to such a perfectly free market wherever customers can be found, who are either unable or unwilling to raise for themselves.

Admitting, for the sake of argument only, that a different course should be adopted with goods imported from foreign countries, it would be very desirable that whatever duties are levied should be of

EQUAL INCIDENCE IN ALL THE PORTS OF THE EMPIRE,

that is, that the fiscal regulations everywhere within its territories should be the same. In the United Kingdom the Irish consumer pays the same as the Scotch, and the English fares the same as both the others. It is possible that local difficulties in the imposition of other taxes, may render this difficult, or even impracticable; yet it would have the effect of making the trade between one colony and another a coasting one, and so free from harassing Customs inspection. Thus, for instance, the commerce between Sydney and Melbourne would be as untrammelled as that between Dublin or Leith and London. If it should follow, upon complete federation, that certain expenditure, say for defence or other purposes, for the benefit of all alike, came to be defrayed out of a common fund, there could be no more equitable way of raising it than by means of Customs duties, which must fall upon each community just in the proportion which, according to its numbers and wealth, it was able to bear. In such a case it would be a matter of utter indifference whether the tax were levied in one port or another, and the transport of commodities from one place to others should be unfettered by troublesome regulations. If federation did lead up to such results, the commercial benefits it would confer would be undeniable.

But there is another way in which a more liberal and uniform treatment of the imports from the mother-country would increase the commerce and serve the

INTERESTS OF THE COLONIES.

The great wants of the United Kingdom are, established customers for her manufactures, and fresh homes for her superabundant children. So long as England was mistress of the markets of the world, she was well able to meet the necessities of her increasing population; but now that she has rivals in the manufacturing industries of other nations, and her output of goods is, if not less in quantity, yet shrunken in the prices they obtain and the profits they secure, she needs to spread abroad both her sons and her wares. On the other hand, the outlying portions of the Empire, north, south, and west, if not the east as well, all require hands to till, and mouths to eat the bounteous supplies that there reward the labours of the husbandman. Many of the Colonies have lavishly expended borrowed money in laying down the iron roads, forming accommodation for shipping, and bringing into cultivation tracts of land, which still need a surplus of labour to render the sunken funds reproductive. This England can well supply, but not, as she has hitherto done, as a free gift. Every adult who leaves this country has cost some one his maintenance and education, all of which is lost to the State if he ceases in his new home to render any return for what he has received. When, however, he raises food or raw material for those whom he leaves behind, and takes in payment that which they can produce for him, but cannot manufacture so cheap as they can, the advantage is mutual. Then the money spent upon him in childhood becomes a good investment, and the mother-country may for years go on breeding and rearing those who shall utilise the abundant resources to be found in her possessions abroad. The community of interest between the two is that on which each so greatly depends for employing the property of both, and this requires freedom of exchange for the commodities which each produces. The contrary course cripples the productiveness of both. Look, for instance, at what is happening in Canada at the present moment. Lancashire spins and weaves cottons far beyond the wants of her home customers. Supported by the sale of these, her operatives bring into the world, and train up to maturity, lads and lasses for whom there is now a lack of employment. The youths may go to the far West, now thrown open by the railway which traverses the country from east to west, there they plant fields and tend herds to supply the wants of the body they have left. The maidens in due time ought to follow, and become the wives and mothers who are to fill the solitudes of the homes and prairies there; but they remain at home to glut the labour market or to swell the pauper roll. Why so? Because every article of clothing the would-be husbands and fathers wear, every tool they use, all that they consume beyond the products of the soil they cultivate, is enhanced in price by protective duties, to foster trades which otherwise could not compete with the manufactures of the very men who have been at the cost of providing the skill and labour thus turned against themselves. This is neither Fair Trade nor Free Trade; it wastes the wealth of productive power on both sides, and a Federal union which should unite the interests of both would surely be a great means of commercial benefit all round. It would help to fill the harbours with ships, crowd the trains with passengers and goods, enlarge the borders of the towns and cities; for there is scarcely any limit to the population, now stunted and destroyed, which it would not fail to create, and furnish with the means of sustaining in comfort. [...]

STE. BOURNE.

'Imperial Federation', *Fair-Trade. A Weekly Journal Devoted to Industry and Commerce*, 1:39 (9 July 1886), pp. 308–9.

FAIR – TRADE.

9 JULY, 1886, pp. 308–9.

IMPERIAL FEDERATION.

HAD it not been for the General Election, much more attention would have been given to the conference and banquet of the Imperial Federation League last week. As it was, in spite of the pressure upon space, our leading newspapers were compelled to give somewhat copious reports, and the interest taken in Federation naturally invited several important leaders. None know better than those, who, amid the greatest obstacles, have been pushing the Fair-Trade cause during recent years, how deeply rooted is the feeling in the English mind in favour of the actual, as well as nominal, Federation of the Empire. When the arguments of the most practiced orators in favour of the reform of our fiscal policy, have apparently failed to overcome the prejudices engendered by habit and education, any reference to the policy by which the commercial interests of the Empire are to be knit together has been certain to elicit applause. The Imperial Federationists, however, who met last week under the presidency of Lord Rosebery, have, it is true, no definite plan of Federation to propound. They talk loudly and plausibly, but openly assert they are only ventilating the subject. In some vague way, indeed, they speak of national, or rather imperial defence, as the chief thing to be attained at present. But any reference to the fiscal or commercial question is carefully tabooed. Strange to say, indeed, that in private conversation many who are deep in the councils of the Imperial Federation League fully agree that it is through fiscal union that the great question must be solved; only these say – not yet! They are afraid to come near the holy ark of Free Trade, for fear of internal divisions, and exciting the wrath of the economical high priests. There are leading lights of the body who dare not, for the life of them, run counter to the fashionable opinion, that aught that rebukes free imports is economic heterodoxy; and we know that in certain circles in London, to be heretic in that so-called science is to be beyond the pale either of criticism or argument. Hence, as we have said, within the charmed circle of those to whom the Federation League owes life, all at present is vagueness. They content themselves with patriotic aspirations, and give expression to respectable sentiments.

But it is remarkable – or, rather may we not say, it is *not* remarkable? – that when outsiders, whose thoughts are not tied and bound by conventionality of opinion on this head, come within the circle, how much more practically they view the whole topic. On the first day of the Conference, for example, two distinguished men spoke

– Professor Seeley and Sir Alexander Galt – the one a learned theoricien, the other a practical diplomatist; the one surrounded by all the prejudices of our national life, the other one of the authors of that Canadian fiscal policy which has renewed the life blood of the Dominion. Professor Seeley's discourse was historical and eloquent. It was far searching in probing the actual conditions of life. It was prescient in seeing what is in store, as the results of science and invention, among increased populations scattered over wide territories. It was correctly styled, 'The object to be gained by the Federation of the Empire.' But not a word did he say or think as to how that actual Federation was to be practically realised. Sir Alexander Galt, on the other hand, whose mind has for years been given to this subject, at once touched the root when he said that 'the commercial union of Great Britain with the Colonies and India should be undertaken and pressed upon the people both at home and abroad, with one leading principle in view – of treating British industry as entitled to peculiar favour as distinguished from that of foreign nations.' This is so precisely the view – and, we venture to say, the only practical view – of the question which Free-Traders have ever specially enforced since the Fair-Trade policy was promulgated, that we cannot too strongly insist on the importance of this opinion of the late High Commissioner for Canada. It is true, as we have already observed, that all reference to the only means by which such Commercial Union can be adopted – namely, the imposition of general, though moderate, import duties against foreign, as distinguished from colonial, products – is studiously kept in the background. Among others, intelligent men like Sir John Lubbock, who presided at the second day's Conference, are apt to shrink from the bare mention of Customs taxation. Even some of the supporters of our creed are content to believe that such policy will follow, instead of being, as we think, the corner stone of the edifice, since, however strong may be the federation sentiment, and however powerful the feelings of kinship, motives of mutual self-interest must ever be the foundation for such policy. In a word, it is by the food custom which the Mother-country has at her command she can only hope effectually to bind her growing Empire together. At present that custom is absolutely given away without thought, whereas if judiciously expended – and it is only by establishing a preferential market it can be utilised – it would buy the goodwill and hearty co-operation of every citizen of the Empire.

It is a singular episode, and none the less singular because accidental, that the holding of such a Conference, within the walls of an Exhibition of Colonial and Indian products, should have been concurrent with a General Election, that turns on the question of the unity of the three kingdoms at home. The problem of Home Rule of itself, and in the abstract, is one indeed involved in that of the practical federation of the Empire. An absolute binding of the whole together in one community, with a central legislative authority for Imperial matters, naturally enough involves Home Rule legislation for all local topics. But that does not mean a particular kind of Home Government, involving ultimate separation, for one part of the Queen's dominion, and not for another. Merely local interests demand local attention, and this is every bit as applicable to England, Scotland, and Wales, as it is to Canada or Australia. The adoption of such local councils – the term, we believe, is Mr. Chamberlain's – would also pave the way, if only by relieving Parliament of much needless labour to the greater federation of the whole Empire. When so great a topic is being discussed in every house in the three kingdoms, it is a notable thing to have seen, as we saw last Saturday; a member of the Cabinet which, under the guise of Home Rule, has introduced a disruptionist policy, presiding at the Federation Banquet, and declaring that 'every week, nay, every day, that we live, by degrees, slow and partial, possibly, but always distinctly in advance, we are marching to the goal of a United Empire.' This indeed we believe to be true, in more senses than even Lord Rosebery meant. It did not then occur to him possibly that the country was even proving his words in action, and indeed it was too early to have given up all hope, as a member of the Cabinet, of Mr. Gladstone's Home Rule scheme being carried. But none the less are the people of Great Britain now giving tongue to the general sentiment in favour of the Unity of the Empire, by rejecting a proposal likely to tend to the dissolution of Unity at home. At the bottom of the whole struggle lies the feeling that united we are strong, but that disunited we must dwindle down to a second-rate Power. People do not all say so, or perhaps think it definitely, but they *feel* that in spite of all our vast commercial strength in the past, we must, if there be no change, give way to other nations that have taken a wiser view of their responsibilities; nations with Governments that have maintained the internal strength of their people, instead of sacrificing so much of it, as we have done, in favour of foreign trade, and from a sickly idea that Cosmopolitanism is a larger and nobler aspiration than Nationalism.

'The Fair Trade Scheme of Commercial Federation', *Imperial Federation*, 2:24 (1887), p. 245.

THE FAIR TRADE SCHEME OF COMMERCIAL FEDERATION.

THE Fair-Traders having been challenged by Lord Randolph Churchill to a definite declaration of policy, replied by a letter from Mr. S. Cunliffe Lister, President of their Association, which was published in the *Times*. We quote the passages in which the trade of the British Empire is discussed, in pursuance of our plan of ventilating all schemes for its furtherance, by whomsoever advocated.

'If there be one point more than another which Fair-Traders believe they have impressed upon the public mind, it is this very question of Commercial Federation between the Mother Country and her possessions, by which British industry could not be placed under the disabilities you mention either in India or Ireland. Throughout the whole of your speech you appear to have borne this in mind yourself, for you have only spoken of foreign manufacturers and foreign goods.

The Fair Trade policy – and I believe this is generally known and understood – is based on having the resources of our Empire to rely upon for such supplies of necessaries as the United Kingdom may require from external sources, and to find work and labour for our people in the full return trade such policy would assure. It is because our Empire can feed the Mother Country, and, with such a market at its disposal, give an adequate return trade, that we are better enabled to retaliate on foreign tariffs and say that we will no longer give a free market place. The United States, embracing an immense territory, with every description of climate, is self-sustaining, and can, therefore, exclude foreign supplies by a high tariff. The British Empire is in a still more commanding position, and beyond its boundaries we need not travel for the supply of all our wants. Let us have Free Trade within the Empire, or as nearly thereto as may be possible, and no longer should we be dependent upon the foreigner who refuses to deal with us. Any questions of detail arising out of special circumstances, such, for instance, as the national danger of corn lands going out of cultivation generally, or the fall of silver, would have to be dealt with separately as they arose; but points of this character in no way affect the general principle of 'Free Trade (as far as possible) within the Empire, and protection against the world.'

In conclusion, let me point out that it is this Commercial Federation of the Empire which furnishes the keynote of the present position compared with the protection of old days, which looked to the United Kingdom being self-contained, self-subsisting, and self-supporting. This latter condition is so absolutely impossible to-day, that we are bound to extend our borders and to treat the

Empire as one; and if it be urged, as it is urged, that some of our possessions cannot for revenue purposes, and will not, dispense with import duties, even against British products, our reply is simple. In such case our hands are free to establish the differential system in lieu of absolutely free imports. In such case our Empire would be still united in commercial bonds, and there is probably no British Colony in existence that would not, in return for a preferential market on our shores, only too gladly give us a preferential market on theirs.'

R. Giffen, 'Commercial Union between the United Kingdom and its Colonies' (BT memo, 1891), PRO, CAB 37/29/7.

Commercial Union between the United Kingdom and the Colonies.

In the demand which representatives of the colonies make for a closer commercial union between them and the mother country, it is constantly assumed that 'preferential fiscal arrangements' among them, as against foreign countries, will promote such a union, and are of the essence of such a union.

Neither proposition is admitted in the mother country; and the contrary is in fact so much taken for granted as axiomatic, in almost all quarters in England, that the colonial arguments hardly attract attention, much less discussion.

The persistent demand of the colonies for preferential fiscal arrangements may thus become embarrassing politically. The contempt for it in the mother country is interpreted in the colonies as indifference to commercial union itself, which is by no means the feeling in the mother country. So far from there being indifference, the existence of the Imperial Federation League, and the support given to it, and to the Colonial Institute and the Imperial Institute, show the strength of the feeling at home in favour of a consolidation of the Empire. Still there is mutual misunderstanding between the colonies and the mother country, and mischief may ensue.

It is not difficult to show that the indifference in the mother country to the colonial predilection for preferential fiscal arrangements, and the colonial arguments for them is entirely justified. The colonial representatives are not well informed as to the facts of the matter, and they are crying for the moon.

Thus, they are under the impression that trade between the mother country and the colonies tends to increase more than trade between the mother country and foreign countries; that we are specially crippled in our commercial development by the tariffs of foreign countries, and should, *therefore*, cultivate the colonial field; that we are blind to our own interest in not doing so.

In point of fact the *proportion* of our trade with the colonies does not increase. Thirty years ago one-third of our exports of British and Irish produce was to the colonies, and the proportion is the same now. Mr. Hoffmeyr, in his speech at the International Conference in 1887, asserted that the proportion to the colonies was increasing, on the strength of a comparison starting from the year 1871 only, about which time the proportion of our exports to the colonies to our total exports had fallen to about one-fourth only; but this comparison only showed that Mr. Hoffmeyr had not surveyed the facts comprehensively enough. There was a sudden enlargement of our continental trade about 1871 which altered for the moment the usual proportions of our exports to foreign countries and to the colonies respectively. The proportion to the colonies is, and has been, chronically about a third.

The facts stated are also the answer to the assertion that foreign tariffs specially cripple the development of our trade with foreign countries. The tariffs of some foreign countries, *e.g.*, the United States, must have a tendency to cripple the development of our foreign trade. But the fact remains that with foreign countries, as a whole, our trade grows as fast as it does with our colonies.

The special case, then, for specially cultivating the colonial field falls to the ground. In none of the facts stated is there any proof that we are blind to our own interest.

Even, however, if there were a special case of the kind described for specially cultivating the colonial field, or if there were other reasons for so doing (as I should be disposed to admit there are), as a closer political connection with the colonies would probably be promoted by more intimate coromercial relations, it would not follow that the way to bring about such relations is by 'preferential fiscal arrangements.' Supposing such arrangements to be in themselves bad for both colonies and the mother country, they might have the very opposite effect to that intended. And there might be other and better ways of achieving the object in view.

The colonial representatives seem to be confused between a real customs union and 'preferential fiscal arrangements,' imagining them to be the same thing, whereas they are essentially different and opposite. A customs union means the abolition of customs barriers within the union. Goods pass to and fro as within the limits of a single country. Especially where a number of states are grouped together with land frontiers, or where they are separated only by narrow straits, the abolition of customs barriers is highly favourable to mutual prosperity. The customs barrier is a nuisance. Hence the benefit of such measures as the German zollverein, which was, in fact, preceded last century by the abolition of customs barriers within the limits of France, and at the end of the century by the abolition of customs barriers between Scotland and England, and between Great Britain and Ireland.

The essential point of a customs union is the abolition of a customs line, and the benefit flows from the unrestricted intercourse within a large area thus rendered possible. It is best when not accompanied by 'preferential fiscal arrangements' directed against any other community.

By 'preferential fiscal arrangements' are, in fact, meant differential duties, and what the colonies have in their mind is the establishment of such differential duties in the mother country in favour of the produce of the colonies, and in each colony in favour of the produce of the mother country and other colonies, as against foreign produce, existing customs barriers, whether upheld by the mother country or the colonies, being otherwise untouched. What is proposed therefore, is not a customs union, viz., the abolition of customs barriers, but the very opposite, viz, a new customs barrier against foreign produce.

I should doubt, indeed, whether a customs union between the mother country and the colonies is possible in their present geographical and economic circumstances; or whether, if possible, it would have the specially beneficial effect of such unions. They are so far apart that there is no room for that growth of local trade between them which makes it so desirable to abolish customs barriers. Economically the colonies are in the position which makes it convenient for revenue purposes to impose duties on manufactures imported from a country like England. Some of them, like India, are so conditioned that they do not consume the same articles of common luxury on which we levy customs and excise duties, so that the pooling of such revenues, which would be the condition of a zollverein, is hardly possible. On the other hand, the wide expansions and ramifications of our trade are such, that unless England is made practically a free port, so that we have practically no customs barrier at all against any country, our trade could hardly go on. We have really no customs duties except on a few articles to support our excise revenue. We could not have a general customs tariff resembling that of our colonies, and which they maintain without any particular harm, without crippling and fettering our world-extended trade.

It is no reproach to the colonies, then, that they do not propose a real customs union; but it is essential that what they do propose should not be covered by that name as if it were something like, and might have similar effects.

To some extent, however, this criticism is fatal to what is proposed, because it is put forward as a measure, as far as it goes, in the nature of a zollverein, and its effects are consequently assumed to be beneficial. [...]

R. G.
9th February, 1891.

Howard Vincent, *Commercial Union of the Empire* (London: United Empire Trade League, 1891).

THE COMMERCIAL UNION OF THE EMPIRE, BY COL. HOWARD VINCENT, C.B., M.P.

THE subject of the British Crown exceed three hundred millions in number. They occupy over seventy territories and islands in every portion of the earth. Their empire is a fifth of the entire world. It either produces, or is capable of producing, upon its various soils and under its varied climates, every substance or article known to man. Everything the population of one part of the British Empire may be unable to supply for their own needs, may be found in some other part of the Empire.

THE UNITED EMPIRE TRADE LEAGUE

urges – that we should make full use of the resources acquired for us by our forefathers without regard to foreign states – engaged, as the Premier recently stated, in every country in interposing new barriers of tariff between British producers and their consumers.

Is it necessary to adduce any argument in support of such plain and common sense views? There is no parallel, either in ancient times or in the present day, for an Empire or State calling itself one, to have no commercial links of Union. The whole object of Empire is Commerce and the extension of commercial relations. It is with this view that India was subjugated, that North America and the West Indies were acquired, that Australasia and South Africa were settled.

Let him estimate who can, the British blood, treasure, long-suffering, and indomitable perseverance involved in this wondrous work. The gain has been great. Vast markets have been opened up, limitless wells of supply have been established. Yet in this year of grace the British Nation finds itself fettered, bound hand and foot, peremptorily prohibited by agreements voluntarily, yet blindly, concluded with foreign states, not to enter into any commercial union within itself. The United Kingdom is powerless to conclude a preferential commercial union with Canada, with the West Indies; or with Australia. We have bound South Africa and India as well as ourselves.

Has the British Empire been established for the benefit of the Universe or for ourselves? Was it to open markets for our rivals and competitors, or for the subjects of the Queen, that the History of Britain has been written in blood, in gold, and heroic adventure.

THE UNITED EMPIRE TRADE LEAGUE

affirms – that the British Empire was established by the British for the British.

In 1845 goods from British possessions were given an advantage in the Mother Country of 50 per cent, over those from foreign lands. In 1853 this preference for Colonial goods was re-affirmed in respect of thirteen classes of articles. In 1860 the privilege was withdrawn. Then, the Ministry of the day, proceeded to tie down, not only ourselves, but also British Colonies, and this without consulation with them. A Treaty of Commerce was entered into with Belgium in 1862, containing this clause: 'Articles, the produce or manufacture of Belgium, shall not be subject-in the British Colonies to other or higher duties than those which are or may be imposed upon similar articles of British origin.' It was repeated by the same Ministry in 1865 in a Treaty of Commerce with the German Zollverein.

Now, although this engagement in restraint both of Free Trade and Commercial Union between the several parts of the British Empire was only concluded in express terms with two Foreign States, the official declaration obtained from the Foreign Office in 1888 by Parliamentary Paper, C 5369, declares:

'That while these two Treaties remain in force these express stipulations are extended to all Countries whose Commercial Treaties with Great Britain contain a most favoured nation clause.' There are upwards of 22 such Treaties. In the interests then of British Trade, in the interests of the United Kingdom, in the interests of the entire Empire, in the interests especially of all engaged in industrial pursuits, whether as employers or employed it behoves Britons forthwith to release themselves from these artificial bonds in restraint of British commercial development.

The moment is opportune. The Treaties of Commerce entered into by this country are undergoing revision. France, Russia, and Spain, have determined to follow the example of the United States, and prohibit, so far as increased duties can do it, the importation of British goods. The details of the Commercial Union which might be possible are for ulterior consideration. The imposition of any arrangement which might be distasteful to the free people of any single colony is not suggested. Nor is the slightest increase in the cost of food, or the taxation of raw material in any way advocated. But the United Empire Trade League submits that it is desirable that the hands of Commerce, stretching from each part of the British Empire to every other part, should be freed from any foreign handcuffs. The most dogmatic and suspicious professor of political economy cannot surely decry the acquisition of this freedom of trading relations with our own kith and kin.

The opportunity is golden because our treaties of Commerce are undergoing review. There is another reason. The great Colonies have declared themselves willing to enter into a Commercial Union with the Mother Country, and with each other. They have spoken through the eloquent voices of prominent Colonial – nay Imperial – statesmen. The names of Privy Councillor Dalley; of Service, Griffith, Galt, Vogel, Rhodes, Hoffmeyr, Thompson, among many others, are proof of this. Let the men of patriotism and foresight, with broad minds unshackled by selfish prejudices,

MEET HALFWAY THEIR COLONIAL BROTHERS.

Soon it will be too late. The situation in Newfoundland; the American propositions to the West Indian Islands; the prospect in South Africa; the Convention for the Fiscal Federation of Australasia against the outer world, are proof of this.

Take note particularly of the situation in Canada.

The Legislature of the United States has passed an Act declaring to the Dominion of Canada, and to the 3,000 miles of conterminous frontier, in the words of her great Minister, Sir John Mcdonald [*sic*] – If you want to trade with us, join us, but so long as you are a portion of the British Empire we will shut you out. Then comes the answer of the majority of the Canadian electorate – a dangerously narrow one, however – Our allegiance to Britain, to the greatest Empire the world has ever seen, is unwavering – and for trade, for new markets, we look to Australia, to the West Indies, to the Mother Country.

Are we – are you as an individual with responsibilities, not alone to the present, but to your nation's future – going to remain silent; apathetic, indolent, indifferent? It was thus that fell the Colonial empires of Greece and of Rome, of Spain and of the Netherlands. Give heed to a warning from over the sea. On the 22nd of June., 1889, the High Commissioner of Canada, Sir Charles Tupper, declared that it would not be easy to keep up the necessary amount of enthusiasm unless some practicable scheme was soon devised of establishing closer and more substantial union between the Mother Country and the self-governing colonies to the advantage of the whole Empire.

This authoritative opinion found recent corroboration at the hands of Sir Gordon Sprigg, so long Prime Minister of South Africa:

'How are the component parts of the Empire to be held together? Having given a great deal of attention to this matter myself, it appears to me that the basis of the Imperial federation of the future must be a Customs Union. Supposing you do not bind together your colonies and dependencies by some such bond as a Customs Union, what guarantee have you that you will hold your Empire together.' It has been doubted whether the colonies are themselves in favour of such a proposal as that at which I have hinted. I will only say this in reply – that in travelling through the country here upon occasional visits I keep my eyes and ears open, and I sometimes think that if I wanted to find illustrations of men who hold fast to the best traditions of old England I would not look for them here in the centre, but I would go to the distant dependencies, where the sons and daughters of England keep watch and ward over the outposts of the Empire.'

The growing volume of Colonial trade is well known. Every Australian for trade purposes is of greater money value alone than a score of foreigners. The Colonies desire to buy of you, to sell to you, they would sooner trade with you and their fellow colonists, if it can be done on mutually advantageous terms, than with foreign nations. Is not the Commercial Union of the British Empire highly desirable? Canada says aye, – Australasia says aye, – South Africa says aye. It has met with recent approval in the City of London, in Manchester, in Sheffield, in Leeds, in Liverpool, in Glasgow, in Bristol, in Belfast, and other great centres of commerce. The manufacturers are with us, the agriculturalists are with us, the loyal masses are with us. 'If England forms a Customs Union with her Colonies,' says a Minister of the United States, 'she will be as independent of outsiders as ourselves, producing everything she wants, and consuming herself everything she produces.' The greater portion of the press has of late adopted this view. Then opinions are well summarised by a popular organ, *The People*: –

'When any Statesman is courageous and sagacious enough to propose' such a Union,' he will have a following which will astound himself, and the greatest Empire the world has ever seen will consolidate with lightning-like rapidity. In our possessions the wide world over we have inexhaustable [*sic*] resources, and all possible variety of products, and nothing but our ruinously absurd laws prevents our making proper use of them. Alter or revoke those laws, and the British Empire is instantly self-supporting, and her sons and daughters will be ten times as prosperous as now.'

Lord Salisbury has declared: – 'We know that every bit of the world's surface that is not under the English flag is a country which may be and probably will be closed to us by a hostile tariff, and therefore it is that we are anxious above all things to conserve, to unify, to strengthen the Empire of the Queen, because it is to the trade that is carried on within the Empire of the Queen that we look for the vital force of the commerce of this country.'

Let the Government hear the voice of the people – says the Prime Minister. 'I feel the deepest sympathy with the objects in view,' (of Imperial Federation,) 'and earnestly desire that means for attaining those objects may be found.' Let British industry speak, says The Chancellor of the Exchequer. Let the country pronounce, and then come to the Ministry, says the President of the Board of Trade.

To elicit the voice of the nation – of the Empire, of the British race – on this great question; to develop the world-wide internal commerce on mutually advantageous terms of the British Empire is the object of

THE UNITED EMPIRE TRADE LEAGUE.

It seeks your support – it hopes for your active sympathy and co-operation in whatever sphere you are, in whatever portion of the realm of Britain and Greater Britain you may be located.

C. E. HOWARD VINCENT,
Hon. Secretary.
HOUSE OF COMMONS,
LONDON.

British Empire League, *Report of Inaugural Meeting of the League held on Wednesday, January 29th, 1896, at the Mansion House* (London, [1896]), pp. 23–4.

REPRINT OF LEADING ARTICLE IN THE 'STANDARD' OF JANUARY 30.

An important meeting was held at the Mansion House yesterday, under the presidency of the Lord Mayor, for the purpose of laying the foundation-stone, so to speak, of the new British Empire League, intended to supply the place vacated by the dissolution of the Imperial Federation League. The object of the association is mainly, though not exclusively, of a commercial character, and is intended to knit together the various portions of the Empire by still closer bonds than those which unite them at the present moment. The means to be employed for this purpose are set out under five different heads, the most valuable of all, perhaps, being the suggested 'periodical meetings of representatives from all parts of the Empire for the discussion of matters of general commercial interest, and the best means of expanding the national trade.' The second suggestion is one that looks extremely well upon paper, but may possibly cover more than appears to lie on the surface. It is to 'consider how far it may be possible to modify any laws or treaties which impede freedom of action in the making of reciprocal trade arrangements between the United Kingdom and the Colonies, or between any two or more British Colonies or Possessions.' In the next place, we are told that it is desirable, as undoubtedly it is, to promote closer intercourse between the different parts of the Empire 'by the development of direct steam and telegraphic communication.' The assimilation of the law relating to copyrights, patents, legitimacy, and bankruptcy throughout the Empire figures fourth on the list; and last, but not least, we are invited to 'devise a more perfect co-operation of the military and naval forces of the Empire, with a special view to the due protection of trade routes.' These are the principal objects which the British Empire League sets before itself; and they were supported in a short but very eloquent speech by Sir John Lubbock. He based the justification of such an association on the paramount necessity of bracing the British Empire together, and making it conscious of its unity at all points. It is on the broad basis of common interests, sympathies, and character that he would weld our scattered Colonial Empire into one Imperial unit, having regard, of course, to the separate local institutions which our Colonies have developed. Sir John Lubbock drew the usual comparison between the Colonies of antiquity and our own, reminding us of Mr. Balfour's reference to the Spanish Empire in his speech last week at Manchester. But it strikes us that Sir John Lubbock must have been thinking also of the Colonial Empire of ancient Athens, which was held together 'by armed force,' and which ultimately fell to pieces through the unpopularity of the very system which, according to Sir Robert Herbert, has been suggested as an example to ourselves; that is to say, the practice of levying contributions on the Colonies towards a general Imperial Defence Fund. Our Colonies would probably resent such a proposal as this as much as the Athenian Colonies resented the demands made upon them. Great Britain has wisely kept clear of this most mischievous precedent; and her policy is evidently appreciated. Mr. Dobell, the delegate from Quebec, said that there 'was no example in history of any country dealing with her Colonies as Great Britain had dealt with hers.' We know very well that there is a not inconsiderable party in the country who think that England has shown herself less responsive to the loyalty of her Colonies than she ought to have done. Their attitude in the present crisis, however, does not seem as if there were much ground for this indictment. And, at all events, whatever may have happened in the past, we may hope that all memory of it will die away under the influence of such bodies as the British Empire League, which ought to be a sufficient assurance to the Colonists of our desire to draw together as closely as possible the bonds which now unite us, be they material, intellectual, or political. In literature, in science, and in the art of government the Mother Country enjoys a pre-eminence which her children should be proud to share, and which, in some future generation, they may be able to emulate.

British Empire League, *Report of Speech of the Right Hon. Joseph Chamberlain, at the Canada Club Dinner on Wednesday, March 25th, 1896* (London, [1896]), pp. 9–11.

FOUR PROPOSITIONS.

I have laid down four propositions which I think cannot be controverted. The first is that there is a universal desire among all the members of the Empire for a closer union between the several branches, and that, in their opinion as in ours, this is desirable – nay, it is essential for the existence of the Empire as such. My second proposition is that experience has taught us that this closer union can be most hopefully approached in the first instance from its commercial side. My third proposition is that the suggestions which have hitherto been made to us, although we know them to have been made in good part, are, when considered from the point of view of British interests, not sufficiently favourable to be considered by this country. My fourth proposition is that a true Zollverein for the Empire, that a free trade established throughout the Empire, although it would involve the imposition of duties against foreign countries, and would be in that respect a derogation from the high principles of free trade and from the practice of the United Kingdom up to the present time, would still be a proper subject for discussion and might probably lead to a satisfactory arrangement if the colonies on their part were willing to consider it. ('Hear, hear,' and cheers.) It has been assumed, in Lord Ripon's despatch and in many other documents, that the colonies must necessarily refuse to consider a proposition of this kind because it would interfere with the necessities of their revenue, that they are obliged to rely upon indirect taxation for the funds by which their Administration is carried on, and that they could not enter on such an agreement as this without providing way and means by methods which, at present at any rate, are altogether unpopular in many of our colonies. I am not convinced of the truth of that statement, and I want especially to point out that the advantages of such a proposal are so great to the colonies, as they would undoubtedly lead to the earliest possible development of their great natural resources, would bring to them population, would open to them the enormous market of the United Kingdom for their products, their food, their timber, their sugar – the advantages, I say, are so important that it appears to me that the colonies themselves would be bound to give to any suggestion, of this kind at all events, a careful reconsideration.

AN INDISPENSABLE CONDITION.

My second point is that we are dealing with an entirely exceptional state of things, and that we cannot, even if we wished, imitate exactly the German Zollverein. We are not conterminous countries, we are countries, as I have said, separated by thousands of miles, in some cases, and the circumstances of our different countries vary considerably that it is evident that in any arrangement as to general free trade within the Empire exceptions must be made in the case of articles that are chiefly taxed for revenue purposes. For instance, we cannot admit free trade in spirits or in tobacco, and to any gentleman who has any experience other articles will suggest themselves, which in one part of the Empire or another are the subject of strictly revenue duties, and might, by common agreement, be excluded from any such arrangement. But the principle which I claim must be accepted if we are to make any, even the slightest, progress is that within the different parts of the Empire protection must disappear, and that the duties must be revenue duties, and not protective duties in the sense of protecting the products of one part of the Empire against those of another part. It seems to me that if that principle were adopted there would be reason for calling a council of the Empire, calling representatives from the different States forming the Empire; and although the subject would be one of enormous difficulty and the greatest complication, still, with the good will that exists and the ultimate goal in view, I cannot but think that something like a satisfactory and a workable arrangement might be arrived at. (Cheers.) And although in such a case the principles of free trade would lose something in their application to the dealings between ourselves and foreign countries, advocates of free trade must remember how much they would gain by its extension to all the States which form the British Empire, States which are after all, whatever may be said of their present position, more likely to develop and increase in prosperity and population and wealth and power and commerce than any of the foreign States with which we have relations.

TARIFF WARS IN EUROPE, c. 1879–1914

Fair trade and imperial schemes for economic unity were both reactions to what by the late 1870s was increasingly seen as the failure of the Cobden treaty system. This had been made most obvious with the return of Germany to protection in 1879, followed by Italy in 1887, and France in 1892, with the Méline tariff.[1] By the late 1880s, few of the commercial treaties which had embraced Europe in the 1870s remained in place. No longer were such treaties conceptualized as peace bonds between nations but, with the wave of neo-mercantilistic thinking which swept Europe in the 1880s, tariffs were now seen as weapons of economic warfare designed to achieve national goals. Such goals included the desire to build up armaments industries, as in Italy and Russia, but tariffs were also now used aggressively as bargaining counters to seek exclusive advantages or to retaliate against the withdrawal of trade benefits. Europe, Lord Salisbury announced in 1892, had entered 'an age of a war of tariffs'.[2]

In a sense tariff wars were the logical consequence of rising tariffs in Europe after 1879. Most such tariff wars were counterproductive, launched, as Conybeare has suggested, by smaller economic powers, who met with swift retaliation by larger ones.[3] After a period in which trade normally declined, agreements were reached which benefited the larger country. Three of these tariff wars stand out. First, the long-running Franco-Italian tariff war of 1886–98 had been sparked off by both countries raising duties on each other's shipping, followed by Italy denouncing her trade treaty with France and imposing higher duties under her 1887 tariff. Both countries then retaliated against each other with higher tariffs, but Italy miscalculated for her agricultural exports to France were less vital than she supposed; Italian exports to France fell by 57 per cent but France's to Italy fell by only 21 per cent. By 1889 financial authorities in Italy urged an end to the war of tariffs but France only slowly relaxed her counter-measures, and most-favoured nation status was only partially restored in 1898. Italy, according to the study of the British Foreign Office in 1904, ended up 'severely wounded'.[4]

The second illustrative case study is that of France and Switzerland between 1892 and 1895, following France's Méline tariff of 1892. The Méline tariff represented a genuine turning-point in France's tariff history, the point at which the survival of the French peasantry became an overriding political goal.[5] But Switzerland was reluctant to accept the higher duties now imposed on its goods and rejected the treaty offered by France, preferring no treaty to a bad one.[6] Even so compromise was soon reached and this did not escalate in the way the dispute with Italy had done.

Much more significant was the third case study, the Russo-German tariff war of 1894. In 1891 Russia had sought tariff rates comparable to those enjoyed by the Habsburg Empire but Germany had refused on the grounds that Russian tariffs were prohibitive. In 1892 Russia had introduced minimum and maximum rates, applying the higher to Russia, who responded with 50 per cent penalty rates on Russian goods. Germany replied in kind before climbing down in 1894, when she agreed to lower her own duties on 120 articles by 17–30 per cent (fixed for ten years) in return for most-favoured nation status.[7]

The impact of tariffs wars in Europe is, however, difficult to quantify. In most cases, it seems likely that only a small percentage of trade was affected, but in Russia's case the tariff war may well have accounted for the substantial replacement of Russian grain exports to Germany by American ones. In theory too successful retaliation might open up markets (as the fair traders argued), although available studies emphasize the negative effects of tariff wars. But the real significance of such tariff wars was in undermining an earlier view of the *douceur* of commerce in which the extension of commerce was the extension of civilization and peace; by 1900 it was clear that trade had become part of the machinery of states geared to war. Hence the paradox that while in some ways Europe enjoyed unparalleled rates of economic growth in the period 1890–1914, at the same time, as Sidney Pollard wrote, it seemed increasingly divided into hostile economic blocs, with the emphasis especially in Russia and Germany on autarky.[8]

In Germany, for example, although the tariff remained a battlefield between industrializers and agrarians whose ramifications remain outside the scope of this work, the new general tariff accompanied by new trade treaties negotiated between 1902 and 1906 suggested that Germany was not simply fostering a self-sufficient domestic economy but the creation of a central European market bloc; Mitteleuropa was now a self-conscious goal of many, while the rye tariffs continued to cause resentment in Russia, contributing, as Gerschenkron argued, to the 'envenomed international atmosphere of 1914'.[9] Autarky and Mitteleuropa reflected the primacy of an economic vision which anticipated trade as warfare, not the pursuit of peace through the economic interdependence of nations.[10]

The conspicuous exception to these trends was Great Britain which, despite the yearnings of fair traders, federationists and later tariff reformers, remained firmly attached to free trade. In part this was the result of continued popular loyalty to free trade which was deeply rooted in British political culture. But it also reflected the result of sober analysis by British civil servants. For example, the leading Board of Trade official Sir Robert Giffen, although later a qualified supporter of imperial preference, at this stage believed that the growth of protection abroad had not significantly reduced Britain's ability to trade.[11] Later on, too, officials viewed European tariff wars with relative detachment, although once Joseph Chamberlain had raised the possibility of Britain reintroducing tariffs, the Foreign Office's study of the tariff wars led resoundingly to the conclusion that the tariff 'revolver' should be resisted, and that, as the famous Eyre Crowe memorandum of 1907 put it, '[In] proportion as England champions the principle of the largest measure of freedom of commerce, she undoubtedly strengthens her hold on the interested friendship of other nations'.[12] Chamberlain's supporters, such as William Hewins, were keen to devise a scientific tariff as the basis of a national productive and imperial strategy,[13] but this was a form of interventionism which had few attractions for the bureaucratic elite; more usually tariffs were still considered as a threat to peace, and at variance with the tradition of British diplomacy.

To some extent therefore attachment to free trade made Britain a spectator in the tariff battles of Europe, but not entirely so. First, the growing demands of her own businessmen, mobilized in increasingly powerful organizations, necessitated some activity on the diplomatic front, even if this only took the form of appointing a first commercial attaché for Europe, and a committee of the Board of Trade to observe treaties.[14] At one point, especially after Lord Salisbury's Hastings speech of 1892, a more active policy seemed signalled but this did not materialize. The nearest Britain therefore got to an active commercial policy was when in 1897, following domestic and colonial pressure, she agreed to the abrogation of the Anglo-German and Anglo-Belgian commercial treaties of the 1860s, a sign that Britain was now distancing herself from her earlier policy. Nevertheless, the growing demand, even before Chamberlain, for reciprocal trade agreements, despite some support within the civil service, did not turn itself into a new commercial system. Interestingly Britain did engage in long commercial negotiations with Germany between 1902 and 1905 but with little prospect of success given Germany's attachment to high protection. At the same time, Germany did grant Britain most-favoured nation status, while pursuing an aggressive policy against Canada, having launched a tariff war against the Canadian granting of preference to Britain in 1897. This 'war' simmered in the first decade of the twentieth century, an augury of the conflict that a switch from free trade to imperial preference might entail.[15]

By 1906, however, it did seem to many that Europe was increasingly coming under German trade 'domination', against which Britain remained impotent.[16] This was to be an important theme in tariff reform rhetoric, which at times made free trade look passé. Nevertheless, free traders remained equally keen to advertise the currency of their trade vision and in particular the calling of the first international free trade congress in London in 1908 served as a globally-supported riposte to the tariff reformers by displaying the considerable support which Cobdenite free trade still enjoyed among Liberal statesmen, publicists and a genuinely cosmopolitan intelligentsia.[17] The need to counter tariff reform at home and German trade policy abroad also encouraged Britain to seek new treaties on the old model – with abortive negotiations with France in 1908 (to complement the entente of 1904) and Portugal, but successful ones with Serbia (1907), Montenegro (1910) and Japan (1911). Before 1914 therefore Britain continued to offer a policy of free trade as a public good for the world, although increasingly within Britain it was urged that she should abandon free trade as 'wishy-washy philanthropy' in favour of the creation of her own autarkic imperial bloc, which would better fit her for survival in the new Social-Darwinian world of tariffs and trade wars envisaged by the tariff reformers to whom the next section turns.

Notes

1. See the section on 'The Rise and Fall of Fair Trade in Britain', above; for an overview, see P. Bairoch, 'European Trade Policy, 1815–1914', in P. Mathias and S. Pollard (eds), *Cambridge Economic History of Europe. Volume VIII: The Industrial Economies: The Development of Economic and Social Policies* (Cambridge: Cambridge University Press, 1989), pp. 1–169.
2. Speech at Hastings, 18 May 1892, *The Times*, 19 May 1892, 10b.
3. J. A. Conybeare, *Trade Wars* (New York: Columbia University Press, 1987)
4. Tariff Wars between European States: Report on the Franco-Italian Tariff War, 1888–99; Report on the Tariff War between Germany and Russia; Summary of the Franco-Swiss Tariff War, 1893–5, *Parliamentary Papers* (1904), below, pp. 96–105, on p. 99.
5. See the Introduction, above.
6. E. Dérobert, *La Politique Douanière de al Confédération Suisse* (Geneva, 1926).
7. Tariff Wars between European States, below, pp. 96–105; E. Zweig *Die russischer Handelspolitik seit 1877: unter besonderer Berücksichtigung des Handels über die europäische Grenze* (Leipzig: Duncker and Humboldt, 1906).
8. S. Pollard, *The Integration of the European Economy since 1815* (London: University Association for Contemporary European Studies, 1981), pp. 58–60.
9. F. Naumann, *Central Europe [Mitteleuropa]* (1915; London: King, 1916); the Introduction, above; A. Gerschenkron, *Bread and Democracy in Germany* (Berkeley, CA: University of California Press, 1943), p. 87.
10. For a different perspective, see C. Torp, *Die Herausforderung der Globalisierung: Wirtschaft und Politik in Deutschland 1860–1914* (Göttingen: Vandenhoeck and Ruprecht, 2005).
11. R. Giffen, 'The Relative Growth of Free Trade and Protection', Cabinet Memo, 25 May 1892, below, pp. 88–9.
12. Cited in K. Bourne, *The Foreign Policy of Victorian England* (Oxford: Oxford University Press, 1970), p. 482.

13. Beatrice Webb believed that Hewins foresaw his role as 'arranging tariffs, and tariff wars, and tariff treaties ... hurrying from continent to continent, in close and confidential intercourse with Ministers and great financial personages – one long delightful intrigue with the World Empire as the result', *The Diary of Beatrice Webb. Volume 3: 1905–1924, The Power to Alter Things*, ed. N. Mackenzie and J. Mackenzie (Cambridge, MA: Belknap Press of Harvard University Press, 1984), 28 January 1906, p. 23.
14. J. W. T. Gaston, 'Trade and the Late Victorian Foreign Office', *International History Review*, 4 (1982), pp. 317–38; F. Trentmann, 'The Transformation of Fiscal Reform: Reciprocity, Modernization and the Fiscal Debate within the Business Community in Early Twentieth-Century Britain', *Historical Journal*, 39 (1996), pp. 1005–48.
15. 'It is the old and senseless game of throat-cutting on both sides', *New York Times*, 28 April 1903, p. 8.
16. Hewins, 'The New German Commercial Treaties', *National Review* (June 1905), pp. 693–704.
17. *Report of the Proceedings of the International Free Trade Congress, London, 1908* (London: Cobden Club, 1908); Howe, *Free Trade and Liberal England*, p. 276.

TARIFF WARS IN EUROPE, 1880–1914

'Protection in Germany', *Economist*, 39:1999 (17 December 1881), p. 1555.

PROTECTION IN GERMANY.– It is very evident that Prince Bismarck fears to have his new commercial policy subjected to independent criticism. In their reports for 1880, a digest of which we published last week, the German Chambers of Commerce denounced with remarkable unanimity the new protective tariff. Its operation during the past year, which was the first during which it was in force, had, they declared, been most injurious. It had restricted trade, and at the same time enormously enhanced the cost of subsistence, thus materially deteriorating the condition of the people.[1] For this expression of opinion some of the Chambers have already been sharply censured; but not content with mere reprimand, Prince Bismarck now seeks either to coerce them into silence, or failing that effectually to gag them. He has, it is announced, sent a circular to all the local authorities calling upon them to prescribe that for the future the various Chambers of Commerce shall send their annual reports in to the Government before the end of June each year, and shall not publish them until four weeks afterwards, so as to give the Ministry time to alter and amend them if necessary. That Prince Bismarck will succeed in this new effort to stifle public opinion is not very probable. But that he should make the attempt is in itself the strongest possible condemnation of his new fiscal policy. That, it would appear, is so bad that it is impossible to allow the truth to be told as to its results.

---

1 [Ed.: See 'The Results of Protection in Germany', *Economist*, 39:1998 (10 December 1881), pp. 1521–2.]

Trade and Treaties Committee, First Report, 24 January 1891, *Parliamentary Papers* (1890–1), lxxviii, Cmnd 6286.

TO THE LORDS OF THE COMMITTEE OF PRIVY COUNCIL FOR TRADE

MAY IT PLEASE YOUR LORDSHIPS,

1. In conformity with your directions, your Committee have commenced their inquiries into the probable effects of the approaching expiry of various European Commercial Treaties in connexion with British trade.
2. We found, at the outset of our inquiry, that the commercial system of France was the one which had the most immediate claims on our attention, not only because her trade with Great Britain amounts to more than that of any other continental country, but also because the future commercial policy of other continental countries is closely bound up with that of France.
3. Briefly stated, the position of France is as follows: she has two Customs Tariffs, one – the General Tariff – which can be modified at the will of the Legislature at any time, and which is applied to the goods imported from such countries as do not enjoy most-favoured-nation treatment in France; the other tariff – the Conventional one – is the combination of the various special tariffs granted by France to other countries. Corn, live stock, and many raw products have not been included in these special tariffs, and have, therefore to pay the rates of the General Tariff, even when imported from countries which enjoy most-favoured-nation treatment in France.
4. The Conventional Tariff rates are usually about 24 per cent. less than those of the General Tariff, and Great Britain enjoys the benefit of this lower tariff by law, and not by the Treaty of the 28th February 1882, which has no reference to the Customs Tariff, though it includes many important provisions in regard to shipping, personal rights, Customs formalities, brokerage, &c. Up to the 1st February 1892, Great Britain will pay on her manufactures the rates mainly of the Belgian and Swiss Tariff Treaties with France, unless the French law of the 27th February 1882, under which Great Britain enjoys the benefits of most-favoured-nation treatment, is previously modified or repealed.
5. We are informed that all these *tariff* treaties are likely to be denounced by the French Government in a few days' time, and several have, in fact, been already denounced, so as to expire on the same date, thus leaving France free to impose whatever duties she may think fit by General Tariff, or to negotiate fresh Tariff Treaties with the various Governments.

6. This situation is, however, likely to be changed in a manner injurious to the interests of British trade and to the commercial intercourse betwixt the two nations, should the 'Projet de Loi' which has been presented to the French Legislature by the Government be passed in its present shape. By the provisions of this Bill, there are to be two tariffs – a General Tariff, which will, in its nature, correspond to the present General Tariff, but will contain considerably higher duties on most articles; and, second, a Minimum Tariff, which the Government will have power to apply to those countries only whose tariffs are considered correspondingly favourable to French trade, and who give French goods their lowest tariffs.
7. The position will thus be, that in negotiating with foreign countries, the French Government could offer them at best only the duties of this irreducible minimum, and would be prevented from granting more favourable terms under any condition, unless it was prepared to submit the new treaty for ratification by a special law. Any material increase of duties in the Minimum Tariff from the *status quo* of the present Conventional Tariff would, therefore, be regarded as an act of commercial hostility to other countries, and would tend to provoke a general rise of tariffs in Europe.
8. Immediately after the receipt of copies of the French Tariff Bill, we took steps to communicate statements of the present and proposed duties confidentially to the various Chambers of Commerce and Commercial Associations of the United Kingdom, so that the Committee might obtain from them full information as to each branch of trade and industry, and might supplement these written Reports from the various Associations by personal statements from their expert representatives. The principal Chambers of Commerce and Trade Associations, besides representative private firms, have now furnished reports, but there has not been time, in the few days which have elapsed since these statements have been furnished, to take oral evidence. We have, however, made an examination of the documents, sufficient to convince us that the proposed Minimum Tariff presents important increases of duty on most of the chief articles of British manufacture exported to France, notably on cotton yarns and tissues and on woollen tissues. Not only have these minimum duties been raised generally to the level of the General Tariff of 1881, *i.e.*, about 24 per cent. above the present Conventional Tariff, but more complicated classifications have been introduced, which will cause disputes, and, consequently, delay and friction, between the French Custom-house officials and the importers. In many particular instances, the duties are raised much more than the above-mentioned 24 per cent., the extra rates for bleaching, dyeing, printing, embroidering, and generally for all processes which involve more labour as distinguished from mere material, being considerably increased.

9. We have also been informed that in the passage of the Bill through the Customs Committee of the Chamber of Deputies further increase of duty on many articles of interest to British trade have already been approved by the Committee. For example, light woollens (weighing 250 to 400 grammes per square metre), which now pay 1 fr. 40 c. per kilog., are raised by the Government proposal to 2 fr., and by the Committee's to 2 fr. 20 c.
10. While the French Government do not appear to have offered any great resistance to these proposals to increase the rates provided for by their Bill, they have hitherto strongly opposed the attempts of the agricultural interests to tax raw materials such as skins, wool, silk, and cotton, and to reimburse the manufacturer by allowing drawback on the export of the finished article, or by extending the system of temporary admission which is now granted to certain textiles for bleaching and such like processes in France.
11. This disagreement between the government and the agricultural interests appears to be the only hindrance to the early passing of the tariff 'Projet de Loi,' a measure which would shut the door to commercial negotiations with France by fixing an irreducible Minimum Tariff from which no reduction might be made.
12. The effects would, no doubt, be injurious not only to British trade with France, but to our trade with the Continent generally, although the chief injury, we may assume, will be to the French people themselves. Whatever the extent of the direct losses to ourselves may be, the general tendency of the measures threatened must be injurious, while one of the worst effects would be the excitement among European nations of a spirit of commercial war, which the policy adopted thirty years ago had done much to allay, with advantage to all the nations concerned.
13. The extent of the primary losses to be inflicted on our own trade, apart from the more general mischiefs referred to in the previous paragraph, is naturally the subject of very serious complaint from the special interests concerned. In various trades, especially in the woollen, worsted, and other textile trades, the representations made to us are that the proposed tariff will, in effect, prohibit the export of certain articles of manufacture from this country to France, and greatly restrict the export of many others.
14. A measure which can be described as having such effects is, as already indicated, an act of commercial hostility to the country affected; and this attitude towards English trade is, indeed, hardly disguised in discussions of the subject in France.
15. We have, therefore, felt it our duty to make this interim Report to Her Majesty's Government, without waiting for a more detailed examination of the special industries affected by the tariff, in order that the Government may be in possession of the facts as set forth in this Report, and of the views of the

Committee thereon, and thus be in a position, if they think fit, to deal with the subject at the earliest opportunity.

(Signed)

A. J. Mundella (Chairman)

Lowthian Bell

C. E. Bousefield

Frederick Brittain

Wm. L. Ewart

R. Giffen

David Guthrie

Edward S. Hill

C. M. Kennedy

Joseph C. Lee

A. E. Bateman, *Secretary*, 24 January 1891

R. Giffen, 'The Relative Growth of Free Trade and Protection', Cabinet Memo, 25 May 1892, Gladstone Papers, BL, Add. MS 44258, fol. 282.

SUMMARY

The conclusions of this memorandum may be set forth very shortly:

1. It is not true that protectionist policy is gaining ground on free-trade policy. The contrary is true. Free trade is gaining ground against protection.
2. As regards protection by means of import duties the proceedings of some protectionist countries in this respect have made a good deal of noise during the last few years, but, apart from this, an astonishing progress has been made in the free-trade direction during the last century and a half. (*a.*) Customs barriers within the same political frontier which existed a century ago, even in such advanced countries as the United Kingdom and France, have been all but universally, if not universally, abolished, thereby promoting free intercourse. (*b.*) The same promotion of free intercourse has been effected by extensive political consolidations, and the creation of large districts in which there is internal trade, of which illustrations are furnished by the United States, the German Zollverein and Empire, and the Indian Empire. (*c.*) Bounties, differential duties, restraints on navigation, export duties, and other protectionist devices, which were prevalent last century, have also been generally abolished – a few bounties and one or two occasional differential duties only surviving. (*d.*) Free trade has been further aided by the modern development of facilities of communication – the railway, the steamship, the telegraph, &c. – which are continually neutralising *pro tanto* the artificial barriers set up by import duties. (*e.*) Fifty years ago England adopted definitively a free-trade policy in everything, import duties as well as other matters, and as this policy governs the Crown Colonies and possessions of the Empire, including India, the step was an important one towards free trade in conjunction with all others. (*f.*) By means of the Cobden Treaties another important step was taken towards free trade, and in spite of the recent recrudescence of protectionist ideas and policy the situation created by the Cobden Treaties between 1860 and 1870 has not been substantially changed; protective duties on the Continent generally are less protective than they were forty years ago. The United States, also, is not any more protective now than it has been during the century, and the McKinley Tariff did not sensibly aggravate protection there in spite of all the noise made about it.
3. It is untrue, also, that England is isolated in its policy of abolishing protective import duties. As a matter of fact, half the world carries on its foreign

trade free of protective import duties; and protection by no means commands that area it is supposed to command. The imports and exports of the free-trade and protectionist groups of nations are about 2,000,000,000*l.* each group, imports and exports being nearly balanced.

4. The increase of the imports and exports in the free trade group has, however, been much greater than in the protectionist group in the last ten years, the increase in the case of the imports and exports respectively being 200,000,000*l.* whereas in the protectionist group the increase is less than 100,000,000*l.* The increase in the imports of the free-trade group is mainly in the imports of countries other than the United Kingdom and as a matter of fact the increase of our exports in the last ten years has been mainly to free trade and not to protectionist countries, though to those latter there is also an increase.

5. Protection by means of import duties is more ineffective and less extended in protectionist countries than it is commonly supposed to be; and it is doubtful if more than 2 per cent of the industry of leading protectionist nations like the United States and France is, or can be, protected. This means that only 1 per cent of the industry of the world is protected. The rest is carried on under free-trade conditions.

6. There is a reason of substance for the ineffectiveness of protection by means of import duties in the fact that by a process of evolution the leading manufacturing nations find themselves in such circumstances that they must obtain free of import duties the raw materials and food they import, and as they manufacture so much for export and import manufactured articles very little by comparison, the result is that the bulk of their trade must be carried on under free-trade conditions. The force of the circumstances described is being felt more and more and ensures the extension of free-trade policy, which is not due to any propaganda of free trade, but to the immediate pressure of practical considerations. This view is held by leading protectionists themselves and is obviously indisputable.

R. G.
25*th May*, 1892.

Memorandum on Terminating the Belgian and German Commercial Treaties, 10 June 1897, PRO, CAB 37/44/26.

Printed for the use of the Cabinet. June 10, 1897.
CONFIDENTIAL

Memorandum on terminating the Belgian and German Commercial Treaties.

THE step of terminating the Belgian and German Commercial Treaties, unless new Treaties are at once negotiated, will no doubt be a serious one. It will place a considerable portion of the foreign trade of both the United Kingdom and the Colonies outside the pale of Treaty Regulation, and this will be a great change, although no actual mischief may arise. Both Belgium and Germany, in their own interest, may, without a Treaty, continue to treat us much as they do now with a Treaty; but they will no longer be prevented by Treaty from discriminating against us.

GERMANY.

To take Germany first, as the more important country, the change will be as follows: –

1. Apart from import duties altogether we shall lose the benefit of the following stipulations respecting our trade with Germany (see the Treaty with Germany, Appendix I).

    (a.) The general privilege of British subjects residing temporarily or permanently in Germany to enjoy the same rights in respect to the exercise of commerce or trades as the subjects of any third country, and to be subjected to no higher or other taxes (Clause I of Treaty). This is a usual clause in Commercial Treaties, and is of course valuable as establishing the position for commercial purposes of British subjects in Germany. The Colonies, of course, have the benefit of this as well as the United Kingdom.

    (b.) Clauses II and III of the Treaty stipulate for equal treatment in all respects as compared with other countries of goods of the United Kingdom imported into Germany and of exports from Germany to the United Kingdom, not merely in regard to customs duties but in all other respects. The Colonies have the benefit of this under Clause VII. This most-favoured-nation clause accordingly extends to other matters, as well as to the customs duties, and whatever benefits we derive from it will be lost when the Treaty is at an end.

(c.)   The transit of British goods is now free from duties in Germany (Clause IV). This may be important. We do some trade with Russia, Austria, Switzerland, and Italy, and perhaps more remote countries through Germany; and although in the statistics this may all appear as trade with Germany, the fact that a portion shown in the statistics is transit trade through Germany only may be important. By the termination of the Treaty *we* lose specifically the right of transit.

(d.)   Any favour, privilege, or reduction in the Tariff of duties which Germany may give to any country is by the Treaty extended immediately and unconditionally to the United Kingdom and to the Colonies (Clauses V and VII). This will be lost if the Treaty is terminated. Germany may then give preferential treatment to other nations as compared with the United Kingdom and its Colonies.

Of the same nature is the stipulation that no prohibition of import or export is to be applied to the United Kingdom and Colonies that is not applied to other countries (Clause V).

(e.)   Both the Contracting Parties engage not to prohibit the export of coal or to levy export duties on it. This clause, though reciprocal, was no doubt originally meant to secure Germany English coal for use in manufactures; but it is reciprocal in form, and cannot be passed over here.

(f.)   In trade-marks the subjects of one of the Contracting Parties have in the other country the same protection as native subjects – national, and not merely most-favoured-nation treatment.

All these privileges conceded by Germany not merely to the United Kingdom but to the Colonies will be swept away if the Treaties are terminated. *Per contra* Germany will lose the like privileges in the United Kingdom and the Colonies, for the stipulations are reciprocal; but it is, of course, a serious change that the commercial relations between us and so important a unit as Germany should cease to be explicitly friendly. It will continue to be the interest of both to treat each other well, but the risk of friction will be increased.

2. The main question, however, is the Tariff, as to which, when the Treaty terminates, we shall no longer have most-favoured-nation treatment (Clauses II and III). It will be understood, however, from what has been already said, that the Treaty is not merly a Tariff Treaty, but the privileges as to import duties are only a part of the whole, and derive their value in part from their combination with other privileges.

We have now to examine, then, the amount of trade, imports and exports, which will be affected by the Treaty terminating.

The exports from the United Kingdom to Germany in the latest year (1896) were as follows: –

	£
British and Irish produce	22,244,000
Foreign and Colonial produce	11,741,000
Total	33,985,000

And the exports of the principal Colonies direct to Germany, according to the German Trade Returns, were, in the latest year for which there are figures, 1895: –

	£
Exports from India	8,106,000
" " Cape of Good Hope and Natal	855,000
" " British North America	104,000
" " British West Indies	422,000
" " Australasia	5,684,000
Total	15,171,000

This would make a total of 49,000,000*l*. exported from the United Kingdom and its Colonies to Germany annually. There is apparently, however, some duplication as the total imports into Germany from the United Kingdom and the above-named Colonies, according to the German Returns, only to about 42,000,000*l*., so that apparently some goods from the Colonies going to Germany viâ the United Kingdom, while they appear in our Returns as exports to Germany, are entered in the German Returns as imports from the Colonies. But whether we take the figure of *49,000,000l.* or *42,000,000l.* as the annual exports of the United Kingdom and the Colonies to Germany, there is clearly a large trade to be affected if Germany, when free from the Treaty, chooses to discriminate against us.

The same of the exports from Germany to the United Kingdom and the Colonies, amounting as follows, according to the German Returns, which it is the most convenient to employ.

Exports from Germany in 1895.

	£
To United Kingdom	33,776,000
" India	2,223,000
" Cape of Good Hope and Natal	652,000
" British North American	816,000
" British West Indies	51,000
" Australasia	1,143,000
Total	38,671,000

We seldom think now of a nation discriminating against another by means of exports duties or prohibitions on exportation, and we should probably in the worst event get from Germany whatever we want by indirect routes. Still the possibility of friction when Treaties are at an and is to be considered *quantum valeat.*

This is not the whole matter. Part of the trade we carry on with Germany is carried on viâ Belgium and Holland, and appears in the statistics of our trade those countries, though the exact amount cannot be separated. The total trade between the United Kingdom and Germany, Belgium, and Holland is shown in the Appendix III. But it will be understood that it is not all trade between this country and Germany, while it is also subject to the observation above stated as to transit through Germany.

Is the mischief actually arising from the termination of the Treaties likely to be very great? Possibilities are one thing and must not be left out of sight, but we must also look at the matter according to the probabilities of what will happen having regard to the self-interest of all countries concerned.

It will be to our interest in the United Kingdom at least, as we always view it, not to discriminate against German trade in comparison with the trade of any third country. As far as we are concerned, therefore, we shall probably be willing to give to Germany without a Treaty what we now give by a Treaty, especially if Germany will do the like. We do not discriminate against any nation, because we feel it to be to our interest to buy in the cheapest market. This applies to the miscellaneous stipulations of the Treaty, and not merely to the special stipulations regarding import duties.

On one side, therefore, trade with Germany, as far as the United Kingdom is concerned, it may be assumed, is likely to go on after the Treaties are terminated as before, and this will go a long way to force the other side of the trade into the same groove.

What the Colonies may do is less certain. But India and the non-self-governing Colonies will, of course, be guided by the mother-country, so that as regards a very large proportion of the colonial trade with Germany, that trade, also, on one side will go on after the termination of the Treaties as before.

The question then arises as to what Germany will do. I should say that it will be clearly Germany's interest to continue the treatment it now gives to us by the Treaty. It has practically the same *quid pro quo* as before, not only from the United Kingdom but from most of the British possessions, and why should it make a change? I cannot understand, I may say, why Germany objected to leave out of the Treaty the special clause which is so objectionable to the Colonies. German goods were not in fact as a rule going to be differentiated against even as compared with the United Kingdom after the clause was struck out. It would have been easy also to stipulate that no Colony should receive the benefit of the Treaty which so differentiated against German goods and leave that Colony out of the arrangement. At any rate, when the Treaty is terminated, Germany ought soon to find out that practically it is no worse off than before as regards the United Kingdom and the Colonies generally.

As regards the United Kingdom, moreover, Germany might be expected to give weight to two considerations. The first of these is the great importance to Germany of the United Kingdom market. We are Germany's best customer. The United Kingdom alone takes a fifth to a fourth of Germany's exports, and if we add what is taken by British Colonies the figure is certainly about a fourth. Germany, if it consults its own interest, would certainly hesitate before treating England and English subjects worse than others. The second is that as regards the goods which Germany imports from the United Kingdom and Colonies they are mostly coal and raw materials, or semi-manufactured articles, such as leather, and cotton and woollen yarns, where the existing duties are presumably levied in Germany's own interest, and could not be increased except to Germany's disadvantage.

The following is a list of the leading exports from the United Kingdom to Germany: –

			£
1.	British and Irish produce –		
	Coal		1,785,000
	Cotton yarn		2,069,000
	Cottons		1,785,000
	Herrings		793,000
	Machinery –		
	Steam engines and other sorts		1,788,000
	Woollen and worsted yarn		3,515,000
	Yarn, alpaca, mohair, and other sorts		914,000
	Woollens and worsteds		1,134,000
	Leather		338,000
	Linen yarn		246,000
	Linens		287,000
	Wool		934,000
2.	Foreign and Colonial produce –		
	Caoutchouc		735,000
	Coffee		626,000
	Wool		4,050,000
	Skins		892,000

Many other smaller articles might be inserted, but these are enough to show that while there is a miscellaneous export to Germany, our chief export is raw material, or semi-manufactured articles, without which Germany could not carry on her own trade.

It is difficult to see, therefore, in what way Germany would find it expedient to discriminate against English trade.

On the whole, then, there is some ground for thinking that no very serious result would follow if the Treaty with Germany should come to an end.

It should be added on this head also that apparently legislative action would be necessary if Germany is to discriminate materially against us. There is a General and a Conventional Tariff in Germany, but the Conventional is not much lower than the General, and many articles imported from England are the same in both Tariffs, while coal is free.[1] The fact that legislation will be necessary if Germany is to discriminate against us makes discrimination less likely.

I assume, also, that if we decided to give notice to terminate the Treaty, we should propose at once to enter into new negotiations, so as to avoid even the appearance of the notice notice being unfriendly, which it is not. Perhaps the giving of notice to terminate might be averted by an immediate negotiation if Germany was assured that we meant business.

It should be understood that in the case of one important country – France – we are already without a Treaty, but France finds it to be to her interest to treat us as well as it treats other nations, because we treat her as well. There is no reason why trade should not go on between different nations in a friendly manner even if there were no Tariff Treaties.

While stating the case thus generally, however, I have to draw attention to the peculiarity of the Constitution of the British Empire, which *may* give the Administration in Germany power to discriminate against us. Germany may choose to regard the British Empire, for diplomatic action, as a unit, and in that case, if any one of our Colonies discriminates against Germany as compared with any foreign country, or as compared even with the United Kingdom only, the Administration in Germany might perhaps take action against the United Kingdom and every other part of the Empire under the following clause in the Tariff Law: –

'Goods proceeding from States that treat German ships or products less favourably than those of other States, may, in so far as existing Treaties are not thereby violated, be burdened with a surtax ranging up to 100 per cent. of the Tariff duty imposed on such goods. Goods free of duty in virtue of the Tariff may, under the same conditions, be burdened with a duty not exceeding 20 per cent. *ad valorem*.

'The levying of this surtax and, as the case may be, of this duty, will, with the consent of the Bundesrath, be enforced by an Imperial Ordinance.

'This Imperial Order is to be communicated at once to the Reichstag, or, if the Reichstag be not in Session, when it next meets.

'The same shall no longer be enforced when not approved by the Reichstag.'

(Article VI of the German Tariff Law [...])

---

1   See Appendix IV annexed.

Tariff Wars between European States: Report on the Franco-Italian Tariff War, 1888–99; Reports on the Tariff War between Germany and Russia; Summary of the Franco-Swiss Tariff War, 1893–5, *Parliamentary Papers,* **95 (1904), Cmnd 1938, pp. 7–9, 11, 13, 39–40, 72, 77, 78–9.**

Report on the Franco-Italian Tariff War, 1888–99.[1]

On the 15th December, 1886, the Italian Ambassador in Paris informed the French Minister for Foreign Affairs that he was instructed by his Government to denounce the Traty of Commerce of the 3rd November, 1881, existing between France and Italy, the provisions of which would cease to have effect from the 1st January, 1888.

The Italian Government assigned as the reason for their action that the existing Treaty no longer responded to the present needs of their commerce, and proposed that negotiations should be started forthwith for the conclusion of a new Treaty.

France having accepted this proposal, it was agreed that the benefits of the Treaty of 1881 should continue to remain in force during the negotiations, which took place at Rome from the 31st December, 1887, till the 2nd February, 1888. As, however, the two Governments were unable to come to terms, the negotiations were broken off, and on the 27th February, 1888, the French Government promulgated a Law establishing special duties on Italian produce, and on the 29th of the same month the Italian Government published a Decree imposing heavy duties on French goods entering Italy.

These two war tariffs came into force on the 1st March, 1888, when the Treaty of 1881, which had been prolonged for two months, definitely terminated.

In addition, the maritime relations of the two countries were placed from this date under a severely restrictive régime.

The maritime relations of France and Italy were regulated by a Treaty concluded on the 13th June, 1862, which expired on the 16th July, 1886, and was not renewed. Consequently French shipping at Italian ports was subjected to the provisions of the Italian Law of the 6th December, 1885, which applied differential dues on foreign vessels. On the other hand, Italian shipping was subjected to the French Decree of the 17th July, 1886, which imposed surtaxes equivalent to those embodied in the Italian Decree of the 6th December, 1885.

The system of reprisals thus organized, both as regards the commercial relations and the maritime intercourse of the two countries, continued without change until the month of January 1890. In Italy, a law of the 29th December,

---

1 [Ed.: By Sir Henry Austin Lee, enclosed in Sir E. Monson to the Marquess of Lansdowne, 20 November 1903.]

1889, abrogated from the 1st January, 1890, the provisions of the Royal Decree of the 29th February of the previous year establishing the war Tariff against French imports; while, in France, by virtue of Article 17 of the Customs Law of the 11th January, 1892, the surtaxes imposed on imports from Italy in virtue of the Law of the 27th February, 1888, were repealed.

From this period until the conclusion of the Arrangement of February 1899, the commercial relations of France and Italy were placed under the regime of the general of Maximum Tariff of the respective countries.

The re-establishment of better relations which ensued was much appreciated in the commercial and industrial circles of both countries, but at the same time it was plain that the actual state of affairs could not be considered a permanent solution, and that reciprocal concession on both sides of their lowest Tariff was impatiently awaited.

In 1896 the Italian Government marked the feeling in this direction by concluding with France certain important political and economic Conventions, and, in particular, the Treaties relating to Tunis (28th September, 1896), which put an end to their differences concerning the French Protectorate in that country, and the maritime Arrangement of the 1st October, 1896, in virtue of which the two countries reciprocally granted the benefits of national treatment to shipping, except the coasting trade.

Following the resumption of the normal relations as regards shipping, the Italian Government made overtures to France on the 6th May, 1897, to place the commercial relations of the two countries on a footing of reciprocal most-favoured-nation treatment, which, in practice, meant the application of the Italian Conventional Tariff to French produce, in return for the application of the French Minimum Tariff to Italian produce.

The French Government, however, considered that in exchange for their Minimum Tariff they were entitled to claim from Italy not only the whole of the reductions she already granted to the other Powers by commercial Conventions, but a series of reductions of duties on goods specially interesting their exports to Italy.

France further stipulated that the concession of their Minimum Tariff should not be extended to Italian silk and silk stuffs, and also that Italian wines should be subject to the higher duties proposed on foreign wines.

Italy having accepted negotiations on this basis, an arrangement was concluded between the two Governments on the 21st November, 1898, and a Bill to authorize the French Government to apply the Minimum Tariff to Italian products, with the exception of silk and silk stuffs, was presented to the Chamber of Deputies on the 25th of the same month.

It may be mentioned that the concession to Italy by France of her Minimum Tariff constitutes on the part of France a purely unilateral act, and, consequently on renouncing the advantages of the arrangement, she is free at any minute to revert to such measures as may be considered expedient.

The Bill, embodying the proposed arrangement, came up for discussion on the 22nd December, 1898, and, after some opposition on political grounds, it was carried by 407 to 36 votes in the Chamber and by 248 to 4 votes in the Senate on the 31st January.

In virtue of a Law of the 2nd February and a Decree of the 7th February, 1899, the benefits of the French Minimum Tariff were applied to goods of Italian origin, with the exception of silk and silk stuffs, in return for most-favoured-nation treatment from Italy.

By the rupture of the Franco-Italian commercial relations, Italian trade suffered very severely. According to French customs statistics the imports into France of Italian products, which in 1887 represented a value of 307,709,000 fr., immediately fell in 1888 to 181,163,000 fr., and gradually declined to 131,738,000 fr. in the year 1897. In the space, therefore, of ten years Italian goods destined for consumption in France fell off to the extent of 57 per cent; but in 1898, when the Tariff strife practically ended, there was a slight improvement in her exports to France, which increased to 137, 806,000 fr.

Italy was the first to suffer from the denunciation of the Commercial Treaty with France, but it is certain that French exports to Italy were also seriously affected.

From 1887 till 1897 the loss of trade sustained by France amounted to fully 50 per cent., French exports (according to Italian statistics) to Italy having decreased from 326, 188,000 fr. in 1887 to 155,514,000 fr. in 1888, and to 160,833,000 fr. in 1897. In 1898, however, they fell as low as 116,370,000 fr.

There is no doubt that causes quite foreign to the rupture of the commercial relations can account in some measure for the serious diminution in the French exports to Italy, and it may be remarked that in 1887 the economic situation of the latter country was better than it was ten years later, and that her purchasing power was greater than in 1897.

Italy had also largely developed her industries since 1887, and was able to call on the national production for many manufactured articles which a few years earlier she had been in the habit of importing from France.

It cannot, however, be denied that to the rupture of the normal relations in the commerce of the two countries must be attributed the great decrease in the exports from France to Italy.

In 1887, for instance, the total importations into Italy of foreign goods from all countries amounted to 1,605,419,000 fr., of which France furnished for 326,188,000 fr., while ten years later, in 1897, on a total importation of 1,191,598,000 fr., the part contributed by France amounted to only 160,833,000 fr., so that in ten years France's share in the supply of the Italian market fluctuated from 20 to 13 ½ per cent., a notable portion of Italy's purchases from France having thus passed into the hands of other foreign competitors – principally the United States and Canada, which gained nearly 7 per cent., and to Germany, which advanced 2 per cent.

On the other hand, in the total of Italy's exports in 1897 as compared with 1887 (which advanced 8 per cent.), those to Switzerland increased 9 per cent., to Germany 4 per cent., to Austro-Hungary 3 per cent., and to the United Kingdom 2 per cent. – in all 18 per cent., or about 1 per cent. above the percentage of Italy's reduced exports to France.[1] [...]

Notwithstanding the improved commercial relations between France and Italy since the conclusion of the Arrangement of February 1899, it will be observed from the following Table, showing the trade of the two countries since the year 1881, that the enormous fall in their exchanges caused by the rupture of the Commercial Treaty in 1888 is being very slowly recovered. In the war of Tariffs Italy has been much more severely wounded than France, and now finds the French market practically closed to her exports of silks and wines, which formerly represented the most important part of her trade with France; but this loss has been compensated in some measure by a notable extension of her exports to foreign countries, which show an increase of fully 30 per cent. in 1902 as compared with the year 1897: – ...

Report on the Tariff War between Germany and Russia [2]

The Tariff policy of Russia during the latter half of the nineteenth century was characterized at first by growing liberality; but after 1868–76, during which years the *ad valorem* rate was about 12 per cent., the Tariff was gradually raised till in 1891, after a series of tentative changes, it was fixed at the high rate of 33 per cent. for the avowed purpose of protecting the nascent industries of the country.

Up to 1879 Russia had not to fear reprisals on the part of foreign nations, for food-stuffs, her principal export, were not as a rule subject to a high Tariff. But in that year a change of system took place, and from 1879 to 1890 the rates on Russian corn were raised in Germany for the avowed purpose of protecting agriculture. In 1891 the commercial relations between the two countries were in the following condition: –

Russia, bent on protecting her iron and other industrial enterprises, had drawn up a Tariff of a highly protective character, which bore especially hard on Germany whose export trade to Russia was on the decline.[3] Germany, on the other hand, had inaugurated a new policy. Convinced of the necessity of provid-

---

1 [Ed.: Tables omitted.]

2 [Ed.: By Cecil Spring Rice, enclosed in Sir C. Scott to the Marquess of Lansdowne, 6 August 1903.]

3 The iron exports to Russia fell from 2,100,000*l* to 632,000*l* in 1892 according to the German statistics.

ing for her largely-increased industrial population, she was determined to lower the duties on food-stuffs, but only on condition that the countries exporting food-stuffs to Germany should in return lower the duties on the products of German industry. And although Russia was immensely interested in the German market for her food-stuffs, she was equally interested in protecting the metallurgic industries which were established by direct State intervention. She was thus precluded from granting German trade any facilities which might prove fatal to the industries which she had established, and for which she was responsible.

The consequence of this conflict of interest was that Russia found herself in an exceptionally disadvantageous position. For not only was her export trade subject to a high duty, but the trade of her rivals on the German market was treated with favour in exchange for similar favours accorded to German exports, which Russia was, as she thought, unable to give. In 1891 Germany had concluded Treaties by which she had lowered her Tariff rates on certain articles of primary necessity in exchange for lowered rates on German manufactured goods; and in 1892 Russia found herself practically the only nation interested in the German market, which was excluded from the benefit of the new Tariffs.[1] She found her place in that market being gradually taken by the produce of her competitors, and although she was unwilling to follow their example and accord low rates to German products, she resolved to have recourse to the alternative of force, and raised the duties on all German goods by 50 per cent. Germany replied by raising her own Tariff – already higher for Russian exports than for those of any other country – against Russian goods. The Tariff war thus declared lasted from August 1893 to March 1894, when, as a result of negotiations (which had never ceased since they were first begun in 1890), hostilities were terminated by an agreement, by which Russia consented to lower her Tariff on the principal products of German industry, and Germany admitted Russia to the benefits of the Conventional Tariff as fixed in her Agreements with other nations.

The Treaty was to remain in operation ten years, and as was anticipated by the German Government, the stability thus introduced into the commercial relations between the two countries resulted in a renewal of the growth of their mutual trade which recent events had interrupted. The share of Germany in the trade of Russia increased from 26 to 32 per cent. in the ten years from 1891–1900; the exports of Russian food-stuffs to Germany and of German manufactures to Russia increased 200 per cent. from 1892 to 1900.

The Tariff war had not lasted long enough to dislocate permanently the conditions of trade, and neither Germany nor Russia lost their place in each other's market for much more than a year. The war took place in the winter, and during most of the time the Baltic ports were closed by ice; moreover, the Regulations as to certificates of origin seriously hampered the trade of neutrals. But in the

1 Germany concluded Treaties with Austria, Italy, Switzerland in 1891. She had most-favoured nation Treaties with the United States, Argentine, &c. There was no such Treaty between Russia and Germany.

opinion of both Governments a continuation of the war would have led to very serious consequences – some of a political character–and there appears to have been great relief when peace was concluded.

The ten years fixed by the Treaty have nearly elapsed. The same Parties are now negotiating a new Treaty at St. Petersburgh, and each other them is armed with a highly protective Tariff.

With regard to the question as to whether the recent growth of Russo-German trade is due to the Tariff war, the answer depends on whether or no the Tariff peace – which (with the monetary reform of 1896) ensured the stability of commercial conditions necessary to commerce – was or was not possible without the war which preceded it. Without a Tariff war German trade with Russia had steadily increased since the middle of the century from 11 per cent. to 28 per cent. of the entire trade of Russia. But a review of the conditions under which the struggle was conducted, and especially of the points of view of the two antagonists, makes it appear doubtful whether ordinary negotiations, without the sanction of force, would ever have led to a satisfactory compromise, or whether the protective policy of the two nations would ever have been modified except after an experience of the results of protection in its extremest form...

Report on the Russo-German Tariff War of 1893–1894: its origins, history and effects.[1]

The question as to the effect which the Tariff war had on Russo–German trade, invites the further inquiry as to how far it influenced the final conclusion of a Commercial Treaty between the two Empires. The Tariff war lasted only eight months, namely, from August 1893 to March 1894, but from February 1892, and even from a much earlier date, the commercial relations of the two countries had been most strained. It is, indeed, necessary to go back to the end of the seventies to seek the origin of the coolness, which in 1893 culminated in an open declaration of war. In 1877, Russia raised her Tariff 33 per cent. by enforcing the collection of the customs duties in gold. In 1879, Prince Bismarck reversed the policy of moderate Free Trade which had governed Germany's commercial relations since the conclusion of the Treaty with France in 1862. Between 1879 and 1891, when Russia raised her Tariff to the verge of prohibition, increased duties were repeatedly imposed by either side, more especially by Russia. When the new Treaties concluded by Germany with Austria–Hungary and other countries came into force in February 1892, Russia found that she alone among the great exporting States was differentiated against in the German market. Believing, as she did, that she was indispensible [*sic*] to Germany as a purveyor of corn, she declined to purchase the reduced rates of the new conventional Tariff at the price which Germany asked – namely concessions similar to those made by the coun-

---

1 [Ed.: By Mr Buchanan, enclosed in Sir F. Lascelles to the Marquess of Lansdowne, 7 August 1903.]

tries enjoying most-favoured-nation treatment in that Empire. Russia hoped to make better terms for herself, and limited her offer to the reductions which had been granted to France in the Treaty which she had concluded with that Power in June 1893. That Treaty had, however, been drafted so as to include as few concessions as possible on goods in which other third countries were directly interested, and affected but slightly the export trade of Germany. The course of the negotiations which followed has already been described. Both countries were confident in their own strength, and there was a large class in both whose personal interests were best served by the maintenance of high protective duties. Although the importance of the German market to her corn trade had been brought home to her after the bad harvests of 1891 and 1892, Russia, like a bold player, tried to force her adversary to give up the game by raising the stakes still higher, and threatened the application of the maximum Tariff. Germany took up the challenge, and the war broke out.

It had not, however, lasted a couple of months before negotiations were resumed, and the sharpness of the lesson which it taught helped to render both parties more ready to come to terms. As an acute attack of illness is often less hurtful to the human body than a chronic disease, so the Tariff war, in spite of the temporary loss which it inflicted on the trade of both countries, hastened the process by which their commercial relations were restored to a healthy and normal condition under a Treaty which has given so remarkable an impetus to their respective export trades.

The effect of the Treaty soon made itself felt in many important branches of German industry. Even before its final conclusion large orders for iron wares had been executed for Russian houses, and the goods were but awaiting the announcement of its ratification to be dispatched to their destination. The export of iron reached a standard which it had never attained before, while that of coal and coke, of locomotives, sewing machines, skins, hides, drugs, dyes, chemicals, groceries, and woollen goods also increased ...

The Treaty of 1894, which was concluded for a period of ten years, namely, till the 31st December, 1903, may now be denounced by a year's notice on either side, and preliminary negotiations for its renewal have already been opened at St. Petersburgh. The position which Russia occupies at present is no longer the same as that with which she was confronted before the outbreak of the Tariff war in 1893. The minimum duties on wheat and rye fixed by the new German Tariff at 55*s.* and 50*s.* respectively per ton, are not to be levied on Russian corn alone, but on that of all corn exporting countries. Russia is no longer differentiated against, and her rivals in the corn trade will no longer profit by her loss.

The raising of the German corn duties is, however, none the less a matter of great moment to her export trade, and is not likely to be accepted without some countervailing action on her part. The depressed condition of German agriculture has caused the pendulum to swing round once more in favour of a higher form of protection than that embodied in the Treaties negotiated by Count Caprivi. Under the system of what, on the Continent, is termed moderate Protection, German industry has made great progress; but the agrarians look only at the other side of the picture, and are resolved to save German agriculture, if possible, from the fate which has befallen the agriculture of Great Britain.

The raising of the duties on wheat and rye from 35*s.* per ton to 55*s.* and 50*s.* has had the inevitable consequence of causing a general raising of other duties as compensation to the industrial classes, so that the new German Tariff, in its present form, represents a return to a highly protective system. There seems little doubt, however, that it will be mainly used as a weapon by which to extract concessions from other countries, and that it will undergo many modifications in the course of the negotiations for the new Treaties. As regards those with Russia, with which this Report is alone concerned, the danger of a rupture may perhaps be diminished by the experience gained in the short Tariff war of 1893. The lessons then learnt may help remind both countries of the loss which such a war entails, and while Germany, with her great stock of industrial products, has every reason to keep the Russian market open to her exports, Russia, on the other hand, has equally good grounds for desiring to retain what is to her the most valuable of all markets for her surplus agricultural produce ...

Summary of the History of the Franco-Swiss Tariff War, 1893–5[1]

The Swiss Tariff Conventions with France and other countries were due to expire in 1892.

As early as 1890 the Swiss Government embarked upon the revision of their general tariff.

I may explain that the Confederation, having no power to impose direct taxes, is obliged to raise its revenue from the yield of indirect taxation, federal monopolies, and other administrative receipts, of which revenue customs receipts contribute the largest item.

Consequently, the Federal Government were anxious to secure by the revision of their conventions an annual revenue from indirect taxation to balance any deficit in their Budget. Moreover, they were of the opinion that the General Tariff required revision in order to make the incidence of the duties correspond with the changes which had been taking place in the relative position of certain Swiss industries which it was designed to protect; and lastly, they were no doubt influenced by the desirability of being able to use the revised General Tariff as an effective instrument of negotiation for the new commercial Treaties of 1892.

1   [Ed.: Enclosed in Sir C. Greene to the Marquess of Lansdowne, 10 July 1903.]

In France at this time the tendency of public feeling in the Chambers was in favour of a largely-extended protective policy, and the Swiss Government realized that these influences would be very likely to prevent the French Government from coming to satisfactory terms with the Confederation in the approaching negotiations of 1892; with the inevitable consequence, in such an event, of a war of general Tariffs except in the case of some few articles of exclusively Swiss and French production.

Accordingly the Swiss Government, while expressing their faith in the abstract principle of free trade, admitted to the country that they had been obliged, in the interest of self-preservation, gradually to depart from the traditions which had been up till now professed by the majority of the Swiss people, and had determined to make early preparations for this struggle for existence by an effectual revision of the existing Tariff.

In the autumn of 1890 the French Government introduced a Bill proposing two new draft Tariffs, but the Swiss Government lost no time in intimating to them that the minimum Tariff which the Republic proposed to offer in return for further concessions in favour of French trade could never be accepted by the Confederation as a Conventional Tariff, and was simply the old General Tariff shorn of the reductions which Switzerland had already purchased by concessions to France in her own Tariff. The Swiss Government considered that, under these circumstances, it would be better for the country to endeavour to subsist without any Conventional Tariff with France, especially as the Tariff, under the last French proposals, would be always liable to termination or revision at the will of the French Legislature, and would thus introduce an element of instability, which would, in their opinion, be most prejudicial to the trade between the two countries.

In January 1891 the French Government denounced their Treaty of Commerce with Switzerland of the 23rd February, 1882, but proposed to the Federal Government to conclude a Convention reviving all the stipulations of the Commercial Treaty just denounced, which had no reference to Conventional Tariffs.

The Federal Government, however, declined to give any encouragement to this suggestion; and, further, declared that they were not prepared to conclude any binding engagement with France which might secure to that country 'most-favoured-nation treatment' in return for simple admission to the benefits of the minimum French Tariff at that time under the consideration of the French Legislature.

The revised Swiss General Customs Tariff was then submitted to popular Referendum, and accepted by a majority of 60,000 votes out of a total of 369,226.

In January 1892 the Federal Council applied to the Federal Chambers and obtained their permission to negotiate an unconventional *modus vivendi* with France, whereby Switzerland should, by an autonomous act, apply to France 'most-favoured-nation treatment,' and France should similarly apply her minimum Tariff to Switzerland, as a provisional measure, and in order to give time for the conclusion, if possible, of a more satisfactory and binding Agreement. The *modus vivendi* was, however, subject to cancellation at any moment, and to the application to France by Switzerland of her new general Tariff instead of the provisional 'most-favoured-nation treatment.'

Further negotiations for an understanding proceeded between the two Governments during the autumn, but in December the Arrangement which had been the outcome of these 'pourparlers' was rejected by the French Chambers.

Thereupon the Federal Government published a Decree on the 28th December, stating that, in consequence of the above rejection, goods of French origin would after the 1st January, 1893, be subjected to the rates of the Swiss General Tariff, while higher differential rates would be levied on some 200 articles of French trade and agriculture, and certificates of origin would also be required for certain classes of goods.

War was thus declared, and continued uninterruptedly during 1893, no relaxation being granted on either side excepting the introduction of an Arrangement, agreed to in June, for the differential treatment of goods from the free zones of Gex and Haute Savoie.

Matters remained in the same state during the whole of 1894, and indeed up till the summer of 1895, notwithstanding various attempts which were made on both sides to restore the old relations of the two countries. However, in June negotiations which had been proceeding quietly for several months resulted at last in an Agreement being come to between the two countries, and notes embodying it were officially exchanged on the 24th June between the Federal Government and the French Ambassador at Berne. This Arrangement was accepted by the Swiss Chambers by very large majorities on the 10th August, and the Tariff war which had been in operation for two years and seven and a-half months thus came to an end.

A Federal Decree was promulgated on the 16th August whereby French products were, under the new Arrangement, to enter Switzerland from the 19th August subject only to payment of duties fixed by the 'Tarif d'usage' (most-favoured-nation Tariff), and certificates of origin were no longer to be required. Swiss products, on the other hand, were to enter France on the basis of the minimum Tariff reduced in favour of certain articles.

It may be observed, in conclusion, that the Arrangement thus arrived at, and which is still in force, was in no sense a Treaty of fixed duration, but only a *modus vivendi* terminable by either party at any time.

  (Signed)   CONYNGHAM GREENE.

'Commercial Diplomacy 1860–1902' (n.d.), PRO, T 172/945.

SECTION 2. – LATTER-DAY PROTECTION: ITS INFLUENCE ON COMMERCIAL DIPLOMACY.

CHAPTER III. – INTRODUCTORY.

The history of commercial diplomacy in Europe during the last thirty years is very different from the triumphant progress between 1860 and 1870 that was described above. In the ten years which preceded the Franco-Prussian War most of the important nations of Europe made Treaties with one another, embodying considerable reductions of customs duties. Since 1870, commercial Treaties have been proportionally less numerous and individually of less moment than the Treaties of the sixties. The States which between 1860 and 1870 took what seemed to be first steps in the direction of Free Trade have taken no second steps. Either they have remained at the point to which those first steps carried them, or they have returned towards Protection.

The principal causes which make commercial diplomacy difficult to-day, in countries where forty years ago it was easy, may be summarized briefly as follows: –

1. Formerly economic opinion in these countries was in a state of flux, and tended on the whole towards Free Trade; to-day the economic opinion of the majority is decisively in favour of Protection.
2. The essence of the old Protection was privileges granted by the Government in a more or less haphazard way. To-day Protection is, in form at least, democratic; tariffs have been debated and voted by representative Assemblies, and represent something not far removed from the will of the majority.
3. In the Parliamentary manœuvres which attend the construction of a modern Tariff, the sections of producers whose interests are more or less opposed have struck their bargains with one another and with the Government. It is more difficult now than forty years ago to break up their alliance. They recognize a common interest against the foreigner and against the domestic free trader, and are fully alive to the danger of being beaten in detail attendant on any important split. The remedy for an exporting industry which is selected by the foreigner for retaliation is, in most cases, ready to hand, viz., increased protection in the home market.

It may seem remarkable that, with such views prevailing, the policy of commercial Treaties has been able to subsist at all. As was said above, the Treaties which have been concluded since 1870 have not been of the same importance as the Treaties which were concluded between 1860 and 1870. The most important are those which have been negotiated by France and Germany; a short sketch of the commercial policy of these two countries will be supplied presently. But before entering upon this detailed exposition a few general remarks may be made.

1. The Protectionist doctrine admits the profit to be derived from an interchange of goods between countries whose products are – as the phrase goes – 'supplementary' to one another. There is thus room (*a*) for Treaties between States whose manufactures are advanced and States whose manufactures are not advanced, especially where certain of the natural products of the former are not produced at all in the latter; (*b*) for Treaties between States whose manufactures have reached a similar stage of development if any of their natural products are 'supplementary.'
2. Governments have in some cases been less Protectionist than majorities, and have fought hard for retaining the principle of commercial Treaties, even when the new Treaties could contain no reductions of duties, or even where they contained increases of duties. A breach with the system of Treaties has in certain cases been feared also as likely to lead to political estrangement from countries with which Treaties had formerly been concluded.
3. The protectionist majorities in many countries have worked out a system by which it is possible to have Treaties without abandoning immoderate protection. The most complete development of this system is to be seen in the 'maximum and minimum' Tariffs of France and Spain; its first stage is the almost universal practice of fixing the general Tariff so high that concessions may be made without abandoning an ample margin of protection.

But though the practice of concluding commercial Treaties has continued, the importance of these Treaties in relation to international trade is very different from what it was between 1860 and 1870. From being a machinery for effecting a general reduction of Tariffs they have become a mere fly upon the wheel of protection. The nations of Europe have concluded many Treaties with one another since 1880, but European Tariffs as a whole are far more protectionist now than they were then. The Treaties may have checked the reaction – though opinion differs on this point. They have never been able to stay it entirely, far less have diplomatists succeeded, whether by threats or reasoning, in converting convinced protectionists into free traders.

CHAPTER IV. – THE TARIFF POLICY OF FRANCE SINCE THE FRANCO-GERMAN WAR.

The history of French commercial policy during the last thirty years may be told briefly. It is the story (1) of the consolidation of a national Protectionist party embracing all important sections of French producers; (2) of the capture by this party of the machinery of Government; (3) of the establishment of a Tariff system in conformity with the views of the party.

The culmination of the Liberal movement in France coincides with the quinquennium immediately succeeding on the Franco-German war. The reform of 1860, which was at its outset opposed to the wishes of most Frenchmen,[1] had ended by converting the nation. From the evidence given by textile manufactures at the Commission of 1869 into the workings of the new system, it is plain that the principle upon which the duties had been assessed in 1860 was accepted almost universally. Complaints were directed against details; particular duties were declared to be too low; but it was agreed on all hands that French manufactures should be content with the minimum duties necessary to equalize the conditions of production in France and in foreign countries.

In the early seventies M. Thiers attempted some return towards high protection. His attempt failed, partly through the opposition of Austria and Great Britain (to which countries France had contracted Treaty obligations), but principally from the opposition of the vast majority of French manufacturers.

Again in 1875, when a Circular was sent to the Chambers of Commerce and to the Consultative Chambers of Arts and Crafts to know their opinion as to the workings of the Treaties of 1860, an enormous majority were in favour of the renewal of the Treaties.

From this time on, however, the French nation as a whole has grown steadily more protectionist. The main lines of this movement of opinion have been these: –

1. The growth of protectionism among manufacturers.
2. The conversion of the agriculturists.
3. The conversion of the wine growers.

1. In or about the year 1875 began what is known as 'the great depression.' The conclusion of the Franco-German war had been followed by a boom in all manufacturing industries, particularly in the iron trade. This was followed by a depression which affected every branch of manufacturing industry, and with the progress of this depression the demand for protection increased.
2. Agriculturalists in France (as in Germany) had been in favour of Free Trade (or at least of moderate Protection) so long as they were not themselves exposed to foreign competition. Towards the end of the seventies the exports of American agricultural produce to Europe began to alarm them. Even those countries which did not feel the new competition directly in their home market were affected by it indirectly, inas-much as it drove them out from the English market. Hence in France, as in Germany, the agricultural interest came to desire

---

[1] Cobden declared in 1860 that it would be impossible to find among any ten representative Frenchmen more than one in favour of the Treaty.

Protection for themselves, and could no longer oppose the grant of it to other producers.
3. The wine growers had always been in favour of Free Trade. In the eighties, however, French vineyards were to a great extent destroyed by the phylloxera. France became, for the time being, a wine importing country, and the cry for Protection arose. The conditions were thus favourable for the growth of protectionism in France. The Government and the permanent officials remained for a long time staunch in their adherence to the policy of the sixties, but the misfortune of that policy was that though on the whole Liberal it had no basis of principle which would afford arguments against an increase in Protection corresponding to the growth of foreign competition. As has been shown, the Government in its most Free Trade period had never abandoned the position that it was desirable to protect the home producer. The utmost of its liberalism was contained in the plea that the Protection so granted should be the minimum necessary. It only remained, therefore, for the protectionists to demonstrate that the prices at which foreign goods were offered had fallen considerably.

The reaction in French feeling did not really control the Government until the early nineties, though, as has been shown, it had been gathering force since the middle of the seventies. The Government which concluded the Commercial Treaties of 1882 was still under the sway of the policy of the Second Empire; it had indeed fought staunchly against the reaction, and had succeeded to some extent in stemming it. At the same time it had given the Chambers certain pledges relative to the negotiation of Commercial Treaties, the most important being a promise to preserve a certain minimum rate of duties beyond which reductions should in no case be made. The plan of fixing minimum duties by law, which is foreshadowed in this undertaking, is of so much importance that it may be well to consider it in some detail.

It will be remembered that at the time when the Cobden Treaty was negotiated the French Government possessed the right of reducing the Tariff by Treaty without reference to the Chambers. This right was lost to the Executive at the fall of the Empire; from the seventies onwards, in France as in the other great States of Western Europe, full control over all modifications in the Tariff became a prerogative of the Chambers. The conditions for the negotiation of Tariff Treaties were thereby altered considerably. A protectionist majority in the Chambers had the right to veto the concessions which a more liberal Executive might make, and it naturally follows that a majority in this position is strongly tempted to fix beforehand limits beyond which no concessions may be made. This practice recommends itself as likely to save friction between the Government and the

Assembly; in certain cases, too, as a safeguard where the Government may be suspected of coquetting with Free Trade.

The complete machinery of maximum and minimum Tariffs was not developed by the French until 1892; yet the difference between the double Tariff of that year and the Arrangement of 1882 is in fact of the slightest. In 1882 the Government agreed that none of the duties in the new Tariff should be reduced by more than 25 per cent. In 1892 two Tariffs, a maximum and a minimum, were worked out in all their details. The prospective minimum duties of 1882 were, however, more moderate than the minimum duties of 1892.

The reaction towards Protection in France found its first opportunity over the reconstruction of the general Tariff, which had been undertaken in the first instance as a further step in the direction of Free Trade. The Conventional Tariff which arose out of the Treaties of the sixties applied of course to those countries only with which Treaties had been concluded. Behind it there still remained the old general Tariff with its prohibitions and excessive duties. Under this Tariff fell the trade with all countries which had not entered the Treaty network. Now, so long as the Treaties subsisted, this was not of much moment, though trade with some important countries – *e.g.*, Russia and the United States – was of course impeded. The danger rather lay in this; that if, after the Treaties expired, any interval should elapse before the conclusion of new Treaties, foreign trade would be hit severely and important foreign countries seriously annoyed.

The need then of reconstructing the general Tariff on liberal lines was imperative, and in the first instance it was intended to make the existing Conventional Tariff the basis of the new general Tariff. This design was defeated by the first beginnings of the protectionist reaction, and the duties in the new general Tariff, when it at last took shape, averaged 25 per cent, more than the duties in the Conventional Tariff. The undertaking then of the Government, that none of the new duties should be reduced by more than 25 per cent, was equivalent to an undertaking that no concessions should be made beyond the limits of the existing Conventional Tariff. It is plain that the French Government had intended, in the first instance, to go further than this. In their first proposals to the British Government they suggested as a basis for the negotiation 'an improvement in the *status quo* in the direction of Free Trade.' The British Government accepted this basis; they persuaded the House of Commons to approve of a reduction of the wine duties[1] (in case they should come to terms with the French), but they pledged themselves not to conclude any Treaty which included higher duties on any important British commodity than those granted in 1860. This undertaking by the British Gov-

---

1 A resolution was passed by the House, and clauses were included in the Budget Bill of 1880 which would have enabled the wine duties to be reduced if the negotiations with France were concluded by August in that year; but the clauses were dropped when it was seen that the negotiations would not be settled in time.

ernment was sufficient in conjunction with the pledge given to the Chambers by the French Government to make the conclusion of a Treaty impossible. The minimum rates which the French were able to offer were, on the average, at least as favourable as the *status quo*,[1] but on certain lines of British exports they were higher than those of the old régime. The negotiations, therefore, after lasting (with intervals) for several years, were given up at the beginning of 1882. Nevertheless, the records of these unsuccessful negotiations are interesting, as showing how much depends in such matters on the feelings of the foreign Government, and how little on the concessions which the home Government can offer.

The French were anxious to conclude a Treaty, partly for political reasons, partly through loyalty to the policy of the Empire. The concession offered by this country on the wine duties was only important as giving some appearance of a 'bargain' to the negotiation. Sir Charles Dilke, it would appear, made little mention of this side of the matter. His general procedure was to interview in the morning the representatives of some French industry; to persuade them that a low duty on some article was to their advantage, and to urge them to point this out to their Government. In the afternoon he negotiated with the French Government, and often found that the seed sown in the morning had borne fruit.[2] It is noteworthy that some of the duties offered to Sir Charles by the French Government were actually lower than those granted subsequently in negotiation with other nations who had much more 'bargaining power' than this country.

It has been said that the negotiations between France and this country were abandoned. In place of a Treaty the French passed a law conferring on us most-favoured-nation treatment. The new Conventional Tariff which resulted from Treaties with Belgium, Switzerland, Italy, Portugal, Holland, Norway and Sweden, and Spain, was not far removed from the old Conventional Tariff, the duties being in some cases a little higher, in others a little lower. This Tariff remained in force until 1892.

The protectionist reaction which had commenced in the latter 'seventies, gathered force in the 'eighties. In particular the old cleft between manufacturers on the one hand, and agriculturists and wine growers on the other, was closed up. American wheat and the phylloxera produced a union of French producers irresistibly strong.

The various Treaties had not 'bound' the duties on cereals, sugar, and animals, and it was therefore possible for the distressed agriculturists to obtain protection without awaiting for the date fixed for the expiration of the Treaties. In 1884 the sugar producers obtained a rearrangement of the export-drawback

1 Sir Charles Dilke has told me that he could at any moment have concluded a Treaty which would have been, on the average, better than the *status quo*.
2 It is doubtful whether this kind of negotiation would be possible at the present day – at least in France; where the actual rates of the minimum duties have been settled in detail already there is obviously less scope for it.

which gave them a bounty similar to that already enjoyed by their German competitors. In 1885, and again in 1887, the duties on live animals and cereals were raised. Meantime the manufacturing protectionists had not been idle. Their own protection could not be increased until the Treaties expired, but by sympathetic treatment of the demands of the agriculturists they paved the way for a junction of the two parties. This junction seems to have been effected formally at the elections in 1889. Strong protectionist majorities were returned. M. Tirard, who favoured the *status quo*, resigned his post as Minister of Commerce to M. Jules Roche, an adherent of advanced protection.

The Tariff system, which was adopted in 1892, is interesting as being the logical outcome of Protection – the most perfect machinery for effecting the ends of Protection which has yet been devised. The protectionist is in favour of Tariff Treaties in so far as they prevent other countries from raising their duties, but they have, in his opinion, two serious drawbacks – (1) the Government in negotiating may make too great concessions; (2) if the conventional duties are in technical language 'bound,' i.e., if the contracting country enters into an obligation not to raise certain duties during the lifetime of the Treaty, it may happen that duties which, at the time when the Treaty was concluded, were thought amply large for protective purposes may become in course of time too small, owing either to a change in prices or to an alteration in the conditions of production.

Against these two dangers the French double Tariff (maximum and minimum) was devised as a perfect remedy.

1. The minimum duties defined accurately the limits beyond which the Government might not make concessions.
2. The minimum Tariff, like the maximum, was intended to be autonomous, i.e., it was to remain open to the Chambers to increase at any moment any individual duty which might seem insufficiently protective.

Such a system, it is plain, is ideally satisfactory to Protectionists. To it all protectionist countries will tend more and more to approximate.[1] It would seem therefore desirable to determine its importance as regards the commercial diplomacy of the future.

1. The minimum rates prescribed being considered amply sufficient for protective purposes there is no inclination to withhold them from countries whose Tariffs are moderate. The French minimum Tariff in its entirety was offered to Belgium, Switzerland, Norway and Sweden, and other countries

---

1 It was imitated in 1892 by Spain. The Austrian and German Tariffs of 1902 contain 'maximum' and 'minimum' duties on cereals. The Dingley Tariff Act made a 20 per cent. reduction the limit of all concessions. The Russian Tariff of 1902 contains, strictly speaking, no 'minimum' rates, but the duties levied on many commodities when imported by the Western land frontier are in excess of the duties en the same commodities when imported by sea. This excess is plainly meant to leave a margin for reductions to Germany and Austria.

in exchange for most-favoured-nation treatment, and was extended without question to the United Kingdom.
2. The business of securing reductions on the minimum rates is particularly difficult, however serious the counter threats may be. A threat passed in diplomatic language between two Governments is not very serious, since it is kept secret from the public, in most cases, until the event is decided. But to secure a reduction in the French minimum Tariff it is not enough to 'reason gently' with the French Government.

The utmost the Government can do is to propose to the Chambers that the duties should be reduced; for this proposal it must give reasons; and in giving the reasons it is difficult to conceal the fact that the chief reason is fear. In other words, the threat has to be made public. Once it is made public the controversy is lifted above economic issues; the national honour is at stake; and the two countries are fortunate indeed if they escape without a Tariff war.

As this system gains ground in Europe – and the principal protectionist countries have been working steadily towards it during the last ten years – it is plain that each country, in relation to its neighbours, will be driven more and more to adopt one of two courses: either to accept with the best face possible the minimum duties offered to it, or to engage in a Tariff war. The Protectionist is at least as clever as the diplomatist who relies upon 'bluff', and he is perfecting a very pretty piece of machinery to render the policy of bluff impossible.

Up to the present time the French have made concessions beyond their minimum duties in three instances: –

1. To the Swiss after a Tariff war of three years' duration.
2. To the Italians after a Tariff war, which, beginning in 1888, continued until 1898.
3. To the Russians – the concessions here being small, and made for political considerations.

Into the details of these Tariff wars we need not enter, the following tables of the 'special' trade of France with Italy and Switzerland speak for themselves: –

	French Imports.* Merchandize only, for home consumption. Million fr.			French Exports. – Domestic produce, merchandize only. Million fr.
From Italy –			To Italy –	
1885	262		1885	177
1886	309		1886	192
1887	307		1887	192
1888	181	}Tariff War{	1888	119
1889	133		1889	143
1890	121		1890	149
1891	123		1891	125
1892	132		1892	132
1893	151		1893	128
1894	121		1894	98
1895	114		1895	134
1896	126		1896	115
1897	131		1897	150
1898	137		1898	143
1899	158		1899	191
From Switzerland –			To Switzerland –	
1890	104		1890	242
1891	103		1891	234
1892	91	}Tariff War{	1892	227
1893	74		1893	172
1894	66		1894	129
1895	67		1895	163
1896	75		1896	179
1897	78		1897	190
1898	80		1898	202
1899	92		1899	215

* From the Statistical Abstract for Foreign Countries.

FREE TRADE VERSUS TARIFF REFORM: THE EDWARDIAN BATTLEGROUND

In 1903 Joseph Chamberlain launched his frontal assault on the tribal god of free trade, setting in train the tariff reform crusade, which would divide the Conservative Party as well as families, firms and friends for a generation. Tariff reform succeeded where fair trade and imperial federation had failed in achieving electoral plausibility, becoming the official policy of the Conservative Party in 1910. The Conservatives lost all the elections they fought on this issue, and when the programme devised by Joseph was put into practice by his son Neville as Chancellor of the Exchequer in 1932, it was as the policy of a national government which had appealed for a 'doctor's mandate'. However, after 1903, especially in the elections of 1906 and 1910, tariff reform had provided a vital electoral battlefield and had engendered a deep debate within British political culture, a debate carried on at all levels from academic treatises, parliamentary debates, student unions, leaflets, films, cartoons and even picture postcards.[1]

The depth of public engagement in the tariff reform issue belies any simple interpretation in terms of rival economic interests. Although some historians have suggested that the covert interests of the City of London allied to the economic orthodoxy of the bureaucracy deprived the tariff reformers of any scope for influence, there was in fact no consensus within the City that free trade was the most desirable policy and increasingly the City was prepared to accept tariffs in order to avoid the increasingly 'socialistic' financial policies of the 'new' Liberal party.[2] Although it may be argued that the case for tariff reform constituted a 'national productive strategy' by which British industry would be reconstructed behind tariff walls, and so be able to modernize and defeat growing foreign competition, this was a recipe which only appealed to select industries, especially in Chamberlain's own bastion of the West Midlands, expanding more widely to many, but by no means all, sections of the iron and steel industries.[3] Moreover there continued an essential ambiguity within the tariff campaign, for the evidence suggests that many businessmen were much more interested in retaliation against say Germany and the United States, the case Arthur Balfour supported in his *Insular Notes of Free Trade* (1904), rather than Chamberlain's fully-fledged campaign for imperial economic unity.[4] But beyond that, since Britain's prosperity was essentially based on her exports of goods and services, many industrialists as well as financiers believed that free trade retained the benefits that had commended it in the 1840s, that competition was the best spur to innovation, that Britain had the most to gain from the maximum extent of free trade in the world economy, the most to lose in a potentially global tariff war, and that free trade ensured cheap food as the basis of working-class prosperity.

Nevertheless, although we now have much evidence as to how industries lined up on this issue, the battle for tariff reform was fought and lost at the electoral level; in May 1903 Chamberlain left the Conservative cabinet and fought an extra-parliamentary campaign, ironically modelled on that of the Anti-Corn Law League in the 1840s, hoping to convert the party and the electorate to tariffs. The case for tariff reform which he put forward may be summarized succinctly as a recipe for economic modernization, agricultural revival, working-class welfare and imperial consolidation, all of which would ensure Britain's survival as a 'Great Power'.[5] Why did this attempt at a German-style *Sammlungspolitik* fail?

Generalizing across the elections of 1906 and 1910, the tariff reform case appears to have had most success in the south of England (not the industrial north) and Chamberlain's own West Midlands duchy; at the same time, whereas many middle-class voters had abstained or supported free trade candidates in 1906, by 1910 the fiscal strategy of the Liberal party, with the resort to increased direct taxation in the budget of 1909, had alienated many of the propertied who were now prepared to swallow tariffs rather than face confiscatory taxation. But the real failure of tariff reform was in its inability to mobilize the working classes, despite its promises of revenue for social reform and of full employment held out in its headline slogan, 'Tariff Reform means work for All'. Two weaknesses were crucial. First, the 'Chamberlain bubble' confronted the ideals of the emerging Labour Party but seemed much more geared to the needs of capital than labour, so that however much the nascent Labour Party might dissent (in theory) from the economics of liberalism, it had no political choice other than to support the progressive alliance against tariffs. This was a policy fully in keeping with organized Labour at all levels and perhaps the most conspicuous failure of tariff reform was not to win over many trade unionists, as the fate of the Trade Union Tariff Reform Association showed.[6] The second, related, weakness of tariff reform was the electorally disastrous association of tariffs with 'dear food'; the cry of cheap food, or the big loaf versus the small one, remained markedly effective, as the threat of a return to the 'Hungry Forties' was brilliantly orchestrated by Liberal publicists. Bread remained at heart of the working-class diet, and free traders successfully appealed to women as the guardians of domestic budgets in an effort to extent the appeal of free trade as a 'woman's issue'. Again the tariff reformers riposted with a women's Tariff Reform Association but the Women's Free Trade Union seems on the whole to have been more effective.[7] Besides these central weaknesses, Liberal propaganda also successfully picked up other themes – the link between tariffs and political corruption, the poor standard of working-class living in tariff-based economies (German horsemeat), the link between free trade and peace, even the idea of free trade as an authentically 'British' cause, although here tariff reformers were equally ready to clothe themselves in the garb of John Bull repelling foreign invasion and resisting the lures of cosmopolitan capitalism.[8]

If the tariff battle in Edwardian Britain was decided as a popular electoral issue, its ramifications were also imperial. Arguably Chamberlain's leading concern in 1903 was to use tariff reform combined with imperial preference as the basis of an imperial strategy, which would mobilize the resources of the empire as a whole, so helping Britain to counteract the growing power of the states based on large land masses, Germany, the United States and Russia. His keenest supporters were therefore the so-called 'constructive imperialists' who wished to preserve and consolidate Britain's imperial power.[9] Here too it is important to see tariff reform as a genuinely empire-wide policy designed to appeal to constituencies in Montreal and Melbourne as well as Manchester. Tariff reform harmonized with the sentiment which had led to the granting of preference by Canada in 1897, a policy which had growing support in Australasia in the early twentieth century. Hence, despite the failure of tariff reform in the 1906 election, the 1907 imperial conference was seen as a key opportunity to put forward the imperial strategy of preference.[10] This had no immediate chance of success in Britain but in 1907 the hopes of the tariff reformers were kept up when preference for Britain was added to the 'new protection' package which Alfred Deakin had devised for the fledgling Australian federation.[11] Significantly, even erstwhile keen Cobdenite free traders, such as Bernhard Wise, now saw the needs of imperial consolidation as uppermost.[12] Nevertheless, for the Liberal free traders, the Empire was not a sufficient economic base, with at best only a third of British trade linked to it, while their vision of Empire emphasized sentiment, not material linkages. They had no truck therefore with the growing number of 'trade warriors' such as Dudley Docker, who would nevertheless become a growing force in British politics during the First World War, when it was much easier to see trade as an extension of anti-German warfare. In the longer term too, as the section on The Ottawa Economic Conference, below, will show, while the imperial strategy of tariff reform proved abortive before 1914, ultimately it was to succeed at Ottawa in 1932.

Notes

1. See E. H. H. Green, *The Crisis of Conservatism* (London: Routledge, 1995); A. J. Sykes, *Tariff Reform and British Politics, 1903–1913* (Oxford: Clarendon Press, 1979); A. Howe, *Free Trade and Liberal England* (Oxford: Clarendon Press, 1997), ch. 7.
2. P. J. Cain and A. G. Hopkins, *British Imperialism: Innovation and Expansion, 1688–1914* (London: Longman, 1993), pp. 214–24; cf. Howe, 'The Liberals and the City of London, 1900–1931', in R. Michie and P. Williamson (eds), *The British Government and the City of London in the Twentieth Century* (Cambridge: Cambridge Unviersity Press, 2004), pp. 135–52.
3. A. J. Marrison, *British Business and Protection, 1903–32* (Oxford: Clarendon Press, 1996).
4. See F. Trentmann, 'The Transformation of Fiscal Reform: Reciprocity, Modernization and the Fiscal Debate within the Business Community in Early Twentieth-Century Britain', *Historical Journal*, 39 (1996), pp. 1005–48; for Balfour, see E. H. H. Green, *Ideologies of Conservatism* (Oxford: Oxford University Press, 2002), pp. 18–41.
5. See especially Green, *The Crisis of Conservatism*; also A. Klug, 'Why Chamberlain Failed and Bismarck Succeeded: The Political Economy of Trade Tariffs in British and German Elections', *European Review of Economic History*, 5:2 (2001), pp. 219–50.
6. F. Trentmann, 'Wealth versus Welfare: The British Left between Free Trade and National Political Economy before the First World War', *Historical Research*, 70 (1997), pp. 70–98; K. D. Brown, 'The Trade Union Tariff Reform Association, 1904–13', *Journal of British Studies*, 9:2 (1970), pp. 141–53.
7. J. Cobden-Unwin, *The Hungry Forties* (London: Unwin, 1904); Howe, *Free Trade and Liberal England*, pp. 246–56.
8. See especially F. Trentmann, 'National Identity and Consumer Politics: Free Trade and Tariff Reform', in D. Winch and P. K. O'Brien (eds), *The Political Economy of British Historical Experience, 1688–1914* (Oxford: Oxford University Press, 2002), pp. 215–40.
9. P. J. Cain, 'Wealth, Power and Empire: The Protectionist Movement in Britain, 1880–1914', in P. K. O'Brien and A. Clesse (eds), *Two Hegemonies: Britain 1846–1914 and the United States 1941–2000* (Aldershot: Ashgate, 2002), pp. 106–15; P. J. Cain, 'The Economic Philosophy of Constructive Imperialism', in C. Navari (ed.), *British Politics and the Spirit of the Age* (Edinburgh: Edinbugrh University Press, 1996), pp. 41–65.
10. A. S. Thompson, 'Tariff Reform: An Imperial Strategy, 1903–1913', *Historical Journal*, 40:4 (1997), pp. 1033–54; J. D. Startt, *Journalists for Empire* (Westport, CT: Greenwood Press, 1991).
11. J. A. La Nauze, *Alfred Deakin*, 1 vol. edn (Melbourne: Angus & Robertson, 1979), pp. 425–6.
12. See B. R. Wise, *Free Trade and Imperial Preference* (1905), below, pp. 133–7.

FREE TRADE VERSUS TARIFF REFORM: THE EDWARDIAN BATTLEGROUND

R. D. Denman, 'The City and the Tariff Question', *Westminster Gazette*, 23 June 1903, p. 71.

THE CITY AND THE TARIFF QUESTION

'MENACED BY TEMPORARY CONDITIONS.'

To the EDITOR *of* THE WESTMINSTER GAZETTE.

SIR, – Lord Rosebery will have difficulty in discovering the City's view of the Tariff question, because there exists no body which the mass of business men regard as representative of them. From so individualistic a collection you can get no more than individual opinions. Yet I believe I am not singular among City men in lamenting that the political knights are battling somewhat confusedly and without that precision of aim the contest demands.

Any scientific war against Mr. Chamberlain's dragon will recognise that the monster possesses several distinct heads, by no means all equally ugly, and capable of independent life; and that to deal indiscriminate blows upon the body of the creature is both unjust and ineffective.

Two heads in particular need the sharpest possible distinction. May I label them?
1. The reciprocal-preferential-treaty problem.
2. The tariff problem.

For the moment I wish to neglect the first head, merely suggesting that the sooner it is cut off the better – the better even for head No. 2 – and that the irresistible weapon against it is this: That if a 'tie of interest' means a bond whereby both Britain and her Colonies profit as a whole, and not simply particular industries in each, then it is a glaring economic fallacy to maintain that preferential tariffs can conceivably create a 'tie of interest.' Any preference given by one country to another represents a financial sacrifice made by the preferrer to the preferred, and the most subtle balancing of financial sacrifices can never produce a profit for both sides.

It is, however, to the second head viewed quite alone that I wish to call attention. The tariff problem proper is concerned solely with the disadvantages that Britain suffers from being the 'dumping-ground' of foreign nations. Of course this subject has received a certain amount of incidental notice recently. It has been pointed out that our industries have no bulwarks of defence against unfair competition, that they are apt to lead a precarious existence at the mercy of rival States and trusts. The danger that a couple of years ago threatened even so powerful an industry as our tobacco manufacture is in everyone's memory. And it certainly appears desirable that the State should possess the means of insuring the safety of any industry menaced by temporary conditions in which reasonable competition has given place to commercial war. But it is the object of this letter to point out that a tariff with these aims has no natural connexion whatever with Zollverein schemes, and that it would place a small import duty on *manufactured goods only*. If this particular problem is to be given fair consideration it must be severed entirely from the problem of preferential treaties based on the taxation of foodstuffs which has obviously nothing to do with the defence of our industries. Indeed, unless it is secured from such 'misapprehension' as ruined the corn-tax, it seems likely to remain a question of academic interest. Its prospects would be more imperilled by the support of Sheffield than by the opposition of the Cobden Club.

Two practical points suggest that much work must be done before a manufacture-tariff can be brought well within the political horizon.

(*a*) Britain will not for some years be in a fit condition to work a tariff. In this country commerce suffers more than any branch of activity from lack of organised knowledge. Remarks upon the ignorance and inefficiency of the Board of Trade (except as a life-preserving apparatus) and of Chambers of Commerce are City commonplaces; perhaps they are yearly becoming less just. But until we have some body of men with sufficient knowledge to wield a tariff weapon, until some institution is developed that possesses as accurate an acquaintance with commercial conditions as, for example, the Admiralty has with naval, tariff legislation would no doubt be a greater curse to trade than even the Merchandise Marks Act was.

(*b*)) Leaders of Industry should recognise that, according to the spirit of English life, the reform of commercial ignorance rests with them rather than with the Government. If they make the Chambers of Commerce efficient, and weld them firmly into an association with annual public meetings and discussions, they will create a store of knowledge that would enormously facilitate whatever trade legislation might be shown to be necessary. At present commercial knowledge usually remains in scattered fragments with individual business men, and it rarely gets collected into serviceable form. – I am, Sir, your obedient servant,

R. D. Denman

Lloyd's, E.C., June 19.

Philip Snowden, *The Chamberlain Bubble* (London: Independent Labour Party Tracts for the Times, 1903) **pp. 13–15.**

Tracts for the Times – No. 1.
The Chamberlain Bubble.
Facts about the Zollverein,
WITH
An Alternative Policy.
BY
PHILIP SNOWDEN
But it will raise Wages!

The most absurd of Mr. Chamberlain's claims is that it will raise wages. That it will raise the cost of living he admits, but he points out that if under this scheme it costs a working man's family three shillings a week more to live, the working man will benefit if his wages are raised three-and-sixpence a week. Mr. Chamberlain says that this is the argument to which those who oppose him will have to give serious attention. But it is not worth serious attention An ounce of experience is worth a ton of Mr. Chamberlain's rhetoric, and there is not a working man in the country but knows that his wages would not increase with the cost of living. Mr. Chamberlain points to the United States and Germany, and repeatedly states that in the former country the workman has more left after paying for all necessaries than a British workman. Mr. Chamberlain invariably refrains from claiming that there is a larger margin between wages and the cost of living in Germany than in Britain. But if there is a difference in favour of the workman in the United States, and if this be due, as Mr. Chamberlain assumes, to Protection, why is it not so in Germany? The case of the United States is exceptional. We may admit, though it is a debatable point, that the American workman can save more than an Englishman, but the reason is not Protection, but the fact that America is a new country with vast, almost undeveloped, resources, and cheap productive land. The competition of a profitable agriculture has kept up wages in the manufacturing industries in America. Were it not for this, the American workman would be worse off than the British, for even now he works longer hours and at a much greater strain. Countries like France and Germany show what effect protection would have on the condition of the British workman. In those countries they work equal to a working day a week longer than here, and at lower wages. From a recent return published by the Royal Statistical Office of Wurtemburg (Germany) we find the wages paid for the following classes of workmen are: Turners 24/- a week; Fitters 23/-; Boilermakers 25/6; Joiners and Wheelwrights 23/-; Saddlers 24/-; Labourers 16/-. And from a report recently sent to our Foreign Office by the British Consul at Mannheim we learn that protection in Germany has increased the cost of living. The commercial development of Germany is due not to protection but to attention to education and smarter business methods. But during the last few years Germany has been in a trade depression more severe than we have experienced during the present generation. At present, both Germany and France have far more unemployed than we have. In France the returns of employment for February last (1903) showed 11 per cent. unemployed, in March 7.5, while in this country our returns for the same periods were 4.8 and 4.3. For 1902, of the eleven leading German Shipping Companies four paid no dividend, and the rest an average reduction of 2 per cent. on the dividends of the previous year. The German elections just held have been contested on Protection and Militarism, and the Socialists who opposed both have enormously increased their vote. The German workers are clearly sick of Protection. Mr. Chamberlain is unfortunate in his references to the prosperity of the workmen and nation in protected countries.

Mr. Chamberlain reserves the right to change his opinions, or we might quote innumerable extracts from his former speeches to show that he once held the opinion that protection would raise the cost of living, reduce wages, raise rents and enable the big capitalists to make larger profits. But he surely has not changed his opinion since January last, and on the 18th of that month in a speech at Johannesburg, he said that 'the first obstacle in the way of those who wanted to make their home in the Transvaal, was the high cost of living.' And he promised that this obstacle should be removed, and since then he has been taking steps to remove the obstacle by 'inducing' cheap black labour into the mines.

The contention that wages will increase with the increase in the cost of living is not worth serious attention. But it may be mentioned that during 1900 and 1901 the cost of living in this country, according to Sauerbeck's tables, was 17 per cent. higher than from 1894 to 1896. Did the wages of the workpeople increase in proportion? If they did Mr. Chamberlain is right. If they did not Mr. Chamberlain is wrong. Answer from your own experience. In 1901, according to the Board of Trade returns, British workpeople suffered reductions in wages amounting to £1,580,000.

We have now done with the criticism of Mr. Chamberlain's Zollverein. It is supported by a set of self-contradictory contentions. If carried into effect it could not make a self-supporting empire; it would not increase, but decrease our exports to the colonies; it would ruin our trade with foreign countries, and add millions to the ranks of the unemployed: it would raise the cost of living and reduce wages, lower the physical condition of our people and lessen their industrial efficiency; it would provide no funds for social reform, but by accentuating the bitterness of our foreign relationships it would necessitate a still larger unproductive expenditure on our army and navy.

A New Departure Needed.

But the time has come for a change in our commercial policy. Free Trade, though a sound principle, is not a salvation. It is a condition of national prosperity, but not the only or even the most important condition. The idea of the Free Traders that free imports, cheap labour, and cheap living would for ever give us pre-eminence and keep our population in comfort by manufacturing for export, has been proved by experience to be fallacious. Free Trade has not brought prosperity to the masses[.] The present condition of half our population after fifty years of Free Trade proves that Free Trade alone cannot ensure prosperity. We have now to recognise that no nation can maintain a monopoly of anything but its own natural resources. Technical skill, formerly our monopoly, is now international. A country which has to import raw material for manufacturing purposes cannot hope to maintain its commerce in competition with nations possessing the same machinery and technical skill, and the raw material close at hand. For forty years every one of our staple industries, with the exception of the coal and iron industries, has been declining in relative volume. Our coal and iron trades have been sustained because of the development of other countries as manufacturers. Every loom and spindle sent abroad puts one loom and one spindle out of use at home. During the last ten years the actual number of persons employed in the cotton trade in Lancashire has fallen by over 20,000. The Yorkshire woollen and worsted trade employs 28,735 fewer persons than it did ten years ago. With the exceptions stated, our other industries tell the same tale of declining commercial pre-eminence. This is the serious problem demanding the attention of statesmen.

How is it to be met?

Our commercial system cannot be changed at once. The loss of any portion of our foreign trade without providing other employment for those now engaged in it will entail great privations. Recognising that the loss of our export manufacturing trade is only a matter of time, we should begin at once to adopt two courses to avert the consequences. We must throw off all the unnecessary burdens which hamper British foreign trade, so as to preserve as much of it as possible until we are in a position to be largely independent of a vast foreign trade. To bring us to that desirable condition we must set to work to develop the resources of our own country.

Editorial on Labour Representatives and the Tariff Commission, *Morning Post*, 16 January 1904.

Mr. CHAMBERLAIN'S great speech to the Tariff Commission yesterday afternoon was one of the most admirable statements of his policy he has delivered during the fiscal campaign. He was particularly happy in the circumstances in which it was delivered. He has throughout based his advocacy of an Imperial policy not on the exigencies of party politics but on the results of an impartial examination of present tendencies in British trade and commerce. He is not interested in academic discussions of the meaning which professors may attach to the terms Free Trade and Protection. He wishes to get down to the facts of business, and to express the Imperial ideal which inspires his action in terms to which the ordinary business man can give precision by reference to his accounts. Mr. CHAMBERLAIN'S opponents say that this simply means that he is appealing to the selfish instincts of what they are pleased to regard as the most selfish class in the community. No charge could be more absurd. An ideal which is incompatible with a sound balance-sheet has, we may be sure, weak points somewhere. Mr. CHAMBERLAIN combines in an extraordinary degree the capacity for expressing the highest ideals of the British race with the practical instinct which is necessary for realising them, and his audience yesterday afternoon was of just the character which he would have chosen for the exposition of his policy. His opponents are obliging enough to show their unfitness to organise the commercial system of the United Kingdom by revealing their condition of ignorance as to who are the leading men of business. The truth is, they carry their devotion to the principle of *laissez faire* to such a pitch that they would entrust the commercial destinies of the Empire to men of leisure. Efficiency is to them an excellent idea as long as it is dealt with from the point of view of the amateur or made the subject of an after-dinner speech. They will never forgive Mr. CHAMBERLAIN for keeping his promise to take business experts into his confidence. It is safe to say that since the Seventeenth Century there has been no serious attempt to bring together representatives of the various trading interests of the United Kingdom with the view of shaping its commercial policy. The Board of Trade, which originated in the commissions of the STUART Monarchy, is now, we believe, reduced to the President, who is not always a business man, and the Archbishop of Canterbury. But when the policy which formed the basis of British commercial supremacy was fashioned the advisers of the Government were practical men, such as Mr. CHAMBERLAIN has now brought together.

Mr. CHAMBERLAIN'S opponents' have tried to depreciate his commission by suggesting that only convinced supporters of his views are to be invited to give evidence. Such a charge originates in a complete misconception of the stage which the fiscal controversy has now reached. The Tariff Commission must get through its business as rapidly as possible. Otherwise if it desired entertainment nothing would be more delightful than the cross-examination of the leaders of the Opposition on the materials laboriously accumulated for them by their private secretaries. To have Sir HENRY CAMPBELL-BANNERMAN examined by Mr. CHARLES BOOTH on the statistical investigations of the latter, would add to the duration of life of all the commissioners. The Earl of ROSEBERY on the corn trade would provide an excellent send-off for the agricultural committee announced by Mr. CHAMBERLAIN. Mr. ASQUITH on the woollen industry of the West Riding might be handed over to the tender mercies of Mr. W. H. MITCHELL, and one of the most delightful experiences the commission could have would be the cross-examination of Mr. HALDANE by Mr. LEVINSTEIN, late President of the Manchester Chamber of Commerce, on the functions of a Charlottenburg. Sir ALEXANDER HENDERSON might discuss ton-mile statistics with Sir EDWARD GREY, while Sir ALFRED HICKMAN might examine Sir HENRY FOWLER on the state of the iron trade in his constituency. Unfortunately the Tariff Commission means business and there will not be time for these delights. As Mr. CHAMBERLAIN explained, the limitations of the terms of reference must be constantly kept in mind. Irrelevancies must be strictly ruled out; mere opinions, however strongly supported by academic authority, do not count for much in making a tariff; the commission wants the facts of business; and whether they come from the Free Trading iron manufacturer or his Protectionist partner they are equally valuable for the purposes of the commission. The commission might even enlist the co-operation of the economists who signed the August Manifesto. Professor MARSHALL, Professor EDGEWORTH, and the others are scientific men, accustomed to examine hypotheses. Why should they not abate their merely human rancour against Mr. CHAMBERLAIN and accept the Tariff Commission as the incarnation of a purely scientific assumption? The fact is, as Mr. CHAMBERLAIN explained, the commission does not care one jot or tittle what the views of its witnesses are on tariff reform. It is not going to discuss the academic merits of Free Trade versus Protection, but to make a tariff, and presumably the Free Traders represent a 'conflicting interest' which must be 'harmonised.' One of the most encouraging signs of the future success of the commission is that some of the Free Traders who some people think might be on a rival body are exceedingly disappointed that they were not at the Whitehall Rooms yesterday afternoon.

Mr. CHAMBERLAIN devoted part of his speech to the subject of Labour representation on the commission. As a matter of fact it would have been perfectly easy to include any number of labour representatives. As Mr. and Mrs. SIDNEY WEBB have explained in their work on 'Industrial Democracy,' the Trade Union Congress and official trade unionism generally do not represent the views of the working classes on the great questions of the day. Mr. CHAMBERLAIN'S commission has not been constructed on the basis of class representation or the idea of currying favour with any group of 'interests.' If any working man has figures at his command which will guide the commission in formulating a fair tariff his evidence will be welcomed. Whatever decisions are reached by the commission must obviously be referred to working men for their approval, and no tariff can ever be adopted which does not win their support. We know that Mr. CHAMBERLAIN's proposals are nowhere being discussed with more interest and enthusiasm than by working men in the manufactories where they are employed. The criticisms of the Free Traders are based on the idea that the 'Labour interest' should be represented as such. If that idea is accepted we must have employers' associations, railway interests, middle-class interests, investors' interests, and so on represented. Mr. CHAMBERLAIN will not accept this view of the constitution of his commission. He rightly insists on the solidarity of the British community, and wants the men who can give the data he requires because they are recorded in the accounts of which they have the custody. It is quite impossible even to recommend a tariff of which working men disapprove, because the ultimate appeal is to them. It might no doubt have been well from the electioneering standpoint to include some prominent 'Labour leader' in the commission. But Mr. CHAMBERLAIN has not had that idea in view. Grant that fiscal reform is desirable, he does not care in the least where the evidence comes from. He is satisfied that the case for his policy is incontrovertible. What has to be done now is to work out the details, and no one is more convinced than his opponents that this work will most assuredly be accomplished. They reveal the strength of their conviction that this is the case in the impotence of their criticism. Even extreme Free Traders rejoice that he has set a precedent that no Government will dare to ignore.

'What Co-Operative Women Think', *Free Trader*, 23 October 1903, p. 102.

WHAT CO-OPERATIVE WOMEN THINK.
By Margaret Llewelyn Davies,
General Secretary of the Women's Co-operative Guild.

Working women, although non-existent as a political factor, form the largest element in our country, and are those in closest touch with the primary essentials of life. A little while ago they had no means of expressing their views, but now they can speak – and should be listened to – through their own organisations.

One of these, the Women's Co-operative Guild, has a special claim to be heard at this moment. The Guild, numbering 16,200 members and 330 branches, is a self-governing body of working women, who are either shareholders themselves or the wives and daughters of members of co-operative societies. The two million co-operators trading for themselves may be described as the guardians of the people's food, and the Guild women have consistently denounced its taxation.

The following resolutions, passed at the annual congresses of the Guild, show what the attitude of the women has been:

'THE TAX ON SUGAR. – That this congress protests against the tax on sugar, which falls most heavily on working women and children; and wishes to express its strong disapproval of taxing a staple article of food, instead of so adjusting the burden that wealth in various forms bears its fair share.' (Passed at Blackpool Congress, 1901.)

According to the results of an inquiry made among Guild members at the time, the tax increased the average weekly expenditure by from 3d. to 5d., according as the amount of sugar consumed was from 6lb to 10lb.

Then came the Corn Tax, and at the Newcastle Congress in 1902 a resolution was passed

'indignantly protesting against the proposed tax on grain and flour, as an unjust and economically unsound method of taxation, by which the food of the people is taxed, while powerful interests and monopolies are left untouched.'

This year, 1903, at the Lincoln Congress, strong speeches in favour of Free Trade were made, and the following resolution was unanimously carried:

'That this Congress of Working Women expresses its emphatic disapproval of any proposal for interfering with the policy of Free Trade by a system of Preferential Tariffs, which it believes would enrich monopolists, impoverish the people, corrupt public life, and embitter international relations.'

As chancellors of the family exchequers, providing the daily meals and drawing up the weekly budgets, women are most particularly concerned with the present taxation proposals. One of the Guild members writes as follows:

'There is one point that stands out quite plain to my mind, that whether it be the food or the clothing or any other articles that will be taxed it will be the working classes that will suffer the most, and the women the greatest of all.... We should choose the tax to be on tea rather than on bread... Bread does not play such an important part on the rich man's table as on the poor man's. There are many substitutes for bread on the former's table that the poor man cannot purchase.'

Now that we know what is proposed as regards taxing bread, meat, dairy produce, and fruit, and partially remitting the taxes on tea, sugar, coffee, and cocoa, we are in a position to see what the cost would be to working-class families.

From the facts given by co-operative women we get the following results. The average income in the particular budgets taken is about two guineas, and the average number in the families from four to five persons. The average amount spent weekly on bread and flour is 3s. 6d., and on meat, eggs, butter, and cheese, 11s. The extra taxes, calculated on import prices, amount to 7d. a week on these articles.

The average amount of tea bought weekly is 8½ oz., of sugar 6 lb., of cocoa ¼ lb., while coffee may be estimated at ¼lb. and jam and syrup at 7d. The taxes saved on these would amount to 5 ¼d. a week, *giving a net loss of* 1 ¾d.

In addition there is, of course, the 10 per cent. tax on manufactured articles, the additional cost of which it is impossible to estimate.

The above figures do not take into account that the present taxes on tea and sugar are war taxes. If we compare the loss with the ordinary peace taxation *the net loss would be 5 ¾d. a week.*

There is another point which appeals to co-operative women. International co-operative intercourse has been rapidly growing within the last years, and the spirit of friendship which is fostered is entirely opposed to the enmity with foreigners which is the new gospel we are asked to accept. One of our members in speaking at our last Congress asked: 'Were we going to be separated from our fellow co-operators in France and Germany? The people of this country were asked to work for the brotherhood of their colonies, but co-operators were working for the brotherhood of all nations.'

The present crisis is helping to burn into the minds of working women the injustice of their position, of being taxed without representation. But though without direct power they will do what they can in protesting against the return to any form of Protection. The Guild is organising a Free Trade demonstration on November 11 in the Free Trade Hall, Manchester, and has also arranged for five sectional conferences to be held shortly in different parts of England. These gatherings will show what co-operative women think.

C. Booth, 'Fiscal Reform', *National Review*, January 1904, pp. 689–93.

FISCAL REFORM
III

The conflict between national aspirations and Free Trade ideals is marked. No nation will adopt Free Trade so long as it holds the belief that to do so will restrict its own industrial development. Whether rightly or wrongly this is the general belief, and those nations which have most strenuously pursued the policy of Protection appear to be satisfied with its success economically as well as politically. If any reversal of the policy is to come it will come as the action of a man who kicks away the ladder by which he has mounted. There is no sign of reaction from the application of the spirit of nationality to industrial interests.

Our Free Trade propaganda has failed to convince. Nor, indeed, have we ourselves been consistent Free Traders. We halted between the two systems; first throwing away our weapons as only an embarrassment, and then humiliating ourselves by resorting to persuasion in the attempt to interfere with courses of action which might well have been left alone, since, according to the theory we upheld, they could only result in loss to those who pursued them. If others disregarded their true interests in this matter, or took a different view of them, it was not to be supposed that they would change their policy to oblige us. The recognition of the necessity for treaties could not, however, be withheld, and with nothing to give except fair words, nor anything to withhold except gibes, our disadvantage has been great. The position which we abandoned because at that time we did not value it we can still recover if we will.

National aspirations have conflicted more with the ideal than with the practical side of this question; since the enlargement of national areas, and the consequent increase of population living under one system, has done much to provide a very real measure of free exchange. This tendency may go still further, and we may see it extended beyond national limits on the Zollverein plan when commercial interests are sufficiently identical. It is also possible, and may prove to be increasingly so, that tariff walls may be lowered by mutual concession as the result of negotiation, especially if England is enabled to throw the advantages she can offer into the scale.

Our unqualified reception of imports has done much to encourage the protective system of others, especially in Europe, and a change in this respect might now do much in the opposite direction. The industrial development of all the European countries and that of the United States are now so nearly equal as to make mutually high tariff walls almost an absurdity. Stripped of its ideals Free Trade may still triumph.

But one of these ideals, which must for the present be abandoned, is the dream of Free Trade within the British Empire. The time is not yet ripe for this great consummation. The welfare of the whole Empire requires the full individual development of every part, and only by means of protecting their industries can this development be fully secured. This at any rate is the Colonial ideal and fixed intention, and, however we may regard it, has to be accepted; the fiscal independence of its component parts being one of the conditions upon which the British Empire rests.

IV

The objects to be sought from a revision of our present fiscal policy are:
 (1) Trade preference within the Empire.
 (2) Some degree of protection for home production.
 (3) The gradual modification of excessive obstruction to international trade.

I shall seek to show that there is nothing inconsistent in these aims, but that on the contrary they may be regarded as supplementing and supporting each other, and that when thus balanced and combined they are safeguarded from dangerous results. To accomplish this I am obliged to sketch a tentative programme, but it will be of the simplest description.

(1) To be efficient in linking the Empire together, and to be at the same time fair all round, the preference should, I think, apply equally to all inter-imperial trade transactions without exception, and I see no reason why we should shrink from this logical application of principle. The incidence of preference must be uniform, but the amount need not be great. Five per cent. *ad valorem* would suffice; and if suggested by England would, I do not doubt, be heartily welcomed. The advantage of even a small preference in the supply of the wants of Great Britain in food and raw material and the many needs of different portions of the Empire, would be of great commercial value, and would be fairly met in every case by a similar advantage given in return; whatever the imports might be. Imperial production and inter-imperial trade would receive a great impulse; the ties which bind the Empire would be strengthened, and its wealth increased.

(2) As regards England there would be many advantages in an absolutely uniform protective tax such as would be the natural and automatic result of a uniform system of inter-imperial preference; and a tariff wall of 5 per cent. would be sufficiently high behind which to operate industries for the home trade, while manufacturers working for export might claim a return of duty paid on the raw material or on the value of raw material represented by

manufactured or partly manufactured imports, being thus placed on an equality with their foreign competitors in outside markets, while enjoying an advantage of 5 per cent. throughout the British dominions. Any advance on the 5 per cent. basis of import tax would be levied, as regards the Colonies no doubt for the sake of sectional Protection, but in our case solely for the purposes of revenue or retaliation.

(3) The minimum of 5 per cent. would represent the best terms we could offer to any foreign nation, and might well constitute our side of every commercial treaty, with an equally uniform 10 per cent. to be levied in the absence of any treaty. The ordinary revenue taxes would not be affected, except that an advantage of 5 per cent. *ad valorem* would be given to all products of the Empire, reducing to that extent the yield of the taxes. Only if any of these taxes did not amount to 10 per cent. *ad valorem* it would require to be increased to that amount in the case of non-treaty imports.

The permanent advantage of 5 per cent. should be sufficient to safeguard our industrial position in our own markets, but would not, and would not be intended to, *exclude* foreign competition; and to be able to trade with England on easy terms could not but be still accounted a great advantage. Treaties with us would be sought, and it would be our desire to make treaties. The penalty of a 10 per cent. tax where no treaty could be made is hardly to be termed retaliation when compared with the duties commonly charged against us, but would not the less be effective since no competitor for our trade could afford to be at any disadvantage in it compared to others. We should not obtain all we wanted at first, but gradually, at each revision, better conditions would be granted; first by one and then by another; competing for the trade and goodwill of our Empire.

The dangers to which the opponents of preferential treatment of the Colonies usually point are these: That the terms of preference would arouse jealousies and lead to disruption rather than to closer union of the Empire; that in some cases there might be an unwillingness to reciprocate at all; that there would need to be distinct agreements to govern the relations of each part with the rest; and that any negotiations with foreign Powers would be greatly complicated if all these interests had to be taken into account.

None of these fears seem to attach in any serious manner to a preference applicable uniformly to all inter-imperial trade transactions, and subject to which each unit of the Empire would be free to fix its own tariff. The dangers named, so far as they are real at all, apply mainly to proposals which are not real, but are put forward with no other object than to be demolished.

It is also said, and with more justification, that beyond its economic cost, whatever that may be, the protection of home industries involves some danger of the struggling of sectional interests for special fiscal consideration, and might induce an unwholesome reliance on the support thus obtained, which would be likely to lead to continually extended demands, and that it is thus a dangerous gate to open. These risks apply little if at all to the broad uniform lines of action imposed by Imperial preference as here suggested in place of the special consideration of individual trades, which even if more scientific would be infinitely more difficult to arrange and administer.

Again, it is claimed that retaliatory measures recoil on the heads of those who adopt them, and that tariff wars rarely lead to lower duties; but the assertion does not apply if the utmost form that hostility assumes is the non-conclusion of a treaty and the utmost penalty an additional 5 per cent. duty.

The fear that change of fiscal policy will have an immediate revolutionary effect on our trade relations, very disturbing and detrimental to business, would also be groundless; nor with moderate proposals based on simple and intelligible principles need uncertainty due to lack of finality be dreaded. Finally, if it be claimed that such measures will be ineffective, if it be said that if they are harmless they will also be useless, I join issue. We are dealing with far-reaching tendencies and the results looked for can only become apparent in time.

The course of events during the past sixty years has left us with free imports in place of free exchange, and to the Empire has brought absolute fiscal disunion. The reversal of this, by the establishment of a common Imperial system, and by the acknowledgment of mutual consideration as the basis of our commercial relations with foreign states, is the object in view. The realisation can only be gradual, but the need for a change of policy presses.

B. R. Wise, *Free Trade and Imperial Preference* (Letchworth: Garden City Press, 1905), pp. 7–13.

17th Oct. 1905.

Sir,

I owe too much to the Cobden Club, and particularly to its founder, Mr. T. B. Potter, to lightly take any course which is displeasing to its members. I recognise, too, the courtesy of your recent communications.

I am, however, unable to admit that because, like Sir Wilfrid Laurier (who remains, I believe, a member of the Club), I advocate the policy of preferential trading between Great Britain and the Colonies, I have in any way lost my claim to be regarded as a Free Trader. On the contrary, I maintain that the question of 'Protection' *v.* 'Free Trade,' as it was understood by Mr. Cobden, is not raised by this proposal to bind the Empire together by ties of commerce as well as sentiment; and that Mr. Cobden, who was pre-eminently a great Englishman and of great sagacity, would be found, were he alive to-day, supporting Mr. Chamberlain in his efforts to consolidate the Empire, even at the risk, in doing so, of being expelled from the Cobden Club.

You will recall that in 1861 Mr. Cobden took a similar risk when he negotiated the French Commercial Treaty without regard to what Mr. John Morley has termed, in narrating the episode, 'the verbal jingle of an abstract dogma,' and that he in consequence incurred the hostility of the 'Cobdenites' of his own day.

Moreover, I have the less reason to suppose that my views are inconsistent with the principles of the Cobden Club, because in my work, *Industrial Freedom*, which was published and circulated by the Club in 1891, I repeatedly pointed out – not, I admit, with prescience (for who could foresee the stirring of the dry bones?) but from the stress of logic – that high political considerations must always impose a limit to the practical application of Free Trade principles; and I particularly instanced the cases of National Defence and Imperial Unity. In 1903 the Secretary of the Club requested my permission to publish a new edition of this book, which I readily granted, provided that the passages in which I had enforced this doctrine, and to which I specifically referred in my reply were not altered. I have not yet received an answer to this letter, but I notice that a new edition of *Industrial Freedom* has not appeared!

Your letter compels me to pursue this matter a little further.

The distinctive feature of my book, as was recognised both by your Committee and reviewers, was the clearness and consistency with which it separated, for the first time, the economic arguments in favour of Free Trade from the political. The nature of this difference is thus expressed (pp. 77–80).

'Neither Protection nor Free Trade can be discussed as a purely economic question. Each policy involves political as well as economic considerations... Viewed as a question to be settled by economic arguments, the test of either policy is its result upon the production of wealth. ... If it increases the aggregate of wealth possessed by a country, a fiscal policy is economically good; if it lessens the aggregate, it is economically bad. Viewed, however, as a question of politics, the test of a fiscal policy depends upon the determination of the question, 'What is best for the well-being of a nation as a whole?'... In many ways political considerations may override conclusions of economic reasoning... The welfare of a nation is composed of many elements, and the paths towards it are extremely numerous, so that many aspects of a political question must of necessity lie beyond the range of any purely economic argument ... Even the most extreme Free Trader would hesitate before he allowed a foreign line of steamers to have the exclusive carriage of the ocean mails between Great Britain and the Colonies. ... Another familiar instance of the over-riding of the economic by political considerations is afforded by the salutary practice of subsidising ocean-going merchant steamers of a high class on condition that ... they can take their place as cruisers in time of war. ... Occasions must also arise in the history of a nation when motives of humanity, regard for safety, or other urgent reasons compel wise rulers to subordinate consideration of economics.'

I would also refer you to pp. 93, 103, 109, 121, 262–3, and 312, where the same idea is developed.

I believe that the economic argument in favour of Free Trade is unassailable, and that it can be mathematically proved that free imports both cause a more rapid accumulation of immediately exchangeable commodities, and also contribute to their more equal distribution at a given moment. Since, however, the economic argument deals with the statics of commerce rather than with its possible and probable developments, the practical question to be determined is not only 'Which policy, Free Trade or Protection, causes the larger accumulation of wealth presently or in the immediate future?' but 'Which, taking all things into consideration, namely – the accumulation of wealth, its distribution, the industrial development of the community, its position relatively to foreign powers both commercially and politically, etc., etc., – is most conducive to the highest form of national development?'

These two lines of argument are obviously distinct; Adam Smith, for instance (whose right to be called a Free Trader would hardly be questioned by the Cobden Club), writes in *The Wealth of Nations*, 'Defence is of more importance than opulence,' and justified, by reference to this saying, his support of the Navigation Laws; and Cobden showed himself equally free from slavery to phrases when he advocated the use of the King's ships for the transport of emigrants to the British colonies.

It is true that, while inquiring in *Industrial Freedom* into the validity of the political arguments, I did not examine in detail those which are based upon considerations of National Defence or National Unity; and for this omission I must plead as an excuse that I had not the gift of prophecy. Who, in 1891, when the book was printed (it was begun in 1885), could have foreseen those changes which have taken place in the conditions of international commerce during the last 14 years? Or that out of the new perils to which England is exposed there would grow through all the Empire a new spirit and a new force finding and making clear the path of safety in Union? I admit that I never dared indulge in such a day-dream as I have seen made real within the last few years.

Now, I presume the Club will agree with me (1) that it is essential that England should retain her commercial supremacy, on which her political supremacy depends, and (2) that the union of the British Empire is desirable.

Once grant these two objects of our policy, and the inquiry becomes at first one into facts. Is it true that the commercial supremacy of England is being threatened? On this point I felt doubt until I had studied with care the voluminous returns presented by the Board of Trade when it became as plain to me as I believe it will become to all who will follow my example, that grave injury has been already done to England's trade by foreign tariffs, and that the future is full of danger. It would be impossible within the limits of a letter to justify this belief, but I would refer you to a short work by one who, like myself, is a convinced and trained Free Trader, Professor Ashley, who's book, entitled *Tariff Reform*, should remove many prejudices.

Suppose, then, that facts do prove that all is not well with British trade, and that foreign tariffs largely cause the evil, surely I may, without inconsistency, conclude that this is a case in which political considerations might so far outweigh economic as to justify retaliation against foreigners in the belief and hope that by this means trade will be made freer? And if you reply, 'Why, then, in your book did you not advocate retaliation?' my answer is that since I wrote the conditions of international commerce have wholly altered, owing mainly to the growth of trusts and to the organisation of States, through the use of tariffs, into competing units.

I may be wrong in my facts and conclusions, but I cannot fairly be charged with inconsistency, because under present conditions and for certain limited purposes I would favour retaliation.

But the most important aspect of preferential trade is the Imperial. Here, again, you may dispute my view that preferential trade will be an aid to closer union, but if I believe (as I do most strongly) that not only will this bring us closer together, but that without closer trade relations the Empire may drift apart, then I am guilty of no inconsistency; because no stronger case can be made out for that supersession of economic by political considerations which is assumed to be admissible in certain cases in every chapter of *Industrial Freedom*.

I wish, indeed, that this question could be discussed without the prejudice which is created by the terms 'Protection' and 'Free Trade.' To my mind the question is one of politics. Germany attempted to punish Canada by putting a penal duty on her imports into Germany, because Canada, in the exercise of her right of self-government, preferred to trade with kinsfolk. Can England submit to this? What was Canada's turn yesterday may be Australia's to-morrow. And how does the most learned disquisition on the economic value of free imports help us to a conclusion as to what should be our conduct in such a case. It is not a matter at all of Free Trade or Protection, but rather of national honour and self-preservation in which the abstract conclusions of economy offer no guide. But here, again, suppose you disagree with me and think that Germany should be allowed to hit at England's trade through Canada exactly as she pleases, yet still you must admit that legislation like that which Germany has directed against Canada, denies the very existence of the British Empire, and a follower of Cobden might surely believe that in such a case, if one had to choose between free imports and a free Empire, one should prefer a free Empire.

I would like to add that I do not understand why my remarks about the changed attitude of a section of the Liberal party towards new political developments should arouse the susceptibilities of my fellow members. For I have always understood that the Cobden Club was disassociated as a body from the accidental divisions of party politics. Consequently I cannot admit that I can be called to account as a member of the Club for having pointed out that in regard to the essential differences of politics, Liberals and Conservatives appear to have been changing places during the last 20 years, and that which was formerly the party of inquiry and progress is in danger of becoming the party of negation and drift.

In conclusion, may I express the hope that the Club will continue to perform the high duty of using its traditional authority to encourage a spirit of impartial investigation, and thus mitigate the more than theological acrimony which is becoming a characteristic of economic discussions.

I am,
Yours faithfully,
(Signed) B.R. WISE.
G. H. Perris, Esq.

Oct. 31st., 1905.

Sir,

I laid your letter before the Committee of the Cobden Club at its last meeting, and I was instructed to thank you for the courtesy of its tone. They appreciate also the clearness with which you express your views. The Committee cannot, however, accept your statement of economic facts as accurate, or admit that your represent the views of the Club; and they do not believe that the ties between the several parts of the Empire are likely to be drawn closer by the means you propose to adopt. The Committee prefer, however, to leave it to yourself to consider the question of remaining a member of the Club in view of its principles and policy.

    Faithfully yours,
    (Signed) G. H. Perris.
The Hon. B.R. Wise.

Tariff Commission Memo, 'Colonial Preference and Imperial Reciprocity', 22 July 1908, Tariff Commission Papers, British Library of Political and Economic Science, MM35, pp. 1–6.

MM35/22/7/08
THE TARIFF COMMISSION
COLONIAL PREFERENCE AND IMPERIAL RECIPROCITY

(A) NOTES ON THE GROWTH OF THE POLICY OF PREFERENCE

Preference was an established principle of the older Imperial policy of England from the beginning of Colonial enterprise until the Free Trade era, and the first tariff preferences were granted to the Colonies as long ago as the reign of James I. With the progress of the Free Trade movement the old preferences were abolished contrary to the wishes of the Colonies. This fact is brought out clearly in the correspondence between Mr. Gladstone, when Colonial Secretary in Sir Robert Peel's administration of 1846, and Earl Cathcart, then Governor-General of the United Provinces of Canada. Lord Cathcart pleaded for the continuance of the preferences on the ground that their withdrawal would seriously cripple Canadian commerce with England, bringing about its diversion into United States channels, and also 'greatly affect the consumption of British manufactures in the province, which must depend on the means of the farmers to pay for them.' He asserted: 'An increased demand and consumption has been very perceptible for the last two years, and it is mainly attributable to the flourishing condition of the agricultural population of Upper Canada.'[1] Mr. Gladstone, in reply,[2] defended the policy of the administration and urged the natural advantages Canada possessed in her export trade. In the following passage Mr. Gladstone admitted the great stimulus given to Canadian production by the preferences and predicted that the price of wheat in England would not fall below the 50s. then current:–

> 'It is beyond doubt that Canada has felt a very invigorating influence from the augmented facility of access to the British market which she has enjoyed since the Act of 1843 and that it has perceptibly stimulated the extension of her agriculture. But the average prices of wheat during the years 1843, 1844, 1845, have been only 50s. 10d., 51s. 3d., and 50s. 1d. respectively. Not presuming to anticipate, within any very close limits, what are likely to be the ruling prices of this grain after a perfect freedom of trade shall have been established, I yet venture to think that the most competent

1   Earl Cathcart to Mr. Gladstone, January 28, 1846. Official dispatches.
2   Mr. Gladstone to Earl Cathcart, March 3, 1846. Official dispatch.

persons are not generally of opinion that they will exhibit any reduction which shall place them greatly below the rates I have just cited, and as I trust we may look forward to some diminution in the cost of conveyance between the place of growth or grinding, and Montreal, I cannot participate in the apprehensions of those who conceive that the measure now under consideration will involve ruin, or anything approaching to it, to the trade in Canadian corn and flour.'

In a memorandum of 1851 Mr. Gladstone explained that in 1843 he was strongly in favour of the extension to all the Colonies of the preference which had thus encouraged Canadian production. He said: 'In 1843 I pleaded strongly for the admission of all the Colonies to the privilege then granted to Canada.'[3]

In 1854–66 the diversion of Canadian trade towards the United States which Earl Cathcart anticipated actually took place under the stimulus of the reciprocity treaty negotiated with the United States by Lord Elgin. The aggregate interchange of commodities between the two countries rose from an annual average of $14,230,763 in the years previous to 1854 to $33,492,754, gold currency, in the first year of the treaty; to $42,944,754, gold currency in the second year; to $50,339,770, gold currency, in the third year; and to $84,070,955 at war prices in the thirteenth year when it was terminated by the United States.[4]

In its modern form the preferential movement may be traced to the following main causes:–

1. The creation of large States – the United States, Germany, &c. – each pursuing its own national policy, conceived in its own individual interests.
2. The adoption by these large States of scientific tariffs as an essential feature of their policy and the consequent economic pressure upon the United Kingdom to find within the Empire new markets for British manufactures in the place of markets threatened by the industrial development of competing foreign nations.
3. The realisation by the self-governing portions of the Empire – Canada and Australia, New Zealand and South Africa – of the imperative necessity of their national development. The competition to which they have been subjected by highly developed foreign States, and the necessity for security during their time of growth has led these Colonies to the conviction that their fullest development is to be obtained under the ægis of the British Empire.
4. The growing dependence of the United Kingdom upon foreign sources of supply of raw materials and food and the necessity of developing the vast natural resources with the Empire.

Preference is thus only one aspect of a general movement towards the consolidation of the British Empire. The development of the autonomous powers

3   Morley's 'Life of Gladstone,' vol. 1, p. 255.
4   'Lord Elgin.' By Sir John Bourinot. p. 200.

of the several self-governing Colonies has made it necessary that any commercial arrangement with them should be the result of negotiations between the Imperial and the several Colonial Governments as representatives of co-ordinate British states each having special regard to its own national interests as well as the interests of the Empire as a whole.

This desire for the readoption of preference in a form adapted to modern conditions and arranged on a reciprocal basis has found formal expression at five Conferences between British and Colonial statesmen held at intervals since the year 1887, at each of which trade relations with various parts of the Empire has been an essential subject of discussion. [...]

(F) SUMMARY STATEMENT

Surveying briefly the facts and figures of this Memorandum it is seen that: –
   (1) Preference is not a new movement. It was the historic policy of England, and the old preferences were withdrawn in deference to the Free Trade ideal and in opposition to the wishes of the Colonies.
   (2) The anticipations of Canadian statesmen in 1846 that the abolition of the English preferences would divert Canadian trade into United States channels were realised under the 1854 – 1866 reciprocity treaty between Canada and the United States, when the annual average interchange of commodities between the two countries rose from 11¼ to 84 million dollars.
   (3) During the period of this treaty and after its termination at the instance of the United States in 1866 Canadian statesmen again pressed upon British Governments the desirability of the re-adoption of Preference adapted to modern conditions and arranged on a reciprocal basis as between the United Kingdom and the Colonies and as between Colony and Colony. Canada having adopted her protective tariff, Sir John Macdonald and his colleagues while in London in 1879 made a definite proposal for ' a reciprocity treaty which England' which however went no further.
   (4) At each of the five Colonies Conferences beginning with that of 1887 Colonial proposals for preferential trade within the Empire have been submitted to British Ministers without result, and at the later Conferences Colonial statesmen particularly urged the denunciation of the treaties with Belgium and Germany, which gave to these countries the benefit of any tariff concessions granted by the Colonies to the United Kingdom.
   (5) In 1897 the Canadian Parliament enacted a preference in favor of the United Kingdom and any reciprocating countries. In the same year Lord Salisbury denounced the treaties with Belgium and Germany, and upon their termination in 1898 the Canadian preference was confined to the United Kingdom and certain other parts of the Empire. New Zealand,

South Africa and Australia have since followed the Canadian example and the principle of Preference is now embodied in their tariffs.

(6) In 1902 the Colonies asked through the Colonial Conference for British reciprocity 'either by exemption from or reduction of duties now or hereafter imposed in the United Kingdom' and this Colonial Ministers undertook to grant further preferences to the United Kingdom. This Colonial desire was repeated at the Conference of 1907. It was admitted by British Ministers that great and increasing benefit had accrued to the industries of the United Kingdom from the Colonial preference in force, but they refused to accede to the preferential resolutions of the Conference in so far as they implied that it was 'necessary or expedient to alter the fiscal system of the United Kingdom.'

(7) Colonial Ministers have indicated the general lines upon which they would be prepared to move towards inter-Imperial reciprocity. Their tariffs must be so designed as to bring in the revenue needed for administration, and they must have regard for Colonial interests as British Ministers must have regard for the economic interests of the United Kingdom. But beyond these primary objects Colonial Governments are prepared in their tariff policy to go the fullest lengths to encourage importation from the United Kingdom rather than from foreign countries. The character of their trade of the Colonies and the structures of their tariffs provide a large margin for the extension of preference.

(8) Meanwhile negotiations have taken place between Canada and foreign countries and a treaty of commerce between Canada and France was concluded in the autumn of 1907 but awaits ratification and is therefore not in force. This treaty by bringing into operation certain rates of duty of the Canadian intermediate tariff and by special concessions reduces the British preference on competitive goods.

F. W. Hirst, 'The City and Tariff Reform', *Free Trader*, May 1910, p. 124.

The City and Tariff Reform

By F.W. Hirst, Editor of *The Economist*.

The majority of City men call themselves Tariff Reformers because the majority of City men belong to the Conservative party, and Tariff Reform, was through the agency of Mr. Chamberlain, made a plank in the platform of the Conservative party.

That the introduction into the greatest commercial country in the world of this fiscal revolution should be called a conservative measure is, of course, in the highest degree paradoxical and absurd, but the system of party politics often prevents business men from really examining political proposals. If only they had done so when Mr. Chamberlain started Fiscal Reform, and if only they would do so even now, there is every reason to think that Mr. Balfour, as Member for the City and leader of the Conservative party, would be very willing indeed to put Tariff Reform in the background and allow the two parties to fight on the old lines without this dangerous and disturbing factor. But if the Tariff Reform League, whose mainspring is Birmingham, contrives to keep permanently from out of the Conservative party those genuine Conservatives who wish to conserve the traditional Free-trade policy of Great Britain, then we must contemplate the possibility of Tariff Reform being actually introduced. Upon this assumption, I will, on the invitation of the Editor of THE FREE TRADER, make a few observations with special reference to City men.

First of all, it will readily be admitted that Tariff Reform can only assist those who are producers in the strict sense of the word. If a man lives in England and produces corn, or beef, or bacon, or cotton goods, or machinery and tools, you can obviously put a duty upon corn, cloth and machinery coming in from abroad, so that – granted a steady import of these articles from outside competitors – prices will be raised as far as sales in England are concerned to the full extent of the duty. It is easy enough to show that most of our manufacturers would suffer in the end even by a system which is specially intended to benefit them; and that our most successful manufacturers (those who export most) would be damaged or ruined by the substantial rise in the 'cost of production,' which of necessity follows the imposition of a general tariff, is a proposition that does not really require argument or admit of dispute. But manufacturers are not the main element upon which great ports and entrepots, like London and Liverpool, subsist and flourish. The City swarms with a population of bankers, brokers, bill discounters, insurers, merchants of all kinds, both wholesale and retail, auctioneers, accountants, and the like. A veritable army of assistants, agents, clerks, doorkeepers, office boys, messengers *et hoc genus omne* serves and surrounds them. Hundreds of great houses have their hundreds of thousands of branches and agents in Great Britain, in Britain beyond the seas, and in foreign countries all over the world. Am I exaggerating when I say that any one out of the hundred different forms of a Protective Tariff, with their 'scientific' sea-walls of various strength and varying height, and their 'scientifically' constructed gaps for the free entry of 'scientifically' defined raw materials, would inevitably injure, and in some cases ruin, ninety-nine out of every hundred merchants and business men in the City of London?

London is quite as much the financial and commercial centre of the world as it is the centre of the Empire or the centre of England. It is the greatest bank, the greatest shop, the greatest warehouse, the greatest Stock Exchange, the greatest market, and very nearly the greatest port of the world. Perhaps its chief rival as a port is Hamburg, and why? Not only because Hamburg is finely situated at the gate of Germany, but because the port of Hamburg is free from all customs and duties, a 'free port' like Singapore in the fullest sense of the word.

Our banking supremacy, though assisted by the prudence and skill of our bankers, the abundance of capital, the organisation and differentiation of the discount market, etc., has grown up under Free-trade, and with the disappearance of Free-trade it must decline and disappear. The mark of our financial supremacy is the number of foreign and colonial banks which find it profitable to have large establishments in the City of London, within easy reach of the Bank of England and the Stock Exchange. A few years ago New York professed to be on the point of challenging London's financial supremacy. Last year when I was in New York I looked with curiosity at the banks clustered round Wall Street. Practically no foreign banks were to be seen. They were nearly all New York banks, and nearly all of them were absorbed in purely American trade and speculation. That is the natural consequence of a high Protective Tariff. Another consequence of that tariff has been the decline of a mercantile marine, which, when we adopted Free-trade, was rapidly overhauling our own.

During the last year a cry has gone up that we are ruined by exports of capital. The Tariff Reformer can stop that and smash the leading finance houses of London. These exports are the visible signs of our overflowing prosperity and the visible proofs of British commercial enterprise. The immense profits which British enterprise has reaped from rubber are all founded upon exports of capital and of British managers who go abroad to look after that capital and to see that the profits find their way home. The rubber boom will doubtless go the way of all booms, but when it is over, perhaps some members of the Stock Exchange who call themselves Tariff Reformers will have the grace to recognise how largely their fortunes have been made for them by our fiscal system.

TARIFF BATTLES IN NORTH AMERICA, 1880–1914

As we have already seen, North America impinged in two major ways on tariff debates in Britain. First, Canada, while still in many ways linked with the British economy, had abandoned the metropolitan policy of free trade in favour of her own national policy, designed to encourage the growth of domestic industry. At the same time, strong imperial sentiment encouraged support for imperial preference, and it was in the wake of the Colonial Conference of 1902 that Joseph Chamberlain determined to build on such support to devise Britain's imperial strategy of tariff reform.[1] Such an imperial partnership had the additional advantage of counteracting the growing demand for economic cooperation with the United States, a policy once encouraged by Britain (with the Reciprocity Act of 1854) but which had acquired the taint of disloyalty and annexationism later in the century. But second, the United States had itself been identified by the fair traders as what would later be termed a 'free-rider' within the British free trade world, able to trade freely and so develop her own export markets, while excluding British goods by a highly protectionist tariff.[2] American economic debate too was often inflected by the tones of a strident economic nationalism, with proponents of free trade identified as 'un-American' advocates of British interests.[3] Two key tariff battles therefore dominated North America – that between free traders and protectionists over the content of the American tariff, and that between those who saw Canada's future allied to the United States within a North American Free Trade Agreement (NAFTA)-style economic arrangement and those who sought on the contrary to reinforce Canada's imperial economic ties.

The American tariff had assumed its remorselessly protectionist shape during and immediately after the Civil War. As the American economist (and future chairman of the first United States Tariff Commission in 1917) F. W. Taussig put it, 'the extreme protectionist character of our tariff is an indirect and unexpected result of the Civil War'.[4] Nevertheless the 1880s had seen growing public support for tariff revision, with pressure group campaigns, academic support and a new journal, the *American Free Trader*. This was the prelude to the so-called

'Great Debate' on the tariff in the 1888 presidential election, started by the Democrat candidate Grover Cleveland (in protectionist propaganda, 'England's Candidate for the American presidency' or 'the Anglo-Maniac').[5] The defeat (albeit narrow) of Cleveland led to the rising of tariff levels to a new peak in the McKinley tariff of 1890, although, since the United States itself was now producing far more manufactured goods for export, the Republicans now turned to reciprocal tariff negotiations as the best way to cement their economic progress. While Gladstone therefore called in 1890 for the United States, now the world's most productive economy, to take over Britain's role as free trade 'hegemon', James Blaine, the Republican Secretary of State, looked above all to force America's way into the hitherto British-dominated markets of Latin America by means of reciprocity treaties. Nevertheless, the McKinley tariff, for Taussig 'a radical extension of the protective system',[6] also encouraged a new wave of popular opposition to tariffs, especially for the sectional benefits which they bestowed on specific economic interests.

This popular reaction led to the partial liberalization of the tariff with the return of the Democrats to office in 1894, but this proved purely temporary for in 1897 the Dingley tariff reinforced what the president of Harvard described as the 'commercial barbarism of protection'.[7] The Dingley tariff, devised by Nelson Dingley, a doctrinaire protectionist, set the highest American tariff levels before the Smoot-Hawley tariff of 1930. He also revived the policy of reciprocity abandoned in 1894, but reciprocity, rather than being a form of liberalization as it had been in Britain in the 1820s, was regarded as scientific protection, a means of forcing open foreign markets and, in mercantilist fashion, increasing American treasure.[8] In other words, the United States maintained high protection at home while seeking to benefit from and extend free trade abroad. Although reciprocity was soon dropped (under Theodore Roosevelt), the Dingley tariff remained in place until 1909, becoming the longest-lived of American general tariff acts between 1789 and 1914.

The Dingley Act survived despite growing criticism. Significantly a number of bodies including New England manufacturers were ready to campaign for freer trade, while the Republican party under William Taft also modified its protectionist stance in the Payne-Aldrich Act of 1909, which abandoned the reciprocity provisions of the Dingley tariff but gave the executive new powers to combat discrimination against American goods abroad. A tariff commission was now set up to investigate foreign tariffs and trade practices; American trade negotiators now no longer sought exclusive advantages abroad but simply an open door; the liberal rule of non-discrimination in foreign trade, previously sought by Great Britain, was now adopted by the United States, newly confident in her own ability to succeed in foreign markets without special favours. In this sense the Payne-Aldrich Act, although, according to Taussig, bringing 'no essential change in our tariff system', was nevertheless a decisive turning-point in American commercial diplomacy.[9]

The presidency of Taft was also marked by the desire to renew reciprocity with Canada, partly for reasons of foreign policy, including the need to counter the tariff reform drive to British imperial consolidation, while access to Canadian raw materials was also an important consideration. Even so this produced a strong protectionist backlash in the United States, with one Senator complaining the proposal, negotiated in secret, threw open 'markets of 90,000,000 ... prosperous people to the meager markets of less than 9,000,000'.[10] Taft was opposed by many in his own party but the proposals passed with Democrat support. They met a different fate in Canada, where reciprocity once more stirred up fears of annexation, but perhaps more importantly imperial sentiment in Canada was growing, and Canadian manufacturers feared an American threat to their domestic market. The imperial vision in Canada proved stronger at a time when the prospect of a North American common market or free trade area was still remote.[11]

Finally, however, American policy itself was to shift decisively when the Democrats under Woodrow Wilson returned to office in 1912. Ever since the high tariffs of the 1890s, a groundswell of public discontent had grown and Wilson had readily aligned himself with the muck-rakers' analysis that tariffs benefited economic interests at the expense of consumers and that in effect they stemmed from political corruption. Free trade became increasingly linked to political virtue and consumer welfare as it had been in Victorian Britain.[12] This was the prelude to the Underwood-Simmons Act of 1913, which reduced American tariff duties substantially and unilaterally. For this reason it was welcomed in Britain as the United States' equivalent of the repeal of the Corn Laws and the evidence of a significant shift in American sentiment.[13] As its American critics charged, and as the British manufacturer Swire Smith hoped, it also gave great opportunities to British firms, although these were to be opportunities abruptly cut short by war. Nevertheless, the ideological link now made in American policy between free trade, peace and economic power would prove an enduring, if fitful, one in the twentieth century.[14]

Notes
1. See the headnote to the section Free Trade versus Tariff Reform, above, pp. 115–18; J. Amery, *The Life of Joseph Chamberlain, Volume 5: 1901–1903* (London: Macmillan, 1969), pp. 39–55.
2. D. A. Lake, *Power, Protection, and Free Trade: International Sources of U. S. Commercial Strategy, 1887–1939* (Ithaca, NY: Cornell University Press, 1988).
3. E. J. Crapol, *America for the Americans: Economic Nationalism and Anglophobia in the Late Nineteenth Century* (Westport, CT: Greenwood Press, 1973).

4. F. W. Taussig, *The Tariff History of the United States*, 5th edn (New York: G. P. Putnam's Sons, 1910), p. 193.
5. See J. R. Reitano, *The Tariff Question in the Gilded Age: the Great Debate of 1888* (University Park, PA: Pennsylvania State University Press, 1994).
6. Taussig, *The Tariff History of the United States*, p. 283.
7. C. E. Eliot to James Bryce, 18 June 1897, cited in A. Howe, 'Free Trade and the International Order: The Anglo-American Tradition, 1846–1946', in F. M. Leventhal and R. Quinault (eds), *Anglo-American Attitudes* (Aldershot: Ashgate, 2000), pp. 142–67, on p. 150.
8. P. Wolman, *Most Favored Nation. The Republican Revisionists and U. S. Tariff Policy, 1897–1912* (Chapel Hill, NC: University of North Carolina Press, 1992).
9. Taussig, *The Tariff History of the United States*, p. 407 cf. A. Eckes, *Opening America's Market: U.S. Foreign Trade Policy since 1776* (Chapel Hill, NC: University of North Carolina Press, 1995), pp. 82–3, 88–9; Lake, *Power, Protection, and Free Trade*, pp. 131–6.
10. Quoted in Eckes, *Opening America's Market*, pp. 83–4.
11. See especially S. J. Potter, 'The Imperial Significance of the Canadian–American Reciprocity Proposals of 1911', *Historical Journal*, 47:1 (2004), pp. 81–100.
12. For the development of Wilson's ideas, see W. J. Diamond, *The Economic Thought of Woodrow Wilson* (Baltimore, MD: Johns Hopkins University Press, 1943)
13. Eckes, *Opening America's Market*, 85–6; Lake, *Power, Protection, and Free Trade*, pp. 153–9.
14. A. Eckes and T. W. Zeiler, *Globalization and the American Century* (Cambridge: Cambridge University Press, 2003).

TARIFF BATTLES IN NORTH AMERICA, 1880–1914

W. E. Gladstone, 'Free Trade', *North American Review,* 150 (1890), pp. 24–7.

VII. THE MORAL ASPECT OF THE SUBJECT.

I am sorry to say that, although I have closed the economical argument, I have not yet done with the counts of my indictment against protection. I have, indeed, had to ask myself whether I should be within my right in saying hard things, outside the domain of political economy, about a system which has commended itself to the great American state and people, although those hard things are, in part at least, strictly consequent upon what has been said before. Indeed, the moral is so closely allied to the economical argument as to be intertwined with it rather than consequent upon it. Further, I believe the people of the United States to be a people who, like that race from which they are sprung, love plain speaking; and I do not believe that to suppress opinions deliberately and conscientiously held would be the way to win your respect.

I urge, then, that all protection is morally as well as economically bad. This is a very different thing from saying that all Protectionists are bad. Many of them, without doubt, are good, nay, excellent, as were in this country many of the supporters of the Corn Law. It is of the tendencies of a system that I speak, which operate variously, upon most men unconsciously, upon some men not at all; and surely that system cannot be good which makes an individual, or a set of individuals, live on the resources of the community and causes him relatively to diminish that store, which duty to his fellow-citizens and to their equal rights should teach him by his contributions to augment. The habit of mind thus engendered is not such as altogether befits a free country or harmonizes with an independent character. And the more the system of protection is discussed and contested, the more those whom it favors are driven to struggle for its maintenance, the farther they must insensibly deviate from the law of equal rights, and, perhaps, even from the tone of genuine personal independence.

In speaking thus, we speak greatly from our own experience. I have personally lived through the varied phases of that experience, since we began that battle between monopoly and freedom which cost us about a quarter of a century of the nation's life. I have seen and known, and had the opportunity of comparing, the temper and frame of mind engendered first by our protectionism, which we now look back upon as servitude, and then by the commercial freedom and equality which we have enjoyed for the last thirty or forty years. The one tended to harden into positive selfishness; the other has done much to foster a more liberal tone of mind.

The economical question which I have been endeavoring to discuss is a very large one. Nevertheless, it dwindles, in my view, when it is compared with the paramount question of the American future viewed at large. There opens before the thinking mind when this supreme question is propounded a vista so transcending all ordinary limitation as requires an almost preterhuman force and expansion of the mental eye in order to embrace it. Some things, and some weighty things, are clear so far as the future admits of clearness. There is a vision of territory, population, power, passing beyond all experience. The exhibition to mankind, for the first time in history, of free institutions on a gigantic scale, is momentous, and I have enough faith in freedom, enough distrust of all that is alien from freedom, to believe that it will work powerfully for good. But together with and behind these vast developments there will come a corresponding opportunity of social and moral influence to be exercised over the rest of the world. And the question of questions for us, as trustees for our posterity, is, What will be the nature of this influence? Will it make us, the children of the senior races, who will have to come under its action, better or worse? Not what manner of producer, but what manner of man, is the American of the future to be?

I am, I trust, a lover of human advancement; but I know of no true progress except upon the old lines. Our race has not lived for nothing. Their pilgrimage through this deeply shadowed valley of life and death has not been all in vain. They have made accumulations on our behalf. I resent, and to the best of my power I would resist, every attempt to deprive us either in whole or in part of the benefit of those accumulations. The American love of freedom will, beyond all doubt, be to some extent qualified, perhaps in some cases impaired, by the subtle influence of gold, aggregated by many hands in vaster masses than have yet been known.

> Aurum per medios ire satellites,
> Et perrumpere amat saxa, potentius
> Ictu fulmineo.

But, to rise higher still, how will the majestic figure, about to become the largest and most powerful on the stage of the world's history, make use of his power? Will it be instinct with moral life in proportion to its material strength? Will he uphold and propagate the Christian tradition with that surpassing energy which marks him in all the ordinary pursuits of life? Will he maintain with a high hand an unfaltering reverence for that law of nature which is anterior to the Gospel, and supplies the standard to which it appeals, the very foundation on which it is built up? Will he fully know, and fully act upon the knowledge, that both reverence and strictness are essential conditions of all high and desirable well-being? And will he be a leader and teacher to us of the old world in rejecting and denouncing all the miserable degrading sophistries by which the arch-enemy, ever devising more and more subtle schemes against us, seeks at one stroke perhaps to lower us beneath the brutes, assuredly to cut us off from the hope and from the source of the final good? One thing is certain: his temptations will multiply with his power; his responsibilities with his opportunities. Will the seed be sown among the thorns? Will worldliness overrun the ground and blight its flowers and its fruit? On the answers to these questions, and to such as these, it will depend whether this new revelation of power upon the earth is also to be a revelation of virtue; whether it shall prove a blessing or a curse. May Heaven avert every darker omen, and grant that the latest and largest growth of the great Christian civilization shall also be the brightest and the best!

——————— W.E. GLADSTONE.

MR. BLAINE:

THERE can be no doubt that Mr. Gladstone is the most distinguished representative of the free-trade school of political economists. His addresses in Parliament on his celebrated budget, when Chancellor of the Exchequer, in 1853, were declared by Lord John Russell 'to contain the ablest exposition of the true principles of finance ever delivered by an English statesman.' His illustrious character, his great ability, and his financial experience point to him as the leading defender of free trade applied to the industrial system of Great Britain.

Mr. Gladstone apologizes for his apparent interference with our affairs. He may be assured that apology is superfluous. Americans of all classes hold him in honor: Free-Traders will rejoice in so eminent an advocate, and Protectionists, always the representatives of liberality and progress, will be glad to learn his opinions upon a question of such transcendent importance to the past, the present, and the future of the Republic.

Editorial, *The Times*, 9 October 1890, p. 7f.

SHEFFIELD AND THE AMERICAN TARIFF.
(FROM OUR SHEFFIELD CORRESPONDENT.)

Sheffield is already experiencing the bad effects of the M'Kinley Bill. cutlery to the amount of about £360,000 is annually exported from that town to the United States, and its is the general opinion that the greater portion of this trade will be lost under the new condition of things. Evidence continues to come to hand respecting the altered conditions of affairs. The agent of a large Sheffield house, writing from New York, states that when freight charges and brokers' fees are added to the heavy duties to be levied in the future upon cutlery of all descriptions, the cost will be too high for successful competition with American goods, unless the prices in the States are largely increased. He also states, 'I leave you to imagine the condition of things, cut off from doing business at present and not knowing what the future will being forth. I have thought over the situation long and carefully, with the result that, although there exists, and will exist, a demand for fine English goods, the demand will not be large enough to support an agency. The general impression among Sheffield men here,' he concludes, 'is that the Bill will about shut up the trade.' There are further evidences tending to support this conclusion. American travellers who have up to the passing of the Tariff Act bought largely in Sheffiled have since either pased through the town without deigning to make inquiries, or have visited the manufacturers with whom they have had dealings and stated that they were not to able to offer Sheffield prices in face of the increased tariff charges. The only ray of hope to the Anglo-American cutlery trade, so far as it relates to the cheaper kinds of cutlery ware, is that there is a tendency just now in American trade circles to raise prices. If values continue to rise English manufacturers may again obtain a foothold, but the outlook is very unpromising, for it cannot be expected in the opinion of a large American exporter, that the successful competition of the past few years will be repeated. A letter from New York received by the last mail states that knives which could have been purchased there a fortnight ago at 14 or 15 dollars a dozen are now being disposed of at 21 dollars, an increase of 50 per cent on previous prices. In face of the congested condition of the United States market it cannot be expected that the inflated values will remain long in operation, as manufacturers who cannot afford to keep their capital locked up will in many instances be forced to sell their stocks. It is thought that fictitious values will rule for some time to come, and that it will be a question of months before prices adjust themselves to the requirements of the market. In the meantime Sheffield manufacturers are trying to cut down prices as much as possible, but there is not much hope of their succceeding very greatly in this respect on account of the difficulty which is sure to arise with the trades council if the cutlers are asked to accept a reduction of wages. Numbers of men have been sounded on the subject, but their reply has invariably been that they must consult the leaders of their union. It is estimated that about 2,000 workmen are engaged, directly or indirectly, in the American trade, and if these men are thrown upon the market wages must be reduced. The competition between England and Germany in the lighter branches of cutlery has been so severe of late years that the increased pressure of the M'Kinley Bill will be felt very seriously in both countries. New markets can be found only with the greatest difficulty, and the chipping down of values which will result in consequence of increased competition will be the least pleasant effect of the strongly protective policy adopted in the States.

A. K. McClure, *The McKinley Tariff Robbery and Fraud* (Philadelphia, PA: The Record, 1892), pp 1–3, 32.

THE McKINLEY
Tariff Robbery and Fraud.
SPEECH OF
A. K. McCLURE,
IN REPLY TO
GOVERNOR McKINLEY,
Delivered in the Philadelphia Academy of Music
September 26, 1892.

Ladies and Gentlemen:
In response to the invitation of the Tariff Reform Club of this city, I appear to-night to answer the recent address by Governor McKinley, in which he attempted the impossible task of justifying the McKinley tariff law; and I shall proceed with directness to the purpose. I shall not deal in partisan platitudes, nor glittering generalities, nor special pleading of any sort, but in plain, incontrovertible facts.

Let us take our latitude fairly at the start so that all can intelligently judge results. I am here to arraign the so-called Republican protection to labor as presented in the McKinley tariff, as mingled robbery and fraud. [cheers.] It is a deliberate fraud in its pretense of protecting the labor of American workmen, and it is as deliberate robbery of the great masses of the people for the benefit of the few of favored classes. [Applause.] It has bastardized the honest protection of our fathers by subtle hypocrisy and insatiate greed, until it is to-day simply the festering maggots of monopoly. [Prolonged applause.] These are strong words; and I fully appreciate the fact that if I fail to justify them in answering Governor McKinley, I must justly forfeit public respect.

I followed the tall white plume of Henry Clay with all the idolatry of boyhood in his advocacy of his great American System half a century ago. I was then, have ever been and am to-night a Clay protectionist [applause], and there is no more similarity between the McKinley and the Clay theories of protection than there is between the soaring eagle and the mousing owl. Clay protected labor when our manufacturing industries were in their infancy; McKinley protects capital when industries are fully established, breeds monopoly and trusts, limits our markets, oppresses labor by lessening employment and increased taxes on the necessaries of life, and his most conspicuous products are rapidly multiplying millionaires and tramps. [Applause.]

The Clay protective tariff of 1842 levied a lower rate of protective taxes than the Mills bill that McKinley now calls a free-trade measure, and in his defence of protection to labor he never claimed the right to enact anything but a revenue tariff, with incidental protection for a very brief period, as he held that continued taxation for the benefit of any class was unjustifiable. He held free raw materials as one of the integral parts of protection to labor and continued taxes on some of them for a season only to develop them fully, and as early as 1833, when urging the passage of the compromise tariff, he said in his Senate speech of February 12, 1833: 'Now give us time: *Cease all fluctuations for nine years and the manufacturers in every branch will sustain themselves against foreign competition.*

Then our manufactories were in their infancy. They were unable to cope with the established industries of centuries abroad. Washington recognized the need of incidental protection and under his administration tariff taxes of from fifteen to seventeen per cent. were levied. During Clay's compromise of 1833 the taxes averaged about thirty-two per cent., gradually reducing until less than twenty-six per cent. in 1842. His protective tariff of 1842 ranged from twenty-eight to thirty-six per cent. The Mills bill, with judicious protective features left tariff taxes at little more than forty per cent. and the McKinley bill has increased these taxes from forty-six per cent. in 1888 to fully fifty per cent. Clay wanted tariff taxes of thirty-three per cent for nine years to establish our manufacturing industries, when, as he assured the Senate and the country, 'the manufacturers in every branch will sustain themselves against foreign competition.' McKinley increases tariff taxes, after our industries have been fostered for thrice nine years, by higher tariff taxes than Clay ever dreamed of, and assumes that the people must perpetually pay these taxes to maintain our industrial prosperity.

I believe in fostering every industry that promises to advance the prosperity of the whole people; but I quite agree with Colonel Ingersoll when he said that he believed in protecting infant industries, but when the infant industry gets to wearing No. 12 boots, and proposes to get up and kick him all around the room if he stopped rocking the infant's cradle, he thought it about time to call a halt. [Laughter and applause.] [...]

WHAT HIGH TAXES HAVE DONE.

They Have Hindered Industry, Bred Monopoly and Labor Unrest.

The McKinley tariff has now been in operation two years, and the same baleful policy of excessive taxation of the people has been maintained since the necessities of war ceased, with the McKinley tariff increasing its oppressive features. That restrictive policy drove American commerce from the seas of the world for a generation [applause], and now the same insane policy is illustrated by trying to revive commerce by paternalism and taxation. With free ships we would have had the stars and stripes floating over our commerce in all the waters of the world [applause], and long ere this, with free opportunities, we would have been building our own ships. It has abolished the sailor industry that once gave us 100,000 of the best sailors of the oceans. It has increased the cost of the necessaries of business by the madness of taxes on raw materials, and thus increased the cost of American products, reduced their consumption and necessarily lessened the demand for labor. It has increased needless taxes on the necessaries of life to satiate the greed of combined capital, without increasing the wages of the workman. [Applause.] It has given us monopoly combines to control prices of nearly all the products we consume. It has built up the plutocracy of centralized wealth here that dated the decline and fall of Rome, then the mistress of the world [applause], and it has made the common mind familiar with three alliterative words of fearful import – tariff, trusts, tramps! [Cheers and applause.] It has given labor unrest in all the industries it professes to protect, and bred labor disorders in every section of the land. It teaches labor that it is protected by the taxes levied upon all in the name of protection, and labor has finally awakened to the fact that it is robbed of its protection while oppressed by increased cost of living. It is this now generally known fact in labor circles that crimsoned the records of our State with murder at Homestead; that filled the mountain regions of Tennessee with outlaws bent on bloodshed, and that halted the great building industries of New England and New York for half the season. [Applause.] It has benefited the few who paid the price of political debauchery to win such legislation, and it has oppressed the many until the sullen murmurs of revolution come up from the cheated workmen of the country. [Applause.] Such is the record, such the achievements of high war taxes levied in time of peace, and on this record I here arraign the McKinley tariff policy as mingled robbery and fraud [applause], and carry the appeal to the sober convictions of this intelligent audience, and to the considerate judgment of the American people. [Long continued cheers and applause.]

Edward Atkinson, 'Arguments in Favor of such Discrimination in Framing the Tariff as shall Best Promote Domestic Industry and American Labor', in Arthur B. Farquhar, Edward Atkinson and Harvey N. Shepard, *Arguments Against the Dingley Bill* (New England Free Trade League, 1897), pp. 28–31.

ARGUMENTS IN FAVOR OF SUCH DISCRIMINATION IN FRAMING THE TARIFF AS SHALL BEST PROMOTE DOMESTIC INDUSTRY AND PROTECT AMERICAN LABOR.

ADDRESS OF MR. EDWARD ATKINSON

Gentlemen, I declared my purpose to appeal to you for the promotion of domestic industry and the protection of American labor, worthy and rightful ends, which should be considered with suitable discrimination by every Committee on Ways and Means and by every Congress that may be summoned to frame measures of taxation. These ends are to be gained by economy in the public service, by so framing measures of taxation that all taxes that the people pay the government shall receive, by refraining from taxing industry at the source, and by opening the way for the ever-increasing exports, now amounting to more than a billion dollars' worth a year, giving support to more than 10 per cent. of our entire population. In support of these ends I have exposed the Dingley Bill, its purposes and its methods. I challenge any man, be he Republican or Democrat, to meet this case and to justify his vote, if he sustains that act.

Gentlemen, there are ways and means by which a revenue of five dollars ($5) per head or a revenue of six dollars ($6) per head can be secured without any considerable burden falling on a prosperous State, under a simple act that shall be free of the taxation for private ends which is the motive force behind the Dingley Bill. At either rate, we should be the lightest taxed nation for national purposes in the civilized world. I would most heartily sustain a tax of six dollars ($6) per head, – five dollars ($5) for national expenses, lessening year by year as they might with the falling in of pensions; the remainder to be applied as rapidly as possible to the reduction of our debt, – not only the bonded debt, but the demand debt. I should be glad to begin next year, and to apply the seventy, eighty, or ninety million dollars (which under this measure will be taken from the pockets of the people in order to support private enterprise and augment private profits) to the only rightful purpose of taxation, at the rate of a dollar to a dollar and a quarter ($1.25) a year, for the public purpose of bringing this country in a few short years out of debt. Why, gentlemen, think of it. If we began now to tax ourselves at the rate of a dollar a head for payment of debt instead of private bounties, and applied it absolutely to the reduction of our debt, in less than eight years we should be free from bonded, and in less than fifteen years we should be free from any debt of any kind, either bonded or payable on demand; and we should then have silver which had cost us over five hundred million gold dollars ($500,000,000) lying in our vaults, subject to such disposal as the nation might make of it.

Gentlemen, when you requested me to speak to you to-night, I thought my work for the time had ended, and was preparing for a month's rest; but I felt it to be my duty to grant your request. I speak under many embarrassments. I am identified very closely with the manufacturing industries of New England. I am not entitled to represent them. I speak for myself only. Some of my closest business associates and personal friends support the Dingley Bill, and are themselves petitioners for an advance in the rate of duty. Others think it unwise to oppose it. Many, and an increasing number, would take the ground that I have taken, were they here. Whom are we addressing? There are in the Massachusetts delegation men of independent character and sincerity of purpose on the Republican side, some of whom would not be there except they had received the votes of the sound money Democrats, of the free traders, and of the tariff reformers. We asked no pledges from them. We were glad to vote for them, in order to save the honor of the country. There are also in that House of Representatives more than enough members to change the balance of power who have been elected under the same circumstances, and who would not have been where they are except for the votes of the sound money Democrats. The President himself would be a private citizen to-day except for that support. While such are the conditions, although we expect every man to vote according to his conscience and his view of right, we may also demand the most earnest consideration for the facts which I have presented and others which are being put before them from every part of the country. I have great confidence in the judgment of many of these new members. I believe that they may take the same independent course which was taken by the conscience Whigs, – Charles Francis Adams, Charles Allen, and many others away back in our history, – when they refused any longer to subject themselves to partisan power. I believe they will take the same independent course that was taken by Summer and Wilson, by the late Judge Hoar, and by our present honored senator, when, joining with the conscience Whigs, they also broke away from partisan alliance and laid the foundation of the very Republican party which some of the same men now represent. I think we may safely call upon such men to pause and ponder well before they run the danger of wrecking that party by submission to the dictation of those who are attempting to control it for private interests.

I feel to-day more solicitude for the immediate future than I did at any time down to November, 1896, when I see the urgent questions of currency and banking, of civil service and of good government, deferred and treated as if they were of little relative importance, while this bad measure – a mere policy, not sustained by any principle of right – is put forward, and the attempt is made to force it upon the country without hearing, without consideration, and without regard of protests. The sound money Democrats yet hold the balance of power, and we can yet exert it. Although we may have two or four years of distrust and uncertainty before us; yet, holding as we do to all that makes for good government, for sound money, for civil service reform, and for just and equal taxation, we may be sure that we shall in the end compel either or both of the existing political parties to adopt and sustain the measures that we support, or else die, as parties have died before from their own inherent faults and from the utter lack of comprehension or statesmanship in their leaders.

J. A Hobson, *The Fruits of American Protection* (London: Cassell, 1907), pp. 9–11, 51–6.

THE FRUITS OF AMERICAN PROTECTION
The Effects of the Dingley Tariff upon the Industries of the Country, and especially upon the well-being of the People
BY
J. A. HOBSON
5. The Dingley Tariff.

The return of the Republicans to power in 1896 was followed by a renewal of Protectionist pressure, and the Dingley Tariff Act of 1897 is the high-water mark of tariff achievement. It emerged a far stronger measure of Protection than its original draft indicated.

Mr. Dingley, in summarising the provisions of the Bill he introduced, estimated that in general the duties it imposed, though higher than those of the Wilson Act, were lower than those of the McKinley Act.

During the consideration of the Bill no opportunity for general criticism was afforded, the time allotted for amendment was consumed in discussion of the first schedule, and the Democrats were disabled from moving the reduction or removal of the tariffs on wool, sugar, and other debated articles. The original form of the Bill restored wool, lumber, and most other important free raw materials, with the exception of hides, to the dutiable lists, increased the duties on luxuries, like liquors, tobacco, silk, and laces, raised the duties on flax and linen beyond the 1890 rates, restored the schedules on earthenware, glass, and agriculture to about the 1890 rates, leaving iron, tin, cotton, and many other duties somewhat lower than the McKinley rate. When the Bill emerged in its final shape, hides were restored to the dutiable list, and a general lift was given to the rates, especially on manufactured goods. These amendments, made mostly in progress through the Senate, where the organised manufacturing interests have their stronghold, were generally accepted by the House, and the Bill, as it was actually passed, represented a higher scale of Protection than either of the original Bills in the House or the Senate.

Protectionists justly contend that the high tariff of 1897 has not ruined the foreign trade of the United States, which, both on its import and its export side, has exhibited a great advance. But when they go further and insist that the general effect of the Dingley Act is to increase and to diffuse wealth and thus to create conditions which lead to larger importations, they ignore not only the necessary operations of economic laws, but certain important facts relating to the diffusion of wealth. It is obvious that there are many other important factors determining the creation of wealth and the expansion of foreign trade besides tariff policy; in particular the development of large new areas of rich natural resources in the West and South, the application of improved machinery and new sorts of power to great backward industries, the rapid advance of railroads and other modes of transport over the country, the great accessions of industrial population, especially in the Middle-West, the strain imposed upon all industrial factors by the reconstruction of great cities on a basis of steel and electrical apparatus – Such are a few of the most evident sources of the great productivity of recent years, a productivity which, tariff or no tariff, would exercise a strong impulsion towards increase of foreign trade. Free Traders, or low-tariff men, contend that, under a tariff-for-revenue policy, both the increase of natural productivity and of foreign commerce would have been greater than they have been. It is as impossible to gainsay this contention as it is to prove the opposite by a mere appeal to facts. [...]

20. How the Protected Interests Maintain Their Privilege.

By an accumulation of statistical and other evidence drawn from various sources, we have shown that the high protective tariff of the United States is injurious to the material and moral welfare of the population of that country, that the wage earners in particular have been hurt by it, in respect to wages, prices, and regularity and security of employment; that the public revenue has shared to a comparatively small extent in the enhancement of prices occasioned by protection, and that the chief beneficiaries are a small number of capitalists in those industries which, being most strongly organized for purposes of political 'pull,' have succeeded in obtaining from the federal legislature the power to tax the general consumer for their private profit.

In the face of testimony so overwhelming, how do the protected interests succeed in maintaining that privilege? In answer to this question, it must suffice to explain briefly the inertia in American Democracy which has enabled the protected interests to resist recent attempts to lighten the burden of tariff taxation.

We may set aside as a negligible factor the pretence occasionally put forward by Protectionist politicians, that the present, or indeed any past American tariff is a 'scientific' tariff adjusted to a disinterested consideration of national economy by the fostering of infant industries in proportion to present workers and future work, and by the protection of older but still struggling industries against the 'unfair' competition of foreign businesses based on sweated labour or public subsidies. The ideal of the United States as a virtually self-sufficing economic system with all essential industries developed in due proportion, independent as far as possible of foreign markets, either for buying or for selling, and thus secure from political entanglements which attend the large world commerce, an ideal never consciously held by any considerable number of Americans, must be considered to be definitely and finally abandoned, in view of the growing international position which the Government and people of the United States are taking both in politics and industry.

Even in earlier times it was not seriously contended that the formation of a tariff was really demanded either by the needs of the general exchequer or by the public advantage which might accrue from various measures of Protection accorded to the different domestic industries. Knowledge of the actual pressure which moulded the tariffs in passing through the Committees at Washington, suffices to dispel any such illusion. A tariff never was based on a 'scientific' interpretation of 'national economy.' Still less is such a notion tenable to-day, for the great recent development of an export trade, not only in raw materials but in manufactures, has removed the foundation of a 'national economy,' such as Carey contemplated. The great protected industries are themselves chiefly responsible for the recent rapid extension of the export trade, involving, if not immediately, at any rate in the long run, a corresponding extension of imports and a consequent dependence of the United States upon other countries for some considerable number of commodities.

21. Present State of Public Opinion.

This new trend of events has helped to open the eyes of the American people. The old widespread belief that a protective system was a right financial counterpart of the political system, which aimed at minimising international relations, has disappeared. Few thoughtful men, even among the habitual adherents of the Republican Party, believe in the honesty or impartiality of the Dingley Tariff Act. The ordinary attitude of business men throughout the country is one of cynical disbelief in the possibility of a 'scientific' or even a 'fair' tariff. Working men everywhere are aware that it is a form of capitalist plunder.

Although it would be incorrect to affirm that any definite apprehension of the Free Trade theory is widely accepted in any quarter, there has been for some years past a growing disgust with the inequalities of the tariff and a desire for a large measure of tariff reform. But the fierce and growing animosity against Trusts has helped to retard the efficacy of the movement, for Trusts have other supports and other modes of extortion more galling to the mass of American citizens even than the Tariff. The direct control exercised over oil, coal, meat, wheat and other necessaries, by conspiracy with the railroads, has served to direct public feeling into another channel than tariff reform. The fierce prolonged attack upon illicit practices of railroads, into which President Roosevelt and some other reforming Republicans have thrown their energies, has procured a respite for Protection.

Then again even the keenest enemies of the Tariff hesitate to press their attack at a time of great and general prosperity among the business classes of the country. For though, as we have seen, the great mass of the workers are not better off, there has been a great growth of wealth in the country, shared in different degrees by those engaged in the organisation and control of industry, transport and distribution, by the professions, the growing number of public employees, and, in general, by most of the influential and vocal classes of the community. Although their prosperity is not due to the Tariff, it appears to be consistent with its maintenance, and the prospering American business man or professional man will not strike such a blow at the Tariff as would cause even a temporary disturbance of business at such a time.

But it is right to recognise that the real strength of American Protection lies in a certain equilibrium of business interests represented by the Dingley Tariff Act. This indeed is the nearest approach to 'Science' that American Protection can claim, the attainment of an adjustment of interest among the industries which count politically, strong enough to resent the attacks of specialist reformers. Regarded thus as a work of political art the Dingley Tariff is worthy of admiration. Its prophets and high priests, such as Senators Aldrich and Lodge, have succeeded in persuading the several sections of Republicans, who at sundry times and places have favoured the free admission of competitive raw materials, reciprocity in non-competitive goods, and general treaties of reciprocity with particular countries, that such disturbances of the scientific equipoise of interest at any point would bring down the whole protective tariff with a crash. Farming interests are set off against manufacturing, East against West, crude manufacture against finished commodity, so as to maintain a plausible appearance of a justly and a delicately contrived adjustment.

While no one acquainted with the political process of making a tariff supposes that this balance of interests is just, while every competent observer knows that the real adjustment was one of political influences measured by 'pull,' not of economic needs or advantages, the false pretence of scientific harmony has been so successfully maintained on the stage of politics as to crush revolts within Republican ranks.

In fact, Protection has hardened itself since the passing of the Dingley Act. There is good reason to know that neither President McKinley nor the bulk of the Protectionist leaders in 1897 really intended that the fiscal system of the United States should be operated on this high tariff without flexibility or discrimination. Not merely was President McKinley personally a strong advocate of reciprocity, but he believed that he had provided in the Dingley Act the machinery for operating a series of reciprocal arrangements which would have the effect of leaving the Dingley rates applicable only to exceptional countries which refused to treat with the United States on liberal terms.

'Reciprocity is the natural outgrowth of our wonderful industrial development under the domestic policy now firmly established. . . . . Reciprocity treaties are in harmony with the spirit of the times; measures of retaliation are not. If, perchance, some of the tariffs are no longer needed for revenue or to encourage and protect our industries at home, why should they not be employed to extend and promote our market abroad?'

Indeed, attempts were made on President McKinley's initiative to arrange reciprocity treaties with a number of foreign countries in accordance with the fourth Section of the Dingley Act, which permitted this reduction of duties by as much as 20 per cent. in return for reciprocal concessions. Mr. Kasson, on behalf of the Government, completed such arrangements with France, Barbadoes, British Guiana, Turks Island, Jamaica, the Bermudas and Argentina. The Foreign Relations Committee of the Senate reported favourably in each case (except Argentina), but a rally of special interests in the Senate made it impossible to secure the necessary vote of two-thirds for ratification, so that the treaties were withdrawn. Thus it came to pass that for the last nine years the United States has been fettered by a more rigorous protective tariff than was intended by the makers of the Dingley Act, and special interests favoured beyond their needs have thriven under it and, entrenching themselves in the high places of politics, offer uncompromising opposition to all reform.

The first duty of the American people is to break these fetters.

'Tariff Reform in Canada', *Nation*, 20 August 1910, pp. 725-6.

'TARIFF REFORM' IN CANADA.

IT ought to be no matter of surprise that the Liberal Party in Canada, under Sir W. Laurier, should be swinging back to their old political moorings, tariff for revenue and reciprocity with the United States. This was their traditional policy up to 1897, when a special and a quite intelligible stress of circumstances drove them to a temporary abandonment. For a quarter of a century they had struggled against the so-called 'National' policy, of which a high protective tariff, directed primarily in hostility to the United States, was the chief instrument. Even after their defeat upon reciprocity in 1892 they clung closely to their Free Trade professions, fighting and winning the contest of 1896 mainly on this issue. But the conjunction of the rising tide of Imperialist sentiment throughout Great and Greater Britain in the 'diamond jubilee' year with the oppressive features of the Dingley Tariff swept them off their feet. To preserve popularity and power Sir W. Laurier and his associates consented to bow themselves in the House of Rimmon. They covered their defection from Free Trade under the cloak of an Imperial Preference which presented the false appearance of freer trade with the mother-country. So long as the glamor of Imperialism lasted, all went well. The Boer war, the pageantry of the new reign, the fervor of Imperial defence, served to maintain the double illusion that Canada was equipping herself for a great part in the drama of a self-sufficing British Empire and that she could 'do without' the United States. In truth she was handing herself over to the dictation and manipulation of groups of Ontarian manufactures, merchants, and speculators, who worked politics for their own pockets, imposing duties, securing bounties, and operating land and railway deals on highly profitable lines. So long as the great Eastern cities were sucking in an increasing share of the population, while the new settlers in the West were too dispersed and too much immersed in business to organise for politics, these little capitalist groups had the game in their hands. The arrogance and the oppressive fiscal policy of the United States helped them to play Imperial Preference for ten times its real worth, while the general tone of confidence which followed the discovery of the vast potentialities of the new North-West allayed all apprehensions of the future.

But things have moved rapidly within the last few years. Large sections of country in Manitoba and the two new provinces have filled up rapidly with a population of energetic, intelligent, and prosperous citizens who show no intention of lying still, a helpless prey of manufacturing trusts and railroads. Though large numbers of them consist of recently arrived peasants from the continent of Europe, probably an absolute majority are American or British born, and carry with them traditions of self-government and habits of revolt against injustice and oppression. It is absurd to impute this great Free Trade awakening, as the 'Morning Post' attributes it, to a conscious conspiracy for the Americanisation of Canada. But there can be no question but that the large migration of experienced and prosperous farmers from Minnesota, Kansas, Iowa, and the other middle-Western States of the Union has largely contributed to the new movement. It has developed in Canada the organisation of Growers' and Farmers' Associations which have played so important a part in the politics of the United States. With the grants of railroads, an enterprising Press, and that new bond of local union, the telephone, the agricultural electorate is for the first time able to make its voice effective. No longer distracted by idle controversies upon education, Dominion politics formulate themselves in a few strong, simple, definite demands. Chief among them are the call for open markets for the machinery and other farm appliances, for the clothing and other manufactured goods, which they want to buy, and the pressure for suitably open markets across the American frontier for the grain, lumber, hides, coal, and other raw materials, which they want to sell.

Every year transfers more patently the balance of political power in Canada from Montreal and Toronto and the manufacturing East to the great expanding North-West. There can therefore be no question of the wisdom of Sir W. Laurier's reversion to the policy which always held his heart and intellect, and which now again chimes with his sense of political expediency. That the true interests of the people lay in the direction of land duties and reciprocity has always been evident to students of the national structure of the country. Canada from East to West is a series of developed patches, severed from one another by vast stretches of wilderness. Each of these important clearings, with its industrial and rural population and its rising cities, is flanked by a contiguous section of industrial development across the United States frontier. The manifest drive of economic and social intercourse is everywhere North and South rather than East and West. The great European markets for agricultural produce would doubtless in time have justified the creation of a direct railroad service along the routes taken by the Canadian Pacific and the Grand Trunk. But the forcing of these routes, to the comparative neglect of the American routes and markets, has been 'against Nature.' And Nature, through the play of mutual interests, is now beginning vigorously to assert herself.

The scare-monger of the 'Daily Mail' is doubtless right in his assertion that 'Everywhere, the opinion is held that within the next two years a treaty of reciprocity will be concluded between the United States and Canada,' though his interpretation of this highly commendable measure as marking 'the first step towards imperial disintegration,' is a ridiculous *non sequitur*. It is possible that such an arrangement may involve a partial withdrawal of British Preference. Though Sir W. Laurier no doubt quite honestly disclaims any intention of revoking the imperial preference, the logic of reciprocity may oblige him to make such concessions to the manufacturing interests of the United States as virtually to cancel the advantage which the present preference gives to our machinery and metal exporters. In the most profitable branches of textiles we should doubtless continue for some time to hold our own. But those who have followed the actual history of the Canadian preference are aware that it is eventually an ephemeral policy. A nation with the manufacturing ambitions which Canada entertains will not long be able to make the preferential policy for British manufacturers fit in either with a Protectionist or a Free-Trade policy.

The demand of the farmers for tariff reductions and reciprocity must find an early expression in Canadian fiscal policy. But it is probable that English Free Traders may be deceived in their interpretation of the pace of the Canadian movement towards free importation. While Canada is not precluded by constitutional obstacles, as is the United States, from finding through direct taxation substitutes for import duties, she must continue for some time to depend largely on this source of revenue. Nor is it likely that, maintaining a tariff for revenue, she will apply the full logic of Free Trade by rigorous insistence upon excise duties to offset the import duty in the case of goods where competition of home industries is involved. What we have to expect is an early revision of the present tariff, with general reductions on manufactured goods, and an arrangement with the United States which will admit American manufactured goods at low rates. Both measures very conceivably involve a reduction of the Imperial Preference. This fact, taken in conjunction with the explicit and repeated declaration of Canadian farmers that they seek no British Preference for their agricultural exports, practically destroys the Imperial plank in the platform of our Protectionists. They will shortly be driven to throw aside their thin cloak of patriotism and stand forth as the pocket-politicians they are, content to help their paymasters to get value for their contributions to the propaganda of Tariff Reform. But they will not succeed. The revolt of the Canadian farmer will go far to expose the meaning of Protection to our rural electorate, and they, when once it is made manifest that nothing can be done for them, will focus their intelligence more clearly on the proposal to make them pay higher prices for the manufactured goods they buy.

Canadian National League, *Reciprocity with the United States* (Toronto: The League, 1911), pp. 2–3.

The Canadian National League

Why it was formed – What its Objects are – How it will promote them.

THE CANADIAN NATIONAL LEAGUE was formed following the Protest against 'Reciprocity with the United States of America,' which was signed by eighteen supporters in Toronto of the Liberal Party in Canada, and published in the press on February 20th, 1911.

The objects of the League are:–

> To oppose the adoption of the proposed Reciprocity Agreement between Canada and the United States of America and to support such measures as will uphold Canadian Nationality and British Connection, will preserve our Fiscal Independence and will continue to develop our present National policy of interprovincial and external trade, under which the Dominion has achieved its present prosperity.

The basis upon which the League has been formed is Canadian Nationality, British Connection and Fiscal Independence.

It is non-partisan in character, and opposes the Laurier Government because it believes that in negotiating this Agreement with the United States, and in endeavouring to have it adopted by Parliament, the Government is not upholding Canadian Nationality and British Connection, and is not preserving our Fiscal Independence. The League would oppose any Government, whether Liberal or Conservative, for the same reasons.

While opposing this Agreement upon the principles stated, the Agreement is also opposed upon economic grounds, because any present benefit to any section of Canada, or to any interests or individuals therein, which might accrue from it, would be more than offset by the loss and injury which would accrue to other sections, and interests, and individuals; and because the result to Canada as a whole, would be greatly injurious.

Believing that the people of Canada desire accurate and nonpartisan information upon the questions involved, and that the surest way to defeat this Agreement is to supply such information, the League is engaged in collecting facts and statistics which will be embodied in pamphlets and distributed. The readers of these pamphlets may rely upon the accuracy of the statements of facts and figures, whether or not they agree with the arguments and inferences drawn from them.

We wish it to be understood that in opposing this Reciprocity Agreement no charge of bad faith or disloyalty is brought against the Government, or any member of it, or against any of those who believe it to be their duty to support the Government's action. Nor is there any unfriendly feeling against the Government of the United States or their people.

We give both Governments credit for thinking that they are acting in the best interests of their respective peoples; but we believe that the Government of Canada is sadly mistaken, that it acted without sufficient information upon the questions involved, and without giving sufficient thought to the consequences, and under the erroneous belief that our people now want Reciprocity.

We believe that our Government failed to appreciate properly the present position and condition of Canada, contrasted with its position and condition when Reciprocity would have been welcomed, and that it lost sight of the fact that the principles underlying its own policy for years past are utterly inconsistent with the principles underlying this Agreement.

In the present pamphlets, and in those to follow, nothing will be said intentionally to wound the feelings of any one, and no offensive personal allusions will be made. The subject is above party and persons, and will be so kept and treated.

The opposition will be kept up until the people have pronounced upon the question. Should they pronounce in favor of Reciprocity then we shall have to accept the verdict for the time being. Should they pronounce against it, our opposition will be the sooner justified and we shall be encouraged to continue our work and to support such measures as will uphold for all time Canadian Nationality and British Connection and preserve our Fiscal Independence.

The President of the United States said in transmitting the Agreement to Congress, and in a subsequent speech, 'Canada is at the parting of the ways.'

From evidence submitted in the accompanying pamphlet it will be apparent that this statement is only too true. Canadians must now choose which way they will go:– Shall we continue along the path which has led us to our present prosperity and to our proud position as the keystone in the arch of a United British Empire; or, Shall we take the path which leads to Washington?

The answer to this question will, we hope, be found in this pamphlet, which is devoted to this branch of the subject. In future pamphlets we shall deal with the economic side, and we may again refer to the questions now discussed.

TORONTO, April, 1911.   Z. A. LASH, *Chairman*.

'Canada's Answer', *The Standard of Empire,* 29 September 1911, p. 3.

THE STANDARD OF EMPIRE.
LONDON, FRIDAY, SEPTEMBER 29, 1911.

Canada's Answer.

Apart altogether from any question of the merits or demerits of the primary issue at stake, the action of the Canadian public in the General Election just completed in the Dominion fully justifies the claim made in this column some months ago that this would be the most important Parliamentary election in modern Greater British history. We claimed then that the immediate political prospect in Canada overshadowed, in Imperial significance, any other issue before the people of the Empire, not even excepting the Constitutional controversy then raging in Great Britain over the House of Lords. And during the past week the people of Canada have made good that contention to the very hilt. We remember that, a few weeks ago, a public speaker in Toronto urged upon his audience the suggestion that by the rejection of the U.S.A. Reciprocity Pact, Canada and Canadian trade would obtain the best and largest kind of advertisement they had ever received. The contention might have been deemed fanciful. The event has proved it strictly correct. But that is a minor point.

The President of the United States, in urging the adoption of the Pact upon the public in his country, argued that Canada stood at the parting of the ways. The opportunity would never recur, he said. It was the only opportunity which would offer of 'scotching' the 'Chinese Wall' of All-British commercial union, based upon Preference within the Empire. Captains of industry and leaders of thought and action throughout the United States united to drive the lesson home, and added their own quite natural reflections as to the Pan-American union which would grow out of the Reciprocity Pact; 'one flag from Arctic to Panama,' and so forth. Canada listened. The world listened. And, even here in the Mother Country, there were not lacking men and journals so saturated in economic prejudices as to be able complacently to endorse the Reciprocity idea in the face of the plainly described ambitions behind it, which United States leaders avowed. (One of the London journals which most warmly and fatuously approved the Pact, accomplished its volte-face after the election results were announced by saying that, whatever we might think of it from an economic standpoint, we must rejoice in Canada's proof of loyalty to the Empire! We must, and do, from our very hearts; but with the reverse of thanks to those English organs which before the election forgot their patriotism in their desire to further at any cost at all their own brand of fiscal faith.)

And, at 'the parting of the ways,' how has the premier Dominion of the British Empire comported herself? With a steadfastness and deliberately calculated patriotism which, in our opinion, deserves a high place among the records of the most splendid episodes in the history of the Empire. For the moment we are not concerned with the economic aspect at all. We are taking the broader view, and we say with all deliberation that no community within the Empire has ever more finely proved its solid worth, its national integrity, its high Imperial status, than the Canadian people proved theirs during this election. And we say that for this reason: The Canadian people were invited, upon the one hand, to choose a course which they were assured would bring them immediate material gain, commercial profit, economic advantage; and, upon the other hand, to choose the course involving rejection of all this, in the interests of their national future, and their Imperial obligations as leader among the Dominions of a world-wide Empire. And, not doubtingly or grudgingly, not with reservations or hesitation, but with absolutely overwhelming enthusiasm and decision, the Canadian people elected to tread the path of Imperial patriotism and of devoted loyalty to the future destiny of their own nation, irrespective of all considerations of immediate gain. We would ask for no more satisfactory assurance of the future progress and greatness of our race and Empire than the knowledge that in similar circumstances all British peoples would act as our brethren in Canada have acted in this crisis of their national development.

Two points we desire to lay stress upon, though readers who have followed these columns for any length of time may find the emphasis redundant. The British public throughout the Empire implicitly trusted Canada. We have repeated the statement during the past month, because, in what we believed to be the Empire's interest, we felt called upon to show what we regard as the dangers to All-British unity of the U.S.A. Reciprocity Pact. We stated no longer ago than last week our positive conviction that if Canada as a nation saw danger to the Empire in the Pact their rejection of it would be quite certain. Then came the election results, proving the truth of our conviction. If Canada had accepted the Pact, that fact would have meant that Canadians saw in it no danger to the Empire. The other point we desire to emphasise is the Empire's frank and hearty rejoicing in Canada's patriotic rejection of the Pact; the intensity of the wave of relief which news of the election-results brought; this contained not the smallest spark of unkindness toward Sir Wilfrid Laurier and the able statesmen associated with him, nor any abatement of so much as one single jot of the high respect and esteem in which these great Canadian leaders are held by their fellow subjects throughout the Empire. The 'Standard of Empire' can never relinquish any portion of its gratitude and respect for Canada's great father and creator of Preference; for Mr. Fielding, who carried Preference into effect and administered it; or for Ministers like Mr. Oliver, whose bold and practical statesmanship has done so much towards the prosperous settlement of the Canadian West.

We believe that a mistake was made in the estimate of the United States attitude and aims in Reciprocity, and of the ultimate effects that measure would have produced. We rejoice that Canada has safeguarded herself, as premier British Dominion. And we believe firmly that, upon the path she has chosen to tread, her present leaders will carry Canada to greater heights of prosperity and true national well-being than could have been attained under Reciprocity with the United States. But we abate nothing of our respect for Canada's previous leaders, and we deeply regret the somewhat unsportsmanlike attitude of that section of the United States Press which seeks relief from the irritation of defeat in an unworthy endeavour to belittle a very honourable opponent. The Canadian public, however, is quite astute enough to rate at their true value these lapses of taste and discretion on the part of angry journalists and others who should have more self-control. In the past week, even as in the harder days of thirty years ago, Canada has lived greatly and chosen well. It is for the statesmen and people of the Mother Country to show, with the least possible delay, Britain's understanding and practical appreciation of Canada's choice for inter-Imperial Preference as against extra-Imperial Reciprocity.

'The New American Tariff', *Economist*, 3633 (12 April 1913), pp. 867–8.

The new Democratic Tariff Bill presented to Congress on Monday is the heaviest blow that has been aimed against the Protective system since the British legislation of Sir Robert Peel between 1842 and 1846. The changes proposed are undoubtedly more sweeping than those of any single tariff introduced either by Sir Robert Peel or by Mr Gladstone, though it is, of course, to be remembered that even at the beginning of the hungry 'forties the English tariff was in most respects less burdensome upon the consumer than is the American tariff of to-day, with the very important exception of wheat. Our optimism has so far been entirely justified as against the various correspondents who doubted our contention that President Wilson and the Democratic party intended to redeem their pledges, and to take a very large step towards Free-trade. It is, of course, premature to express an opinion of the prospects of the measure; but so far as can be judged at present they are favourable, especially if the support of Mr La Follette and his friends in the Senate can be counted upon. Mr Woodrow Wilson's brief and telling address, personally read to Congress, conveys an impression of victory, and his whole attitude is that of a great man who feels that he is endowed with popular authority to execute a large measure of commercial and economic emancipation.

The first feature of the new tariff is free food. Meat, wheat and flour, milk, cream, fish, potatoes, salt, maize, and meal are all placed upon the free list, save that a duty of 10 per cent. is proposed on the flour of countries which levy a duty on flour. This provision will operate against the Canadian flour mills, which are, of course, protected against the American article. As regards sugar, which produces a very large revenue, the policy of Sir Robert Peel in regard to corn is to be followed, though in a less scientific manner. There is to be an immediate reduction of 25 per cent. in the duty, and after three years sugar is to be placed on the free list.

The second feature of the new Bill is the placing on the free list of many raw materials, of various kinds of machinery; and of important articles of consumption which enter into the budget of the working classes in town and country. Among the raw materials to be placed on the free list we notice raw wool, lumber and various lumber products, coal, iron ore, leather, wood pulp, sulphur, soda, tanning materials, and various acids. To these are added certain kinds of machinery and finished articles which play a prominent part in agriculture, transportation, printing, &c. Among them may be mentioned agricultural implements, cheap printing paper, typewriters, sewing machines, type-setting machines, cash registers, steel rails, fence wire, nails, &c.

A few articles now on the free list are to be taxed – furs, coal tar products, volatile oils, spices, rough diamonds, and precious stones.

The third feature of the Bill is a great and general reduction upon manufactures, more especially upon the common necessaries of life. An idea of the general reduction may be formed from a few instances:–The average duties on cotton cloth fall from about 42 to about 26 per cent., those on underwear from 60 to 25 per cent., on blankets from 72 to 25 per cent., on flannel from 93 to 30 per cent., on women's dress goods from 99 to 35 per cent., on rubber manufactures from 35 to 10 per cent., and on common soap from 20 to 5 per cent. On knives, scissors, &c., the duties are nearly halved. It is, of course, impossible to predict how far the general fall in prices throughout the United States will correspond with the fall in duties. But the correspondence will be very close in all those numerous branches of trade – especially textiles – where the tariff has been fully capitalised and exploited by trusts and agreements between manufacturers. It must be remembered that since the McKinley tariff the working classes and the lower middle classes of the United States have hardly known such luxuries as underclothing, or garments, or blankets, made of wool. Cotton and shoddy have been the principal raw materials of the so-called 'Woollen Companies.' The wealthy who travel have been in the habit of buying suits and dresses in England, and carrying them home duty free for personal use in their trunks. Consequently, if this new tariff passes there will not only be a general fall in prices, but also an introduction of many goods which for some time have been practically unknown to the shops of the United States.

The deficiency caused by these enormous reductions is estimated to be only $80,000,000, which will be more than met by a new federal income-tax, estimated (perhaps optimistically) to yield nearly $100,000,000. The existing company or corporation tax of 1 per cent. on corporation incomes exceeding $5,000 is retained. The new income-tax exempts all incomes of less than £800. Incomes from £800 to £4,000 will pay 1 per cent., from £4,000 to £10,000 2 per cent., from £10,000 to £20,000 3 per cent., and those above £20,000 will pay 4 per cent. Thus the highest incomes in the United States will begin by paying a little more than 9d in the £. Here again, the Fiscal Reformers of the United States are following the precedent of Sir Robert Peel, who revived the income-tax for the benefit of trade and consumption.

Swire Smith, *The New American Tariff (Simmons-Underwood) and the Wool Industry of Bradford* (Keighley, 1914).

The Simmons-Underwood Tariff, 1913,
AND THE
Wool Industry of Bradford.

The new United States Tariff is a measure of far-reaching influence in many directions. In its relation to the trade of the United Kingdom, and especially to the wool industry of Bradford, it may prove to be the most important act of commercial legislation that has been passed since the Civil War.

The Great Resources of the United States.

The material resources of America, ever since its discovery by Columbus over four centuries ago, have been mainly developed by British colonists and capital; and even at the present time it is estimated that £500,000,000 of British capital are invested there. The United States is the richest country in the world. In extent and productiveness it is equal to more than twenty Britains rolled into one. Its resources in agricultural land and minerals surpass those of any other country. Its varied climate enables its people to produce within its own borders nearly everything that they require. It has a population of nearly a hundred millions, rapidly increasing, the best paid, the most highly equipped, and the most intelligent and energetic in the world – more lightly taxed than our own people. In spite of all the fluctuations of trade, the competition of the great States of Europe, and the hindrances of tariffs, the United States and Britain for a century past, have exchanged commodities and bought from each other overwhelmingly more than from any other countries. It is hoped that this interdependence upon each other will continue and increase to their mutual advantage.

America's Inheritance of Supremacy.

This very Underwood Tariff that now arrests the world's attention, with its sweeping clearance of duties upon food and raw materials, brings America nearer by many steps to her great inheritance of agricultural and industrial supremacy, which will benefit the world, and from which it is not likely that she will turn back. She will find it to be more and more profitable to produce the crops that her soil and climate are best adapted for, and exchange them for those products which some other country can produce more advantageously. As for example: she will buy wheat from Canada and give more attention to cotton and maize at home; and in the great domain of manufacturing, in which in most branches she is destined to take the lead, she will remove, consistently with her revenue needs, the restrictions which militate against her exchange of manufactures with those of other countries.

British and American Commerce.

In all this movement towards a wider commerce, Britain, next to the United States, will be the greatest gainer. In 1912 the oversea trade of Britain – imports and exports – amounted to the stupendous sum of £1,342,000,000, of which over £200,000,000 (about one-sixth) were with the United States. Germany came next with £102,000,000. These are the two foreign countries that do most trade with Britain, and more especially with this district; but it is obvious that America is the field that offers the most highly successful business in the future. For many years before and since the Civil War, the United States was Bradford's chief market for wool goods, and but for the tariff with its frequent changes and fluctuations, would probably have remained so. The returns of the exports of this district are entered at the American Consulate at Bradford. There are separate returns at Huddersfield and other centres of the wool industry, but the Bradford figures are the most available and the conclusions from them apply to Britain generally.

History of Wool Tariffs.

The history of the wool tariffs of America illustrates the methods by which in all countries the tariffs instituted primarily for the raising of revenue have been made the instruments for the protection of favoured industries. Britain might be quoted as an early example. The first import duty on wool goods in the States goes back nearly 100 years, and for a time served the double purpose of raising revenue and protecting an infant industry. But there gradually grew around the infant an organization whose aim it was to raise the tariff, not for revenue but for protective purposes. More and more protection was demanded for the 'infant' the older it grew. The movement was opposed by the representatives of the consumers, and thus the tariff, a generation ago, became the football of American politics, dominating all other considerations. There were 19 tariff laws in the last century – one in every five years – tinkering the import duties up and down, but almost invariably up. After each advance the victors invariably prayed for peace, for time to allow the business of the country to be pursued without further unrest or change, while all the time their defeated opponents agitated for reduction or repeal. Thus, as I shall show from statistical evidence, the tariff has always been a disturbing influence, upsetting and seriously injuring the commerce not of America only, but of the world. The Morill Tariff of 1861 followed by the War Tariff of 1864 – both of which were highly protective – stimulated the development of the worsted and woollen industries in the States. Factories modelled on those of Bradford were extensively built, with machinery, and in many instances operatives and overlookers from this neighbourhood.

Exports from Bradford to America.

As far back as 1866 there passed through the American Consulate at Bradford, exports to the United States valued at £3,000,000. No country took so large a share of the products of the district of which Bradford is the centre. During the Franco-German War the average for the four years 1870–1873 was £3,270,000 a year. The wool industry of Bradford at that period enjoyed exceptional prosperity. Beginning about 1875 there came the tragic effect of the Franco-German war and a terrible depression fell on Bradford. There was a great fall in values, there were many failures, and the exports to America dropped to an average for the four years 1876–1879 to £1,342,000 a year, less than one-half. The American Consul in his report to his Government in 1881 declared that the prospects of the Bradford trade were 'most dismal,' and that the rapidly dwindling exports suggested the not distant time when America would be independent of Bradford altogether.

McKinley Tariff.

It is difficult at this date to realise how the whole district suffered at that time. But in the early eighties, without any lowering of the United States tariffs, trade revived, and from 1884 to 1890 the exports from Bradford to America averaged £3,643,000 a year, nearly threefold those of 1876–1879. There was much complaining among the American manufacturers of British competition, and a successful agitation for raising the tariff resulted in the passing of the McKinley Act which came into operation in October, 1890, the exports from Bradford in 1889 having reached £4,689,000. Under the McKinley tariff a heavy duty was levied on wool (equal to about 60 per cent.) and on tops, noils, yarn and goods, in some instances ranging beyond 100 per cent. It is not surprising that in 1891 the Bradford exports dropped to £2,391,000, about one-half, and some Bradford industries were paralysed. But it was not only that our trade with America was affected; German exports of goods to America made from Bradford yarns were diminished on a similar scale, and the local spinning industry suffered accordingly. There is an old saying that 'those people do not permanently hurt us who compel us to put forth our best.' Bradford, in despair, had to find new markets or 'go under.' It turned its attention to home and colonial markets, that it had neglected. It gave more and more attention to technical education, which in the previous good times it had ignored – as witness the Technical College and the Technical Schools of Huddersfield, Halifax, Keighley, Batley, etc., not forgetting the great Cloth-workers' Institution at Leeds – which were attended by thousands of young men engaged in the wool industries. A new spirit arose, the attention of trained specialists was given to designing, to dyeing, to new styles, to economy of production, and to efficiency in every department of production. These efforts began to tell; Bradford goods found favour in wider fields, and, to adopt the old simile, 'as one door closed another opened.'

Gorman Wilson Tariff.

The McKinley tariff undoubtedly stimulated to a remarkable degree the making in American factories of the Bradford goods shut out by the tariff, and just as the American Congress and Senate had yielded to the agitation of the high protectionists, so under another agitation, which resulted in Cleveland's election in 1892, a sweeping reduction was made in the tariff, making wool free and reducing the duties on goods from, in some instances, 100 per cent. to about half. The Gorman-Wilson tariff, as it was called, came into operation on January 1st, 1895, and in the course of the year, beginning without excitement in the spring, up went the exports from Bradford from £1,686,000 in 1894 (under McKinley) to £5,697,000 in 1895, an increase of over £4,000,000. It may be imagined what a difference this made to Bradford – and doubtless it made a difference to the competing manufacturers in America. One need not dwell upon the advances in wool, nor upon the mischief that was done by the excesses of speculators during the brief period that the fever lasted. In two years the boom collapsed, owing largely to causes unconnected with the tariff – an unprecedented agricultural depression, under which thousands of farm mortgages were foreclosed; a financial crisis aggravated by the silver question which was felt acutely throughout the whole country. Great numbers of factories were closed and their workpeople thrown out of employment, while at the following election the pendulum swung back, the Dingley Bill was carried, and up went the duties on wool, tops, yarn and goods to a height that had never been reached before. The Gorman-Wilson Bill operated from January 1st, 1895 to July 24th, 1897, but taking the three years 1895–6–7 Bradford exported to the United States wool and tops valued at £3,407,000 and yarn and goods at £8,509,000, a total of £11,916,000.

Dingley Tariff.

In the following three years 1898–1899–1900 under the Dingley Bill, the exports were – wool £683,000, yarn and goods £1,773,000, a total of £2,456,000, representing a fall in the three years of £9,460,000, or 80 per cent. One can imagine the dislocation of business, the anxiety, worry, and loss, that had to be endured by the various branches of the Bradford Trade and their workpeople during these trying years, and through causes absolutely beyond their power to control. The blow fell not only on the manufacturers, but almost as heavily on the spinners who supplied large quantities of yarn to Germany, there to be made into goods for export to America.

The charge is often made that Britain suffers more from these high tariffs than countries like France and Germany, because unlike them, she does not possess bargaining power and she cannot retaliate under her free trade system. As a matter of fact Germany suffered more acutely from the Dingley tariff than Britain, and made no attempt either to bargain or retaliate. So it was with France. German exports of wool goods to America in 1898 fell to less than one third those of 1897, while in the case of France they fell to nearer a fourth than a third.

Bargaining Power of Tariffs not effective.

With regard to the bargaining power of a tariff, to which so much importance is often attached, it is instructive to observe that throughout the protracted discussions at Washington on the Underwood Bill, no suggestion, so far as I have heard, was made of bargaining for privileges or preferences with other countries. The 'big revolver' was never mentioned, although if there had been any magic in this weapon, no country could have used it so effectively. In making food and raw materials free, she did not consider how much preference she was giving to any other country, it was enough that the real preference was going to her own people. And so in reducing the duties on manufactures the advantages were secured to her own consumers irrespective of the tariffs of other countries.

Bradford Exports of Superior Goods not shut out by Tariffs.

To return to the Dingley tariff, the total exports from Bradford for the first four years 1898–1901 averaged £1,485,000 while during the last four years 1910–1913 under equally adverse conditions, they advanced to an average of £2,768,000 a year – nearly double. Thus it would appear that no tariff, even doubling the price of superior goods and novelties of Bradford, has been able to permanently shut them out of the American Market. The same fate has not been enjoyed by the makers of the 'goods for the million' which in days gone by employed so many Bradford spindles and looms. These have lost the American trade, but after much tribulation they have happily found customers in our colonies and in other countries, and for some time have been steadily employed. Indeed, but for the recent depression caused by the war in Eastern Europe the new and latest act of the American industrial drama would – except for its effect on raw material – have almost escaped observation.

Underwood Tariff – Fluctuations.

But the act has commenced, and if we may in any degree mirror the future from the past, a brief summary of the fluctuations caused largely by American Tariffs within memory, may not be uninteresting. They exerted a profound influence not only over America, but over every other manufacturing country. I will only refer to their effect on the wool industry of Britain. In 1889, the year before the operation of the McKinley Bill, our total exports of wool products amounted in round figures to £30 ¼ millions. In 1891, the first year of the McKinley tariff, up went the American duties and down went our exports of wool products to £26 ¾ millions. In 1895, on the passing of the Gorman-Wilson Bill, making wool free and considerably lowering the duties on manufactures, our exports immediately rose again from £26¾ millions to £30½ millions; while on the passing of the Dingley Bill in 1897 they fell in 1898 to £24 millions, with consequent disasters. Since that time, now 16 years ago, in spite of the disturbing influences of the Aldrich Payne Bill, our total exports of wool products have grown from £24 millions in 1898 to £44 millions in 1913, an increase of 83 per cent. The figures show that the late American tariff, although intended to be prohibitive, had to a large extent lost its sting, so far as this country was concerned.

In the meantime, the prosperity of America – which no legislative enactments can destroy – has raised a large class of consumers who do not allow the tariff to prevent them from buying what they want. Even with the excessive duty, America imported in 1913 wool of the foreign value of £6 millions and wool manufactures of the foreign value of £9 millions, or nearly £18 millions on passing the American Custom Houses, against an import of £5 ¾ millions of wool products in Britain, the one country that opens its ports freely to the world.

Disturbing Influence of Tariffs.

Without questioning the right of any country to regulate its fiscal policy in its own interests, we may complain against the unsettlement of business and the losses entailed through the frequent changes in the American tariff. There are many who believe that the higher the American tariff, the greater is the safeguard of this country against American competition in the neutral markets of the world and in our own. The tariff which acts as a barricade against imports by our most formidable rival, is equally a barricade against its exports. There are others who hold the view that in proportion as restrictions are removed the greater will be the prosperity and amity between nation and nation, and who consequently welcome the lowering of the American tariff as a great promoter of friendship and goodwill. But whether the American tariff be high or low, it is fair to ask in the interests of all concerned, on both sides, that there should be some reasonable permanency in its duration. Most of us would rather endure the hardships of a permanent tariff however high, than have to suffer from the fluctuations caused by the rapid changes from a low tariff to a high one. It will be a serious calamity should the Underwood Tariff result in an inflation such as occurred under the Gorman-Wilson Bill of 1895, to be followed in the next Administration by such a disastrous fall in our exports as was caused by the Dingley Bill of 1897.

America has turned the Key of Economic Advantage against Herself.

It is said of America that she holds the key of industrial supremacy, but that she has turned it against herself. This has been undoubtedly her position with regard to wool, which she has shut out by an exhorbitant duty – a complete disappointment so far as regards the production of domestic wools, which has not increased during the last twenty-four years – and a serious handicap of the manufacturers in restricting the variety of their productions by depriving them of free access to the various qualities of foreign wool.

Marvellous Progress of America.

But in spite of this drawback, during the last thirty years, the wool industry of America in all its branches has made marvellous progress in extent and efficiency. The largest and best equipped worsted factories in the world are undoubtedly in America, and, in my opinion, helped as they will be by the tariff when the adjustment of the economic conditions of labour and the cost of production have been assimilated with those of this country, those great factories will hold their own in efficient and economic production against all their competitors. The sheet anchor of the Underwood Bill lies in its broad and generous provision for the benefit of the consumer in removing the taxes from food, and for the manufacturer in free raw materials and machinery, from which one may hazard the opinion that neither consumer nor producer will go back. And yet it is not likely that the agricultural classes and the general public who, under the free food clauses of the new tariff get no protection, will willingly consent to the continued protection of the manufacturers. There is an increasing desire among all producers for an export market, and this is not to be secured in conjunction with high protection. The way to encourage exports is to encourage imports.

Tariff has made Clothing Dear.

The abnormally high price of wool and wool goods in America has made clothing exorbitantly dear, and has led to an adulteration of cloth and dress goods by a stealthy admixture of cotton and shoddy. The result is shown in a greatly reduced consumption of wool, which at the present time is recorded as five pounds per head in the States, against much more than double that weight per head in this country.

Free Wool means Cheaper and Better Wool Goods.

Strange to say, the effect of the tariff has been to depress the price of wool throughout the world outside America, by to so large an extent closing against the outside producer the largest and wealthiest market. The first effect of free wool will be to stimulate the wearing of wool apparel throughout America, which will increase consumption and provide fuller employment for the domestic factories, and will soon be felt in the wool producing countries. It is said that already there has arisen in America a demand for New Zealand and Argentine mutton as well as wool, and the Panama Canal will open up new markets in the Far East and South of immense importance to America.

A New Market for Bradford.

The Underwood Bill has come into operation at a time when there has been no assault on the protective system of America except from within. The rebellion against high prices has provoked the conscience of a great nation, and brought about results more drastic than were dreamt of a few years ago. Whether this great step will lead forward to further freedom or will be retraced depends upon the patriotism and judgment of the American people, and the general prosperity of the country during the next few years. To this district the lowering of the American tariff at this time is equivalent to the opening of a new market, for the sudden depression in the East is at least temporarily turning many eyes Westward in the hope that relief may be found in that quarter. The effect of the tariff is already being felt in wool; the great fact is before us that the wool manufacturers of America can now buy British and other wools for practically 6d. per lb. less than they paid for them a few months ago. The spinners of America, who, for the last 16 years, have been prohibited from buying imported tops, can now buy them at a duty of 8 per cent. The weaver who found it impossible to import foreign yarn, can now buy it at 18 per cent. duty, while the importer of finished goods, who in many instances paid a duty doubling their price, can now effect his purchases on payment of a duty of 35 per cent. But the greatest gainer by this transformation is the American citizen, the man in the street and on the farm, with his wife and family – numbering 100 millions of people – who have been compelled by the outrageous tariff to be clothed in high-priced goods of doubtful quality, and who will soon have the choice of the world placed before them on thousands of shop counters throughout the Union at prices 20, 30 or 40 per cent. lower than they have been paying. Does not this change point to a greater production of wool the world over, and in the first instance to an enlarged field for the American manufacturer at his own door? Does it not point also to larger exports from Bradford of all the commodities that find a market in America and that give employment to the people of this district?

THE PARIS ECONOMIC CONFERENCE, 1916

Although British free traders had fought off the first serious assault of the tariff reformers in the elections of 1906 and 1910, the onset of the First World War put the British government's commitment to free trade under additional pressure. The financial requirements of wartime and concerns about Germany's potential as an economic rival in the post-war environment raised concerns about Britain's relative economic position and lowered the attractiveness of free trade arguments about lower prices and the aggregate gains from trade. Already in Britain, the 1915 McKenna duties on luxury goods such as cars and clocks – a deviation from traditional Liberal support of free trade – were designed and presented as temporary wartime measures, although they ultimately lasted into the 1930s. As the war dragged on into its second year, it had become abundantly clear to all the participants that the demands of modern warfare necessitated substantial economic as well as military efforts. Britain and France were already conducting an economic blockade of the Central Powers with the aim of limiting Germany's access to raw materials and foreign exchange. In practice, this meant not only the detention and impounding of merchant vessels bound for German ports, but also supervision and restrictions on neutral commerce with Dutch, Danish and Swedish ports for fear that Germany would trans-ship war materials via these non-combatant nations. Producers in the United States and Latin America particularly chaffed at such wartime restrictions. Despite the efforts of the British and French authorities, several Allied Powers – Japan, Russia and Italy foremost among them – were not viewed by either London or Paris as being sufficiently rigorous in the prosecution of the economic war.

The French in particular were keen for their allies to implement wartime measures that would enhance the economic blockade of Germany, thus serving to continue depriving the Germans of vital war supplies. In response to the French request for economic talks, Britain's predominantly Liberal Cabinet responded affirmatively but warily. Prime Minister H. H. Asquith wanted wartime cooperation, but did not want to be bound to a particular set of post-war policies foisted upon him by wartime exigencies. In contrast, tariff reformers, Dominion politicians and many members of the Conservative Party saw the Paris Conference as an opportunity to use the war and Allied pressure to implement protectionist policies within the British Empire. With his Allies in the Dominions calling for action and a Conservative press pushing for tougher anti-German policies, Asquith sent a 'balanced' delegation consisting of two supporters of protection and imperial preference: Prime Minister William M. Hughes of Australia and the Colonial Secretary (and Conservative Party leader), Bonar Law; and two free traders: the Canadian Finance Minister George Foster and Lord Crewe, Lord President of the Council (also the leader of the Liberals in the House of Lords). However, despite the stature of the participants, the British Cabinet insisted that any resolutions emerging from the Conference be non-binding.

The Paris Economic Conference met in June 1916 to coordinate the prosecution of the economic war against Germany better and to lay the groundwork for a post-war economic settlement that would continue to benefit the Allies' position. With a military victory on the battlefield proving elusive, the economic war came to have greater salience as a means to strike at Germany. The Allies also had to confront the possibility that an inconclusive peace might leave major swathes of their own countries devastated by war while simultaneously leaving the German industrial heartland unscathed and ready to re-enter the international economy on particularly advantageous terms. In these circumstances, a peace settlement might be more of a temporary armistice that left major political conflicts unresolved and left the enemy unvanquished. Consequently, Allied planners sought to prioritize wartime economic cooperation, set post-war reconstruction priorities and prepare a framework that reduced Allied reliance on Germany and restrained Germany's future economic opportunities.[1]

The Allies were not alone in thinking in terms of a post-war economic combine, similar ideas were percolating in Germany as well. Many tariff reformers saw the Paris Conference as providing an Allied response to the ideas of a Continental economic union outlined by Friedrich Naumann in his book *Mitteleuropa*. Arguing that the future belonged to large, continent-sized political groupings such as the United States, Russia and the British Empire, Naumann envisioned a free-trade area consisting of the German and Austro-Hungarian empires under the umbrella of an economic and military union.[2] The Paris Resolutions were, in part, the Allied response to perceived plans for a post-war German-led Mitteleuropa.

The Paris Economic Conference looked to the post-war environment in which the Allied powers remained concerned about the economic dynamism of Germany and its future war-making potential. The French sought to cripple the Germany economy after the war, depriving Germany of the large, nearby Allied markets and constructing a post-war Allied economic alliance of privileged access between the Allies. In the French view, the Allies would liberate themselves from economic dependence on Germany and strengthen their own economic position in any future struggle with the Central Powers.

However, Allied solidarity was far from complete. While the Belgian government-in-exile did not welcome the prospects of returning to the economic embrace of an enemy who at that moment was occupying most of Belgium and threatening its very existence, it also recognized that the Belgian economy had long been highly dependent on its larger and wealthier neighbour. Any attempt to isolate Germany without corresponding compensation would be financially ruinous to the Belgians. In its aim of extracting itself from dependence on Germany, Belgium turned first to Britain, rather than France, as the markets of the British Empire promised greater access to resources and larger markets for Belgian products.

Many domestic interests in other Allied countries did not see isolating Germany and establishing preferential arrangements with their wartime allies as inevitably a wise course of action after the war. The Japanese government – which had been allowing trade with German and Austrian nationals prior to the conference – tepidly endorsed the Paris Conference's wartime measures and pointedly refused to commit itself to any policy that extended past the cessation of hostilities. The Russians were likewise less than enthusiastic about binding themselves to British finance and British and French trade in the post-bellum period. As one Russian financier warily commented: 'Our enemies as well as our friends ... will endeavour to get the most favourable conditions for their imports. We must take care to defend ourselves not only against our enemies, but also against our friends.'[3]

The Russian concerns were certainly well founded so far as the British were concerned. Although support for the Paris Resolutions was lukewarm among the leaders of the Liberal Party, Conservatives took them as an indicator that protection would be the policy of the future.[4] Many Conservatives foresaw a situation in which the post-war Allied economic bloc provided the superstructure to a system of imperial preference within the British Empire. In this fashion, Britain would first create a special economic area out of the empire and Dominions, and buttress that core bloc with another exclusive system based around its Continental allies. The empire would be secured first and foremost and the allies' security would be secondary. Both would reinforce Britain's central role in the international economic system.

British policymakers were extremely sensitive to their dependence on imports and financing from the United States. They also recognized the extent that continued American prosperity was a function of American trade with the British Empire. This mutual interdependence made discriminatory policies difficult to impose by either party for fear of hurting their own domestic interests at least as much as the target of any economic sanctions.

Across the Atlantic in the neutral United States, public and political opinion was strongly against the Allies' economic plans, although they did not rate it as a serious threat to America in a post-war environment. If the Allies sought to limit trade with Germany, that would simply make it easier for the Americans to export raw materials to the former Central Powers and import German manufactures into the United States. Of somewhat more concern was the potential for Allied discrimination against neutral powers in favour of each other. In this regard, the United States and the Latin American republics might find their raw materials suffered under new tariffs and quotas. However, the added costs to Allied industry would likely make the goods they desired to export to the western hemisphere more expensive than German products and domestically produced items. At the same time, the consequences of such policies also included the heightened risk that the United States would retaliate against the Allies and enter into either reciprocal or preferential trade agreements with Germany – in practice joining the German economic alliance.[5] Once the United States joined the war as an 'Associated' rather than an 'Allied' power, the aims of the Paris Resolutions became more complicated. The Americans would not countenance a post-war Allied economic cartel as part of the peace settlement and the Allies themselves came to the conclusion that extracting direct cash payments in the form of reparations from Germany was a more efficient means of economic control.

Notes
1. R. E. Bunselmeyer, *The Cost of War: British Economic War Aims and the Origins of Reparation* (Hamden, CT: Archon Books, 1975), pp. 37–8.
2. F. Naumann, *Central Europe* (1916; New York: Alfred A. Knopf, 1917), pp. 216–83.
3. See 'The End of the War and After', *Economist* (1916), below, pp. 197–200.
4. J. Turner, *British Politics and the Great War: Coalition and Conflict, 1915–1918* (New Haven, CT: Yale University Press, 1992), p. 337.
5. This point is advanced in 'The Allies' Economic Combine', *New Republic* (1916), below, pp. 215–17.

THE PARIS CONFERENCE, 1916

Foreign Office Note of Invitation from the French Ambassador for the British Government to Participate in an Economic Conference in Paris, 10 February 1916, PRO, CAB 37/142/29.

CONFIDENTIAL:

In a note dated the 22nd December, 1915, the French Ambassador in London on behalf of the French Government, invited His Majesty's Government to take part officially in a conference at Paris between the Allies to discuss economic questions arising out of the war. Among the questions which might be discussed, M. Cambos cited:–

1. Legislation regarding prohibition of trading with the enemy.
2. The regulation of export prohibitions in such a way that the Allies should afford reciprocal assistance to one another.
3. The measures to be taken by the Allies for the reconstitution of the necessary machinery for the resumption of normal trade.
4. The study of measures for the liberation to the fullest extent of the Allied countries from any economic dependence on the German States.

The Russian and Italian Governments have accepted the invitation of the French Government, but the Japanese Government, who have also been invited, have not yet replied.

Foreign Office, February 10, 1916.

Foreign Minister Edward Grey's Memorandum on British Participation in Paris Economic Conference, 11 February 1916, PRO, CAB 37/142/29.

THE French Ambassador came to see me on the 10th February, and urged that His Majesty's Government should send a representative or representatives to the Conference the objects of which are set out in the annexed memorandum.

I told him that it was impossible for the Cabinet to examine thoroughly the larger questions which the Conference was to discuss, and he replied that he quite understood this, but that, as the Conference was simply to study the questions, instructions were really unnecessary. He hoped, therefore, that His Majesty's Government would arrange for representatives to attend even without instructions, as the French Government were anxious that cold water should not be thrown on the plan.

E. G.

Foreign Office,

February 11, 1916.

Confidential Correspondence between Edward Grey and Sir Francis Villiers, British Ambassador to Belgium, 6 March 1916 and 5 April 1916, PRO, CAB 37/158/3.

CONFIDENTIAL

[44505] No. 1.

Sir Edward Grey to Sir F. Villiers.

(No. 18, Commercial, Confidential.)

Foreign Office, March 6, 1910.

Sir,

THE Belgian Minister spoke to me to-day on the subject of the Economic Conference which the French Government had proposed should be held at Paris before long.

With one of the two main subjects of discussion, viz, the best methods of carrying on trade during the progress of the war, Belgium unhappily could have no concern; but his Government were deeply interested in the other branch of the subject, that of the commercial projects and prospects of the Allies after the conclusion of peace. Belgium, as I was aware, would find herself in a peculiar situation owing to the close association which had existed before the war between many of her industries and Germany. Her exports must always form a large part of her national life, and if the avenues of trade with the Central Powers were to be closed or narrowed in the future, fresh roads must be opened, or it could not be expected that business men would refuse to employ the old ones. In these circumstances the Belgian Government looked towards Great Britain and the British Empire with the utmost hope, and they would be glad if some preliminary conversations could be held with us before the conference took place. He had assumed that we were going to take part in it with the other Powers.

I said that we had received an invitation to the conference and should no doubt take some part in it, but to what extent, or with what representation, was not yet decided. So far as I knew, it was not at present hoped to do more than open up the ground and examine some of the main problems, leaving definite decisions until later.

I enquired whether the Belgian Government had contemplated engaging in any similar conversations with France before the conference itself took place.

M. Hymans replied that he would speak quite frankly and in confidence. His Government fully appreciated the friendship of France in this and other matters, but they considered that on this subject in particular they stood in a closer relation to us, both on account of the past fiscal policy of our two countries, and because the prospects of future commercial co-operation with the British Empire seemed to be the most promising that existed.

I said that I would consult the President of the Board of Trade on the question of some preliminary conversations, and would communicate with the Minister again as soon as possible.

I am, &c.

E. GREY

[60806] No. 2.

Sir Edward Grey to Sir F. Villiers.

(No. 21, Commercial, Secret and Confidential.)

Foreign Office, April 5, 1916.

Sir,

WITH reference to my despatch No. 18, Commercial, of the 6th ultimo, I have to inform you that the Belgian Minister called to see Mr. Runciman on the 27th March on the subject of the forthcoming Economic Conference in Paris for a preliminary conversation, on the ground that at the conference Belgium and the United Kingdom would be the only Governments with a recent Free Trade policy. Mr. Runciman asked M. Hymans to state what hearing this had on the conference, and on the present attitude of the Belgian Government, and M. Hymans thereupon described the extent to which trade between Belgium and Germany had expanded in the last twenty years. He said that, geographically, Belgium was bound to be mainly dependent on Germany for her inward and outward trade. She was a country of transit, and the port of Antwerp would be a small port, instead of being, as it is, one of the greatest, if transit trade to and from Germany by way of the Scheldt were impeded or prohibited. M. Hymans quoted many figures from their trade returns to support this, the most important being those of the imports from Germany into Belgium, which in 1913, according to his statement, reached the sum of 600,000,000 fr., which were paid largely for coal, for tools and machinery, for half-finished products, as well as fully manufactured articles. He said that if Belgium were to refuse to receive coals, tools, and machinery from Germany after the war, she would place her industries under great disadvantage, unless the tools and machinery could be supplied more cheaply from England or America. In the restoration of Belgian industry, the Belgian Government regarded the cheapness of the supplies which they purchased essential to their success.

Belgian exports to Germany were 350,000,000 fr., and M. Hymans declared that any policy which prevented Belgium selling her goods to this extent would be most damaging to the country, and could only be contemplated if she were offered new and equally remunerative markets elsewhere. When Mr. Runciman pressed him on this point he said that what his Government meant by that was that there should be no tariff in England against Belgian goods or produce, and that the tariffs in the dominions which affected Belgian goods should be removed. He desired to see the treaty which was in force up to 1896, and which permitted Belgian goods to enter the dominions on the same terms as British goods, restored. This would to some extent compensate Belgium for the loss of her export trade to Germany.

With regard to Antwerp, Mr. Runciman called attention to the fact that the best quays and berths were reserved for German vessels previous to the war, and stated that His Majesty's Government hoped this preferential advantage in Antwerp would not be given to German lines in future. M. Hymans replied that he had no instructions on that subject, but he pointed out that Antwerp existed largely on traffic which came into port on its way to Germany, and on the carriage of goods away from Antwerp which originated in Germany, the loss of which none of the Allies could make up to Antwerp.

Mr. Runciman acknowledged that these were difficult problems to solve, and that the peculiar geographical position of Belgium made her problems different from ours or those of the other Allies. M. Hymans was anxious to assure His Majesty's Government that the only difference was geographical, and that the sentiment against all Germans was so pronounced in Belgium that it would not die out for generations or possibly for centuries, which would in itself act as a preference against Germany. He desired to lay stress on this point, but to draw the attention of His Majesty's Government to the facts regarding Belgian trade and its peculiar position.

Having spoken on these subjects from his notes. M. Hymans went on to say, quite unofficially, that in Belgium there was a certain amount of feeling against a Zollverein with France. He did not express himself clearly on this subject, but he wished to state that Belgium would not like to be brought under the economic influence of France, though he did not explain what he meant by this. M. Hymans said that further instructions would be given to him by his Government in the course of a week or two, and that that he would like to communicate them to His Majesty's Government. They would be based on the data collected by Professor Waxweiler, who, by method of questionnaire, was making enquiries of Belgian traders, manufacturers, coal-owners, iron-masters, &c., which were now being condensed for official use.

I am, &c.

E. GREY.

J. A. Hobson, 'The New Protectionism', *War and Peace*, 3:31 (April 1916), pp. 104–5.

WAR AND PEACE

Vol. III. No. 31.
April 1916

The New Protectionism
By J. A. HOBSON

WAR-TIME is the opportunity for every reactionary cause to recover lost positions and to invade fresh territory. Free speech, free Press, freedom from arbitrary arrest, voluntary service, with other civil liberties, are killed or mutilated. Free trade is now threatened. How should it escape? Protectionism is the commercial counterpart of militarism. It was therefore to be expected that Protectionists should seize this opportunity to obtain by indirect pressures what they failed to obtain by open appeals to the electorate. The atmosphere of fierce passions and clouded judgment is favourable to their cause. They need not meet the free trade logic which has so often pierced their fallacies and exposed their selfish scheming. They can plead the present emergencies of war-economy, the urgent need to curb our imports, the shortage of our shipping, the necessity to fortify direct by indirect taxation. Indeed, the argument which was hitherto most fatal to their cause, that the consumer pays, they are quite ready to admit for the nonce. For they can turn it to account. The rise in prices which a tariff brings will serve two desirable war purposes – reducing consumption and enabling the workers out of their enhanced war-wages to make a considerable contribution to the cost of the war! This attitude is ingeniously adapted to the politically valuable purpose of winning over the support of former free trade organs, politicians and business men. Liberals are called upon to lay down free trade, like their other liberties, as a patriotic sacrifice. It is necessary, they are told, in order to win the war, and to secure the country afterwards against the vengeful policy of Germany. Some illrooted free traders have allowed themselves to fall into a trap baited with such highly flavoured patriotism. German financial and commercial policy has been exclusively governed by the military purposes of the State, and will continue to be so governed in the future. This country, therefore, in close concert with her Dominions and her Allies, must organise a fiscal and commercial policy which will obviate this danger. Germany must be kept continuously weak after the war, so that she cannot on the one hand pursue abroad her Machiavellian trade policy, or, on the other, find ample home resources to reconstruct her shattered military and naval power so as to drag Europe into another war.

It will be observed that, in order to utilise the war emergency, our Protectionists are driven into proposals a good deal more complicated and mutually destructive than those rejected by the country in 1906 and 1910. It was then chiefly a problem of harmonising British protection with imperial preferences. There were only three parties to consider – Great Britain, the Empire and the rest of the world. But the new war situation breaks up the outer world into three groups, allies, neutrals and belligerents, and this new discrimination must be injected into the required tariff arrangements. The rotund oratory of our Chambers of Commerce and the generalisations of the *Morning Post* are designed to rush the country and the Government into committals to our Allies and our Dominions before the essential discords of the new Protectionism are made manifest. Security is to be the watchword. Defence against the future machinations of the Central Powers is to mould the policy. German trade and finance are to be excluded from the countries of the Alliance (or reduced to safe and negligible shapes), and are to be prevented from extending their influence over neutral countries. Economic self-sufficiency is to be the basis of defence. But in the statement of this basic principle the utmost haziness prevails. Sometimes it is argued that our fiscal arrangements must aim at producing or storing within this country all the essential requisites for life and for defence. For this purpose we must stimulate our agriculture to the utmost, keep huge stores of the foods and materials which we are compelled to import, and preserve in sufficient size all 'key industries,' alike for war requisites and for other products needed for our civil needs of life and trade. Others stress more the unity and self-sufficiency of the Empire, hoping to make it virtually self-sufficient for all our major wants. What we cannot procure within the limits of the Empire, we should procure, if possible, from our Allies, partly to do them a good turn, partly to preserve and strengthen the alliance in view of future emergencies. Reflection, however, compels the admission that it will be necessary and desirable to do profitable trade with neutral countries, though not on terms of equality with our Allies.

Now the political and defensive motives play havoc with the economic structure of Protectionism. A mere citation of some of the contradictions and absurdities must here suffice. In order to work the proposed fivefold discrimination, a general tariff will be necessary. Is it suggested that free trade within the Empire is feasible? Would our agrarian party be satisfied merely to keep out the wheat of foreign countries, such as Argentina and Russia (our Ally!)? Would Canada and Australia admit all our manufactures free? Even if we were prepared to continue our free importation of imperial products, only taxing foreigners – how would that policy please our Allies? However preferential the terms given to these Allies, as compared with neutrals, the fact would remain that French wines would for the first time, in a time of deep impoverishment, be taxed higher than Australian wines, while Russia, whose trade we particularly desire to cultivate, would find a tariff on her wheat while Canadian and Australian wheat entered our ports free. Would such facts cement the Alliance? That complete free trade within the Alliance is practicable could not be suggested by any informed person, having regard to the existing fiscal system and the after-war financial needs of Russia and of France. On the other hand, will any of our Protectionists be content to grant one-sided free trade, both for our Dominions and our Allies, without getting any reciprocal advantages from the latter? Are French motor-cars, silks and jewellery to enter absolutely free? All the proposals I have seen assume, on the contrary, a low general tariff on allied imports, a higher one for neutrals, and a prohibitive one for belligerents. But these difficulties in adjusting the respective claims and interests of the Dominions and the Allies are exceeded when we come to the case of neutrals and belligerents. In order to punish Germany and to prevent her economic recovery, we are to impose terms which virtually keep her trade out of our markets. We will neither buy nor sell with her, nor will our Empire or our Allies. That will no doubt injure Germany. It will injure us and our Allies precisely as much, for the loss of foreign trade on both sides will be equal and opposite. There is no reason to suppose that Germany gains more by an act of exchange across her frontiers than other countries. There is thus no reason to suppose that a boycott of German trades adds one jot or tittle to the comparative economic strength of the Alliance. What it clearly does is greatly to stimulate the external trade of Germany with neutral countries. This it does in several ways. For Germany, being *ex hypothesi* excluded from her former large profitable trade with her great neighbours, will be under extreme pressure to open up larger markets in neutral countries. The competition of her traders in these countries would naturally become intense, and prices would be lowered in order to push trade. But this lowering of prices might not be necessary. For Germany could now make commercial arrangements with neutral countries on terms more advantageous to her traders than to ours. Neutral countries, no longer getting most favoured nations' treatment from the Allies, would retaliate by raising their tariffs against Allied goods, and would admit German goods at lower rates. The elaborate tariff of this country would make it particularly inelastic for negotiating treaties with such a neutral as the United States. Again, if Germany is required to pay any large indemnity, this payment can only be made by means of foreign trade. If the Allies refuse to take the indemnity direct in the shape of imports from Germany, they will only be able to get it on condition of an immensely expanded trade of Germany with neutral countries, which in their turn will have to find means of sending in great quantities of goods into the Allied countries, over the tariff walls erected to keep them out. These goods will either be German goods, sent by indirect processes, or they will will be neutral substitutes for German goods, liberating neutral goods for export. In any case we shall not have stopped German foreign trade, but only directed it into circuitous ways of reaching this country. This would be a more expensive way of exacting an indemnity – more expensive to us as well as to Germany. If the Allies intend to get out of Germany a really substantial contribution towards the damages, they can only do so by giving Germany good facilities for making payment in the only shape it can be made – *i.e.,* by import trade.

The whole fabric of the new Protectionism is riddled with foolishness and ignorance. It is quite impracticable to seek suddenly to reverse the intricate processes by which international trade has grown within recent generations. No important staple trade in this country is independent or can be made independent, as regards all its materials, tools and processes, of foreign countries outside the Empire or the Alliance. To put this tariff ramrod into the delicate machinery of international trade and finance at a time when the first need of every nation is industrial and commercial recovery would be an act of criminal folly.

To engage in this reactionary exploit under the name of defence is a particularly impudent perversion of the truth. If it could be put into operation, this Protectionism would do nothing to increase the relative strength of the resources of the Allies. For reasons I have indicated it would be extremely likely to sow dissension among the Allies. Historically war has proved an exceedingly unreliable cement of friendship, and when allies become business partners the relations are not rendered more but less secure. But suppose a strong, close economic alliance could be maintained. Would it make for security in Europe? It would compel the Central Empires to organise themselves as powerfully as possible, and to strengthen this economical and political position by using the means I have cited to win over neutrals. Europe would be broken into two independent hostile groups, competing in all parts of the world for markets and for power. The economic antagonisms which have lain at the root of every dangerous trouble of this generation would be further developed and intensified. A policy thus negativing at the outset all possibility of any European concert for the equitable settlement of differences would close the door to all possibility of future peace.

'The End of the War and After', *Economist* (17 June 1916), pp. 1134–5.

THE END OF THE WAR AND AFTER.

THERE is more and more speculation week after week as to what will follow the end of the war. The eager anticipations of soldiers, the artful speeches of politicians, the yearnings of anxious homes, and, finally, the calculations of business men all turn upon this one question. Just now we are living in fictitious prosperity upon borrowed money. After the war people will have to try to earn their bread, butter, and jam in the usual way. Profits will disappear as the war trades vanish and competition returns. Employment will become scarce. Wages will fall as trade declines. Many prices which have been sky high will fall to the ground. Private credits will be scrutinised with a new severity, and the longer the war lasts the greater will be the difficulties. Unfortunately, those difficulties cannot be overcome by Governments. It is only by long years of patient work that the individuals who support the vast and costly machine of administration will be able to repair the ravages of this war.

Modern Governments, of course, have to pretend that they can make trade and spread prosperity. This favourite fallacy inspires the Economic Conference now in session in Paris. 'To conquer,' says M. Briand, 'is not enough. The new world which will arise from victory will demand a new conception in all fields of the methods suitable to the circumstances created by the great changes which are coming upon us.' The task of the Conference was, after having organised the necessary defence against a common danger, 'to consider the conditions of the practical utilisation of our internal economic alliance.' What this means is not as yet very clear. The guarded phrases of the *Times* Paris correspondent (June 14th) are a moderate edition of the theory which is founded on the Australian zinc trade:–

The Paris Conference cannot hope to do more than agree upon the main principles and recognise that all the Allies shall have the first claim upon each other's resources in natural produce, metals, capital, and means of transport.

Even Mr Hughes, in his interview with the *Matin*, although fulminating against the German vampire, 'does not pretend that we shall never again do any business with Germany.' His trade views seem, indeed, to have caused some apprehensions in France. If exceeding politeness towards a colonial politician has prevented our economists and statesmen from openly resenting the attempts of Mr Hughes to overthrow our commercial structure and to destroy our free markets, the Paris newspapers evidently do not intend to be so reticent. French business interests are thoroughly alarmed. The *Matin* has questioned Mr Hughes closely respecting his proposals; and the *Journal des Débats* – next to *Le*

Temps undoubtedly the most influential paper in France – publishes a significantly plain hint in its issue of the 13th inst. The adoption of Protection by Great Britain would naturally affect the interests of our Allies; for not even the words of Mr Hughes can alter the ordinary laws of supply and demand. The *Journal des Débats* says: 'His (Mr Hughes') idea is by means of preferential tariffs to create a sort of Customs union between Great Britain and her colonies – a union recalling the famous colonial agreement which, after many struggles, was definitely abandoned by our neighbours and Allies across the Channel in the middle of last century... The ideas of Mr Hughes have rather alarmed the French industrial and commercial groups which are more particularly engaged in business relations with Great Britain.......... Every delegate to the Conference who arrives in Paris with absolute and uncompromising opinions will be obliged to recognise that in economic matters, as in many others, the policy of solidarity of interest ought to dominate all extreme and exclusive ideas on the subject.' Can we wonder that the French manufacturers of silk goods and hats and other luxuries are as little favourable to the new Tariff Reform as were the Belgian glass manufacturers when they heard of the proposed 50 per cent. tariff on foreign glass?

What the predominant interests in Russia want is more capital in order to acquire what is called industrial independence. To attract capital it is quite possible that the high Russian tariff will be raised after the war. The *Daily Chronicle* (May 5th) quoted several representative views expressed by Russian manufacturers and bankers. 'The aims of French or English commercialism have nothing whatever to do with those of Germany, but from a purely economic point of view there is no difference between the two,' says the Petrograd *Bourse Gazette*. Other authorities in Russia have already stated openly that trade with Germany must be resumed immediately after the signing of peace, for Russia is admittedly in want of manufactured goods of all kinds; and it will be a long time before the new industrial policy can provide them. It will be seen, therefore, that the extreme views advocated by Mr Hughes will have to be considerably qualified in practice; for the complete ostracism of Germany and her Allies is out of the question – even the *Morning Post* does not ask for that. 'Our enemies as well as our friends,' says M. Krestovnikoff, member of the Council of Empire and president of the Moscow Stock Exchange, 'will endeavour to get the most favourable conditions for their imports. We must take care to defend ourselves not only against our enemies, but also against our friends.' Our own business men should take note of these facts and opinions.

Earl Beauchamp's letter, following on the previous suggestions by Earl Brassey and Earl Loreburn, is a powerful plea for the substitution of a rational attitude towards peace proposals, as distinguished from a policy founded upon passion, however natural, and revenge, however just. The time seems to have come when rulers will have to consider the true interests of their subjects or fellow citizens in this regard, and when the State which has claimed the right to exact from the individual his life or his property, will have to reduce its pretensions and abate the struggle for glory and prestige, not because they are worthless and undesirable, but because a State which had lost its men and its money could hardly call itself victorious; for after it had imposed peace as a conqueror it would be compelled for years to play second fiddle to other Powers. Every neutral observer realises that the aggressive designs of Prussian militarism are already defeated, and that in Austria and Germany the war is already regarded as a defensive one. Even the Ministers have to represent themselves to their own people as struggling for a tolerable peace. No sooner has the deadlock turned in their favour on the Italian front than it turns against them in Galicia. Germany's naval and commercial position is very bad. If the carnage continues for another year it may collapse. On the other hand, even if all future calculations of the Ministers responsible for the Dardanelles and Mesopotamia prove correct, and if all their promises are made good, yet at the end of a three or four years' war the position of Great Britain as a military, naval, and commercial Power, saddled with a debt charge as great as its old revenue, and with an income-tax rising to 10s or 15s in the pound, would be immeasurably weaker than before. The Prime Minister and Sir Edward Grey are the principal actors; it is upon them that the main responsibility for the management of the war must fall. They are the diplomatic and political managers of the Alliance, and they do not give us a very large supply of information. But their stake is the lives and fortunes of their fellow-citizens, and the future of Great Britain and of the British Empire. These considerations are sufficient to explain the patriotic inquiries put forward by Earls Brassey, Loreburn, and Beauchamp in our columns. Of course you want to crush your enemy in war. Of course you want victory. Of course you wish your enemy to admit that he is beaten, and to sue for peace. But equally of course, unless you are misled by a false and flimsy rhetoric, you do not want to destroy the society, the traditions, the wealth and the happiness of your own people. You do not wish to see your Allies ruined for the sake of reducing an enemy to abject despair. So when attrition and exhaustion have reached a certain point, you are willing to discount the future and to take counsel with the still small voices of reason and common sense. In short, you do not shut your eyes to the facts, or close your ears to overtures when those overtures seem likely to lead in the direction of a favourable settlement and a stable peace which will guarantee the main objects of your endeavours, though they cannot fulfil all expectations.

We have always tried to maintain the standpoint of enlightened national self-interest, because we doubt if there is any other ground on which the leaders of a nation are entitled to declare or carry on war. But we cannot refrain from adding here 'An Appeal for Co-operation Towards a Lasting Peace' which has reached us from the President of Stanford University, California. It is extensively signed by hundreds of American students, and it puts the view of thoughtful and interested neutrals:–

We, the undersigned, loyal citizens of the United States of America, ourselves or our immediate ancestors born in some one of the countries now at war, are confronted by the following facts:–

1. That the great war is bringing ruin to Europe and to civilisation everywhere, since it is working unparalleled havoc in the best racial elements in each nation concerned, thereby exhausting the near future and entailing impoverishment, both physical and mental;
2. That, by the continuance of the war, an increasingly intolerable burden of sorrow and misery is thrown on the non-combatants, men, women, and children of all nations concerned, those who had no part in bringing on the war and no interest to be served by it;
3. That, in our judgment, no gain, political, social, or spiritual, which may possibly result can compensate for the immeasurable loss of human blood, intellect, and energy the war entails, nor for the overwhelming material waste and distress it has already caused, or counteract the feelings of fear, hatred, and revenge which it everywhere engenders;

Therefore, irrespective of issues originally involved, we are convinced that hostilities should be brought to an immediate close. We cannot believe that a sweeping victory for either side will offer real or final solution of any problem, since attempts to gather fruits of victory would leave an increasing legacy of fear and hate, the seed for future wars. We question whether military operations can of themselves bring the war to an end, and the longer it continues, the more insistent and complicated become the problems involved.

We therefore urge all people within the United States to lay aside passion and prejudice, and to use all possible means towards casting the undivided influence of this great neutral nation on the side of an immediate and a lasting peace, based on the principles of international justice and not dependent on the fortunes of war.

This appeal deserves respectful consideration not only for its contents, but also because it appears to represent the views of the leaders of both the great political parties in the United States.

'Who Were Our Best Customers?', *Economist* (17 June 1916), pp. 1135–6.

WHO WERE OUR BEST CUSTOMERS?

The meeting, this week, of the Economic Conference of the Allies in Paris makes opportune a review of the course of our export trade in recent years. Clearly, if we for any reason abandon the policy of free imports, which has caused the immense development of our overseas trade, it is certain that those countries upon whose imports it may be proposed to place a tariff will in self-defence (as they will think) do all they can to make us regret our new departure.

From the year 1904 onwards our statistical tables have published the values of our exports *consigned* to each foreign country and British possession, as distinguished from the values of goods exported. As a result, Switzerland appeared in the list of our customers, and the value of the exports to Belgium was seen to be materially higher than the value of the consignments. In the case of our imports, much greater discrepancies were apparent; and the present system is a very great improvement upon the old. How rapidly our export trade with our best customers has grown, despite hostile tariffs, is seen from the following table, comparing the total values of our exports plus re-exports in 1912 with those of 1904:– (Values in Thousand £)

	1904. £	1912. £	Increase in 1912 Over 1904. Actual. £	%	1913. £	Increase or Decrease in 1913 Over 1912. £
United States	39,272	64,637	25,365	64.58	59,453	- 5,184
British India	41,544	59,775	18,231	43.88	71,670	+ 11,895
Germany	36,425	59,572	23,147	63.54	60,500	+ 923
Australia	19,841	38,281	18,440	93.0	37,829	- 452
France	21,578	37,532	15,954	73.93	40,882	+ 3,350
Canada	12,248	27,320	15,072	123.0	27,307	- 13
Union of South Africa	19,471	23,280	3,809	19.56	24,046	+ 766
Russia	15,286	21,741	6,455	42.22	27,694	+ 5,953
Argentina	11,572	21,325	9,753	84.28	23,437	+ 2,112

The above table comprises British India, our three chief self-governing Dominions, and the five principal foreign countries. In 1904 our best customer was British India, which took goods valued at 41½ millions sterling. Although the great Dependency increased its purchases in 1912 to 59¾ millions, showing an increase of £18,231,000, or 43.88 per cent., the United States had risen to the first place, having increased its purchases from 39¼ to 64⅔ millions, an increase of £25,365,000, or 64.58 per cent. Germany stood third in order in each year, and increased its purchases from 36 425 to 59½ millions, an advance of £23,147,000, or 63.54 per cent. Australia stood fifth in order in 1904, but rose to the fourth place in 1912, having increased its purchases from 19 841 to 38¼ millions, an advance of £18,440,000, or 93 per cent. France fell from the fourth to the fifth place, although it had increased its purchases from 21½ to 37½ millions, an advance of little less than 16 millions, or 73.93 per cent. Canada, which was eighth in order in 1904, rose to the sixth place in 1912, having increased its purchases from 12¼ to 27⅓ millions, an advance of £15,072,000, or 123 per cent. The Union of South Africa increased its purchases from 19½ to 23¼ millions, an advance of £3,809,000, or 19.56 per cent.; Russia increased its purchases from 15¼ to 21¾ millions, an advance of £6,455,000, or 42.22 per cent.; and Argentina increased its purchases from 11½ to 21⅓ millions, an advance of £9,753,000, or 84.28 per cent. Taking their percentage increases, our customers stood in the following order:– Canada, 123 per cent.; Australia, 93 per cent.; Argentina, 84.28 per cent.; France, 73.93 per cent.; the United States, 64.58 per cent.; Germany, 63.54 per cent.; British India, 43.88 per cent.; Russia, 42.22 per and the Union of South Africa, 19.56 per cent., or practically one-fifth. Thus Canada more than doubled its purchases; Australia nearly did so; and the other six countries increased their takings from four-tenths to four-fifths in gradation.

The last two columns of the table indicate that the year 1913 showed an increase in the value of our exports to six out of the nine countries, ranging in amount from £11,895,000 in the case of British India, £5,953,000 in the case of Russia, £3,350,000 in the case of France, and £2,112,000 in the case of Argentina, to sums under a million in the cases of Germany and the Union of South Africa. The decline in the value of our exports to the United States exceeded five millions sterling, was approaching half-a-million in the case of Australia, and amounted to the mere trifle of £13,000 in the case of Canada.

The next table shows the countries to which we exported goods valued at between 10 and 20 millions in the year 1912:–

(Values in Thousand £)

	1904. £	1912. £	Increase in 1912 Over 1904. Actual. £	%	1913 £	Increase or Decrease in 1913 Over 1912. £
Belgium	12,230	19,556	7,326	60.0	20,660	+ 1,104
Netherlands	12,807	19,364	6,557	51.2	20,522	+ 1,158
Italy	9,222	15,011	5,789	62.8	15,622	+ 611
Brazil	6,219	13,172	6,953	111.8	13,021	- 151
Japan	5,043	12,471	7,428	147.3	14,827	+ 2,356
New Zealand	6,897	11,186	4,289	62.2	11,790	+ 604
China	8,890	10,889	1,999	22.5	15,010	+ 4,121

From this table it will be seen that Japan increased its purchases from the United Kingdom in 1912 by £7,428,000 above the value of its purchases in 1904, an increase of 147.3 per cent., and considerably exceeding the 123 per cent. increase by Canada in the same period. Brazil did almost as well, increasing its purchases by £6,953,000, or 111.8 per cent. Italy increased its purchases by £5,789,000, or 62.8 per cent.; New Zealand by £4,289,000, or 62.2 per cent.; and Belgium by £7,326,000, or 60 per cent. The Netherlands increased their purchases by £6,557,000, or 51.2 per cent. Six out of these seven countries are thus seen to have taken from more than half as much again to more than double the amount which they purchased in 1904. Further, China increased its purchases by 22.5 per cent., and in 1913 still further improved its position as a customer by taking £4,121,000 worth more than it did in 1912, showing an increase of 68.8 per cent. upon the value of its purchases from the United Kingdom in 1904. Moreover, the last two columns of the table show that, with the exception of a slight falling off in the value of the purchases made by Brazil in 1913, the other five countries followed the lead of China in taking a larger amount of our goods in 1913 than they had taken in 1912. The case of Brazil is a remarkable instance of improved trade; firstly, because Brazil does not grant us a most-favoured-nation agreement, and, secondly, because its territories extend over some 3,000,000 square miles of South America – the continent with which a few years back we were said by Mr. Bonar Law almost to have ceased to do any trade!

The third table contains nine foreign countries and one British colony, each of which took exports and re-exports from the United Kingdom in 1912, together exceeding £5,000,000:–

(Values in Thousand £)

	1904.	1912.	Increase in 1912 Over 1904.		1913.	Increase or Dec. in 1913 Over 1912.
			Actual	%		
	£	£	£		£	£
Egypt	8,431	9,597	1,166	13.8	9,964	+ 367
Turkey	7,587	8,333	746	9.8	8,012	- 321
Sweden	5,529	8,104	2,575	46.6	9,235	+ 1,131
Spain	4,911	7,678	2,767	56.3	8,631	+ 953
Chile	3,496	6,510	3,014	86.2	6,369	- 141
Denmark	4,031	6,416	2,385	59.2	6,343	- 73
Java and Dutch Possessions in Indian Seas	3,479	6,162	2,683	77.1	7,302	+ 1,140
Austria-Hungary	2,568	6,153	3,585	139.6	5,780	- 373
Staits Settlements	3,183	6,006	2,823	88.7	7,388	+ 1,382
Norway	3,123	6,030	2,707	81.5	6,666	+ 636

Seven out of these 10 countries increased their takings from the United Kingdom in 1912 by more than 50 per cent. of the value which they purchased in 1904. Even Sweden took 46.6 per cent. increase upon the value of 1904. Austria-Hungary's percentage increase of 139.6 places it second only to Japan, whose increase in the eight years was 147.3. The increased values of our exports in 1913 to Sweden, Spain, Java, and the Straits Settlements were very considerable.

The following table practically summarises our export and re-export trade with the world. It comprises our 34 best customers, and it compares the values of our exports and re-exports in 1913 with the average values of 1910 to 1912:–

	Average Value 1910 to 1912. £	Value in 1913. £
British India	53,524,000	71,670,000
Germany	57,299,000	60,500,000
United States	60,972,000	59,453,000
France	36,480,000	40,882,000
Australia	34,631,000	37,829,000
Russia	21,760,000	27,693,000
Canada	24,220,000	27,307,000
Union of S. Africa	22,138,000	24,046,000
Argentina	20,116,000	23,437,000
Belgium	18,668,000	20,660,000
Netherlands	18,306,000	20,522,000
Italy	14,686,000	15,622,000
China	10,821,000	15,010,000
Japan	11,664,000	14,827,000
Brazil	14,126,000	13,021,000
New Zealand	10,396,000	11,790,000
Egypt	9,642,000	9,964,000
Austria-Hungary	5,773,000	5,780,000
Sweden	7,787,000	9,235,000
Spain	6,387,000	8,631,000
Turkey	8,965,000	8,012,000
Straits Settlements	5,297,000	7,388,000
Java and Dutch Ind. Possessions	5,256,000	7,302,000
Norway	5,298,000	6,666,000
Chile	6,263,000	6,369,000
Denmark	6,197,000	6,343,000
Switzerland	4,377,000	5,088,000
Hong Kong	3,527,000	4,555,000
Ceylon	2,690,000	4,316,000
Nigeria	3,442,000	4,011,000
Portugal	3,455,000	3,934,000
Bh. W. Indies and Bh. Guiana	3,704,000	3,336,000
Cuba & Porto Rico	2,946,000	3,067,000
Uruguay	3,000,000	3,012,000

In 30 out of the 34 countries in the list above the value of our exports and re-exports had increased in 1913 above the average of the three preceding years. In the United States, Brazil, Turkey, and the British West Indies trade was not so good. The previous tables have shown the enormous growth of our trade since 1904. Hostile tariffs had absolutely failed to shut us out. Our fiscal system left us with a fleet of merchantmen equal to the combined fleets of the rest of the world. Our policy bound our colonies to ourselves in the closest bonds of affection. We never interfered with them, and imposed no restraints upon their produce entering our ports. Our resulting wealth has grown so enormous that upon our shoulders has fallen the burden of financing our Allies.

'The Paris Economic Conference and After', *New Statesman*, 7:168 (24 June 1916), pp. 268–9.

THE PARIS CONFERENCE AND AFTER

No immediate change of policy, so far as this country is concerned, is heralded by the resolutions of the Paris Economic Conference. With one exception, a clause about 'enabling contracts entered into with enemy subjects and injurious to national interests to be cancelled unconditionally,' – which smacks of Mr. Hughes and Broken Hill, the measures recommended for the war period are those which Great Britain has long enforced. In regard to the blockade of Central Europe, and also in regard to the trading-with-the-enemy question, our Government has been the target of much home criticism. We have been told almost daily that it does not go far enough. In point of fact it has gone so far, that when a conference of all the Allies meets to thresh these problems out, it can find nothing better than to exhort them all to do what Great Britain does. Nor is the exhortation superfluous. France has throughout gone with us; but the practice of some of the Allies, notably Italy, has been much weaker, and it will be a gain to have it equalised.

The rest of the Conference's programme is post-war, and most of it is vague. The 'permanent measures of mutual assistance and collaboration' are left quite in the raw state. It might be excellent, for instance, to get a uniform law about patents and trade-marks in the Allied countries; but the difficult task of doing so is passed on untouched to a proposed technical conference. It might be excellent, again, if the Allied countries could make themselves independent of Central Europe in regard to 'the raw materials and manufactured articles essential to the normal development of their economic activities.' But the Paris resolution settles nothing as to how it should be done; it merely gives a brief catalogue of the imaginable methods, and says that the Allies will adopt whichever they please, 'according to the nature of the commodities and having regard to the principles which govern their economic policy.' Controversy is avoided by being postponed.

It could not be so easily avoided in the case of 'transitory measures' for the period of post-war reconstruction. And here it is that the real difficulties in front of a trade Alliance begin to show themselves. The Conference delegates realised that the first years following the war would present economic problems not the less, but perhaps the more, important because they would not be permanently present, but would be in the nature of opportunities, perils, partings of the ways, to be encountered once for all with results more or less irrevocable. They realised that this fateful period would be comparatively brief; that it would begin immediately on the declaration of peace; and that certain broad principles must be laid down beforehand if Allied action was to keep pace with events. Hence the programme had to be more definite; and the differences between the interests of different nations are at once felt.

Take, for example, the proposal that the Allied countries shall withhold most-favoured-nation treatment from the Central European Powers for a number of years to be fixed by mutual agreement among themselves. Read with it the proposal to fix by similar agreement a period of time during which the trade, the goods, and the ships of Central Europe should be 'subjected either to prohibitions or to a special regime of an effective character.' To Australia these proposals may involve little inconvenience. Mr. Hughes seems to regard German trade as nothing but a poison, which his people would be better without. Even in France such a view is tenable. But what of Belgium? Belgium before the war owed an appreciable part of her prosperity to being a coast State with Germany for hinterland. Antwerp was the rival of Rotterdam as an emporium for shipping and selling Westphalian and Rhenish goods. Is the rivalry to be terminated after the war by Belgium's own act? Is it conceivable that for the sake of remaining in line with her war Allies she should surrender a monopoly of this lucrative trade to Holland? Nobody can think so who knows the long and tragic story of the forced closing of the Schelde, and the close coincidence between its liberation and the modern revival of Belgian prosperity.

But what is true of Belgium is true in only a less glaring degree of Great Britain. Geographically the fortune of this country is that it lies off Central Europe on the way to America. It is the stepping-stone for a great volume of trade. London owes to this as much as to anything the fact that she, and not New York, is the world's financial capital. If one wanted to transfer London's position to New York after the war, perhaps the likeliest way to do it would be to adopt in a drastic form the proposals which we are discussing. Let nobody suppose that either Belgium or ourselves could be saved by the Paris resolution's proviso in favour of the Allies' assuring to each other 'so far as possible compensatory outlets for trade' in hard cases. Pious provisos do not in practice annihilate geography. The coalfields of Germany, having regard to their size, their accessibility by water, and the neighbouring iron deposits, are by far the most important on the Continent. While they last and the utilities of coal last, Germany must remain an immensely important – probably the most important – centre of Continental production, and the one whose trade contains the greatest economic possibilities for us. Before the war she was Britain's best customer, and Britain was hers; it is absurd to talk of such a state of things as if it were artificial, or as if its advantages were confined to one side.

Some of the other 'transitory' measures which look attractive on paper may or may not be workable, when the pressure of war is past. Such is the clause whereby the Allies propose to give each other during the reconstruction period a first claim on their natural resources, i.e., their spare raw materials. Great Britain and her Dominions have recognised such a claim during the war in regard to various substances, such as rubber and wool, to the very great benefit of the Allies. If Russia during the reconstruction period would recognise a similar claim in regard to timber, it might be of material benefit to Belgium and France. One of the most important 'transitory' problems is not mentioned in the resolutions, though it appears to have been discussed at the Conference. It is that of the exchange. If the war ended this year, the pound sterling would return almost immediately to the top of the tree; the franc would soon follow; and the lire might not be far behind. On the other hand, the mark and the rouble, if left to themselves, would remain some time together in the depths. This would give Russian buyers an overwhelming inducement to buy in Germany, where they could get for £8,000 what would cost them £10,000 in Great Britain or France. The Germans would at once recover, and recover for good, all and more than all their pre-war primacy in Russian trade.

The only way to prevent this and restore the Russian rate of exchange would be to create enormous credits in favour of Russia in this country. In other words, having financed our Allies through war, we should continue the process through the first years of peace. Translated from terms of finance into terms of production, it would mean that for some years a considerable part of Great Britain's productive resources would be working for Russia without any fructifying return. Could we stand the strain, in addition to that of all the other claims which will then press on us? Perhaps, yes; perhaps, no. The stake is a big one. The Russian market is probably the greatest future market in the world; and predominance in it is not unlikely to grow in importance every year for the next half-century.

As to Allied tariffs, there is no hope of economic prosperity in them, unless accompanied by Allied Free Trade. If you have two rival combinations of States, which are alike in that each has a tariff against the other, but unlike in that one has Free Trade among its members and the other has not, the former must have an overwhelming advantage over the latter. The pith of the Naumann conception of an economic 'Central Europe' stretching from the Baltic to Bagdad is not merely that there should be a tariff on its borders, but that there should be Free Trade within them. The two ideas are indispensable to each other. Until our Allies and Dominions show some disposition to accept the Free Trade side of the arrangement (of which there is not at present the faintest sign), we should be more than foolish to consent to commit ourselves far on the tariff side.

Commercial Correspondence between Edward Grey and Sir Francis Villiers, British Ambassador to Belgium, 27 June 1916, PRO, CAB 37/150.

CONFIDENTIAL

Sir Edward Grey to Sir F. Villiers.

(No. 51. Commercial.)

Foreign Office, June 27, 1916.

Sir,
    BARON DE BROQUEVILLE came to see me with the Belgian Minister.
    He spoke of the necessity of Belgium being rich and strong after the war to protect her own territory, but commercially the Germans would again, after the war, acquire great hold in Belgium as they had done before the war unless the Allies took special measures to favour Belgian trade. He spoke with considerable force on the danger of the Germans getting commercial control and thereby political influence in Belgium in a few years, and on the need for the Allies to avert this danger.
    In reply to questions from me he said that individual cases, such as that of Belgium, had not been discussed at the Paris Conference, but he had had conversation with Lord Crewe and Mr. Bonar Law, and had found them sympathetic.
    I asked him whether he had any precise proposals to make, and he suggested that, if Belgium were put on the same footing with regard to British trade as British dominions and colonies, this would be regarded as something satisfactory. He said that he had spoken to Mr. Hughes, and Mr. Hughes had said to him: 'Expel all German capitalists from Belgium, and Australia will do everything for you.'
    I did not discuss this proposition, but said that the Cabinet had delegated to Lord Crewe and Mr. Bonar Law authority to deal with the economic question at the Paris Conference, and that, if proposals were to be made arising out of that Conference, they would probably be brought before the Cabinet by Lord Crewe and Mr. Bonar Law.

I am, &c.

E. GREY.

Report on the American Press's Response to the Paris Conference, June 1916, PRO, CAB 37/152.

(2.) The Paris Conference.

Comment on the Economic Conference of the Allies is considerable in amount though restrained in tone. Both friendly and hostile journals are at pains to prove that the resolutions taken by the Conference are not only vague in intention but are impossible to carry out in fact.

The state of public opinion in America is so disturbed over the Conference proposals that it would be well for our Government to make a specific statement that the United States would not suffer in any action taken by the Allies against Germany and Austria. There is an evident alarm, which will become a danger, if there is no further announcement by our Government. No other than a Government statement will do.

Private correspondence from important people who are our friends insists on the seriousness of the situation, and our Government will do well to pay heed to the ill-based warnings or apprehensions, and ease the minds of our American friends.

On the 28th June, for instance, the New York *Times*, in an article entitled 'AFTER THE WAR' declares that:–

'The economic programme of the *Entente* Allies deserves to be added to the catalogue of the illusions of the war. Even the exhausted South would have found breath for another last-ditch struggle if it had been advertised that the North plotted its economic inferiority after the war.'

The article goes on to demonstrate by examples that the conclusion of military struggles has never been followed by the continuance of economic war-measures, and concludes:–

'The erection of a new protection upon the ruins of nations is an idle dream. More trade is the remedy, not less; more natural trade, not a controlled trade.'

The unfriendly *Evening Mail* heads its article 'ETERNAL WAR,' and declares:–

'Those who hope that this war will be the last war, gaze with dismay at plans which lay the basis of certain wars in the future....

Germany is now challenged to fight against a proposed starvation and destruction of half her people, after the war is over....

For belligerents who take these measures to say that they do not desire the destruction of Germany, but only the destruction of 'Prussian militarism,' is to play with words. This programme proposes a dismemberment of the German Empire in a sense more complete than any military success could hope to attain.

Germany now knows she must win the war or face a permanent crippling of her national life.'

The conclusion to which the article leads is as follows:–

'The present neutrals of the world will be stranded in No Man's Land, between the trenches, exposed to the cross fire of both sides and offered the protection of neither.'

On the 28th June the friendly *Evening Post* attempts to defend the resolutions of the Conference by laying stress upon their vagueness.

'The means specified are named as measures to which the Allies 'may have recourse.' As a 'platform' this may evidently mean anything or nothing.'

The *Evening Post* then suggests that the programme 'strikes one rather of mutual aid than of injury to the common enemy.' But it cannot refrain from registering a warning as follows:–

'The mere idea, to be sure, of a contemplated permanent division of the European nations into two groups fronting each other as economic enemies is one that cannot be entertained without deep regret.'

There are two weighty articles on the same subject in the New York *Journal of Commerce*. On the 28th June the *Journal of Commerce* writes on the theme of 'CHERISHING ENMITY AFTER WAR,' and takes the line that the resolutions of the Conference are *prima facie* war measures. It therefore accepts without demur the 'Measures for Duration of the War,' although it remarks in passing that:–

'It may be difficult to reconcile all this with the rights and interests of neutrals and the maintenance of friendly relations with them.'

With regard to the ulterior proposals, however, it declares that:–

'Notwithstanding the presumed ability of the eminent persons who engaged in this Conference, this scheme would prove quite impracticable to maintain in most of its features. It is a matter of national boycott on a huge scale, the effect of which, if it should be effective, could not be confined to enemy countries, and would be calculated to create unfriendliness, if not enmity, in new quarters.'

It concludes as follows:–

'There could hardly be a more effective way of perpetuating enmity, preparing for hostility and alienating friendliness. Nothing could be worse as the result of this war than what is recommended by this Conference at Paris.'

On the 1st July, on the other hand, the *Journal of Commerce* takes Senator Stone to task for his resolution raising the question of the Paris Conference as it affects the United States. It censures such action as premature on the widely accepted ground that:–

'That there will be anything like the scheme proposed at the Paris Conference is a remote possibility, not a probability at all.'

'The Economic War', *War and Peace*, 3:34 (July 1916), p. 158.

WAR AND PEACE

Vol. III. No. 34
July 1916

The Economic War

By Our City Correspondent

TO take too seriously the resolutions of the Economic Conference of the Allies, held in Paris from June 14th to 17th, would probably be a mistake. The delegates were not plenipotentiaries; their recommendations, at once so violent and so vague, are recommendations only. Free Trade England, for instance, was represented by a doubtful Free Trader and two Tariff Reformers; and it remains to be seen how far the recantations of members of the Cabinet have really affected the House of Commons. It is probable that the strength of the realisation in this country of England's real interest in Free Trade has been underrated, as Mr. Chamberlain underrated it. On the other hand, to neglect the danger involved in this propaganda would be the height of folly. All the old protectionist pleas have now behind them not only the anti-German feeling which the Press incites, exaggerates and, to a large extent creates, but also the growing belief in the power of the State, in particular its power to make trade and spread prosperity, which we have learned to a large extent from our enemies, but which is, illogically, held with energy by those very people, and expounded by those very organs, which declare that the war must go on in the economic sphere after it has ceased on the field of battle.

Retaliation is the battle cry of the Conference's unanimous recommendations. The justification of their whole policy is found in their belief 'that agreements are being prepared for this purpose between their enemies which have the obvious object of establishing the domination of the latter over the production and the markets of the whole world and of imposing on other countries an intolerable yoke.' This 'grave peril' causes the representatives of the Allied Governments to endeavour 'to secure for themselves and for the whole of the markets of neutral countries full economic independence and respect for sound commercial practice,' and to organise their economic alliance on a permanent basis. To this end they propose during the war a tightening of the blockade by the complete stoppage of imports to and exports from the Central Powers, and an increased stringency in all legislation governing trading with the enemy, including the sequestration and control of enemy prices. Further, in the transition period, the natural resources of the Allies are to be conserved for their own use, and enemy subjects excluded from 'industries or professions which concern national defence or economic independence' (the latter phrase recurs frequently throughout the document, but a precise definition of what it may mean is nowhere given). The gist of the proposals under this group (*B*) is that most-favoured-nation treatment is not to be granted to any of the enemy Powers 'during a number of years to be fixed by mutual agreement'; on the contrary, a period is to be fixed 'during which the commerce of the enemy Powers shall be submitted to special treatment, and goods originating in their countries subjected either to prohibition or a special *régime* of an effective character.' This 'special *régime*' is apparently extended to shipping. The suggestions under *C* 'Permanent measures' are too vague to be capable of summary. 'Economic independence is, somehow, to be secured for the Allies, by subsidies, bounties, prohibitive duties, temporary or permanent, or by all these methods in combination.'

That the task of achieving 'economic independence' is no light one is admitted by Mr. Hughes himself. Resolutions which propose 'fundamentally to change the trade relations and economic arrangements of 600 millions of the world's inhabitants' are, he says, 'mere empty words unless Great Britain takes immediate steps to give effect to them. The other Allies look to her to lead the way.' Whether they indeed do so is more dubious. The articles published on the Conference by the Paris press have been rather cautious. French manufacturers of silks, hats, etc., are by no means clear as to the advantage to them of Tariff Reform on Mr. Hughes's lines (we do not say Australian lines, for there is a good deal of evidence that Australian opinion, especially labour opinion, is decidedly unfavourable to him). These ideas, on the contrary, according to the *Journal des Débats*, one of the most influential journals in France, 'have rather alarmed the French industrial and commercial groups which are particularly engaged in business relations with Great Britain.' That Italy can, and is prepared to try to, do without German and Austrian trade after the war, few who know the internal conditions of that country will be prepared to believe. The case of Russia is equally clear. What the predominant interests in Russia want is more capital. To attract capital it is quite possible that the high Russian tariff will be raised after the war. The *Daily Chronicle* (May 5th) quoted several representative views expressed by Russian manufacturers and bankers. 'The aims of French or English commercialism have nothing whatever to do with those of Germany, but from a purely economic point of view there is no difference between the two,' says the Petrograd *Bourse Gazette*. Other authorities in Russia have already stated openly that trade with Germany must be resumed immediately after the signing of peace, for Russia is admittedly in want of manufactured goods of all kinds; and it will be a long time before the new industrial policy can provide them. 'Our enemies as well as our friends,' says M. Krestovnikoff, member of the Council of Empire and President of the Moscow Stock Exchange, 'will endeavour to get the most favourable conditions for their imports. We must take care to defend ourselves not only against our enemies, but also against our friends.'

It is thus more than doubtful whether our Allies would really thank us for the prodigious sacrifices we should have to make in the attempt to secure what is so euphemistically called the 'economic independence' of the Allied combination. The assumption that such an independence could be attained is far from established; all the facts of the normal trade relations of Europe go to suggest that it could not, that the attempt to secure it would create such friction as must break up that union on whose permanence the notion of its desirability is based. But is it desirable that Europe should continue, after the war, divided into two camps, whose lines of demarcation perpetuate the sufferings, the bitterness, the waste of the war, and render impossible the inauguration of any system to replace that European anarchy in which Mr. Lowes Dickinson has diagnosed the root cause of the present struggle? To organise an economic war to last after the war, to form part of the permanent machinery of European government, is surely wantonly to abandon every hope, every decent idealism, and to prepare in cold blood for a repetition of the catastrophe.

'The Allies' Economic Combine', *The New Republic*, 7:88 (8 July 1916), pp. 239–40.

The Allies' Economic Combine

AMERICAN commentators are not taking very seriously the reported plans of the Entente Powers for the economic strangulation of Germany after the war. If all the world were in league with the Entente and were willing to pay the cost of keeping Germany impoverished, the project might be feasible. But the countries not involved in the war, including much of the territory most sought after by commercial strategists, will not be easily convinced that they stand to gain through a boycott of Germany. The United States needs Germany as a market for copper, cotton, tobacco and foodstuffs; it needs Germany as a source of supply for an extensive array of manufactures that neither the United States nor any of the Entente Allies can produce so cheaply or so well. Latin America needs Germany as a market for coffee, hides, tobacco, saltpetre, metals, foodstuffs, and it also needs Germany as a source of supply of manufactures. There is nothing that the Entente Allies can offer the United States and Latin America that would fairly compensate them for the losses attending the exclusion of Germany. Nor can the Entente Allies coerce the neutral American nations. They can levy differential duties against our products, but that is a game at which we also can play. In commercial strategy the producer of foodstuffs and raw materials always enjoys an advantage over the producer of manufactures. We should grieve far less over the exclusion of our raw cotton from the markets of the Allies than they would grieve over the exclusion of their cotton fabrics from our markets. For industrial nations to interfere with importation of foodstuffs, beyond the measure needed for encouraging their own production, is to place a handicap upon their export trade. Now, the character of the trade borne eastward across the Atlantic is still prevailingly raw materials and foodstuffs. Even the United States, although now the leading industrial nation, sends to Europe in peace times mainly crude materials, partly manufactured goods, and foodstuffs. The Americas will not discriminate against Germany voluntarily, and they can not be successfully coerced into such a policy.

The Entente Allies are of course free to make arrangements for fostering trade among themselves to the disadvantage of Germany. If these are to involve differential tariff rates against Germany, but most-favored treatment for neutrals, the latter will be given an unreasonably favorable position. The United States will enjoy most favored treatment in both camps. If differential tariff rates are levied against us, we shall of course retaliate and, without intending it, shall be drawn into what would be practically a commercial alliance with Germany. Latin America will find it more advantageous to attach itself to the group of nations including the United States and Germany than to enter upon any exclusive arrangements with the Entente Allies.

The formation of an economic union of the Entente would affect Germany chiefly through forcing her to make new commercial adjustments, establish new markets and find new sources of supply. This would entail serious losses if it had to be undertaken at a time when commercial relations were working smoothly. But we should bear in mind the fact that the German export industries must in any event be built up anew. The German overseas commercial organization, so laboriously constructed in the decade before the war, has completely disintegrated. There is accordingly no scrapping of goodwill involved in the shifting of markets. German industry, too, will be in an extremely flexible state after the war. The labor forces released from the firing line can be set at work on new specifications as readily as on old.

An economic union against Germany would mean practically an economic union against the world. It would be as serious an obstacle to restored prosperity for the Allies as for Germany. Still, the costs would be endurable if the ulterior political effect of such an economic union were certain to be wholesome. This, however, is rather more than uncertain.

The member of the Entente that presents the greatest possibility of commercial exploitation is Russia. Here is a field broad enough to absorb vast quantities of industrial exports. England and France might be pardoned for desiring to reserve this field to themselves. But suppose that they succeeded in doing it. Their gains would appear too patent to be entirely compatible with the rôle of disinterested friends. The Russian nationalist may feel that the feeble industries of his country need tariff defense, but this defense is needed against England, France and Italy as well as against Germany and the United States. Russia will not be content to remain a mere producer of raw materials. The war has taught her the need of a national industry, and those will be her best friends who supply her most cheaply with the machinery she needs and assist her with capital and organization. She can draw heavily upon England and France, but their moral position will be strongest if they demand no exclusive profits.

Russia and the industrial states afford merely one instance of the divergence of economic interest within the Entente. England, Russia, and Japan have divergent interests to reconcile in the trade of China; England, France and Italy in the trade of North Africa. These divergences would become sharply defined if any serious attempt were made to establish commercial union.

The world is not yet ready for extensive economic leagues of the nations. All the lessons of this war point to the desirability of a high degree of national self-sufficiency. It is not safe for one nation to become essentially dependent upon another, no matter how solid the basis of friendship between them may appear to be. Whatever the immediate effect of the war in creating a feeling of economic solidarity, we may be quite certain that the final effect will be a recrudescence of protectionism and economic separatism. From this tendency Germany, as an industrial export nation, may indeed suffer, but only incidentally and along with Great Britain and the United States, equally interested in industrial exportation.

Considered Views of Interdepartmental Committee to Consider Dependence of the British Empire on the United States, October 1916, PRO, CAB 37/158/3.

The Committee considers that this country is at present, and must continue to be, dependent upon the United States for a large proportion of the supplies essential to the conduct of the war. So far as can be foreseen, we shall also henceforward be dependent upon being able to borrow in the United States [...] between one and two-fifths of our total future war expenditure. On the other hand, the effect upon the United States itself of any general restrictions on intercourse with this country would be disastrous. In these circumstances, the Committee has found it impossible to consider the possibility of reprisals in any practical light. They feel that the only probable danger to which we are exposed is the development of a feeling in the United States unfavourable to our loans, and they recommend that every possible step should be taken to prevent the development of such a feeling.

It is obvious, therefore, that in any negotiations with the United States, our present position is extremely weak and must continue to be so unless, and except in so far as, our dependence upon the United States for supplies can be reduced in every way compatible with the efficient conduct of the war.

Confidential Cabinet Report of the Foreign Office on the Interdepartmental Committee to Consider the Dependence of the British Empire on the United States, 31 October 1916, PRO, CAB 37/158/3.

CONFIDENTIAL

I CIRCULATE herewith two memoranda, one embodying the considered views of the Foreign Office on relations with America as recently considered by an interdepartmental conference, and the other a memorandum drawn up in the Foreign Office on the position of the United States from a diplomatic point of view in relation to the resolutions of the Paris Economic Conference and kindred projects. I do not circulate this second memorandum as a considered expression of the opinion of my Department, and I do not press that it should be at once endorsed in all particulars, but it suggests considerations which must be taken into account, and which, in my opinion, it would be disastrous to ignore in any deliberations upon our general economic policy, and especially in determining what assurances it is possible for us to give under the third recommendation of the first memorandum.

Foreign Office, October 30, 1916.

1. The enclosed record of the views arrived at by the Interdepartmental Committee appointed to consider the dependence of the British Empire on the United States raises certain questions on which it is right that the Foreign Office should express an opinion.
2. We have certain controversies with the United States notably regarding the censorship of mails, on which we cannot yield to the United States Government. We have also imposed certain far-reaching restrictions on American trade, and especially on the importation into the United States of raw materials from British sources, which, although not the subject of any immediate controversy except on points of pure detail, are so vital to the maintenance of the blockade that it is of the first importance that they should not be disturbed.
3. The Foreign Office believes that we do not need to yield on any of these points so far as our relations with the United States *Government* are concerned, since the latter do not wish to proceed to extremes, and their only weapons against us are too big for them to use. Even the imposition of embargoes on certain classes of goods, our demand for which threatens to inconvenience important interests in the United States, and might therefore furnish a per-

sonable ground for prohibiting their export from the United States (for instance, wheat and steel), would raise the whole question of commercial relations between the United States and this country. The United States is so dependent upon the British Empire, both as a market for American goods, on which, in present conditions, American prosperity depends, and also as a source of raw materials indispensable to American industries, that it would be, to say the least of it, highly inexpedient for any Government at Washington to raise that question.

4. Consequently, our real danger is irritation of American opinion operating against our loans. This is not a question of our relations with the Government of the United States, but of the feeling of American financial and business interests and of the whole lending public towards us. Irritation in these circles is especially liable to be produced by our censorship and our black list, and above all by apprehensions as to our economic policy after the war. It is true that the more this country borrows from the United States, the more does the latter become our partner in the war, and the less likely is it that Americans will do anything to compromise our success; but on the other hand, as a purely commercial calculation, Americans might well estimate that speedy peace would offer better security for the money they have already invested, than a prolonged war conducted on further American loans.

5. In these circumstances, the Foreign Office makes the following recommendations:–

(1.) No concession should be made to the Government of the United States on any matter of principle. We can, and must, maintain our belligerent measures. If the situation should change for the worse, we might conceivably have to reconsider this position, but at present the best way to prevent such a danger arising is to show a bold front.

(2.) At the same time, the greatest possible consideration, compatible with solid military requirements, should be given to American interests individually in such matters as –

(a.) The censorship, and especially the cable censorship;

(b.) The black list;

(c.) Our coal policy;

(d.) The operation of our trade agreements and guarantees in the United States.

Any standard form of communication that any Department may have for replying to enquiries, such as enquiries relating to missing cables, should be revised where necessary in the direction of greater civility. It is probable that not very much can be done in this direction, but the Foreign

Office will closely examine its own procedure, and would be glad if other Departments could do the same.

(3.) A very early decision should be taken on the extent to which we contemplate applying the principles of the Paris Economic Conference, or other principles on which we have acted during the war, against the United States, at least as far as is necessary to make it possible to give satisfactory assurances, not indeed to the United States Government, but to American business interests.

Foreign Office, October 20, 1916.

Memorandum respecting Commercial Relations with the United States after the War.

1. In connection with the annexed article from the 'New York Tribune.' I should like to raise the whole question of our probable commercial relations with the United States after the war, as bearing upon our present war diplomacy and our future peace policy. It is possible that the war will continue into the year 1918; it is probable that it will not end till the autumn of 1917. These are long periods. We have got to maintain very onerous restrictive measures on American trade – onerous at least to many individuals if not to the country as a whole – in the interests of the blockade so long as the war lasts; and as long as the war lasts we shall in all probability have to maintain the United States as a sure base of supplies for our most essential military and national needs. We cannot do without her. This is the biggest task our diplomacy has to face. And I would suggest this proposition; that our success will depend, above everything, on the prospects of trade development which American business interests believe they can look forward to after the war. If those prospects are bright; if they feel they can rely on considerate treatment from us, whom we have taught them by our war measures to regard, as never before, as the controllers of the world's trade; if they are confident that they will get a 'square deal' from us:– then they will acquiesce in anything necessary to ensure our victory. But if not – if they expect from us, not a 'square,' but a 'raw deal,' – then we cannot guarantee that we can succeed in reconciling the restrictions of our blockade with the preservation of a steady flow of munitions and raw material from the United States and with that general atmosphere of friendliness and confidence necessary to the floating of large loans on a neutral market.

2. The most immediate requirement of foreign policy in America is therefore a decision on our commercial policy towards the United States after the war.

3. Before going any further. I should like to make it clear that I do not propose that we should settle our commercial policy on political grounds with a view to truckling to the United States. If we decide our own policy in our own interests we should be able to get it accepted in the United States. You can nearly always force a card on an American, but in that case you have got to know which card you want to force upon him. I assume, to start with, that, in dealing with a highly Protectionist country like the United States, we must have weapons in our hands to induce them to pursue a proper economic policy towards us. The question I am about to raise is rather whether it is wise to tie our hands in such negotiations with the United States by prior arrangements with other parties.

4. Americans make two different criticisms on the Paris Economic Conference; the one, that it will prolong the warlike situation in Europe after peace and prevent any universal league to prevent war in the future, and the other, that it will affect the United States itself.

5. With the first question I do not propose to deal here; it is the kind of thing that can quite easily be met by our general propaganda. It is the second criticism alone – a severely practical one – which demands more definite action on our part.

6. At present, as a result of interdepartmental discussions, about all we can tell the United States is (1) that the policy of the Paris resolutions is defensive and not offensive and is directed to the assistance of our Allies and not primarily to the boycotting of Germany, and (2) that the treaty and other rights of neutral countries will be scrupulously respected. When boiled down to this, our arguments do not amount to much. Germany has consistently urged, with perfect formal truth, that the Triple Alliance was a defensive and not an offensive Alliance; and as to treaty and other rights of neutral countries, the outstanding feature of the present situation is that the United States are complaining most bitterly about those measures enforced by this country, which are admittedly wholly within our rights. The period when we were disputing with the United States about international law as affecting the blockade is now more or less passed, and even the mails controversy is not the one which excites the United States itself. What excites them is precisely the exercise of our undoubted sovereign rights as expressed in our bunker policy, in our trading with the enemy policy, in our cable censorship, and, to a lesser degree, in our policy of restrictions on imports. Some much more definite account of our policy is therefore needed if we are really to proceed on a practical basis to allay American apprehensions.

7. At present there seem to be three views as to that policy. The first is what I should suppose to be the view of the Government here. On the one hand we have got after the war to help our Allies, to protect ourselves, and to

keep Germany within bounds. We do not intend after the war to offer the facilities of our Empire freely, as in the past, to our possible enemies. On the other hand, we are at the present moment utterly and hopelessly dependent upon the United States for many raw materials and this dependence will continue in peace time, up to a certain point, in respect of such necessaries as steel, copper, and cotton. Our Allies will be in the same position, with the added dependence on American resources resulting from the necessity for reconstruction in the actual war areas. Before the war, the United States took some 300,000,000 dollars of goods a year from the United Kingdom alone, while the six Latin American Republics of Central America, with Colombia and Venezuela, imported nearly 3,000,000*l*, a year of manufactured goods from us as against a little less from the United States and only about 1,500,000*l* from Germany. A remodelling of the United States tariff disadvantageous to us and the tightening of the grip of the United States over the 'zone of the Panama Canal,' where we cannot in the long run combat her influence except by open war, would therefore entail losses on us which we certainly cannot afford after the war. Moreover, if we were to adopt a commercial policy unfavorable to the United States in pursuance of the Paris resolutions, we should run the risk not only of throwing the United States into economic alliance with Germany, but – far more certain and serious – of seeing her break up the European Alliance by separate negotiations with our Allies. It is folly to believe that our Allies will not use the United States to the utmost after the war. What are the signs of the times? More than a year ago Russia was about to place enormous ten-year orders for rolling-stock in the United States, in preference to the Canadian firms who tendered at the same time, because the United States firms were able to give better credit terms. We stopped this, I believe, by refusing to approve the contracts under our financial arrangements with Russia, but the latter will fly from our leading strings to the United States with added eagerness after the war. The Guaranty Trust Company of New York are sending one of the ablest practical economists in America to Petrograd to study Russian conditions, and have told him that they are willing, if necessary, to wait three years for his recommendations, in confidence that Russia will form an inexhaustible field for American enterprise. The National City Bank is pursuing less statesmanlike and more 'get-rich-quick' enquiries in the same field. Instances relating to our other Allies might be multiplied. Moreover, we have an Empire which we hope to consolidate, and Canada better as her present feeling is towards the United States, cannot face a long tariff war with the United States unless the Empire is prepared to 'go the whole hog' and back up the resulting tremendous friction with the United States by force of arms. It would be ludicrous to have a European economic alliance which would force us to secure unanimous approval from our Allies for each step in our commercial relations with the United States. We have had some experience of joint diplomacy as conducted by four Great Powers. To apply such methods to our economic relations with the United States would be to ruin the Empire and the Alliance at the same time. We therefore recognise that we must allot to the United States, in relation to the Paris resolutions, a definite place which will satisfy her, and give both to her and to us that measure of certainty and confidence which is vital to business and no less vital to foreign policy.

8. Further, I presume that the attitude of the Government is that, though we should be able very largely to prevent the United States after the war from trading with Germany by the continued exercise of our powers in respect of bunkers and guarantees covering the importation of British raw materials into the United States, we recognise that the exercise of these powers in times of peace would, in practice, arouse such opposition as to make the policy in the long run fatal to our relations with the United States and with other nations neutral in this war. We can, and very probably should, exercise these powers in a very modified form by the imposition of discriminatory port and coal dues on German vessels and perhaps also neutral vessels chartered by German firms and possibly also by allowing certain British raw materials, vitally necessary to our key industries, to go to the United States only under guarantees against export to Germany so long as Germany remains a distinct military menace. But while reserving our right to enforce such modified measures we may as well make it clear at once, in so far as our relations with neutrals during the war make it advisable to do so, that we shall not use these powers to prevent neutrals trading with Germany as distinct from preventing neutrals using German shipping. We can destroy the carrying trade of a nation, and we have done it frequently in our history, but we cannot destroy its industries.

9. If this is the first view of trade after the war, the second view is that widely entertained in America, and expressed in the annexed article. In thinking of the 'transitional' period after the war Americans are chiefly interested in the question how long it is to last, and whether, during it, our present war measures of rationing and controlling raw materials from British sources after entry into the United States, together with our trading-with-the-enemy policy and our bunker conditions, are to continue to be enforced in any form. In thinking of our *permanent* measures after the war, Americans are especially interested in knowing whether the facilitation of the reciprocal exchange of products among the Allies is going to take the form of a minimum tariff or differential export duties, the advantages of which will not be open to any neutral even in return for reciprocal advantages. Even if

the answer to this is in the negative, they will be quite as much perturbed by the prospect of special transportation facilities such as differential freight rates, shipping subsidies differentiating against trade with neutrals, and a discriminatory bunker policy. First and foremost, Americans are interested to know whether predominating British war power is going to be used in future to make this country not the common carrier of the world, but a jealous controller of the channels of trade. To this feeling are added criticisms of measures taken here, which, without having anything to do with the Paris Economic Conference, are classed by Americans under the same head, such, for instance, as our present policy in many instances of excluding all foreign interests (down even to foreign ownership of any of the shares) from any company formed to take over liquidated German concerns. An instance of this, which has been quoted to me by American business men in the City, is the Mannesmann Tube Company.

It may seem absurd that any such views should be entertained in this crude form, but the absurdity will disappear if we examine a third view, which, if I may generalise from a few conversations, is widely held among business men in this country.

10. This third view is that commercial relations in Europe and the Far East are of far more importance to us than commercial relations with America. It is a platitude that the Russian and Chinese markets are of vastly greater value and potential purchasing power than the sparsely populated markets of South and Central America. Further, it is pointed out that our market in the United States itself is not of great importance, because she will always be a strongly protectionist nation, and will always keep out any of our goods which she does not positively need. There is a sentimental feeling that America does not deserve any consideration from us after the war. Further, there exists a well-founded opinion, frequently expressed by our own representatives in South and Central American that the political influence of the United States on the American continent will always be used for the purpose of definite commercial discrimination against European countries, and especially against us. Consequently, we are advised to 'keep our end up against the United States' in South and Central America by every diplomatic means in our power, basing ourselves on the unpopularity of the United States in Latin America, so long as we can; and when, as must inevitably happen eventually in case of open hostility, the United States opens a tariff war and drives us out of the sphere of the Panama Canal at least, we must just cut our losses (which will not mean any great suffering to us) and compensate ourselves in the more important European and Far Eastern markets, which we can successfully keep the United States out of by the full and untrammelled use of our powers over shipping and over many important raw materials.

11. This third view seems to me to be fatal, but I am afraid that it is rather strong, and that we are drifting as a Government into some sort of acquiescence in it for fear of exciting a controversy or laying ourselves open to the charge of weakness. This hesitation on our part to make it clear that we will not after the war use weapons which we know would he ultimately fatal to us is perhaps strengthened by the rather strong antipathy to American policy in South and Central America, which, if I may say so, characterises the Foreign Office. Most of us would be inclined to agree with the violent view expressed by the late Sir L. Carden, before his departure for Mexico in 1913:–

'The history of the period mentioned[1] shows that the interventions of the United States Government in the domestic affairs of their weaker neighbours has only been affected by force of arms, whether by open war as in the case of Cuba or by presenting or aiding revolutions as in Panama, Nicaragua, Honduras and Mexico. In all these cases British interests have suffered severely through the destruction of property and the interference with trade and industry. Nor can it be shown as such interventions have had any effect which is likely to prove permanent in bringing about improved political conditions or removing the causes which have produced unrest in the past.

Moreover, the United States Government have given repeated proofs that far from loosening the open door in Latin America, they view with jealousy the competition of European nations for the trade of these Republics and all their influence has been and is being directed towards mediating such special advantages for their citizens as will ensure for them in much of time a great preponderance, if not a virtual monopoly, in all matters concerned with finance, commerce or public works.

'Finally, American influence has been rarely, if ever, exerted in favour of the settlement of British claims against the Latin American Governments, on the contrary, in the case of the Dominican, Nicaraguan, Hondurasean, and Guatamalan debts the aim of the United States has been to obtain for their own financiers so privileged a position as would enable them to force other claimants to sell them their credits at rates far lower than those which the debtor Governments were prepared or had actually sanctioned with them, to pay'

12. We should certainly agree with the more moderate statement by Sir C. Mallen in his annual report for 1913 on the subject of the Panama Canal:–

'From a commercial sense, the keenest rivalry and no favour is to be expected for the whole period of American policy so far as trade is concerned is to endeavour to obtain advantages over foreign competitors'

1   i.e., the past twenty-five years.

13. Now, I think that though all this is undoubtedly broadly true, yet Sir L. Carden's statements are exaggerated and are coloured more by a long acquaintance with the minor destructiveness of Central American revolutions and the difficulties of Central American bondholders (which, as distinct from more important bondholder questions in Brazil and South America generally, I have never felt any keen sympathy with) than by any detailed consideration of the really important question of British export trade. I rather doubt whether interventions by the United States in Central America have produced any really detrimental effect on British export trade, although United States exports to those countries have certainly grown rapidly in proportion to exports from Germany or the United Kingdom. While the American control over the Nicaraguan Customs, for instance, is certainly an engine which would drive us out of Nichraguan trade if commercial relations between us and the United States became definitely hostile, there is, I believe, no reason why this should happen if our relations are decently friendly. South and Central America are dependent so entirely upon the British loan market for their capital, and the National City Bank has recently found it so wholly impossible to float Latin American loans in the United States that we may fairly say that we are indispensable to Latin America and can make favourable terms for ourselves in agreement with the United States if our commercial diplomacy in reasonably skilful. The Pan-American Union at Washington has on the whole, been a very honest *general* advertiser in regard to Latin American commerce and it claims, with, I believe, justice, that it answers enquiries from Great Britain and Germany with as much freedom and care as it does enquiries from the United States.
14. To sum up, I would urge that, if the first view set out above is in fact roughly the view of the Government, it should be defined as soon as possible in our own minds by a detailed consideration of our needs in relation to the United States, and that the Foreign Office should be given a line on which it can work for the purpose of securing American acquiescence in the blockade. We must be told what assurances we can, if necessary, give as to the future, and we must be told soon. Before long, also, I believe that we shall find it necessary, in order to keep American opinion in the state necessary to enable us to float our loans there, to arrange something in the nature of a semi-official commercial mission to eliminate the apprehensions now felt throughout the whole of the United States as to our intentions after the war. Otherwise, I venture to prophesy that, if the Republican party does not come into power next March, it will certainly come into power four years hence; and that then, if not before, we shall be faced with an upward revision of the American tariff, providing for retaliatory duties against any nation which does not give the United States most-favoured-nation

treatment. This is the policy already being advocated by the United States Chamber of Commerce. The forces which will ultimately produce this will increasingly during the next twelve months, when we shall be more and more dependent upon American financial assistance, indispose the United States to lend us money or even to acquiesce in the blockade. Moreover, advances will be made to Russia for separate commercial arrangements, and the new-born Paris Economic Alliance will have a coach and four driven through it. We shall find the United States adopting a definite forward policy in China at a time when we can only meet such encroachments by a fatal commercial alliance with Japan. Above all, we shall enormously stimulate the American big navy and shipping programme, and we shall be fools if we believe, as an enormous number of business men in this country do believe, that America cannot man a navy and a merchant marine. We are laying ourselves open to all this by an unpractical desire to keep our hands free while we know with certainty that we must come to a commercial settlement with the United States sooner or later.

15. As I have alluded above to the probable influence of the Republican party towards a higher tariff in the United States, I should like to guard myself against any idea that this country is interested in maintaining the Democratic party in power. There are many reasons outside the scope of this memorandum why this country is not interested in the question which party may be in power in the United States at any one moment. I have merely mentioned the Republican party as a rough political embodiment of the high Protectionist party in America. The case might be put even more strongly by saying that if anything could turn the Democratic party as a whole into a high Protectionist party it would be the fear of what might happen out of the Paris Economic Conference.

16. In conclusion, I would emphasise what I have already said in paragraph 3. I am not trying to make a bogey of America, nor do I want to pursue a soft policy towards her, but I am convinced that if anything will make it necessary for us to pursue a soft policy towards her it would be continued indecision as to what our relations with America are to be. You cannot have a strong policy unless it follows a definite line.

E. P.

October 21, 1916.

Confidential Telegram from Sir Conyngham Greene (British Ambassador to Japan) to Edward Grey (Foreign Minister) regarding Japanese Participation in the Paris Economic Conference, 27 June 1916, PRO, CAB 37/154/7.

CONFIDENTIAL

[163741]

Sir C. Greene to Sir Edward Grey. – (Received August 10.)

(No. 299.)

Sir,   *Tokyo, June* 27, 1916.

WITH reference to my despatch No. 190 of the 1st May relative to the participation of Japan in the Economic Conference of the Allies in Paris. I have the honour to report that the proceedings of that assembly have given rise to a considerable amount of comment in the Japanese press.

In view of the almost complete liberty to live and trade in Japan which enemy subjects have enjoyed since the outbreak of war, it is natural that the resolution of the Conference, designed to prevent subjects of the Allies from engaging in trade with the enemy, should have met with a cool reception here, though the more important newspapers do not absolutely refuse to admit this policy as a measure of war if it should be judged to be necessary.

The suggestion of commercial co-operation among the Allies against the Central Powers after the war is, however, still more distasteful to the Japanese press and is unanimously condemned: and in support of this condemnation stress is laid on the difference between the commercial position of Japan and that of the other members of the Alliance.

The Japanese Government have not yet declared their attitude towards the resolution of the Conference, but, with their knowledge of the character of their compatriots, who regard such questions from a completely selfish point of view, they cannot have failed to perceive that the adoption of such measures would be unpopular, it is, perhaps, in order to silence criticism and prevent the development of an agitation which might embarrass them in their consideration of their policy that, in the communication which they made in publishing the resolutions, they lay some stress on the fact that these were passed only *ad referendum,* and are not binding on the Allied Governments.

The 'Asahi,' in an article, translation of which I have the honour to enclose published on the 17th June, before the nature of the resolutions was known, expresses the opinion that an economic alliance between the Allied Powers would benefit none of them but England, and would be especially disadvantageous to Japan because it would involve the application of a system of preferential tariffs to trade between Great Britain and her colonies, the result of which would be the exclusion of Japanese goods.

The 'Chuwo,' writing on the 19th June, expresses scepticism as to the value of the resolutions, and recommends the Allies to beat their enemies after they have done which there will be no need for economic alliances.

The 'Jiji' deprecates the prohibition to trade with the enemy during the war and the attempt to restrict German commerce afterwards. Translation of this article dated the 29th June, is enclosed.

On the 21st June the 'Chuwo' printed an article by Baron Takahashi, a former Minister of Finance, deprecating any commercial measures against Germany after the war. He had not expected much result from the Conference, which had been, however, useful as a demonstration of the co-operation of the Allied Powers. I have the honour to transmit herewith a summary of this article in translation from the 'Japan Advertiser.'

On the 23rd June the Minister of Finance, in a statement in the 'Kokumin' and her papers, printed out that, in view of the peculiar geographical and political circumstances of Japan, which differentiate her position from that of European countries the Japanese delegates had only attended the Conference on the condition that their Government should be free to accept or reject its resolutions and that, in fact, the Government had not yet considered their attitude.

These observations, which seem harmless enough, nevertheless brought about the suspension of the newspapers in which they appeared by order of the Minister of the Interior.

On the 26th there appeared in the 'Kokumin' a somewhat unconvincing attempt by the Prime Minister to explain this drastic measure, in which his Excellency threw the blame on the suspended papers for failing to consider the effect of the publication of Mr. Taketomi's remarks on public opinion at home and abroad, and admonished the press generally to avoid acting on impulse and indulging in license which will bring about a diminution of its influence.

Translations of Mr. Taketomi's statement and Count Okuma's abmonition are enclosed.

The above has not been the only recent instance of the suspension of newspapers for no apparent reason, and these administrative acts have naturally caused a considerable amount of comment. With respect to the present case, for example, it has been observed that the suspension of newspapers by one Minister for reporting the remarks of another is not a sign of remarkable harmony in the Cabinet. I am, however, dealing with the question of the suspension of the newspapers in a separate despatch.

The 'Cuwo' observed on the 24th June that the real result of the Conference will only become visible when the Government have determined their attitude towards the resolutions. Indeed, until that is determined the Conference has no meaning whatever for Japan.

Finally, I have the honour to transmit a summary of three articles published in the 'Nichi Nichi,' by Professor Kiichi Horie, a doctor of law, on the reaching staff of Keio University, which appear to me to express very fairly the trend of instructed opinion here with regard to this question.

Dr. Horie minimises the importance of Japan's commercial relations with Germany, and exaggerates that of Italy's failure to declare war on Germany, in order to find excuses for not prohibiting trade with the enemy in this country; he complains of the demands which the Allies are making of Japan in the economic sphere: he considers that commercial measures against the Central Powers after the war would benefit no nation but England: he asserts that England's responsibility for the restoration to its original state of the territory ravaged by the enemy is greater than that of the other Allies, alleging as one reason that England induced Belgium and Serbia to join the Allies; he accuses England of restricting her financial assistance to the Allies, and he minimises the results of the Conference, with regard to most of whose resolutions he exhorts Japan to reserve freedom of action.

I have, &c.
CONYNGHAM GREENE

Enclosure 1.

Extract from the 'Asahi' of June 17, 1916.

ECONOMIC CONFERENCE AT PARIS.

DISCUSSING the Conference, the 'Asahi' expresses the opinion that of the Allies Great Britain alone takes up a special position, that is to say, she is seeking to make the Conference the occasion to attain the object of commercial unity throughout the Empire. Public opinion in England is now including in the direction of the principle of preferential tariff rates. Should England propose the application of preferential rates between the colonies and the mother-country at the Conference, the relations between the Powers whose interests are not identical must become still more involved, discussions will grow still more heated, and the Conference may end without any decision being reached.

If by any chance this principle should become the framework of an economic alliance between the Powers the result would be solely to benefit England, and the other Powers, especially Japan, would have to suffer a heavy business sacrifice. This preferential tariff principle not only augments Government receipts; its chief aim is establish commercial unity between the colonies and Great Britain, and to secure victory in commercial competition with other countries. At present Japan's best customers are the United States and China, but Great Britain and the colonies together take more Japanese goods than China, and there is some prospect, in view of the increase of Japanese trade with India and Australia, of the British Empire becoming the principal market for Japanese exports. The application of preferential tariffs between Great Britain and her colonies would therefore greatly embarrass Japan. The tariff question is, of course, one of internal administration, and the increased strength of the British Empire would be a source of rejoicing to her Ally. But, speaking solely with regard to trading interests, there is a fear of Japanese goods being driven out of the British colonies.

Enclosure 2.

Extract from the 'Jiji' of June 20, 1916.

THE object of the resolutions is to apply pressure to the Central Powers; but the premise to this must be the non-existence of Allied trade restrictions. These exist, and have of late become increasingly severe. Even supposing these restrictions on the interchange of commodities between the Allies could be removed it would be difficult absolutely to stop trade between Allied and enemy nations. During war such prohibition must be determined by the criterion of national interests, not merely by temporary sentiment. For instance, though in the relation of enemies Japan has not prohibited trade transactions with German subjects because it would be disadvantageous to us. There are circumstances preventing us keeping step with the other *Entente* Powers on this point. Thus while the principle of prohibition may not be prone to objection, a collision of interests would undoubtedly result if the prohibition were put in effect. Again, it is difficult to understand the treatment of Germany as an enemy even after the war. During hostilities pressure on Germany to expedite their conclusion is in order but to extend present conditions until after the war would conflict with the purpose of restoring peace, and is certainly impolite. It is at any rate precipitate to decide a *post bellum* trade and tariff policy without considering the effect of the exclusion of Germany upon one's own country's economical position. In a word the resolutions of the Conference are difficult to put in practice, and their execution would involve the *Entente* Powers in a clash of interests. The 'Jiji,' however, approves the Conference as an opportunity for an interchange of ideas and a means of strengthening their union.

Enclosure 3.

Extract from the 'Japan Advertiser' of June 22, 1916.

Baron Takahashi's View.

THE 'Chuwo' prints an article by Baron Takahashi in its editorial column on the subject of the Economic Conference in Paris.

Baron Takahashi says that he had not expected much from the Conference. So he is not surprised if the Conference ended abruptly and resulted as reported.

'But was the Conference a useless one? By no means. It was useful in showing the close co-operation among the *Entente* Powers. The object of the clause regarding the prohibition of trade with enemy countries refers to bringing pressure economically upon the enemies just as the *Entente* Powers are doing in war. But that is only during the war. Such an agreement cannot be continued after peace is restored. For instance, Japan would not buy chemicals from other than Germany, because of the difference in price and quality. As for the suggestion made in some quarters that a Customs agreement might be arranged after the war; it is rather an impossibility, to say the least. It was proper that the Paris Conference did not refer to things after the war, and it is improper to criticise the Conference because the decisions made by that body appeared poor and insufficient.'

Enclosure 4.

Extract from the 'Kokumin' of June 23, 1916.

THE Minister of Finance says the participating Governments are free to approve or disapprove the deliberations of the Conference at Paris. At the time of the despatch of the Japanese delegates the Japanese Government, taking into consideration the difficulty of giving effect to the resolutions of the Conference, owing to Japan being differently circumstanced, geographically and politically, from European countries, notes the delegates attend subject to the condition of Japan being able to reserve the matter of giving effect to such resolutions. It is therefore a question whether an intention to approve the resolutions should be expressed or not, and the Government have not yet considered this in any way.

Enclosure 5.

Extract from the 'Kokumin' of June 28, 1916.

Economic Conference and Suppression of Newspapers.

COUNT OKUMA to a newspaper reporter, the 25th June, says:–

The Economic Conference was of course favourably viewed by the Powers in that it draws the relations of the *Entente* closer, and considered an economic policy for dealing with the war. The results of the Conference's deliberations have already been published in the form of resolutions; but the text of those resolutions does not embody the whole case, and the attitude to be taken internationally by Japan still requires study and mature consideration. At this juncture some fragments of conversation by Mr. Taketomi, Minister of Finance, have involved newspapers in trouble, but this must be said to be the fault rather of the latter. When the speaker is a Minister of State journalists must already be aware what effect his utterances will have at home and abroad. They must have fully studied the conditions of international relations. If under the momentary impulse of a spirit of levity, they permit themselves license their influence in the domain of public discussion will come to be questioned.

Enclosure 6.

Extract from the 'Nichi Nichi' of June 24, 25, and 26, 1916.

THE 'Nichi Nichi' published three articles on the resolutions arrived at by the Allied Economic Conference at Paris, contributed by a doctor of law. Kilchi Horie who is on the professorial staff of Keio University.

Dr. Horie states that the prevention of enemy trading has hitherto been considered of the greatest importance as a means of bringing economic pressure to bear on Germany, but he thinks that difficulty will be experienced in enforcing the restrictive measures advocated by the Conference. He instances the procedure adopted with regard to the export of wool and rubber from the British colonies to America and expresses the opinion that it is impossible to prevent such commodities from reaching Germany through neighbouring neutral countries. Great Britain prohibited the export of potassium chloride to America with a view to striking a blow at the German syndicate, but as this chemical is largely used as a fertiliser in the American cotton growing districts, it is doubtful which is the better policy to adopt – that of the cotton spinners, who desire free exportation in order to secure supplies of raw cotton, or that of the State, which desires to stop the exportation of a substance used in the manufacture of ammunition.

Dr. Horie points out that until Italy declares war against Germany it will be impossible completely to realise the Allies' policy of isolating enemy countries in economic matters, and he asks why the Conference did not make some firm arrangement on this point. What will be the advantage of Japan, whose trading relations with enemy countries are very slight, joining in the agreement against enemy trading with Italy's attitude causes deficiences in a policy already difficult to enforce? What does Germany's fighting strength gain from the the fact that a few Germans are carrying on their business here under supervision at so great a distance from their own country. Such actions, which is making an international war resemble a private fight between individuals is a contrary in the sentiments of the Japanese.

In his second article Dr. Horie remarks that if Japan did prohibit enemy trading she would suffer economic loss thereby, and consequently she would have to bring the Allied nations to withdraw their restrictions upon import trade with her. Not only is it very inconsistent for the Allies, to make their necessities an excuse for prohibiting exports and imports and thereby cause loss and inconvenience to Japan, to ask her for economic assistance, but it is making her obligations too heavy to cause her to prohibit enemy trading.

Dr. Horie disapproves of the Allies intention of obstructing the enemy's trade on the restoration of the peace on the ground that it is opposed to the fundamental principles of the freedom of trade. He states that it depends upon the special circumstances of each country whether the proposals for the demand of most favoured nations treatment and similar post bellum measures against the enemy will be profitable or not. Nor is he optimistic of the success of plans to meet the demands of one of the Allied nations with the goods of another to the exclusion of German produce, especially in chemical and industrial products. In other articles it might be possible to substitute British for German goods, but it is doubtful whether the prices to a third country would not be higher than at the time when the goods of both countries were competing for the market. The boycott of German goods would give England a good opportunity to a extend the sale of industrial articles, but none of the other countries would be able to profit. Russia, for instance, would lose the German market for her cereals, and would have to complete with other countries in supplying them to England.

Dr. Horie considers that England's action during the war in forbidding the export abroad of colonial products, and her intention to monopolise the supply of them after the war, from which point of view she is advocating a preferential tariff with her colonies, conflict with the meaning of the resolutions adopted by the Conference to preserve natural resources for the benefit of the Allied countries during the period of recovery after the war.

With regard to the joint responsibility assumed by the Allies for the restoration to its original condition of the territory occupied and laid waste by the enemy. Dr Horie contends that England should naturally render assistance to a much higher degree then the other Allies, as her resources are comparatively large and, far from having suffered occupation of any territory, she has expanded her possessions by the capture of German colonies. Her obligations must further more be recognised as very great in view of the fact that she induced Belgium and Serbia to join the Allies by diplomatic methods. He thinks the England's individual responsibility shoud be far greater than the joint responsibilities of the Allies. She should, moreover, at the present time allow the Allies to make free use of her financial power. Dr Horie regards for England's sake that on the one hand she is now restricting the financial assistance she gives to the Allies, and on the other with regard to the recovery of financial power by the Allied countries after the war she is making the responsibility a joint one instead of taking the principle onesupon her self.

Coming to the desire express by the Allied countries to acquire economic independence of Germany and Austria, Dr. Horie states that the effect of the resolution has been destroyed by the failure of the Conference to discuss the question of a Customs Union, the last method of facilitating the transport of merchandise from one country to another. In a word, the interests of the Allies in fighting Germany and Austria have been identical, but the complicated nature of their economic relations will not allow of a similar unanimity. The Conference which was to investigate various complicated matters has dissolved after issuing various vague resolutions which are unaccompanied by any obligation to put them into practice. Dr Horie saw nothing to justify his original anticipation, that the summoning of the Conference was nothing more than a kind of demonstration against Germany and Austria. As to the attitude which Japan will take up requesting the resolutions, Dr. Horie believes it would be in the interests of the country to reserve freedom of action regarding most of them.

Recommendations of the Economic Conference of the Allies Held at Paris on June 14, 15, 16 and 17, 21 June 1916, House of Commons, Parliamentary Papers, Command 8271.

RECOMMENDATIONS
OF THE
ECONOMIC CONFERENCE OF THE ALLIES
HELD AT PARIS ON JUNE 14, 15, 16, & 17, 1916.

Presented to both Houses of Parliament by Command of His Majesty.

LONDON:
PRINTED UNDER THE AUTHORITY OF HIS MAJESTY'S STATIONERY OFFICE BY HARRISON AND SONS, 45–47, ST. MARTIN'S LANE, W.C.,

PRINTERS IN ORDINARY TO HIS MAJESTY.

To be purchased, either directly or through any Bookseller, from WYMAN AND SONS, LIMITED, 20, BREAMS BUILDINGS, PETTER LANE, E.C., and 28, ABINGDON STREET, S.W., and 54, ST. MARY STREET, CARDIFF; or
H.M. STATIONERY OFFICE (SCOTTISH BEANCH). 23, FORTH STREET, EDINBURGH; or E. POSONBY, LIMITED, 116, GRAFTON STREET, DUBLIN; or from the Agencies in the British Colonies and Dependencies, the United States of America and other Foreign Countries of T. FISHER UNWIN, LIMITED, LONDON, W.C.

1916.

Price One Penny.

I.

The representatives of the Allied Governments have met at Paris under the presidency of M. Clémentel, Minister of Commerce, on June 14, 15, 16 and 17, 1916, for the purpose of fulfilling the mandate given to them by the Paris Conference of March 28, 1916, of giving practical expression to their solidarity of views and interests, and of proposing to their respective Governments the appropriate measures for realising this solidarity.

II.

They declare that after forcing upon them the military contest in spite of all their efforts to avoid the conflict, the Empires of Central Europe are to-day preparing in concert with their Allies, for a contest on the economic plane, which will not only survive the re-establishment of peace, but will at that moment attain its full scope and intensity.

III.

They cannot therefore conceal from themselves that the agreements which are being prepared for this purpose between their enemies have the obvious object of establishing the domination of the latter over the production and the markets of the whole world and of imposing on other countries an intolerable yoke.

In face of so grave a peril the Representatives of the Allied Governments consider that it has become their duty, on grounds of necessary and legitimate defence, to adopt and realise from now onward all the measures requisite on the one hand to secure to themselves and for the whole of the markets of neutral countries full economic independence and respect for sound commercial practice, and on the other hand to facilitate the organisation on a permanent basis of their economic alliance.

For this purpose the Representatives of the Allied Governments have decided to submit for the approval of those Governments the following resolutions:–

A.

MEASURES FOR THE WAR PERIOD.

I.
The laws and regulations prohibiting trading with the enemy shall be brought into accord.

For this purpose:

A. – The Allies will prohibit their own subjects and citizens and all persons residing in their territories from carrying on any trade with:–

1. The inhabitants of enemy countries whatever their nationality.

2. Enemy subjects wherever resident.

3. Persons, firms and companies whose business is controlled wholly or partially by enemy subjects or is subject to enemy influence and whose names are included in a special list.

B. – They will prohibit the importation into their territories of all goods originating in or coming from enemy countries.

C. – They will devise means of establishing a system enabling contracts entered into with enemy subjects and injurious to national interests to be cancelled unconditionally.

II.

Business undertakings owned or operated by enemy subjects in the territories of the Allies will all be sequestrated or placed under control; measures will be taken for the purpose of winding up some of these undertakings and of realising their assets, the proceeds of such realisation remaining sequestrated or under control.

III.

In addition to the export prohibitions which are necessitated by the internal situation of each of the Allied countries, the Allies will complete the measures already taken for the restriction of enemy supplies, both in the mother countries and in the Dominions, Colonies and Protectorates:–

1. By unifying the lists of contraband and of export prohibition, and particularly by prohibiting the export of all commodities declared absolute or conditional contraband;

2. By making the grant of licences for export to neutral countries from which export to enemy territories might take place conditional upon the existence in such countries of control organisations approved by the Allies; or, in the absence of such organisations, upon special guarantees such as the limitation of the quantities exported, supervision by Allied consular officers, etc.

B.

TRANSITORY MEASURES FOR THE PERIOD OF COMMERCIAL, INDUSTRIAL, AGRICULTURAL AND MARITIME RECONSTRUCTION OF THE ALLIED COUNTRIES.

I.

The Allies declare their common determination to ensure the re-establishment of the countries suffering from acts of destruction, spoliation and unjust requisition, and decide to join in devising means to secure the restoration to those countries, as a prior claim, of their raw materials, industrial and agricultural plant, stock and mercantile fleet, or to assist them to re-equip themselves in these respects.

II.

Whereas the war has put an end to all the treaties of commerce between the Allies and the Enemy Powers, and whereas it is of essential importance that, during the period of economic reconstruction which will follow the cessation of hostilities, the liberty of none of the Allies should be hampered by any claim put forward by the Enemy Powers to most-favoured-nation treatment, the Allies agree that the benefit of this treatment shall not be granted to those Powers during a number of years to be fixed by mutual agreement among themselves.

During this number of years the Allies undertake to assure to each other so far as possible compensatory outlets for trade in case consequences detrimental to their commerce result from the application of the undertaking referred to in the preceding paragraph.

III.

The Allies declare themselves agreed to conserve for the Allied countries, before all others, their natural resources during the whole period of commercial, industrial, agricultural and maritime reconstruction, and for this purpose they undertake to establish special arrangements to facilitate the interchange of these resources.

IV.

In order to defend their commerce, their industry, their agriculture and their navigation against economic aggression resulting from dumping or any other mode of unfair competition the Allies decide to fix by agreement a period of time during which the commerce of the enemy powers shall be submitted to special treatment and the goods originating in their countries shall be subjected either to prohibitions or to a special regime of an effective character.

The Allies will determine by agreement through diplomatic channels the special conditions to be imposed during the above-mentioned period on the ships of the enemy powers.

V.

The Allies will devise the measures to be taken jointly or severally for preventing enemy subjects from exercising, in their territories, certain industries or professions which concern national defence or economic independence.

C.

PERMANENT MEASURES OF MUTUAL ASSISTANCE AND COLLABORATION AMONG THE ALLIES.

I.

The Allies decide to take the necessary steps without delay to render themselves independent of the enemy countries in so far as regards the raw materials and manufactures articles essential to the normal development of their economic activities.

These steps should be directed to assuring the independence of the Allies not only so far as concerns their sources of supply, but also as regards their financial, commercial and maritime organisation.

The Allies will adopt the methods which seem to them most suitable for the carrying out of this resolution, according to the nature of the commodities and having regard for the principles which govern their economic policy.

They may, for example, have recourse either to enterprises subsidised, directed or controlled by the Governments themselves, or to the grant of financial assistance for the encouragement of scientific and technical research and the development of national industries and resources; to customs duties or prohibitions of a temporary or permanent character; or to a combination of these different methods.

Whatever may be the methods adopted, the object aimed at by the Allies is to increase production within their territories as a whole to a sufficient extent to enable them to maintain and develop their economic position and independence in relation to enemy countries.

II.

In order to permit the interchange of their products, the Allies undertake to adopt measures for facilitating their mutual trade relations both by the establishment of direct and rapid land and sea transport services at low rates, and by the extension and improvement of postal, telegraphic and other communications.

III.

The Allies undertake to convene a meeting of technical delegates to draw up measures for the assimilation, so far as may be possible, of their laws governing patents, indications of origin and trade marks.

In regard to patents, trade marks and literary and artistic copyright which have come into existence during the war in enemy countries, the Allies will adopt, so far as possible, an identical procedure, to be applied as soon as hostilities cease.

This procedure will be elaborated by the technical delegates of the Allies.

D.

Whereas for the purposes of their common defence against the enemy the Allied Powers have agreed to adopt a common economic policy, on the lines laid down is the Resolutions which have been passed, and whereas it is recognised that the effectiveness of this policy depends absolutely upon these Resolutions being put into operation forthwith, the Representatives of the Allied Governments undertake to recommend their respective Governments to take without delay all the measures, whether temporary or permanent, requisite for giving full and complete effect to this policy forthwith and to communicate to each other the decisions arrived at to attain that object.

BOARD OF TRADE.

21st June, 1916.

A. Stanley 'Economic Desiderata in the Terms of Peace', February 1917, PRO CAB 29/1.

ECONOMIC DESIDERATA IN THE TERMS OF PEACE.

Note by Sir A. Stanley.

THE enclosed memorandum, with reference to the economic desiderata in the terms of peace, was prepared in the Board of Trade some little time ago. I think it desirable to bring it to the attention of the War Cabinet, as representing the first tentative and provisional views of the Board on the assumption of a victory to the Allies, though it is fully recognised that much of its contents must be liable to variation according to the course taken by the war and the circumstances in which it is brought to a close.

January 24, 1917.   A.H.S.

Memorandum by the Board of Trade.

THE following memorandum is based on the hypothesis that the victory of the Allies is complete enough to enable them to secure the acceptance by the Central Powers of all reasonable demands, but that the terms of peace will be arrived at by negotiation, and not merely dictated by the winning side. No provision has been suggested which cannot be explained and supported by argument which should carry conviction to neutrals. On the other hand, no attempt has been made to make all the provisions bilateral, although a reciprocal form has been preferred wherever possible. At the end of the memorandum the modifications which would be necessary in the event, of an inconclusive termination of the war are briefly referred to.

Throughout the memorandum the term 'Central Powers' is used for our enemies, 'Allies' for ourselves and our friends.

2. However complete may be the victory of the Allies, the Board of Trade have no desire to impose terms of peace on the Central Powers inspired by motives of commercial revenge. The permanent crushing of the commercial and industrial power of Germany, even were it practicable, would not be to the eventual advantage of this country, while the attempt to effect it (though doomed to failure) would alienate the good opinion and outrage the moral sense of the civilised world. The suggestions, therefore, which the Board of Trade have to make with regard to the economic provisions of the Treaty of Peace are entirely based on considerations of economic defence, and not of aggression.

3. Most of the economic programme of the Allies outlined in the Paris Resolutions can be carried out by domestic legislation and inter-Ally agreements, and requires no definite stipulations in the Treaty of Peace. The exceptions are noted below. Accordingly the first definite suggestion which the Board of Trade have to make as to the treaty is a negative one, viz., that it should (except as specified hereunder) contain none of the usual provisions of a commercial treaty. As regards the most favoured nation clause, this is definitely laid down in the Paris Resolutions, and the principle is equally applicable to all the other usual stipulations, *e.g.*, those conferring national treatment on shipping, and granting subjects and citizens of both nationalities equal rights as regards the carrying on of commerce and industry.

In order to keep our hands free in the reconstruction period we must firmly refuse to tie them in the Treaty of Peace. This applies equally whether the Allies' victory be complete or incomplete.

4. *Territorial Readjustments.*

The next point which it is desired to emphasise is that in settling territorial changes as the result of the war due weight shall be paid to economic and commercial considerations, and that the transfer of territory shall be accompanied by all possible precautions for the maintenance and improvement of our commercial position. The Board of Trade recognise that in determining transfer of territory, military and political desiderata must often outweigh commercial considerations. They have, however, reason to believe that some at least of our Allies (*e.g.*, France) are very fully alive to the commercial point of view, and it is desirable that we should be at least as alert as they, or the ultimate effects of even a victorious war may be to our detriment. Presumably, the actual distribution of ceded territories among the Allies will not be dealt with in the principal Treaty of Peace, in which the Allies on both sides will presumably figure as a *bloc*. However this may be it is not possible to separate the main treaty from the supplementary inter-Ally conventions which will allocate the spoil and regulate its exploitation.

The following notes on the economic side of territorial changes are probably not exhaustive:—

(a.) *Alsace-Lorraine.* – France will, presumably insist on the cession to her of Alsace-Lorraine in the event of a complete Allied victory. This cession will be very important to us industrially, and its prospect raises questions that will need careful discussion before-hand with the French. One of the most complete German monopolies as regards natural products is potash, of which she produces about a million tons annually, the whole production of the rest of the world being comparatively small. There are two great potash fields: (1) Stassfurt, (2) Alsace. The latter is new and only partly developed, but it is believed to have great possibilities, though at present producing less than one-tenth of the whole German product. Undoubtedly, the transfer of this potash field to the Allies will do much to make them eventually independent of Germany for this essential material. (Another tentative proposal to tide over the interval before the Alsace potash field is fully developed is made below (5 *(c)*), on the assumption that we shall be in a position to claim an indemnity from the enemy.) It is desirable that some arrangement should be arrived at with France in accordance with the Paris Economic Resolutions whereby we and the other Allies shall have access to an adequate share in the products of the Alsace potash field.

The Lorraine ore deposits are also of immense value, and their loss to Germany would be a severe blow to her iron and steel trade.

A memorandum on the economic importance of Alsace-Lorraine is appended (Annex IA). It will be seen that the result of transferring the whole of the ore-producing districts of Lorraine to France would be to halve the German and to double the French resources in respect of iron ore, besides transferring a very large pig-iron industry. Germany, unless beaten to her knees, will, of course, be bound to resist with all her power such a complete reversal of relative economic strength as would result from this transfer, and probably some territorial compromise will be necessary.

In any case, it is of importance for us to discuss with France at an early date the conditions under which an adequate proportion of any iron ore produced in the districts to be transferred can be made available after the war for the needs of British trade.

Besides the above resources there is a large cotton-spinning and weaving industry in Alsace, the latter depending largely on British yarns, and a considerable trade existed before the war in British cotton goods exported to be printed at Mulhausen and the surrounding district and thence re-exported. If Alsace is transferred to France the interests of this trade should be safeguarded, since the French regulations for *admission temporaire* are not nearly so favourable as the German, and, moreover, the French tariff on our yarns is more onerous.

(b.) *The Reconstitution of Serbia*. – Without entering into the thorny racial and religious questions which surround the 'Jugo Slav' problem, the Board of Trade would lay down as a matter of great commercial importance that Serbia should have a sufficient outlet to the sea at a good commercial port. With this means of access there seems a good chance of the United Kingdom replacing the Central Powers (and particularly Austria) in the supply of manufactures to Serbia, but without such a port it is practically certain that Serbia must relapse into dependence on Austria. It seems very doubtful if an outlet on the Adriatic can sufficiently meet the case owing to the lie of the country and the inadequacy of the ports. Serbia's natural outlet is unquestionably the Vardar Valley and Salonica, which derives all its importance as a commercial port from the Serbian 'hinterland.' If, therefore, any opportunity offers to detach Salonica from Greece and hand it over to Serbia there is much to be said for such a course.

With Greece neutral such a transfer could presumably only be arranged as an exchange, but Smyrna ought to be a sufficient compensation. How far such a transaction is possible the Board of Trade are, of course, unable to say.

(c.) *Poland*. – The Board of Trade are not aware whether the Allies have come to any understanding as to the creation of an independent or autonomous Polish State, but in view of the Grand Duke Nicholas's proclamation to the Poles at the beginning of the war, and later published declarations, something of the kind seems inevitable. [...]

A note on the economic position of Russia, Poland is appended (Annex I.x): It will be observed from this note that the severance of Poland from the Russian economic system, even of it were followed by inclusion within the German Zollverein would probably be an immediate gain to British industry. It would probably stimulate the demand for British goods including machinery in Poland itself, while it would of course, put the British textile and other manufacturers in a more equal position to compete with Polish manufacturers in the Russian market, which is at the moment free to the latter. On the other hand, the transfer of Poland to German control would greatly strengthen Germany, both as regards food resources and manufacturing power and ultimately we should probably lose whatever temporary trade advantage would result from such a transfer. No doubt, looking at our trade interests alone, the best thing that could happen would be the constitution of a Polish State economically independent alike of Russia and of German. It would, however be reasonable that for a period of years there should be preferential trade relations between Russia and Poland.

(d) Turkish Dominions – The disposition of the Turkish dominions in the event of the Allies being victorious including the regime applicable to Constantinople and the Dardanelles, has already formed the subject of examination by a Foreign Office Committee which the Board of Trade were represented, and also of negotiation with France and Russia as to which the Board of Trade were consulted. The matter is therefore not dealt with in the present memorandum.

(e) The Disposal of German Overseas Possessions. – This matter is now examined by an Interdepartmental Committee, and it seems sufficient to annex a memorandum and supplementary note prepared in the Board of Trade as to the commercial aspects of the question. (Annex II.)

(f) The Danube Navigation – Russia will probably press for the abolition of the Danube Commission in the Terms of Peace. The interests of British shipping are, however, so overwhelming that, if possible, this claim should be resisted. [...] The best course for British interests would be to continue the Commission without the representation of Germany, Austria, or Turkey.

Secret Report on Economic and Non-Territorial Desiderata, Committee on Terms of Peace, Imperial War Cabinet, 24 April 1917, PRO CAB 29/1.

IMPERIAL WAR CABINET.

REPORT OF COMMITTEE ON TERMS OF PEACE.

(Economic and Non-Territorial Desiderata.)

BY Minute 14 of Meeting 9 of the 12th April, 1917, and Minute 9 of Meeting 10 of the 13th April, 1917, the Imperial War Cabinet appointed a Committee to consider the economic and other non-territorial desiderata in the Terms of Peace.

The Committee was composed as follows:–

Lord Milner (*Chairman*).
Mr. Henderson.
Mr. Walter Long.
Mr. H. A. L. Fisher.
Sir R. Borden.
General Smuts.
Sir Joseph Ward.
Sir Edwin Morris.
Sir J. Meston.
The Maharaja of Bikaner.
Sir Eyre Crowe.
Mr. Thomas Jones (*Secretary*).
Sir Hubert Llewellyn Smith attended on behalf of the Board of Trade.
Mr. E. S. Montagu attended as Vice-Chairman of the Reconstruction Committee.

The Committee held five meetings, and reached the following conclusions, which they now beg to submit to the Imperial War Cabinet:–

1. *Paris Resolutions.*

(a.) The Paris Resolutions do not, under present circumstances, provide any stable basis for the guidance of the British Government with regard to the objects to be aimed at in the negotiations for peace. The attitude of some of the Governments who took part in the Paris Conference, and the entry of the

United States into the war, introduce doubtful and new elements into the situation, and further negotiations between the Allies seem to be necessary, if they are to pursue a common policy towards the Enemy Powers when the time of negotiation arrives.

(b.) Nevertheless, at least one of the principles underlying the Paris Resolutions, namely, that of securing economic freedom for the Allied countries, and resisting attempts on the part of the Enemy Powers to obtain for themselves what is known as most-favoured-nation treatment from any of the Allies, is entirely to be commended. It appears to the Committee that it is out of the question that the British Empire should allow itself to be bound in the Terms of Peace to accord such treatment to our present enemies.

2. *Control of Imperial Resources.*

The Terms of Peace should not contain any condition which would prevent the several Governments of the Empire from carrying out the policy designed to control the natural resources of the Empire with a view to their development and utilisation for essential national purposes.

3. *Removal of Treaties.*

The Terms of Peace should comprise a stipulation for the revival or renewal of such and such only, of the treaties and conventions with Enemy Powers, existing before the War, as may be specifically enumerated.

4. *Indemnities.*

The Committee feel unable to make any precise recommendations as to the extent and nature of the indemnity which we should seek to obtain from the enemy in the negotiations for peace. Obviously our demands must take account of the then existing conditions of the enemy countries, the state of their resources and their ability to pay any indemnity, whether in money or kind. All that seems possible at the present time is to indicate the most desirable form of indemnity and to select, among the many competing claims, for reparation on the part of the Allied Nations, those which are entitled to priority of consideration. An indemnity in kind is probably more practicable and is, in many respects, preferable to any equivalent indemnity in money, although the latter form of indemnity should also be exacted so far as is found feasible. Of indemnities in kind, the most practicable seem to be the cession of:–

(1.) Merchant Shipping;

(2.) Rolling-stock, rails and other material for the rehabilitation of territories devastated by the enemy; and

(3.) Certain natural products, such as potash, of which the enemy countries hold something like a monopoly.

If a supply of the last-mentioned articles form part of the indemnity, it appears necessary that the payment should be spread over a short term of years. This applies equally to any money payment which may be demanded.

The greatest difficulty connected with an indemnity is to determine which are the parties possessing the strongest claim to the benefit of it, having regard to the fact that even all justified claims cannot possibly be satisfied.

In the opinion of the Committee, the case of Belgium is one *sui generis*, and among the invaded countries she stands out as having the strongest title to reparation. Probably the next strongest case is that of France, on account of the terrible and in large measure, wanton devastation of her North-Eastern Departments, and that of Serbia.

The only claim of equal strength with those just enumerated is that of Great Britain and other Allied countries for shipping destroyed in a manner contrary to the hitherto recognised laws of maritime war. It becomes daily more improbable that, even by taking over the whole merchant fleets of the enemy countries, the shipping of the Allies could be replaced in the position in which it stood at the outbreak of war. On the other hand, it is just possible that the mercantile fleets of those countries may suffice to replace losses of Allied merchant ships, which, according to our contention have been sunk contrary to the laws of war. But the attempt to distinguish between ships lawfully and unlawfully sunk presents immense difficulties. If every case has to be gone into by an International Committee it would take many years to dispose of all the questions which must arise. The only practical plan seems to be to fix upon a definite amount of tonnage of suitable kinds which could be transferred to the Allies and distributed between them in proportion to their respective losses.

The consideration of the question of indemnities is complicated by the fact that it is impossible entirely to separate it from the question of territorial readjustments. In the case of France, for instance, the reacquisition of the provinces coded in 1871, especially of the rich iron ore-field of German Lorraine, might be regarded as in itself representing some measure of indemnity for the destruction wrought in her territory by the invading armies.

The Committee had before them a proposal that the surrender of the German Navy should be one of the principal objects to be aimed at in the Treaty of Peace. Doubts were, however, expressed whether such transfer would be of much practical value. The Committee think that the opinion of the Admiralty on this point should be obtained.

5. *Settlement of Private Claims arising out of the War.*

The Committee considered the settlement of the numerous claims and counter claims which may arise between subjects of the Allied States and enemy subjects in respect of private rights affected by the war. This head includes the liquidation of debts, the dealing with property which has been sequestrated, and a complicated group of problems such as rights under patents, trade-marks, copyright, &c. The Committee felt unable to enter into the very technical and detailed discussion which would be necessary before definite proposals could be formulated on these subjects. The question of pre-war indebtedness and property is at present being investigated by a Committee under the Chairmanship of Sir H. Babington Smith. While not wishing to anticipate the conclusions of that body, this Committee are of opinion that it will be necessary to make some general provision for the recovery of money, due to subjects of the Allied countries from enemy subjects, in the Treaty of Peace. It would be unsatisfactory to leave individuals to try to recover debts due to them by legal proceedings in the Courts of enemy countries, even if they did not find themselves barred, as many of them would be, by Statutes of Limitation. Without wishing to commit themselves to a general Resolution on the subject, the Committee are prepared to favour a plan under which each Government would be responsible for collecting the sums ascertained to be due *from* its citizens, and would pay the sums ascertained to be due to its citizens, the balance being settled between the Governments. The scheme should, if possible, apply to the British Empire as a whole, and be concerted with the Allies.

In the course of the discussion a very pronounced opinion was expressed that we should, so far as possible, maintain the position, that action lawfully taken within the Empire under Emergency Acts and Rules with respect to enemy property (including industrial property) should not be questioned after the war.

Whether a similar claim on the part of the enemy could be admitted, must depend upon the character of their action in this respect.

6. *The League of Nations.*

The Committee were deeply impressed with the danger of the complete destruction of civilised society which threatens the world if the recurrence of a war like the present cannot be prevented, and with the necessity of devising means which would tend, at any rate, to diminish the risk of such a calamity. They felt, however, that any too comprehensive or ambitious project to ensure world peace might prove not only impracticable, but harmful. The proposal which seems to promise the best results proceeds along the path of consultation and conference for composing differences which cannot otherwise be adjusted. The Treaty of Peace should provide that none of the parties who are signatories to that treaty should resort to arms against one another without previous submission of their dispute to a Conference of the Powers. The Committee think that the details of such a scheme should be discussed with our Allies, and especially with the United States of America, before the conclusion of the war.

7. *The Freedom of the Seas.*

The Committee briefly reviewed the present position of the controversy popularly known as the 'Freedom of the Seas,' and agreed that no fundamental change in British policy was desirable.

The Committee is indebted for assistance to Lord Robert Cecil, Commander Maxwell Anderson, Mr. H. C. M. Lambert, and Mr. W. A. S. Hewins.

(Signed) MILNER, *Chairman.*

THOMAS JONES, *Secretary.*

2, *Whitehall Gardens, S.W.,*

April 24, 1917.

Memorandum by the Board of Trade on Economic Considerations Affecting the Terms of Peace, November 1918, PRO, CAB 29/1.

MEMORANDUM
BY
THE BOARD OF TRADE
ON
ECONOMIC CONSIDERATIONS AFFECTING THE
TERMS OF PEACE.

BOARD OF TRADE,

November 1918.

Summary of Conclusions in Board of Trade Memorandum on Economic Considerations affecting the Terms of Peace.

Future Trade Relations.

(a.) For a period of at least twelve months from the date of exchange of ratifications all imports from the Central Powers shall be prohibited except under license. (This, being a purely transitory measure of defence, with no aggressive object, but intended to safeguard the essential economic interests of the Allies during the first critical months of reconstruction, is independent of any date of admission of the Central Powers to a League of Nations.)

(b.) Until the expiration of five years from the date of exchange of ratifications or until the date of admission of the Central Powers to full membership of the League of Nations, whichever date is the earlier, none of the Allies without the consent of all the others will make or revive any treaty or arrangement with any of the Central Powers entitling them to most-favoured-nation treatment in matters of trade.

(c.) In any Commercial Treaty that may be entered into with the Central Powers after the above date the Allies to reserve full power to safeguard their essential industries and to counteract any unfair methods of competition.

Supplies during Reconstruction Period.

(a.) Recognising the paramount claims of the devastated districts for the full reconstruction of their industrial life, the Allies consider that the allocation by them of any materials and means of production or transport for the use of the Central Powers must be subordinated to the previous satisfaction of the above claims. Accordingly, no materials or means of production or transport of a kind required either for the actual reconstruction or replacement of factories and plant destroyed or injured by the action of the Central

Powers, or for subsequent use in those factories, should be allocated to the Central Powers until the factories referred to, or their equivalents have, so far as practicable, been restored to or have attained a level of productive capacity not less than the pre-war standard.

> Any deviation from the strict application of this principle must be at the discretion of the Allies, and must be conditional on the prompt fulfilment by the Central Powers of their obligations in respect of restoration.

(b.) Subject to the fulfilment of the above conditions, the Allies will be prepared to entertain applications from the Central Powers for a ration of materials and means of production or transport, having due regard to the prior claims first of the Allies, and next of neutral countries for the reasonable satisfaction of their needs.

Principle of Freedom of Transit.

(a.) A proposition on the following lines to be submitted to the Allies for inclusion in the terms of peace:—

'The High Contracting Parties declare themselves in favour of the principle of freedom of transit for persons, goods, and ships, by land, water, and air, across territories belonging to or controlled by them.

'Accordingly every Contracting State will permit persons, goods, or ships appertaining to any other of the Contracting States, and travelling between two points outside its territories, freely to cross its territories, whether by rail, navigable river, or canal, territorial waters, or air, without subjecting them to any tax or duty in respect of transit, or to any restriction except such as may be necessary for sanitary purposes, and as is imposed equally on its own subjects or citizens, or on national goods or ships. Any charges for the use of any means of conveyance, or for the maintenance or improvement of any waterway, or in respect of any other facilities or services incidental to such transit, shall be equal for the persons, goods, and ships of all the Contracting States, including that across whose territories the transit takes place; and no charges, facilities, or restrictions shall depend directly or indirectly on the nationality or ownership of any ship on which any part of the through journey has been or is to be accomplished.'

(1.) FUTURE TRADE RELATIONS AND INTERCOURSE BETWEEN THE ALLIES AND THE CENTRAL POWERS.

THIS is the most important of all the economic questions affecting the settlement between ourselves and our enemies, because it influences the permanent future trade grouping and mutual relations of the commercial nations of the world. Unfortunately it is also the most controversial, and there cannot be said to be any definite and generally accepted doctrine on the subject, either among the Allies or within the British Empire, or even within the United Kingdom.

It is therefore proposed, in the first place, to attempt to narrow the issue by eliminating those courses which appear to be in conflict with such authoritative declarations and decisions as have already been made on the subject, keeping in mind throughout the bearing of possible alternative on our own trade interests.

On the one hand, prohibition of trade with the Central Powers for an indefinite period after the war, even if qualified by some form of licensing, would be absolutely inconsistent with President Wilson's third point (except on the untenable hypothesis that the Central Powers are to be permanently excluded from the League of Nations); and such a policy will probably not be considered practicable, even if desirable. On the other hand, any proposals for the immediate and unconditional resumption of ordinary trade intercourse, and still more for the mutual grant of most-favoured-nation treatment (with or without reservations) or for special tariff stipulations for the purpose of encouraging mutual trade, would be inconsistent with the policy expressed in the Paris Economic Resolutions of 1916.

It is not necessary here to discuss in detail what degree of validity attaches to these Resolutions. Clearly they have no binding force on the United States, and it would probably be open to His Majesty's Government, without breach of faith towards our Allies, to declare that events that have occurred since 1916, and, notably, the entrance of the United States into the War and the defection of Russia, have so altered the situation that the Resolutions are obsolete. Nevertheless, the Resolutions remain as the most definite pronouncement on record of the view, held (at least, recently) by France, Belgium, and (with some qualifications) by Italy and Japan; as well as by the Government of the United Kingdom, whose representatives, it is to be observed, had the active collaboration of the Prime Minister of Australia and the Canadian Minister of Commerce.

On the 2nd August, 1916, Mr. Asquith, as Prime Minister, stated in the House of Commons that the Resolutions had been adopted by the Government.

In April, 1917, Lord Milner's Committee of the Imperial War Cabinet, which deal with the non-territorial desiderata in the Terms of Peace, reported as follows:–

In view of the above conclusions (especially 1 (b)), and also of the facts that the French Government are believed to attach great importance to the Resolutions, and that some at all events of the Overseas Dominions are also interested in maintaining them, it seems desirable to examine their precise effect with regard to the subject now under consideration, as this has been frequently misunderstood.

A careful examination of these Resolutions shows that –

(a.) The only resolutions which relate to permanent post-war economic relations are C I and II, which impose on the Allies the duty of ensuring their freedom from dependence on their present enemies in respect of 'essential' industries, and of encouraging improved means of transport and communication among themselves.

(b.) The other resolutions contemplate a 'period of time' after the war, during which enemy trade will be definitely penalised (B IV), and a 'number of years' during which the Allies shall abstain from giving any treaty guarantee of 'most-favoured-nation' treatment (B II).

(c.) It should be carefully noted that not one, but two different 'transition' periods are contemplated for the two distinct purposes mentioned above, and the choice of different phrases for these periods in Resolutions B IV and B II was the result of deliberate intention, and not of accident. As the resolutions were passed, both periods were left to be determined later by the Allies; but in the propositions as submitted to the conference (in agreement between the British and French Governments), the periods were fixed at *two* and *five* years respectively, i.e., for *two years* there was to be prohibition or a special tariff, while for *five years* the Allies were to abstain from fettering their freedom by concluding any 'most-favoured-nation' treaty with the Central Powers.

The Board of Trade consider that, in principle, the above resolutions are still sound, and correspond with the needs and interests of British trade. There is, however, need to define the action to be taken under them with greater precision.

We begin with the case of the shorter transitory period contemplated in Resolution B (IV).

As regards this period, there appears to be an important distinction between the steps which should be taken in regard to imports from and exports to the Central Powers. As regards imports, there is no doubt a widespread fear that Germany may pursue an aggressive policy and dump goods on our shores by means of the formidable export organisations which she had elaborated before the war and to which she may have added during the war. How far this fear is justified it is difficult to say, but it is clear that we ought to run no risk of the efforts that have been made during the war to render ourselves independent of enemy sources of supply as regards essential commodities, being frustrated by competition of this character. Quite apart, therefore, from any restrictions we may impose generally on imports from other sources, there is a special reason why imports from the Central Powers should be kept under control, and it is suggested that in the first instance, at any rate, the present prohibition of imports of goods of enemy origin of *all* kinds should continue in force, though it will no doubt be found expedient to admit under licence goods of certain descriptions which we may urgently require. In order to secure the effectiveness of such a prohibition, it would appear necessary that all goods on importation into the United Kingdom, at least from continental neutral countries and possibly from even remoter places, should continue to be accompanied by consular certificates of origin.

As regards exports, on the other hand, it does not appear that it would be practicable after the end of the war to prevent goods reaching the Central Powers unless the export of the same goods to neutral countries were also controlled; and it would seem, therefore, that it would be idle to prohibit the exportation of all articles to the Central Powers. We shall have to rest content with prohibiting the exportation of those articles the control of which is necessary to prevent us from being denuded of foodstuffs and materials of industry or to secure that the wants of our Allies shall take first place. This subject is further dealt with in section (2) of this memorandum.

The foregoing proposals are in accord with the recommendations made by Lord Balfour of Burleigh's Committee on Commercial and Industrial Policy regarding the measures to be adopted during the transitional period. These are as follows:–

The Treatment of Imports from the Present Enemy Countries.

'The present regime, whereby importation of goods of enemy origin is prohibited, should be continued, subject to license in exceptional cases, for a period of at least twelve months after the conclusion of the war, and subsequently for such further period as His Majesty's Government might deem expedient. This prohibition would have to be safeguarded by means of a system of certificates of origin for goods imported from countries, at any rate in Europe, other than the present enemy countries....'

The Control of Exports.

'Any general prohibition of exports to present enemy countries after the war and any continuance of the system of rationing neutral countries are impracticable and inexpedient, but the Paris Resolutions can be carried into effect if a policy of joint control of certain important commodities can be agreed upon between the British Empire and the Allies for the transitional period. Any measures should aim at securing to the British Empire and the Allied countries priority for their requirements and should be applied only to materials which are mainly derived from those countries and will be required by them.'

As regards the period during which imports from the Central Powers should be submitted to special prohibition, it should be noted that the Board of Trade are proposing legislation giving them the power of regulating imports and exports for a period after the war. The Board understand that it is considered unlikely that Parliament would assent to a longer period than twelve months, with of course power to extend; and the discussions at the recent Imperial War Conference showed that Canada and South Africa could not be relied on to enact similar legislation. Accordingly, in any undertaking entered into with our Allies, it is suggested that we should not commit ourselves beyond a minimum period of twelve months to date from the exchange of ratifications.

As regards the longer period (the 'number of years' contemplated in Resolution B (II) during which no treaty guarantee of most-favoured-nation treatment may be given), the situation is affected both by certain legislation recently passed in the United Kingdom and by the prospect of the creation of a League of Nations into which the Central Powers may eventually be admitted.

The legislation referred to consists of 'The Non-Ferrous Metals Act, 1918,' and the banking provision in 'The Trading with the Enemy (Amendment) Act, 1918' Annex 3, p.v), which provide expressly for discrimination against persons and undertakings belonging to, originating in, or associated with, the present Enemy States. The former Act operates for five years after the end of the war, the latter provision for the same five years 'and thereafter until Parliament otherwise determines.'

Both these enactments, therefore, point to five years as the most convenient period to adopt.

On the other hand, it seems clear that admission of Germany into the League of Nations would be incompatible with continued penal discrimination against her trade, and it is therefore suggested that the period of agreed abstention should be until the expiration of five years after the war or until the 'Enemy' State may be admitted to the full privileges of membership of the League of Nations, whichever date may be the earlier.

If Germany were admitted to the League of Nations within five years after the war it would be necessary either to stipulate for a temporary exception in the case of metals and banking business until the full five years are completed, or alternatively to repeal or amend the Acts referred to above. Which of these alternatives should be adopted, if and when the time comes, will naturally depend on conditions which cannot be foreseen at present, and which may well be left open.[1]

It is important to remember that it will be necessary, in order to provide for the continued and permanent independence of our essential industries, that any treaty engagement eventually entered into should expressly reserve the right to adopt any measures necessary to safeguard essential industries, or to counteract direct or indirect bounties or other methods of unfair competition.

1 In any case it would not follow that German participation in metal and banking business must be left uncontrolled, but only that its treatment would have to be assimilated to that accorded to other foreigners.

The question arises what attitude we ought to adopt if some of our Allies, e.g., Italy, declare that they are not prepared to abstain from agreeing to grant most-favoured-nation treatment to Germany as soon as the war is over. It is suggested that, while in that event a general inter-Allied agreement as to positive action is not to be obtained, the case for refusing to consider any proposal to grant most-favoured-nation treatment in the Treaty of Peace is not affected, since that treaty will presumably be a collective one, and no term can be embodied in it on which the Allies disagree. But while the actual terms of peace would not be affected, the post-war economic position would be vitally altered. The result would be that each Allied country would be free after the war to make its own terms with each of the Central Powers as regards economic relations, and the chance of a permanent economic Entente amongst the present Allies would be gravely imperilled. It is even possible that one or more of the weaker Allies might be bribed by attractive offers to enter the economic orbit of the Central Powers.

It is therefore of importance, if possible, to obtain the adherence of the Allies to the principle that for a period of five years, or at least until the Central Powers are fully admitted to the League of Nations, none of the Allies shall make any economic compact with any of them granting them most-favoured-nation treatment without the consent of all the other Allies.

It is believed that such a principle would be in accord with President Wilson's expressed view, and it certainly corresponds to the economic interests of this country.

CONCLUSION.

The Inter-Ally Conference should be asked to assent to the principles –
- (a.) For a period of at least twelve months from the date of exchange of ratifications all imports from the Central Powers shall be prohibited except under licence. (This, being a purely transitory measure of defence, with no aggressive object, but intended to safeguard the essential economic interests of the Allies during the first critical months of reconstruction, is independent of any date of admission of the Central Powers to a League of Nations.)
- (b.) Until the expiration of five years from the date of exchange of ratifications or until the date of admission of the Central Powers* to full membership of the League of Nations whichever date is the earlier, none of the Allies without the consent of all the others will make or revive any treaty or arrangement with any of the Central Powers entitling them to most-favoured-nation treatment in matters of trade.

* The position may conceivably arise of one of the Central Powers being admitted to and another excluded from the League of Nations. Whether in this event full most-favoured-nation treatment could properly be accorded to the Power admitted might depend on its commercial relations with the Power excluded. For example, if Germany and Austria have a Customs alliance, and Austria becomes a member of the League of Nations, but Germany remains outside, she would benefit automatically from any treatment accorded to Austria. The point is a remote one, but should not be neglected.

(c.) In any Commercial Treaty that may be entered into with the Central Powers after the above date the Allies to reserve full power to safeguard their essential industries and to counteract any unfair methods of competition.

It should be particularly noted that the intention of the above paragraph (b) is not merely to defer most-favoured-nation treatment for a fixed period, but to decline until the expiration of that period to enter into any most-favoured-nation agreement.

It would not be fulfilled by inserting a provision in the Treaty of Peace guaranteeing most-favoured-nation treatment at the end of five years (at most). It could only be fulfilled by refusing to insert any provision on the subject in the Treaty, except possibly a promise to reconsider the matter at the end of the period in the light of the behaviour of the Central Powers in the meantime.

Note:– The question of entering into commercial relations with new States formed, as a result of the war, partly or wholly from the body of former enemy States (should any such new States be represented at the Peace Conference) requires separate consideration, and would not necessarily be governed by the above conclusion.

THE SMOOT-HAWLEY TARIFF, 1930

Throughout the latter half of the nineteenth century and the early decades of the twentieth century the United States pursued protectionist policies. The high tariff levels stemmed from many sources: developmental, ideological and political. As a largely agrarian economy in the nineteenth century, the United States had specialized in the export of raw materials and foodstuffs to Europe. Many Americans saw dependence on British and European manufactures as detrimental to national development. American policymakers since Alexander Hamilton at the end of the eighteenth century had argued that a range of policies including a national central bank, state-sponsored infrastructure development and restrictive tariffs were necessary to encourage industrialization and economic development. While economists might have disagreed with his analysis, many voters found themselves in agreement with the succinct argument of Republican campaign literature – apocryphally attributed to Abraham Lincoln – that 'when we buy manufactured goods abroad, we get the goods and the foreigner gets the money. When we buy the manufactured goods at home, we get both the goods and the money.'[1]

The Republican Party – the party in favour of a protective tariff – was the dominant political force in the seventy-two years from the time of the American Civil War through the start of the Great Depression (1861–1933). During that time period, the Republican Party controlled the House of Representatives for forty-eight years, held the presidency for fifty-six years and the Senate for sixty years. All told, for sixty-four of the seventy-two years, the Republicans controlled a minimum of one house of Congress or the presidency. This placed them in a position to promote higher tariffs when they were in complete control (forty years) and limit downward adjustments of tariffs in times when the Democrats controlled either the White House or the Congress. Indeed, during that entire period, it was only for a period of six years (1893–5 and 1913–17) that the free trade Democrats controlled all of the Congress and the presidency simultaneously. Upon regaining control of the executive and legislative branches in 1921, the Republicans soon passed the Fordney-McCumber tariff, which increased tariffs at the expense of income taxes implemented by the Democrats in 1913.

American industries thrived throughout the 1920s, not only those that were sheltered from imports through higher customs duties, but also those which were competitive in foreign markets. The overvaluation of the pound after Britain's return to the gold standard in 1925 further enhanced the position of American exporters as established British producers laboured under severe price pressures. The one sector of the American economy that was distressed in the 'Booming Twenties' was agricultural foodstuffs. Having experienced rapid growth when the First World War drove most European farmers from international markets, American farmers suffered disproportionately after the war as Continental countries reintroduced agricultural tariffs to reinvigorate their rural economies. As the 1928 election campaign neared its climax, the Republican nominee, Herbert Hoover, appealed to traditionally Republican farmers with the pledge that he would ask the Congress to help the agricultural sector through investments in infrastructure and additional tariffs on farm products. Hoover's pledge solidified rural support for the Republicans and he won an overwhelming victory, receiving over 58 per cent of the two-party vote.

The politics of the tariff had once again delivered the White House to the Republican Party, and Hoover soon requested Congressional action on his campaign pledges. The Republican majority was quick to begin work on the legislation, but slow to produce a final bill. The 'limited revision' of the tariff that Hoover had proposed during the election was quickly captured in an extravagant game of log-rolling politics on Capital Hill.[2] Thousands of lobbyists representing hundreds of industries descended on the Congress to press for higher customs duties on their foreign competitors.[3] It was not only farmers and Republicans, but light and labour-intensive industries that supported protection from foreign competition. Many companies involved in heavy industry, especially those firms that were geared towards mass-production – such as Henry Ford's automobile company – were typically successful exporters and tended to oppose tariffs.[4]

As the Smoot-Hawley Bill, increasingly laden with additional special provisions to protect more and more American industries, worked its way through the Congress, foreign governments became ever more attentive to how the provisions would affect their economies. European governments were especially concerned as the entire inter-war system of German reparations payments and Allied debt repayment was based around a combination of access to private American loans for investment and the ability to sell products in the United States to earn foreign exchange. The Wall Street crash and ongoing banking crisis led to a withdrawal of American long-term, counter-cyclical financing of the European economies. The Smoot-Hawley Bill indicated that the United States' international trade policies would be as inward looking as its monetary policies. Democratic opponents of the Smoot-Hawley Act, led by Tennessee Senator Cordell Hull, pointed to the threat of foreign retaliation, but proponents were unmoved.[5] The Democrats remained largely united in opposing Smoot-Hawley, with only a handful of their members in either house of Congress voting for the bloated tariff bill. In contrast, Republicans were almost completely united in support of tariffs, a policy that was, in the words of Joseph Schumpeter, the 'Republican household remedy'.[6]

Additional concerns about foreign retaliation were raised by over 1,000 members of the American Economics Association, who famously wrote an open letter to President Hoover urging him to veto the Smoot-Hawley Bill on the grounds that it would damage the economy, raise prices for consumers, put even more people out of work and invite foreign tariff retaliation against American exports.[7] Hoover disregarded their warning; in any event, public respect for professional economists had receded somewhat with the discipline's failure to provide an explanation for, let alone a way out of, the ongoing depression. One of the prominent signatories of the economists' letter, Professor Irving Fischer of Yale University, had been making headlines in the *New York Times* less than a year previously when he authoritatively gave stocks his enthusiastic endorsement just a few weeks prior to the crash of the New York Stock Exchange in October 1929.[8] Consequently, the academics' professional assessment of public policy and current economic events was taken with a grain of salt.

Foreign governments were quick to complain and then retaliate, many of them pre-emptively. The system of international trade quickly went into a downward spiral, contracting steadily in the months after the passage of the Smoot-Hawley tariff until it reached a nadir in 1933 of less than one-third the volume that had existed at the start of 1929.[9] For protectionists – such as Reed Smoot – these foreign tariffs and the subsequent reduction in world trade vindicated the measures undertaken in the 1930 Tariff Act. In Smoot's view, had the United States not introduced tariffs, foreign surplus production would be 'dumped' into the American marketplace, causing even greater unemployment, further depressing wages and lowering living standards. Britain, which in 1931 still adhered to free-trade policies, had seen its balance of trade deteriorate and its industries come under ferocious attack from foreign competitors.[10] Although many economists then and now attributed Britain's weak balance of payments position to its attempts to remain committed to the gold standard at an overvalued parity, the collapse of Britain's trading position was beyond dispute.

As international trade and the domestic economy both deteriorated, the leaders of the Democratic Party stepped up their criticism of Hoover and the Republicans' management of the domestic economy. The recovery measures and protective legislation, heralded as solutions to the economic downturn, were criticized for their lack of success. Franklin Roosevelt, the Democrats' presidential nominee in 1932, was withering in his criticism of Hoover's limited economic measures. Hoover had responded to criticisms of the shortcomings of Smoot-Hawley dismissively, asserting that 'No tariff bill has ever been enacted or ever will be enacted under the present system that will be perfect'.[11] Roosevelt and the Democrats responded during the 1932 election campaign that Smoot-Hawley lay at the heart of the international depression – in the Democrats' argument, the European countries to whom the United States had loaned great sums of money could only repay those loans if they earned dollars from selling goods to American consumers. The high tariffs imposed by the Smoot-Hawley Act prevented them from doing so, and so the economically-thwarted Europeans' demand for American goods dried up and their governments consequently teetered on the brink of defaulting on their war loans. Both outcomes condemned Hoover and the Republicans first for depriving American industry of markets (and jobs) and second for squandering an important overseas monetary asset.

Although the Democrats who opposed the Smoot-Hawley Act were often ambivalent free traders themselves, the Act entered the mythology of the New Deal as an example of how the feckless economic policies of the Hoover administration had contributed to and exacerbated the Great Depression. The institutional arrangements for passing tariff legislation through Congress, which had encouraged such rampant log-rolling also came in for condemnation. The Reciprocal Trade Agreements Act of 1934 removed the power of Congress to amend trade acts with foreign countries and provided a renewable authority to the President to negotiate trade agreements on behalf of the United States; Congressional oversight of the final agreement was allowed only through an unamendable up-or-down vote on the entire agreement in each House.[12] Coupled with the introduction of most-favoured-nation status into American trade agreements, this greatly facilitated a reduction of trade barriers in the post-war era.

Notes
1. F. W. Taussig, 'Abraham Lincoln on the Tariff: A Myth', *Quarterly Journal of Economics*, 28:4 (1914), pp. 814–20.
2. See Herbert Hoover, Statement Upon Signing the Tariff Bill 1930 into Law, below, pp. 290–3.
3. E. E. Schattschneider, *Politics, Pressures and the Tariff* (New York: Prentice-Hall, 1935).
4. B. Eichengreen, 'The Political Economy of the Smoot-Hawley Tariff', *Research in Economic History*, 12 (1989), pp. 1–43.
5. See Official Protests about Tariff Bill 1930 from Foreign Governments, *Congressional Record*, 9 June 1930, below, pp. 275–89.
6. C. Kindleberger, *The World in Depression, 1929–1939* (1973; Berkeley, CA: University of California Press, 1986), pp. 291–2.
7. See '1,028 Economists Ask Hoover to Veto Pending Tariff Bill', *The New York Times*, 5 May 1930, below, pp. 272–4.
8. 'Fischer Denies Crash is Due,' *New York Times*, 6 September 1929; this article can be found in M. Duckenfield (ed.), *The History of Financial Disasters, 1763–1995*, 3 vols (London: Pickering & Chatto, 2006), vol. 3, pp. 26–7.
9. C. Kindleberger, *The World in Depression*.
10. R. Smoot, 'Our Tariff and the Depression', *Current History*, 35:2 (1931), p. 174.
11. See Herbert Hoover, Statement Upon Signing the Tariff Bill 1930 into Law', below, pp. 290–3
12. A. G. Brown, *Reluctant Partners: A History of Multilateral Trade Cooperation, 1850–2000* (Ann Arbor, MI: University of Michigan Press, 2003), pp. 77–9.

THE SMOOT-HAWLEY TARIFF ACT, 1930

Republican Party Platform of 1928, 12 June 1928, selection on tariff, Herbert Hoover Presidential Library.

Tariff

We reaffirm our belief in the protective tariff as a fundamental and essential principle of the economic life of this nation. While certain provisions of the present law require revision in the light of changes in the world competitive situation since its enactment, the record of the United States since 1922 clearly shows that the fundamental protective principle of the law has been fully justified. It has stimulated the development of our natural resources, provided fuller employment at higher wages through the promotion of industrial activity, assured thereby the continuance of the farmer's major market, and further raised the standards of living and general comfort and well-being of our people. The great expansion in the wealth of our nation during the past fifty years, and particularly in the past decade, could not have been accomplished without a protective tariff system designed to promote the vital interests of all classes.

Nor have these manifest benefits been restricted to any particular section of the country. They are enjoyed throughout the land either directly or indirectly. Their stimulus has been felt in industries, farming sections, trade circles, and communities in every quarter. However, we realize that there are certain industries which cannot now successfully compete with foreign producers because of lower foreign wages and a lower cost of living abroad, and we pledge the next Republican Congress to an examination and where necessary a revision of these schedules to the end that American labor in these industries may again command the home market, may maintain its standard of living, and may count upon steady employment in its accustomed field.

Adherence to that policy is essential for the continued prosperity of the country. Under it the standard of living of the American people has been raised to the highest levels ever known. Its example has been eagerly followed by the rest of the world whose experts have repeatedly reported with approval the relationship of this policy to our prosperity, with the resultant emulation of that example by other nations.

A protective tariff is as vital to American agriculture as it is to American manufacturing. The Republican Party believes that the home market, built up under the protective policy, belongs to the American farmer, and it pledges its support of legislation which will give this market to him to the full extent of his ability to supply it. Agriculture derives large benefits not only directly from the protective duties levied on competitive farm products of foreign origin, but also, indirectly, from the increase in the purchasing power of American workmen employed in industries similarly protected. These benefits extend also to persons engaged in trade, transportation, and other activities.

The Tariff Act of 1922 has justified itself in the expansion of our foreign trade during the past five years. Our domestic exports have increased from 3.8 billions of dollars in 1922 to 4.8 billions in 1927. During the same period imports have increased from 3.1 billions to 4.4 billions. Contrary to the prophesies of its critics, the present tariff law has not hampered the natural growth in the exportation of the products of American agriculture, industry, and mining, nor has it restricted the importation of foreign commodities which this country can utilize without jeopardizing its economic structure.

The United States is the largest customer in the world today. If we were not prosperous and able to buy, the rest of the world also would suffer. It is inconceivable that American labor will ever consent to the abolition of protection which would bring the American standard of living down to the level of that in Europe, or that the American farmer could survive if the enormous consuming power of the people in this country were curtailed and its market at home, if not destroyed, at least seriously impaired.

'Hoover Promises to Call Congress to Act on Farm Aid if December Session Fails', *The New York Times*, 28 October 1928, pp. 1, 27.

HOOVER PROMISES TO CALL CONGRESS TO ACT ON FARM AID IF DECEMBER SESSION FAILS
WOULD AID 1929 CROPS
Quick Action Needed, Nominee Declares, to Save Situation.
OPPOSES DRIFTING POLICY
Statement Calls Agricultural Question the Most Urgent Economic Problem.

FOLLOWS BORAH PROPOSAL

Candidate Sees and Hears Himself in Talking Movie of New York Speech.

Special to The New York Times.

WASHINGTON. Oct. 27. – Herbert Hoover, if elected, will call an extra session of the new Congress for the enactment of legislation in aid of farm relief, he announced today, should the December session of the Sixty-ninth Congress fail to take steps to that end.

That Mr. Hoover was in favor of the action he proposed today was forecast yesterday when Senator Borah, after a conference with the Republican Presidential nominee, stated that an extra session of Congress should be called to deal with agricultural problems if the short session made no move in that direction.

Mr. Hoover's Statement.

The statement in which Mr. Hoover definitely aligned himself with those who are urging an extra session was issued from his personal headquarters in Massachusetts Avenue. On Thursday Mr. Hoover had refused to verify a statement made by Governor McMullen of Nebraska that Mr. Hoover had told him there would be an extra session to consider farm relief legislation.

Mr. Hoover's statement, which was issued in his own name, read:

'The question of a special session of Congress after March 4, in event of the return of the Republican Party, has been under discussion for some time. There are a number of questions, particularly agricultural relief, which urgently require solution and should not be delayed for a whole year. It is our most urgent economic problem.

I should hope it can be dealt with at the regular session this Fall, and thus a special session be avoided. If, however, that cannot be accomplished, I would, if elected, not allow the matter to drift and would of necessity call an extra session so as to secure early constructive action.'

Speculation on Short Term.

Mr. Hoover's reference to possible action at the short or final session of the Sixty-ninth Congress caused speculation in Congressional circles as to the form agricultural relief would take if acted on by the present Congress, which has twice passed the McNary-Haugen bill, each time vetoed by the President.

As the membership has not changed, will it again send the McNary-Haugen measure, with its equalization fee, to the President? This question was heard today in Senate and House Office Building corridors and offices. If this course is not followed, will legislation along lines suggested by Mr. Hoover in his acceptance speech and subsequently amplified in his West Branch speech be enacted?

Adoption again of the McNary-Haugen measure would, it is felt, mean a third Coolidge veto, and the situation would remain as it is at this time. In that event, according to Mr. Hoover's statement, the Seventieth Congress would be called into session soon after he took the oath of office.

The program of farm relief advanced by Mr. Hoover, first at Palo Alto and subsequently at West Branch, Iowa, and Elizabethton, Tenn., included the early completion of an inland waterways system to provide cheaper freight rates to the sea, increased cooperative marketing facilities, a Government-financed farm board to handle crop surpluses and increased tariff protection for farm products.

In the opinion of many Republican leaders, the farm question is likely to decide the election. They maintain that, despite optimistic assertions by Democrats, the situation in the farm States is well in hand and that with one or two exceptions all of them are safe for the Hoover-Curtis ticket.

Ralph E. Williams, National Committeeman for Oregon and Vice Chairman of the Committee, was one of Mr. Hoover's callers today. He told him the Mountain and Pacific States were absolutely safe. Former Representative George Edmund Foss of Illinois, another visitor, was equally optimistic as to the prospects in his State. Mr. Foss, who is a native of Massachusetts, was on his way to campaign for Mr. Hoover in that State.

Herbert Hoover, State of the Union Address, 3 December 1929, Herbert Hoover Presidential Library.

GENERAL ECONOMIC SITUATION

The country has enjoyed a large degree of prosperity and sound progress during the past year with a steady improvement in methods of production and distribution and consequent advancement in standards of living. Progress has, of course, been unequal among industries, and some, such as coal, lumber, leather, and textiles, still lag behind. The long upward trend of fundamental progress, however, gave rise to over-optimism as to profits, which translated itself into a wave of uncontrolled speculation in securities, resulting in the diversion of capital from business to the stock market and the inevitable crash. The natural consequences have been a reduction in the consumption of luxuries and semi-necessities by those who have met with losses, and a number of persons thrown temporarily out of employment. Prices of agricultural products dealt in upon the great markets have been affected in sympathy with the stock crash.

Fortunately, the Federal reserve system had taken measures to strengthen the position against the day when speculation would break, which together with the strong position of the banks has carried the whole credit system through the crisis without impairment. The capital which has been hitherto absorbed in stock-market loans for speculative purposes is now returning to the normal channels of business. There has been no inflation in the prices of commodities; there has been no undue accumulation of goods, and foreign trade has expanded to a magnitude which exerts a steadying influence upon activity in industry and employment.

The sudden threat of unemployment and especially the recollection of the economic consequences of previous crashes under a much less secured financial system created unwarranted pessimism and fear. It was recalled that past storms of similar character had resulted in retrenchment of construction, reduction of wages, and laying off of workers. The natural result was the tendency of business agencies throughout the country to pause in their plans and proposals for continuation and extension of their businesses, and this hesitation unchecked could in itself intensify into a depression with widespread unemployment and suffering.

I have, therefore, instituted systematic, voluntary measures of cooperation with the business institutions and with State and municipal authorities to make certain that fundamental businesses of the country shall continue as usual, that wages and therefore consuming power shall not be reduced, and that a special effort shall be made to expand construction work in order to assist in equalizing other deficits in employment. Due to the enlarged sense of cooperation and responsibility which has grown in the business world during the past few years the response has been remarkable and satisfactory. We have canvassed the Federal Government and instituted measures of prudent expansion in such work that should be helpful, and upon which the different departments will make some early recommendations to Congress.

I am convinced that through these measures we have reestablished confidence. Wages should remain stable. A very large degree of industrial unemployment and suffering which would otherwise have occurred has been prevented. Agricultural prices have reflected the returning confidence. The measures taken must be vigorously pursued until normal conditions are restored.

[...]

THE TARIFF

The special session of Congress was called to expedite the fulfillment of party pledges of agricultural relief and the tariff. The pledge of farm relief has been carried out. At that time I stated the principles upon which I believed action should be taken in respect to the tariff:

'An effective tariff upon agricultural products, that will compensate the farmer's higher costs and higher standards of living, has a dual purpose. Such a tariff not only protects the farmer in our domestic market but it also stimulates him to diversify his crops and to grow products that he could not otherwise produce, and thus lessens his dependence upon exports to foreign markets. The great expansion of production abroad under the conditions I have mentioned renders foreign competition in our export markets increasingly serious. It seems but natural, therefore, that the American farmer, having been greatly handicapped in his foreign market by such competition from the younger expanding countries, should ask that foreign access to our domestic market should be regulated by taking into account the differences in our costs of production.

'In considering the tariff for other industries than agriculture, we find that there have been economic shifts necessitating a readjustment of some of the tariff schedules. Seven years of experience under the tariff bill enacted in 1922 have demonstrated the wisdom of Congress in the enactment of that measure. On the whole it has worked well. In the main our wages have been maintained at high levels; our exports and imports have steadily increased; with some exceptions our manufacturing industries have been prosperous. Nevertheless, economic changes have taken place during that time which have placed certain domestic products at a disadvantage and new industries have come into being, all of which create the necessity for some limited changes in the schedules and in the administrative clauses of the laws as written in 1922.

'It would seem to me that the test of necessity for revision is, in the main, whether there has been a substantial slackening of activity in an industry during the past few years, and a consequent decrease of employment due to insurmountable competition in the products of that industry. It is not as if we were setting up a new basis of protective duties. We did that seven years ago. What we need to remedy now is whatever substantial loss of employment may have resulted from shifts since that time.

'In determining changes in our tariff we must not fail to take into account the broad interests of the country as a whole, and such interests include our trade relations with other countries.'

No condition has arisen in my view to change these principles stated at the opening of the special session. I am firmly of the opinion that their application to the pending revision will give the country the kind of a tariff law it both needs and wants. It would be most helpful if action should be taken at an early moment, more especially at a time when business and agriculture are both cooperating to minimize future uncertainties. It is just that they should know what the rates are to be.

Even a limited revision requires the consideration and readjustment of many items. The exhaustive inquiries and valuable debate from men representative of all parts of the country which is needed to determine the detailed rates must necessarily be accomplished in the Congress. However perfectly this rate structure may be framed at any given time, the shifting of economic forces which inevitably occurs will render changes in some items desirable between the necessarily long intervals of congressional revision. Injustices are bound to develop, such as were experienced by the dairymen, the flaxseed producers, the glass industry, and others, under the 1922 rates. For this reason, I have been most anxious that the broad principle of the flexible tariff as provided in the existing law should be preserved and its delays in action avoided by more expeditious methods of determining the costs of production at home and abroad, with executive authority to promulgate such changes upon recommendation of the Tariff Commission after exhaustive investigation. Changes by the Congress in the isolated items such as those to which I have referred would have been most unlikely both because of the concentrations of oppositions in the country, who could see no advantage to their own industry or State, and because of the difficulty of limiting consideration by the Congress to such isolated cases.

There is no fundamental conflict between the interests of the farmer and the worker. Lowering of the standards of living of either tends to destroy the other. The prosperity of one rests upon the well-being of the other. Nor is there any real conflict between the East and the West or the North and the South in the United States. The complete interlocking of economic dependence, the common striving for social and spiritual progress, our common heritage as Americans, and the infinite web of national sentiment, have created a solidarity in a great people unparalleled in all human history. These invisible bonds should not and can not be shattered by differences of opinion growing out of discussion of a tariff.

'1028 Economists Ask Hoover to Veto Pending Tariff Bill', *The New York Times*, 5 May 1930, p. 1.

1,028 Economists Ask Hoover To Veto Pending Tariff Bill

Professors in 179 Colleges and Other Leaders Assail Rise in Rates as Harmful to Country and Sure to Bring Reprisals.

Special to The New York Times.

WASHINGTON, May 4. – Vigorous opposition to passage of the Hawley-Smoot tariff bill is voiced by 1,028 economists, members of the American Economic Association, in a statement presented to President Hoover, Senator Smoot and Representative Hawley by Dr. Claire Wilcox, associate professor of economics at Swarthmore College, and made public here today. They urge the President to veto the measure if Congress passes it.

Economists from forty-six States and 179 colleges, among them Irving Fisher of Yale, Frank W. Taussig of Harvard, Frank A. Fetter of Princeton, Wesley C. Mitchell of Columbia, J. Laurence Laughlin of the University of Chicago and Willford I. King of New York University join in the statement.

Arguing against increased tariff rates they declare that the pending bill will raise the cost of living and injure the 'majority of our citizens,' that under it the vast majority of farmers would lose and that American export trade in general would suffer.

Asserting that America now faces the problem of unemployment, the economists challenge the contention of high tariff proponents that higher rates will give work to the idle. Employment, they state, cannot be increased by restricting trade, and American industry, in 'the present crisis, might be spared the burden of adjusting itself to higher schedules of duties.'

They urge the administration to give regard to that 'bitterness which a policy of higher tariffs would inevitably inject into our international relations.'

The text of the statement is:

'The undersigned American economists and teachers of economics strongly urge that any measure which provides for a general upward revision of tariff rates be denied passage by Congress, or if passed, be vetoed by the President.

'We are convinced that increased restrictive duties would be a mistake. They would operate, in general, to increase the prices which domestic consumers would have to pay. By raising prices they would encourage concerns with higher costs to undertake production, thus compelling the consumer to subsidize waste and inefficiency in industry.

'At the same time they would force him to pay higher rates of profit to established firms which enjoyed lower production costs. A higher level of duties, such as is contemplated by the Smoot-Hawley bill, would therefore raise the cost of living and injure the great majority of our citizens.

'Few people could hope to gain from such a change. Miners, construction, transportation and public utility workers, professional people and those employed in banks, hotels, newspaper offices, in the wholesale and retail trades and scores of other occupations would clearly lose, since they produce no products which could be specially favored by tariff barriers.

The vast majority of farmers also would lose. Their cotton, pork, lard and wheat are export crops and are sold in the world market. They have no important competition in the home market. They cannot benefit, therefore, from any tariff which is imposed upon the basic commodities which they produce.

Predict a Double Loss.

They would lose through the increased duties on manufactured goods, however, and in a double fashion. First, as consumers they would have to pay still higher prices for the products, made of textiles, chemicals, iron and steel, which they buy. Second as producers their ability to sell their products would be further restricted by the barriers placed in the way of foreigners who wished to sell manufactured goods to us.

Our export trade, in general, would suffer. Countries cannot permanently buy from us unless they are permitted to sell to us, and the more we restrict the importation of goods from them by means ever higher tariffs, the more we reduce the possibility of our exporting to them.

This applies to such exporting industries as copper, automobiles, agricultural machinery, typewriters and the like fully as much as it does to farming. The difficulties of these industries are likely to be increased still further if we pass a higher tariff.

There are already many evidences that such action would inevitably provoke other countries to pay us back in kind by levying retaliatory duties against our goods. There are few more ironical spectacles than that of the American Government as it seeks, on the one hand, to promote exports through the activity of the Bureau of Foreign and Domestic Commerce, while, on the other hand, by increasing tariffs it makes exportation ever more difficult.

We do not believe that American manufacturers, in general, need higher tariffs. The report of the President's Committee on Recent Economic Changes has shown that industrial efficiency has increased, that costs have fallen, that profits have grown with amazing rapidity since the end of the World War. Already our factories supply our people with over 96 per cent of the manufactured goods which they consume, and our producers look to foreign markets to absorb the increasing output of their machines.

Further barriers to trade will serve them not well, but ill.

Affect on Investments Abroad.

Many of our citizens have invested their money in foreign enterprises. The Department of Commerce has estimated that such investments, entirely aside from the war debts, amounted to between $12,555,000,000 and $14,555,000,000 on Jan. 1, 1929. These investors, too, would suffer if restrictive duties were to be increased, since such action would make it still more difficult for their foreign debtors to pay them the interest due them.

America is now facing the problem of unemployment. The proponents of higher tariffs claim that an increase in rates will give work to the idle. This is not true. We cannot increase employment by restricting trade. American industry, in the present crisis, might well be spared the burden of adjusting itself to higher schedules of duties.

Finally, we would urge our government to consider the bitterness which a policy of higher tariffs would inevitably inject into our international relations. The United States was ably represented at the world economic conference which was held under the auspices of the League of Nations in 1927. This conference adopted a resolution announcing that 'the time has come to put an end to the increase in tariffs and to move in the opposite direction.'

The higher duties proposed in our pending legislation violate the spirit of this agreement and plainly invite other nations to compete with us in raising further barriers to trade. A tariff war does not furnish good soil for the growth of world peace.'

The signers include many economists connected with banks, public utilities, manufacturing industries, merchandising concerns and other business establishments.

The number signing from leading universities are: Columbia 28, New York University 22, Cornell 18, Harvard 25, Yale 14, Princeton 17, Dartmouth 24, Chicago 26, Wisconsin 23, Pennsylvania 13, California 11. Stanford 7, Illinois 14, Northwestern 9, Minnesota 15, Missouri 15.

ORIGINATORS AND FIRST SIGNERS.
PAUL H. DOUGLAS. Professor of Economics, University of Chicago.
IRVING FISHER, Professor of Economics, Yale University.
FRANK D. GRAHAN, Professor of Economics, Princeton University.
ERNEST M. PATTERSON, Professor of Economics, University of Pennsylvania.
HENRY R. SEAGER, Professor of Economics, Columbia University.
FRANK W. TAUSSIG, Professor of Economics, Harvard University.
CLAIR WILCOX, Associate Professor of Economics, Swarthmore College.

Official Protests about Tariff Bill 1930 from Foreign Governments, *Congressional Record*, 71st Congress, 2nd Session, 9 June 1930, pp. 10295–9.

Mr. THOMAS of Oklahoma. Just a moment, until I make my statement. Then the Senator may answer.

Last summer I introduced in the Senate a resolution requesting the Secretary of State to transmit these protests to the Senate for the information of the Congress. When that resolution was presented the distinguished chairman of the committee objected to its consideration and the resolution went over under the rules. A few days thereafter I again called up my resolution, and again the distinguished chairman objected to the consideration of the resolution. The protests were on file in the office of the Secretary of State. He had been requested by the protesting governments to transmit them to the Congress. They were not here. I was asking for the protests, and the chairman of the committee was objecting. Finally the chairman of our committee made the proposition that if the resolution could be so modified as to have the protests come to the Committee on Finance, he would agree to it. Having no other recourse to secure the data, I consented to the modification, and the resolution was amended to request the Secretary of State to transmit to the Finance Committee the protests filed by foreign nations. The resolution was agreed to, and the Secretary of State sent us the protests, and here is the printed volume that contains protests filed at that time.

This volue contains the protests filed up to the date of September 5, 1929. It contains 250 pages. It contains protests from 38 governments. It contains protests against 300 items of this tariff bill. I want to call attention to some of these protests.

Mr. SMOOT. Before the Senator does that, will he yield?

Mr. THOMAS of Oklahoma. I yield.

Mr. SMOOT. Does the Senator refer only to the protests which were sent under the resolution offered by him, or does he refer now also to any protests he invited from the foreign nations, not through the State Department, but from his own office?

Mr. THOMAS of Oklahoma. I refer to the protests filed by the governments of the world against the provisions of the tariff bill, and the protests which were sent to the Secretary of State, the protests which were requested to be transmitted to the Congress, which meant to the House and to the Senate.

Mr. SMOOT. All the protests which the committee have received were printed in a public document. I suppose that is the document to which the Senator is referring now.

Mr. THOMAS of Oklahoma. All the protests that were received up to September 5, 1929, were presumed to have been sent to the Finance Committee.

Mr. SMOOT. Yes.

Mr. THOMAS of Oklahoma. And such protests filed up to that date are presumed to have been printed in this volume and the volume contains the protests, as I have said, of 38 countries, and contains 250 pages.

Most of the protests are against the terms of the tariff bill on the ground that its provisions form an embargo against the importation of their goods into the United States.

Mr. SMOOT. Mr. President, will the Senator yield further.

Mr. THOMAS of Oklahoma. I yield.

Mr. SMOOT. I want to say to the Senate, and to the country as well, that no tariff bill has been passed since I have been here, and I do not think there ever was any time in the history of our country when a tariff bill was passed, when the same countries did not protest, and yet the tariff walls in those countries are higher, in 90 per cent of the cases, than the tariff walls of the United States. The first time I ever knew of a Senator writing direct to the embassies here inviting protests against a tariff bill was in the case of this tariff bill, as the Senator knows.

Mr. THOMAS of Oklahoma. Mr. President, so far as I know, no invitations were ever sent to any foreign government to file protests, but as one Member of the Senate, I was interested in knowing what objections were being urged to the provisions of the tariff bill then being prepared by the Finance Committee.

I hold no brief for any foreign government, but I do hold a brief for my State. I hold a partial brief for the entire United States, and I speak here now not merely as a Member of the Senate from the State of Oklahoma but I presume to speak as one of 96 Senators of the entire United States. I am protesting against this bill, not because it hurts my State but because I believe the bill if enacted will hurt the United States and the people who make up this great country of ours.

Mr. VANDENBERG. Mr. President –

The PRESIDING OFFICER (Mr. Howell in the chair). Does the Senator from Oklahoma yield to the Senator from Michigan?

Mr. THOMAS of Oklahoma. I yield.

Mr. VANDERBERG. I am very anxious to get this information straight, because it seems to me so astounding. Do I understand that the Senator wrote to the embassies in Washington inquiring whether they had any protests to make against the tariff bill?

Mr. THOMAS of Oklahoma. When the bill was passed by the House, I had numerous requests for copies of the bill, and I sent out a copy to each person who requested one, so far as I could get copies, and I asked every person to whom I sent a copy of the bill to advise me as to how it affected him, or his interests, or his country, as the case might be.

Mr. VANDENBERG. I am referring particularly to the foreign embassies at Washington. Do I understand that the Senator wrote the foreign embassies at Washington and asked them whether they had any protests to make against the tariff bill?

Mr. THOMAS of Oklahoma. I did not.

I now call attention to some of the protests on file against this bill. The index to the volume containing such protests lists the following countries: Argentine Republic; Austria; Belgium; Canada; Czechoslovak Republic; Denmark; Dominican Republic; Egypt; Finland; France; Germany; Great Britain; Australia, Bahamas, Bermuda, Dominica, England, India, Scotland, West Indian Colonies; Greece; Guatemala; Hungary; Honduras; Irish Free State; Italy; Japan; Latvia; Mexico; Newfoundland; The Netherlands; Norway; Paraguay; Persia; Portugal; Rumania; Spain; Sweden; Switzerland; Turkey; Union of South Africa; Uruguay.

Since September 5, when this volume was published, foreign nations have kept sending their protests to the United States. I have here a list filed by some 42 governments, the documents having come to the State Department since September 5 of last year. These communications were filed with the Secretary of State, and, although he had been requested by the nations sending them to send them to the Congress, he did not do so at least not to the Senate. They would not be here, I take it, had it not been for the fact that the Senate passed a resolution asking the Secretary of State to send the protests to the Senate for the benefit of its Members. The resolution was passed, the Secretary of State sent the protests to the Senate, and the copies I now exhibit were procured from the office of the Secretary of the Senate. These protests are supplemental to those published in the book to which I have just referred.

I want to call attention to some of the communications filed by some of these foreign governments, to show why they felt called upon to protest the passage of this bill. I have here a protest from the Austrian Legation.

The Austrian Government protests against the passage of the tariff bill and gives the reason for its opposition. The communication is of date March 26, 1930, and as follows:

AUSTRIAN LEGATION,
Washington, D.C., March 26, 1930.

Mr. JOSEPH P. COTTON,
Acting Secretary of State, Washington, D.C.

SIR: Among merchandise exported into the United States from Austria are cigar and cigarette holders made of paper with quill mouthpiece and of mahalebwood (Weichsel). They are cheap articles, the first mentioned mostly used only once, to be thrown away with the stub of cigars or cigarettes.

The paper holders sell for $2.30 a thousand, the Weichsel holders, 65 cents a gross.

As no special provisions are made for this kind of smokers' articles it would come under paragraph 1552, H. R. 2667, and be assessed with a duty of 5 cents apiece besides 60 per cent ad valorem.

In other words, a duty of 5 cents would be levied on a paper cigar holder costing only 0.23 cent apiece. It is obvious that this duty of 2,238 per cent ad valorem, respectively, 1,168 per cent ad valorem (for Weichsel holder) was not intended by the framers of the bill, the less so as there are no similar products manufactured in the United States requiring adequate protection.

This legation believes that a mere oversight might have been responsible for this provision which not merely entails unnecessary hardship to Austrian trade but would, without special reason or benefit, exclude from American markets a foreign specialty not competing with any of the home products.

I have the honor to request you to kindly bring the aforesaid to the attention of the chairmen of the Finance and Ways and Means Committees greatly obliging thereby this legation.

Accept, sir, the renewed assurances of my highest consideration.

  EDGAR PROCHNIK.

If that is a sample of the tax to be levied against the Austrian imports, then, of course, it can well be seen why the Austrian Government would feel called upon to file a protest with the American Congress.

I call attention next to a protest filed by the Czechoslovakian Government, as follows:

  CZECHOSLOVAK LEGATION,
  Washington, May 8, 1930.
His Excellency the Hon. HENRY L. STIMSON,
  Secretary of the Senate, Washington, D. C.
EXCELLENCY: I have the honor to submit to your excellency a memorandum of Czechoslovak industrial and commercial organizations concerning the proposed tariff in the United States, with a special attention to the Czechoslovak shoe manufacturers.

The public opinion in Czechoslovakia is following with keen interest the proceedings on the tariff bill in the Congress of the United States, and the result reached by the conferees committee substantially increasing the rates on almost all articles imported to this country from Czechoslovakia, which, if put into effect, would practically bar many of these from the United States. The result of these fears is expressed in the inclosed memorandum.

Accept, Excellency, the renewed assurances of my highest consideration.

Ferdinand Veverka,
Envoy Extraordinary and Minister Plenipotentiary of the Czechoslovak Republic.

I call attention to a protest filed by the Government of Finland. This protest is against the increases in duties on granite and bread and matches.

I call attention to the protest filed by the German Government. This protest is directed to the United States Congress, and calls attention to the fact that we have treaty relations with Germany, which this tariff bill, if enacted, will violate. They call attention to the treaty of 1923, the one which terminated the war between the United States and Germany, and they also call attention to the treaty of Geneva of 1927. It is the contention of the German Government that if this bill is enacted the terms of each of those treaties, into which we have entered in good faith, will be violated.

I call attention to the protest filed by the Spanish Government. It is of date September 21, 1929. The Spanish Government is protesting against the increased rate on pearls, and in order to show what this bill does, I desire to read as follows:

[Translation]

Royal Spanish Embassy,

Washington, September 21, 1929.

The Hon. Henry L. Stimson,

Secretary of State, Washington, D.C.

Mr. Secretary: Complying with instructions which I have just received from the Government of His Majesty, I have the honor to write to your excellency to present to you the condition of our industry producing and exporting imitation pearls, in case the new entry duties on the said merchandise are given final approval by the Senate of the United States.

Last year when the American commission charged with the study of the bill of tariff increases met, it changed the original bill in the sense of suggesting a fixed duty of 0.02 of a dollar per lineal inch of pearls, besides a 20 per cent ad valorem duty, instead of the original proposal to apply a 60 per cent duty on the assumed value of pearls manufactured in the United States.

The proposed tariff of 2 cents, equivalent to about 0.14 of a peseta, besides 20 per cent ad valorem, equivalent to one-half centimo (0.01 of a peseta), would mean a total charge of 14½ centimos, or a duty of about 600 per cent on the price of origin while the still existing tariff applies 60 per cent on the value or origin or 1½ centimos per inch of said article. From the foregoing it is understood that under the proposed tariff it would be impossible to import foreign pearls into the United States.

La Industría Española de Perlas de Imitactión, S. A., has four factories at Barcelona, Palma de Mallorca, Manacor, and Felanitz, giving work to some 12,000 workers, and of its total production more than 60 per cent is exported to the United States.

If a new increase in duties should be made in the United States in the manner anticipated, the Industría Española de Perlas de Imitación would be forced to reduce its production and personnel by at least half of its present figure.

In view of this situation the Government of His Majesty wishes to make it clear to the Government of the United States and to its Tariff Commission that the disproportionate increase provided for the said article would cause a very serious crisis for our manufacturers, with the consequent dismissal of 6,000 persons now employed in the manufacture of pearls in Spain.

How much more desirable would a fairer treatment of this merchandise be, inasmuch as the production of imitation pearls in the United States is very small in comparison with the enormous market for this product in the United States.

For the above reasons the Government of His Majesty hopes that the Tariff Commission and the Senate will maintain the type of tariff in force or will accord better treatment to this product than the new duties anticipated.

I avail myself of the opportunity, etc.

MARIANO AMOEDO.

I call attention to a protest filed by Switzerland. This communication is typical of the protests filed by the other nations, and I think the protest filed by the Swiss Government clearly connects the protests with the business relations of the United States. The Swiss Republic raises produce to supply her people with food for only 50 days each year. The Swiss nation must import food supplies to feed their own people for more than 315 days out of each year.

The Swiss Republic must gets its food supplies from the nations with which it trades. Heretofore they have been trading with the United States. Their watch manufacturers sell their products here, and likewise the Swiss lace industry sells its products to the United States. A very large percentage of the watches made in the Swiss Republic come to the United States. A very large percentage of the lace work and the handerchiefs made by the Swiss people come to the United States, and if this bill shall be enacted, the tariff rates will be so high against the Swiss watches, against Swiss laces, and against Swiss handkerchiefs that they no longer could sell them in the United States, and when a new market is found for their products, if such can be found, the Swiss people will likewise find a new source of food supplies, and thus will the American farmers be injured.

I contend that this bill does raise the rates on the Swiss watch and clock industry to such an extent as to bring about a virtual embargo against importations of their product. I make the same claim in regard to laces and Swiss handkerchiefs. If that is true, this bill will affect the producers of food supplies in the United States; it will affect the farmers who raise wheat; it will affect the farmers who produce meat and the other food supplies which heretofore have been shipped to Switzerland.

I could go through this list of 42 nations and show that the protests are all of the same tenor and to the same effect, that if this bill is enacted it will prevent the respective nations from selling their goods to the United States, and in the event they can not sell their goods here they can not buy here. I contend, Mr. President, that that would seriously interfere with the $10,000,000,000 of foreign trade we now enjoy with the nations of the world.

The Senator from Mississippi spoke about reprisals. I know it has been denied that the enactment of this bill would bring about reprisals. But the preparation and consideration of the bill for a year and a half has already brought about reprisals. Over in Great Britain a new party has been formed for the specific purpose of keeping American goods out of Great Britain. The name of this party is the United Empire Party, and its purpose is to keep out of the British Empire goods made in America.

In Australia already reprisals have been adopted. In Canada reprisals are being considered. In France reprisals have been adopted. Even since the bill reached the conference committee a reprisal threatened by the French Government has been successful in reducing the rate upon laces. I saw an account in a paper not very long ago to the effect that in the town of Calais, which I understand makes a large amount of French laces, a day of prayer, protest, and petition was set aside; and on that day laborers to the number of tens of thousands assembled and marched in protest against the passage of this tariff bill. Immediately thereafter the French Parliament took notice of the petition of the lace workers and proposed to raise the tax on American-made automobiles.

I invite attention to the following cablegram which came from Paris to the effect that a bill proposing to raise the rate on American-made automobiles and automobile parts passed the French Parliament practically unanimously, only 2 votes being cast against it. The cablegram is as follows:

NEW FRENCH TARIFF HITS UNITED STATES AUTO TRADE

Paris – A new and higher French tariff on imported automobiles, aimed especially against motor cars of American manufacture, was approved by the Chamber of Deputies by 475 votes to 2.

The new tariff represents increases ranging from 30 per cent to 60 per cent on present duties. Ad valorem duties, as levied at present, are replaced by duties based upon the weight of cars imported. Under the present tariff the minimum ad valorem duty on tourist cars in 45 per cent.

There was very little criticism in any quarter to-day of the Tardieu government's measure, which strikes a heavy blow at the American automobile industry.

The moment that vote was had in the French Parliament, the information was flashed to America. Among the first ones to get the information were the automobile manufacturers. No sooner did they have the information than the motor magnates of the United States organized for action. They evidently communicated with the conference committee, for at once the rates placed upon French lace were substantially reduced in conference. There is a concrete illustration of a retaliatory measure by the French Parliament which was successful in reducing the tariff on lace.

I exhibit to the Senate a picture presumed to have been taken in Biel, Switzerland. It shows a group protesting against the rates in this bill upon Swiss handkerchiefs, laces, and watches. It is stated in connection with the picture that 15,000 laborers in this one town met in protest against the exorbitant rates proposed to be levied by this act.

I invite attention now briefly to another retaliation which has been effective. I want to explain briefly how retaliation can and has been used as an effective weapon against legislative proposals. A few years ago the shipyards on the Atlantic sea-board took notice of the fact that much boat-building business was going to Germany. They saw that when Americans desired to buy a boat, instead of giving the order to American shipbuilders they gave the orders to Hamburg, Germany.

They saw that a very lucrative business was being done by the Hamburg shipbuilders. The American shipbuilders, not wishing to lose this good business, came down to Washington and asked Congress to give them some protection. At that time – in the Sixty-eighth Congress – no tariff bill was pending, so the shipbuilders went to the House Ways and Means Committee and in connection with the tax reduction bill asked the committee to put an excise tax upon foreign-built boats and yachts.

The Ways and Means Committee, thinking the request reasonable, proceeded to give the shipbuilders on the Atlantic seaboard exactly what they requested. They asked that an annual excise tax of $1 per foot be placed upon boats up to 50 feet in length; a tax of $2 be placed upon boats between 50 and 100 feet in length; and that a tax of $4 be placed upon boats over 100 feet in length. In the absence of a tariff bill and taking advantage of the opportunity they placed the amendment in the tax reduction bill. The Ways and Means Committee reported the amendment and the House passed it and in that form it came to the Senate and the Senate agreed to it, thus placing an excise tax upon foreign-built boats and yachts of from $1 to $4 per foot per year.

It was thought that that tax would stop the practice of Americans going abroad to have their boats built. But, Mr. President, during the ensuing two years' time the American shipbuilders did not secure an additional order for a ship of this class and character. During the Sixty-ninth Congress the shipbuilders came back to Washington when another tax reduction bill was under consideration, and asked that the existing excise tax be doubled. On the 50-foot boats they asked a tax of $2, on the boats between 50 and 100 feet a tax of $4, and on boats of over 100 feet in length a tax of $8; in other words, they asked a doubling of the tax. Again the Ways and Means Committee acceded to the request of the shipbuilders and reported a bill containing such a provision, which was passed. Still this doubled tax gave no protection. Not a single additional order came to the shipbuilders of America.

During the Seventieth Congress the shipbuilders came a third time and advised the Congress, 'You have given us two laws; each time you have increased the tax, but still the business goes abroad. We now want that tax raised 500 per cent. We want the tax on the 50-foot boats raised five times and made $10 a foot. We want the tax on the 100-foot boats raised five times and made $20 a foot. We want the tax on boats over 100 feet raised five times and made $40 a foot.' That was only two years ago. The House of Representatives, upon the recommendation of the Ways and Means Committee, accepted the amendment and added that clause to the then tax reduction bill. The bill came to the Senate and was referred to the Finance Committee.

In the meantime the Hamburg shipbuilders, learning of the proposal to raise the tax upon their boats 500 per cent, of course, did not desire to lose this lucrative business to American interests. They knew that if the provision was agreed to raising the existing excise tax 500 per cent, that thereafter they would get no more business from the United States. They did not want to see that contingency come to pass. They began immediately to try to defeat the legislation, and they found a way. Here is what Hamburg did.

Hamburg is a city as well as a State, just as New York is a city as well as a State. The Hamburg authorities saw on their streets and roads some 5,000 American-built automobiles. Motor cars from the United States, under the Hamburg laws, have to be registered.

The Hamburg shipbuilders were influential in having introduced in the Parliament a proposal to deny registration to American-built automobiles. As soon as this proposal was made the agents of American automobile manufacturers cabled immediately to their principals what was being proposed. Immediately the automobile manufacturers of America came to Washington in an effort to learn the cause of this trouble. They found the trouble to be our proposal to raise the tax upon German-built ships 500 per cent, and that in retaliation the Hamburg authorities proposed to exclude American-built automobiles.

Mr. President, when this issue was joined the motor interests of the United States were so much more powerful than the ship-building interests that the Finance Committee decided to reject immediately the amendment proposed by the House of Representatives. Not only did the Finance Committee proceed to reject that amendment, but recommended that no tax whatever be imposed upon foreign-built boats and yachts, and section 431 of the present revenue act repealed all tax upon foreign-built boats of every kind and character.

There is a practical illustration of a retaliatory measure that was successful. If this bill is passed by the Congress and signed by the President, I predict that the 42 nations which have filed protests will devise some means whereby they can force an immediate reduction of some of these tariff rates.

Mr. President, what does it mean to raise a tariff rate against the products of some foreign country? The higher the Congress raises its tariff wall, the cheaper the goods must be produced abroad if they are to be sold in the American market. The producer abroad must buy his raw material cheaper, and he must pay his wage earners less in order to keep the overhead down, to the end that the goods may be produced at such a cost as to permit of the tax being paid and still compete in price with the goods made in America.

I contend that the high tariff rates of America are responsible for the low wage conditions abroad. In other words, the American protective tariff policy has pauperized the labor of the Old World. In retaliation other nations are now proceeding to establish high tariff duties, are raising their tariff walls, and if this policy is carried on it means only one thing and that is that we must reduce our production costs in order to be able to pay the foreign tariffs and still be able to compete with foreign-made goods.

Therefore if the tariff rates are raised in Great Britain, if they are raised in France, Germany, or Italy, or any place we sell, our factories and our exporters must pay the tariff and to do so they must reduce the production costs of the goods made for export.

From whom does that tariff duty come? I contend that it will come from the producers of the raw materials. I contend that it will come from the wage earners. So that if my analysis is correct, the higher the foreign nations raise their tariff walls, the cheaper we must produce our goods here. In other words, the same rule works both ways. If the high duties of America have pauperized Old World labor, then when the Old World raises their tariff walls the same principle will come back to react against American raw materials and labor, and the high tariff rates imposed by foreign nations will reduce the wages of labor in America to the basis that now prevails abroad.

Mr. President, how do these high rates affect the farmers of the country? How will these high rates in America and the high rates abroad affect the wheat growers, for example, in Nebraska and Kansas? The wheat growers of the United States produce annually something like 200,000,000 bushels of wheat for export purposes. We must sell this surplus wheat abroad, otherwise the $1.05 or $1.06 per bushel we are getting for wheat to-day on the exchanges would probably be 50 or 60 cents. If the tariff rates contained in this bill are raised to such a height that foreign nations can not sell their goods here to get money with which to buy our wheat, then, of course, one of two things must happen: We must destroy our surplus wheat or we must stop the production of wheat over and above what we consume in America.

The same thing is true of automobiles. We produce a very large surplus of automobiles. Unless foreign nations can sell their surplus goods here to get money with which to buy our motor cars, the production of motor cars in the United States must be limited to our local demand.

How do the high tariff rates affect the cotton growers of the South? About 60 per cent of the cotton produced in the United States is exported. Our total cotton production is in the neighborhood of 15,000,000 bales per year, 60 per cent of which is 9,000,000 bales, which represents the quantity of American cotton sold abroad. If we raise our tariff rates so high that foreign nations can not sell their goods here, Mr. President, how can those foreign nations buy the 60 per cent of our cotton crop which we have each year for export? They will not buy the cotton. They will either do without it or they will purchase their supply from some other country where cotton is produced; and at this time it is being produced in northern Africa, in southern Russia, in India, in different places in Europe, in Australia, and in South America. If the nations which have a surplus of goods to sell can not trade with us, they will trade with some other nation with which they can exchange their commodities.

Mr. President, I referred to the automobile business. Not so very long ago I was in Helsingfors, which is the capital of Finland, and which is located north of Russia at one of the far points of the Baltic Sea. Helsingfors is a city of 120,000 people. It is a modern town, well constructed, with paved streets. It looks very much like many American cities, especially when one sees on the streets nothing but American-made motor cars. They are as thick there as they are in cities in the United States of similar population. One sees there the same type of car one sees on the streets of Washington, the moderate-priced car in the main. Foreign-made cars, foreign to America, are just as strange upon the streets of Helsingfors as upon the streets of Washington, and I think one will see more foreign-made cars here than he will see cars not made in America on the streets of that city.

Finland sells us granite, sells us bread, and sells us matches. That country has filed a protest against the pending tariff bill. Mr. President, suppose something should be done to divert the motor demand of Finland to Germany or to France or to Italy or to Great Britain, we would lose that good automobile market, and if their protest shall not be heeded, I prophesy that Finland will find some way to buy its cars from some country other than the United States.

Mr. VANDENBERG. Mr. President, before the Senator leaves the subject of motor cars, will he yield?

The PRESIDING OFFICER. Does the Senator from Oklahoma yield to the Senator from Michigan?

Mr. THOMAS of Oklahoma. I am glad to yield to the Senator from Michigan.

Mr. VANDENBERG. Does not the Senator from Oklahoma agree with me that in so far as the effect upon our ultimate export of automobiles is concerned, the greatest hazard is the further expatriation of American capital and the establishment of American factories with American mass production methods in those foreign countries?

Mr. THOMAS of Oklahoma. I am glad the Senator from Michigan has made that suggestion, and in answer I maintain that the passage of the pending bill will make the further investment of American capital abroad inevitable. The action of Henry Ford is a good illustration. Henry Ford now is reported to have abroad 13 factories making motor cars. Why? The reason is that he can make a car in Great Britain cheaper than he can make it here, and he can sell it there. He can make a motor car in France cheaper than he can make it here, and he can sell it there. Henry Ford is a good business man, and he is pursuing good business tactics from his standpoint in building motor cars abroad, using cheaper material and cheaper labor to make his products.

Just as soon as the pending bill shall pass, those who desire motor cars in Finland, in Germany, in Great Britain, in France, and elsewhere throughout the world, I confidently predict, will proceed to patronize the country which treats them fairly in the matter of tariff rates. I predict that, instead of doing the thing the Senator desires done, the automobile companies in America will establish branches abroad. Only recently the General Motors Co. bought the Oppel factory in Germany.

Mr. VANDENBERG. They did that before the bill was passed by the Senate.

Mr. THOMAS of Oklahoma. But they knew the bill was coming on.

Mr. VANDENBERG. They did not do it simply on that account. The Senator knows very well that the process of European invasion preceded entirely the consideration of the pending tariff bill, and represents a definite, specific policy of American expansion. I am sure he will concede, regardless of tariff controversies, that if that process continues without restraint, sooner or later it will kill all opportunity for American export trade regardless of tariffs.

Mr. THOMAS of Oklahoma. Mr. President, if this bill shall be passed – and for the sake of the argument I concede it will be passed – I predict that in a very short time American motor factories will make a sufficient number of cars to supply America, and no more; that American farmers will raise sufficient wheat to supply America and no more; and that American cotton planters will raise a sufficient amount of cotton to supply America and no more. Already concerns which are supplying America are going abroad to produce, to supply their foreign trade. Take, for illustration, the International Harvester Co. We have free trade in farm implements; there is no tariff on farm machinery; the International Harvester Co. is not afraid of a tariff rate; it has no competition; it is a world-wide monopoly.

Take Mr. Ford again, if you please; he went over to Ireland and built in Ireland a tractor plant for the manufacture of the Fordson tractor. That plant not only supplies the British Isles with tractors but supplies Europe and countries on other continents with tractors; and his surplus he ships back to the United States. The tractors thus brought back come in free; there is no tariff on a Fordson tractor; it is classified as an agricultural implement, and as such it comes in free. Yet 15 per cent of the foreign-made Fordson tractors which thus come to America free of duty have their wheels changed and are placed in use in industry as engines and as various power machines and never see the farm.

Mr. VANDENBERG. Mr. President, if I may suggest one further inquiry, the Senator has at least been proceeding on the theory that tariff reprisals abroad are going to be dangerous. I am submitting to him the thought, if American capital demonstrates its willingness to go abroad, that there is thus provided an impulse to raise foreign tariffs greater than any other incentive that has ever existed, because if an increase in a foreign tariff can shut out the American motor car, and as a result induce the American motor-car manufacturer to go abroad with his factory, it seems to me there is a paramount incentive on the part of the foreign country to put up its rates and thus affect our export trade. The thought I am suggesting to the Senator is that, regardless of our tariff attitude, does he not agree that there is a serious menace and a hazard and danger to American labor and to American prosperity in the expansion of the existing system of the expatriation of American capital?

Mr. THOMAS of Oklahoma. Mr. President, we have been trying for a long time to expand our foreign trade. For example, in the Department of Commerce there is a bureau called the Bureau of Foreign and Domestic Commerce. To maintain that bureau costs our Government about $5,000,000 a year; it has agencies in all the principal countries of the earth; it has something like 600 trained men searching the earth, trying to find markets for the sale of American products, the products of American mines, the products of American factories, and likewise the products of the American farm. Off Pennsylvania Avenue, in Washington, there is now being constructed the largest office building in the world, a building covering something like two blocks, and to cost in the neighborhood of $15,000,000. For what is that building being constructed? In the main it is to house the department and its bureaus which seek to extend American markets, which seek to find a place where American manufacturers can sell more tractors, more motor cars, more radios, more flying machines, and more of the products produced in America.

Mr. President. Our goods now go everywhere, and I give credit to the Department of Commerce for extending our trade throughout the world. One can not go any place without finding American goods. Not so long ago in Russia I saw in one warehouse in Moscow 10,000 bales of American cotton. I asked my guide. 'Whence does this cotton come?' He replied, 'From America.' I asked, 'What point in America?' He replied, 'It is assembled at Houston, Tex., and shipped from Houston, direct to Moscow.' Houston, Tex., is the concentration point for Texas and Oklahoma cotton. While I can not say that Oklahoma cotton was in that warehouse, yet I know it was. There were 10,000 bales of American cotton in Moscow.

Mr. President, go to any city, any trading point in the world, and you will see upon the shelves of the stores there goods made in America. If we are to continue the progress we have made, if our trade is to keep on expanding, as it should, in place of curtailing the markets for American manufactured goods they should be extended. I do not believe they can be extended by placing a higher tariff wall around the United States and making it harder for foreign goods to reach the United States. We can not sell abroad unless the nations across the sea can sell here; and if we raise our tariff wall so high that they can not get here, they can not even see our goods, much less purchase them.

Mr. President, the objections to this bill are, first, that it will add very large sums to the living cost of the people of the United States. No one can tell how much that increased cost is going to be, but it is estimated at a minimum of $1,000,000,000 per annum.

It is stated in many places that if the pending tariff bill shall become a law it will be a declaration of economic warfare against the other nations of the world. It remains to be seen whether or not the challenge will be accepted.

If this bill shall be enacted, it will further embitter our international trade relations; if this bill shall pass it will bring about additional reprisals. I said a moment ago that in Great Britain a party is now being formed to keep American goods out of that country. In South America five or six countries have formed a confederacy to oppose the American tariff bill and American tariff rates. We are aware of the proposal for a United States of Europe, the underlying thought back of which proposal is so to unify the countries of Europe that they may combat the high tariff rates proposed in this bill.

If this bill shall be passed, I predict, Mr. President, that it will bring about very soon a definite proposal for the cancellation of the ten and a half billion dollars of war debts that are now owing to this country. If foreign nations can not sell us their goods, they can not pay the interest on the debt which they owe us; if they can not sell us their goods, they can not pay back the principal, even in 62 years. If this bill shall pass, if it shall do what it is claimed it will do – raise the tariff wall and restrict our foreign trade – it will not be long before there will be a pronounced demand, not only abroad but here at home, that this $10,500,000,000 of funded debt now due the American Government shall be canceled. If that should happen, what is the next thing we may expect? Foreign nations will not be able to pay interest on the private loans made by American investors. They will not be able to pay dividends on the funds invested in factories; and, as a result, much of the money loaned to foreign nations and people will be lost and the debts repudiated.

Mr. President, if this bill passes, if it becomes a law, if it does what it is claimed it will do, and it is generally admitted that it will, I make the further prediction that before very long the United States will be proposing to have an international conference, not upon the limitation of armaments, but rather upon the limitation of tariff rates. We will be the aggressor. We will be the one asking for the conference, and not the foreign nations.

Mr. President, if this bill finally passes, and is approved by the President, it is going to cost many jobs in this country. It will cost many wage-earner's jobs. It will cost many jobs of people who now are conducting their own business. It will, in my judgment, cost many jobs of Members of the House of Representatives; and, in proportion, it will cost the same number of jobs here in the Senate of the United States. If the bill passes and is approved by the President; it will cost another job, and that job will be the Presidency of the United States.

Herbert Hoover, Statement Upon Signing the Tariff Bill 1930 into Law; 15 June 1930, Herbert Hoover Presidential Library.

I shall approve the tariff bill. This legislation has now been under almost continuous consideration by Congress for nearly 15 months. It was undertaken as the result of pledges given by the Republican Party at Kansas City. Its declarations embraced these obligations:

> 'The Republican Party believes that the home market built up under the protective policy belongs to the American farmer, and it pledges its support of legislation which will give this market to him to the full extent of his ability to supply it . . . .
>
> 'There are certain industries which cannot now successfully compete with foreign producers because of lower foreign wages and a lower cost of living abroad, and we pledge the next Republican Congress to an examination and where necessary a revision of these schedules to the end that the American labor in these industries may again command the home market, may maintain its standard of living, and may count upon steady employment in its accustomed field.'

Platform promises must not be empty gestures. In my message of April 16, 1929, to the special session of the Congress I accordingly recommended an increase in agricultural protection; a limited revision of other schedules to take care of the economic changes necessitating increases or decreases since the enactment of the 1922 law, and I further recommended a reorganization both of the Tariff Commission and of the method of executing the flexible provisions.

A statistical estimate of the bill by the Tariff Commission shows that the average duties collected under the 1922 law were about 13.8 percent of the value of all imports, both free and dutiable, while if the new law had been applied it would have increased this percentage to about 16.0 percent. This compares with the average level of the tariff under:

The McKinley law of 23.0%
The Wilson law of 20.9%
The Dingley law of 25.8%
The Payne-Aldrich law of 19.3%
The Fordney-McCumber law of 13.83%

Under the Underwood law of 1913 the amounts were disturbed by war conditions varying 6 percent to 14.8 percent.

The proportion of imports which will be free of duty under the new law is estimated at from 61 to 63 percent. This compares with averages under:

The McKinley law of 52.4%
The Wilson law of 49.4%
The Dingley law of 45.2%
The Payne-Aldrich law of 52.5%
The Fordney-McCumber law of 63.8%

Under the Underwood law of 1913 disturbed conditions varied the free list from 60 percent to 73 percent averaging 66.3 percent.

The increases in tariff are largely directed to the interest of the farmer. Of the increases, it is stated by the Tariff Commission that 93.73 percent are upon products of agricultural origin measured in value, as distinguished from 6.25 percent upon commodities of strictly nonagricultural origin. The average rate upon agricultural raw materials shows an increase from 38.10 percent to 48.92 percent in contrast to dutiable articles of strictly other than agricultural origin which show an average increase of from 31.02 percent to 34.31 percent. Compensatory duties have necessarily been given on products manufactured from agricultural raw materials and protective rates added to these in some instances.

The extent of rate revision as indicated by the Tariff Commission is that in value of the total imports the duties upon approximately 22.5 percent have been increased, and 77.5 percent were untouched or decreased. By number of the dutiable items mentioned in the bill, out of the total of about 3,300, there were about 890 increased, 235 decreased, and 2,170 untouched. The number of items increased was, therefore, 27 percent of all dutiable items, and compares with 83 percent of the number of items which were increased in the 1922 revision.

This tariff law is like all other tariff legislation, whether framed primarily .upon a protective or a revenue basis. It contains many compromises between sectional interests and between different industries. No tariff bill has ever been enacted or ever will be enacted under the present system that will be perfect. A large portion of the items are always adjusted with good judgment, but it is bound to contain some inequalities and inequitable compromises. There are items upon which duties will prove too high and others upon which duties will prove to be too low.

Certainly no President, with his other duties, can pretend to make that exhaustive determination of the complex facts which surround each of those 3,300 items, and which has required the attention of hundreds of men in Congress for nearly a year and a third. That responsibility must rest upon the Congress in a legislative rate revision.

On the administrative side I have insisted, however, that there should be created a new basis for the flexible tariff and it has been incorporated in this law. Thereby the means are established for objective and judicial review of these rates upon principles laid down by the Congress, free from pressures inherent in legislative action. Thus, the outstanding step of this tariff legislation has been the reorganization of the largely inoperative flexible provision of 1922 into a form which should render it possible to secure prompt and scientific adjustment of serious inequities and inequalities which may prove to have been incorporated in the bill.

This new provision has even a larger importance. If a perfect tariff bill were enacted today, the increased rapidity of economic change and the constant shifting of our relations to industries abroad will create a continuous stream of items which would work hardship upon some segment of the American people except for the provision of this relief. Without a workable flexible provision we would require even more frequent congressional tariff revision than during the past. With it the country should be freed from further general revision for many years to come. Congressional revisions are not only disturbing to business but with all their necessary collateral surroundings in lobbies, log rolling, and the activities of group interests, are disturbing to public confidence.

Under the old flexible provisions, the task of adjustment was imposed directly upon the President, and the limitations in the law which circumscribed it were such that action was long delayed and it was largely inoperative, although important benefits were brought to the dairying, flax, glass, and other industries through it.

The new flexible provision established the responsibility for revisions upon a reorganized Tariff Commission, composed of members equal of both parties as a definite rate making body acting through semi-judicial methods of open hearings and investigation by which items can be taken up one by one upon direction or upon application of aggrieved parties. Recommendations are to be made to the President, he being given authority to promulgate or veto the conclusions of the Commission. Such revision can be accomplished without disturbance to business, as they concern but one item at a time, and the principles laid down assure a protective basis.

The principle of a protective tariff for the benefit of labor, industry, and the farmer is established in the bill by the requirement that the Commission shall adjust the rates so as to cover the differences in cost of production at home and abroad, and it is authorized to increase or decrease the duties by 50 percent to effect this end. The means and methods of ascertaining such differences by the Commission are provided in such fashion as should expedite prompt and effective action if grievances develop.

When the flexible principle was first written into law in 1922, by tradition and force of habit the old conception of legislative revision was so firmly fixed that the innovation was bound to be used with caution and in a restricted field, even had it not been largely inoperative for other reasons. Now, however, and particularly after the record of the last 15 months, there is a growing and widespread realization that in this highly complicated and intricately organized and rapidly shifting modern economic world, the time has come when a more scientific and businesslike method of tariff revision must be devised. Toward this the new flexible provision takes a long step.

These provisions meet the repeated demands of statesmen and industrial and agricultural leaders over the past 25 years. It complies in full degree with the proposals made 20 years ago by President Roosevelt. It now covers proposals which I urged in 1922.

If, however, by any chance the flexible provisions now made should prove insufficient for effective action, I shall ask for further authority for the Commission, for I believe that public opinion will give wholehearted support to the carrying out of such a program on a generous scale to the end that we may develop a protective system free from the vices which have characterized every tariff revision in the past.

The complaints from some foreign countries that these duties have been placed unduly high can be remedied, if justified, by proper application to the Tariff Commission.

It is urgent that the uncertainties in the business world which have been added to by the long-extended debate of the measure should be ended. They can be ended only by completion of this bill. Meritorious demands for further protection to agriculture and labor which have developed since the tariff of 1922 would not end if this bill fails of enactment. Agitation for legislative tariff revision would necessarily continue before the country. Nothing would contribute to retard business recovery more than this continued agitation.

As I have said, I do not assume the rate structure in this or any other tariff bill is perfect, but I am convinced that the disposal of the whole question is urgent. I believe that the flexible provisions can within reasonable time remedy inequalities; that this provision is a progressive advance and gives great hope of taking the tariff away from politics, lobbying, and log rolling; that the bill gives protection to agriculture for the market of its products and to several industries in need of such protection for the wage of their labor; that with returning normal conditions our foreign trade will continue to expand.

'The New American Tariff', *Economist* (21 June 1930), p. 1378.

The New American Tariff. – The signature by President Hoover of the Hawley-Smoot Tariff Bill at Washington is the tragi-comic finale to one of the most amazing chapters in world tariff history, and it is one that Protectionist enthusiasts the world over would do well to study. The reason for tariff revision was a desire to restore a balance of protection which had been tilted to the disadvantage of the agriculturalist. But so soon as ever the tariff schedules were cast into the melting-pot of revision, log-rollers and politicians set to work stirring with all their might, and a measure which started with the single object of giving satisfaction to the farmer emerges as a full-fledged high tariff Act in which nearly 900 duties have been raised, some extravagantly. Such is the inevitable result of vested interests working through political influence, ending in signature by a President, antagonistic to the Bill, under compulsion of political necessities. No one, except the interests who fancy their own pockets may benefit, wanted the tariff; big business in the East is against it, the economists of America have condemned it in unison; the motor manufacturers have implored Mr Hoover to use his veto; and the fear of its economic consequences at home and abroad was mainly responsible for the heaviest slump of the year in Wall Street. Yet it is now the law of that land, and we have the spectacle of a great country, at a moment of severe trade depression, and faced with a growing necessity to export her manufactures, deliberately erecting barriers against trade with the rest of the world. Here, indeed, is a classic example of what happens to a country which once starts on the slope of protection. Protection, meant to be a good servant, becomes a dominant and costly master. President Hoover, we see, endeavours to coat the pill by suggesting that the 'flexible' provisions will be used to mitigate the effects of the tariff, where it may be found to be irksome. This hope is surely illusory, as similar hopes held out in the past have proved to be. In the first two years of President Coolidge's administration a number of duties were raised, but only two reduced – namely, on the vital items of bran and live bobwhite quail. We are compelled to accept the view expressed some years ago by Dr Taussig that 'the interests involved in tariff-making are so powerful, and can exert such influence on the party in power, that disinterested and non-partisan administration of the flexible provisions is a vain dream.' If there is any comfort to be derived from this latest chapter in tariff folly, it is the belief that American eyes will be forcibly opened to the fact that they are faced by a *reductio ad absurdum*. Incidentally, every week brings new evidence of the realisation by American business leaders of the dangers of the fiscal path which America is treading. In a contribution to the Annals of the American Academy of Political and Social Science Mr Edward A. Filene, while disavowing Free Trade convictions, argues powerfully that a lowering of American tariffs is essential for the stimulation both of world trade in general and American exports in particular. *Magnaest veritas et prevalebit*.

'The United States Tariff and Swiss Trade', *Economist* (28 June 1930), p. 1442.

United States Tariff and Swiss Trade.

– Our Geneva correspondent writes:– The adoption of the new Tariff Bill by the United States Congress is causing widespread discontent in Switzerland, whose exports, in particular those of the watch-making, silk, cotton and embroidery industries, will be hard hit by the new duties. The Swiss industrialists and Government did their very best to draw the attention of the United States Government to the serious consequences which the enforcing of the new duties would have on Swiss economic conditions, but it was in vain. The effects in Switzerland of the general economic slump will undoubtedly be aggravated by the raising of these duties. The question of boycotting United States products has been earnestly advocated here by several groups of industrialists and Chambers of Commerce, while the Swiss Government was at the same time urged to raise, by way of retaliation, all duties on United States goods, especially on motor-cars, typewriters, agricultural machines and implements and petrol; but Swiss Customs duties are already high, and it is difficult to raise them again. Not much seems to be being done here in regard to the organisation of a boycott of United States products, though an attempt is being made at doing without American oil and petrol, especially as the Anglo-Persian Oil Company is now in a position to supply all the needs of the Swiss market. There is, however, a general tendency towards reducing all purchases in the United States. This is clearly shown by the foreign trade returns for April and May. Imports from the United States, which were £760,635 in March, dropped to £757,232 in April and to £677,000 in May. Imports of United States petrol, which rose until last year, show a drop of about 380,000 lbs. compared with the 1929 average, whereas the total import of petrol was about 2 million lbs. higher in May, 1930, than in May, 1929. Persia, Irak, Roumania and Russia are benefiting from the reduction in United States imports. A similar but smaller drop is also recorded in the import of United States motor-cars, and European countries – Great Britain in particular – should seize that opportunity for developing their sales in Switzerland.

Cordell Hull, 'Economic Policies of the Government', *Congressional Record*, 71st Congress, 3rd Session, 16 February 1931, pp. 5045–6.

ECONOMIC POLICIES OF THE GOVERNMENT

Mr. JONES of Texas. Mr. Speaker, I ask unanimous consent to extend my remarks in the RECORD by inserting a copy of a statement prepared by my colleague, Hon. CORDELL HULL, of Tennessee, on economic policies of the Government.

The SPEAKER. Is there objection to the request of the gentleman from Texas?

There was no objection.

The statement is as follows:

Economic problems, including tariff and commercial policy, should come first on any Democratic National Party program during the next two years. The dominant business and political forces have emphatically demonstrated their incapacity to keep this great country free from an unprecedented panic longer than six years after emerging from a preceding one, notwithstanding the fact that no nation in history was ever more completely equipped with safeguards against possibilities of panic conditions than was this country after 1923.

Unlimited capital, boundless natural resources, wonderful transportation facilities, the greatest and most efficient manufacturing plant in the annals of industry, and the position of world creditor were ours. Without the vision to see that completely transformed postwar conditions imperatively required modernized tariffs and commercial policy, instead of the obsolete system of extreme high tariffs which contemplate that every nation shall live unto itself, our dominant political and business leadership has suffered a complete breakdown. Unless our business and economic civilization is a failure, the Democratic Party has an unsurpassed opportunity to give the Nation such sound and constructive leadership as will at least avoid the most devastating panics within 6-year periods.

High tariffs, under changed postwar conditions, greatly obstruct and restrict to the very narrowest channels, commerce between nations. The inability of nations on this account to dispose of surpluses soon results in conditions of vast overproduction of raw materials, foodstuffs, and manufactures, as the case may be, with the resultant decline in prices and the wide unemployment of both labor and capital. Such prevention of trade by tariff barriers also has the inevitable effect of compelling many countries to settle their balance due other countries in gold, which correspondingly saps the strength of their financial structures. The concurrence of these conditions has had the inevitable effect of greatly diminishing the purchasing power of peoples here and everywhere. High tariffs since the war have been by far the most serious barriers to commerce, including the most mutually profitable exchanges of surpluses between nations throughout the world.

It is astonishing to observe that the value of the exports from the 28 countries of Europe with 350,000,000 consumers was $11,985,000,000 for the calendar year 1929, compared with $12,086,000,000 for the year 1913, with the 1929 commerce adjusted to the value of the 1913 dollar. Omitting our own country and with a similar 1913 dollar adjustment for the sake of accurate comparison, the total export trade of 100 nations for 1929 aggregated $20,642,000,000, compared with $17,786,000,000 for 1913, or a purely nominal increase of less than $3,000,000,000 over a period of 16 years. For 1930 these values must have been actually below those of 1913. A like comparison of United States exports shows a total of $3,785,000,000 for 1929 and $2,484,000,000 in 1913, or an increase of only $1,300,000,000 during 16 years, compared with an annual pre-war increase of 5 to 6½ per cent. Even this showing was largely made possible by American loans abroad aggregating $15,000,000,000.

High-tariff walls here and everywhere have constituted the greatest single underlying cause of the present world economic collapse. Had international trade, unfettered by universal tariff barriers, been permitted to increase according to the pre-war ratio, the many millions of unemployed wage earners in this and other countries would to-day be employed at full time. The best remedy for unemployment is for a nation to sell its surplus. This country can no longer depend upon large but temporary programs of building and highway construction or of the expansion of the automobile business, of installment sales, and of American loans abroad, but we must look beyond the seas, where unlimited trade opportunities beckon to us, for vital, stable, and permanent aid to our domestic prosperity. We are impregnable in our domestic market under any moderate or reasonably competitive tariff policy.

Not content with the Fordney-McCumber tariff enactment of 1922, which virtually shut out imports either directly or remotely competitive, the blind and selfish forces of economic isolation proceeded to enact the still higher rates embodied in the Hawley-Smoot measure in 1930, designed to stop every crack and crevice in our tariff wall, chiefly for the benefit of antiquated or over-capitalized or other inefficient industries. Its authors represented at the time of passage that the equivalent ad valorem rate which it imposed would be 41.14 per cent compared with 40.11 per cent which was the height of the Fordney tariff wall. Some person made a colossal blunder in thus calculating the tariff increase of the Hawley-Smoot Act. The figures for the calendar year 1930 reveal the amazing average ad valorem rate equivalent to 48.13 per cent instead of 41.14 per cent, as heretofore represented. This Smoot Act thus furnishes greater tariff benefits in the circumstances than any previous measure. Comparable factors show that the imports of finished dutiable manufactures are less to-day than in 1913, and this is the best test of tariff prohibitions. And, too, this sordid policy of extreme high tariffs has created the widest, deepest, and worst possible spirit of paternalism. It has brought forth a vast crop of bounties, subsidies, rebates, drawbacks, reprisals, and retaliations which irritate and dislocate trade everywhere. It has also hurried peoples in most countries into every sort of wild efforts for embargoes and impossible devices artificially to fix and peg commodity prices with collapses always following.

The Nation urgently needs economic leadership with vision, courage, and capacity. We have to-day hopeless confusion and chaos of economic ideas. It was under American leadership during the past 10 years that most countries have been engaged in a wild and mad scramble for high and still higher tariffs. America should now lead them back. The need is imperative for a reexamination of our tariff-rate structure with the view to its readjustment to a decent level. Theoretical tariff utterances by individuals or political parties do not necessarily mean anything. For all practical purposes there are two, and only two, groups of tariff thought in this country. One group comprises the chief tariff beneficiaries, in close partnership with dominant forces of the Republican Party, always pursuing an extreme high-tariff policy – and one which invariably means tariff revision upward. The other group comprises the opposition to this sordid and sinister combination of vested interest and politics. The opposition group should, as a first step, demand that there shall no longer be government by any political party in notorious partnership with the forces of special privilege. The second step should be a challenge to the fixed Republican policy of tariff revision ever upward, and a demand that the country face in the opposite direction; that such downward revision should be careful and gradual to a moderate or competitive level, with rates so adjusted, with the aid of a fact-finding commission, as to prevent conditions of domestic monopoly on the one hand, and to avoid abnormal or unreasonable imports against efficient industries operating under normal conditions, on the other.

There must be more than mere hair-splitting differences between the two political parties on tariff and commercial policy. They must be fundamental. The record of the Democratic Party is deeply rooted in a very definite and sound economic philosophy which embraces justice and equality. The Republican economic philosophy is steeped in the most aggravated forms of special privilege or governmental favoritism. If the two old political parties are to be merged with respect to this, the major and most powerful special-privilege group, then they should be merged as to all the minor forces of special privilege. There should be no sham fighting in either instance.

Nor can the tariff be taken out of politics through a tariff commission, whether acting under the flexible provision in concert with the President on the one hand or with Congress on the other. High tariffs are a definite part of the ideals of the Republican Party; no Republican agency, however honest, could ever be depended upon to adjust them to a moderate or competitive level no more than a litigant could be expected fairly to try his own law-suit. President Coolidge tried this experiment and had one scandal after another, as it was also tried with failure in 1883. The country can only look to those who fundamentally oppose the philosophy of typical Republican high tariffs for practical revision downward. Mere formulas get nowhere. For either political party, with the aid of a tariff commission, merely to stabilize the rates around the high Republican tariff level will not and should not be accepted by the country as 'taking the tariff out of politics.'

Reed Smoot, 'Our Tariff and the Depression', *Current History*, 35:2 (November 1931), pp. 173–81.

Our Tariff and the Depression
By REED SMOOT

Chairman, United States Senate Committee on Finance; Co-Author of the Smoot-Hawley Tariff Act

NO event in recent history has emphasized the importance of the American tariff so much as has the current economic depression. Abnormal conditions throughout the world have made protective duties the key to industrial stability. In times of prosperity a tariff is essential to equalize costs of production here and abroad, but in this hour of national distress protection is imperative to save American industry from what might otherwise become the most serious upheaval it has ever experienced.

In attempting to elucidate the influence of the tariff on international trade we encounter a labyrinth of economic forces that affect every commercial nation. Tariff barricades that have been thrown up recently on nearly every international boundary are a result and not the cause of those forces. Inordinate production and maldistribution have made customs duties necessary to re-establish the economic balance.

Purchasing power has been reduced on every continent. In countries that produce mostly raw materials incomes have been drastically cut, and purchases in the world market have been consequently reduced. Economic law thus operates to curtail international commerce in direct relation to the slump in domestic business.

One remarkable aspect of this economic derangement is the plethora of commodities on the market. In those years of feverish activity before 1929 vast surpluses of goods were accumulated in nearly every country. When the undertow of fear and pessimism turned the consuming public from normal buying to abnormal saving, and unemployment further weakened purchasing power, the world markets became glutted with commodities of every kind. Each country sought outlets abroad, while most governments took steps to protect their home producers from inundation by this flood of cheap goods.

It is quite natural that every country should give preference to its own industries and its own working men, especially in economic crises. A similar surplus of commodities induced most countries to strengthen their tariff barriers after the World War. France, Germany, Italy and Great Britain had increased their customs duties even before Congress revised the American tariff in 1922. Since that time some European countries have built several elaborate additions to their protective barricades. In the two years since the depression began forty-five nations have made important changes in their tariff rates. Secretary Hyde's remark that beside many foreign tariff mountains American duties amount to nothing but a cluster of molehills was not exaggerated.

In our present stage of industrial development production is easy. We have no difficulty in turning out more food, more clothing, houses, automobiles and other necessities than the consuming public can buy. For this reason the theory that goods should be purchased where they can be produced most cheaply has undergone an ignominious collapse. The great problem today is to find employment for all our people; and, since we live at a higher standard than the rest of the world, this cannot be done unless we allow ample protection to American enterprise.

What would have happened to the United States if Congress had failed to keep pace with this world-wide protective movement? America would have become a dumping ground for all the surplus products of the world, as is Great Britain. Every month that country becomes more dependent upon industries in other lands, while an appalling number of her own working men subsist on doles supplied largely through taxation. Imports into the United Kingdom are valued at about 16 per cent less than they were a year ago. But exports are worth 30 per cent less. The pitiful position of British industry is an inevitable result of trying to fight the battles of modern commerce from a poorly barricaded position, while competitors are intrenched behind domestic protective policies.

Once before the days of quantity production Congress tried to cure an economic slump by lowering customs duties. Clouds of depression spread over the country in 1893. Critics demanded that international trade be unfettered. In 1894 Congress proceeded to remodel the tariff in the direction of free trade. Instead of stimulating foreign commerce and lifting the country out of its slough of despond, this act merely left the government with a huge deficit and the people with more acute economic distress. Even imports fell off sharply in spite of the lower rates of duty. In the last year under the Wilson low-tariff act exports decreased to $1,050,000,000, as compared with $1,730,000,000 for the year before its enactment.

Not until after President McKinley had been elected and called Congress into extra session in 1897 was this era of hard times brought to an end. A new protective tariff was enacted. Prosperity gradually returned, with both imports and exports growing to larger volumes than had ever been known before. Since that time the United States has never been without protection for its domestic industries. Although the tariff rates were lowered in 1913, their effect was not felt, for when the war came and swept all America's chief competitors into a struggle for existence our industries enjoyed complete protection. War acts as a general embargo; not only does it relieve neutral countries of foreign competition in their own markets, but it affords opportunity to multiply exports to the combatant nations.

It is difficult to understand why any one should try to fasten responsibility for the general movement toward higher protective duties upon the United States. Many nations revised their tariffs before Congress passed the Smoot-Hawley bill in June, 1930, and many have increased their duties since. Each country has been prompted by economic considerations of its own. Only the purblind egotist can suggest that the world turned to protection in retaliation against the American tariff. What chiefly distinguishes the Smoot-Hawley act from foreign tariffs adopted since the depression began is its moderation.

Though the tariff of one country cannot be accurately compared with that of another, for a variety of reasons, duties on specific items can be studied with precision and the average height of tariff barriers can be estimated from the amount of duties collected in relation to the total volume of imports. Thus a recent test made by the Department of Agriculture showed that fourteen leading commodities exported from the United States, constituting 28 per cent of our agricultural sales abroad, were taxed in a dozen leading countries at rates double and quadruple any that may be found in our tariff act. Wheat is a good example. In less than a year and a half Germany increased her wheat tariff six times, beginning at 49 cents per bushel and ending at $1.62. The Italian duty has risen from 37 to 87 cents; the French, from 20 to 85 cents; the Mexican, from 66 to 90 cents. The American duty is 42 cents. Foreign tariffs on meats are still more drastic. The United States taxes hams and shoulders at $3.25 per hundred pounds, but Soviet Russia imposes a duty of $70; Bulgaria, Chile and Argentina, from $20 to $25; Brazil, Yugoslavia, Uruguay, Norway, Portugal and Rumania, from $10 to $20.

It is a prevalent but false belief that American duties are the highest in the world. Almost any test will prove that this is not so. How does the total amount of duties collected compare with the value of all imports for the various nations? The United States Tariff Commission has worked out such a calculation, using the average ad valorem equivalents for duties collected in 1930. The Japanese tariff, spread over all Japan's imports, both dutiable and free, amounts to 7.3 per cent; that of France, 8.7; Norway, 10.1; Germany, 11.7; the United Kingdom, 12.6; Spain, 12.9; the United States, 14.8; Italy, 15.4; Argentina, 16.5, and Chile, 23.5 per cent.

It should be noted that the percentage of duty to total imports during the first six months of the new tariff was only 13.7 per cent. This is not, of course, an exact calculation, because the effect of rates that are so high as greatly to restrict goods or exclude them entirely is not felt in this comparison. But it is apparent that European and South American Legislatures are quite as adept at imposing restrictive duties as is Congress. American automobiles, for example, are virtually excluded from many European markets.

There is nothing in the picture to indicate that Uncle Sam is the tariff Shylock. No other nation in the world is so well adapted to a protective policy as the United States; yet several have higher tariffs. If we were dependent upon the outside world for half our food and raw materials, a tariff might be less useful; but our country, with its vast and varied resources and its highly developed market, is almost an economic unit in itself. For this reason, the United States cannot be compared with Great Britain, Italy, Japan or other political units that do not enjoy economic self-sufficiency. Yet, in spite of these ideal conditions for application of the protective principle, America imports more free goods than any other country with the possible exception of the United Kingdom, which lives on trade.

Any attempt to measure the effect of the tariff on foreign trade must take into consideration current economic conditions; that is, we must talk about our foreign commerce in terms of 1931 values. The first question is, not how much the dollar value of exports and imports has diminished, but how America has fared in commerce as compared with the rest of the world. In 1913 American exports amounted to 12.3 per cent of the world's total; from 1921 to 1925, 16.5 per cent; in 1928, 15.6 per cent. Then the boom year of 1929 brought a new spurt and the United States furnished 16.8 per cent of the exports from sixty-seven chief commercial nations. In 1930 the ratio was again equal to that of 1928. For the period since the Smoot-Hawley act was passed statistics are available for only the fifty-six foremost commercial nations, but they are sufficiently clear to indicate the trend. During the first six months under the new tariff the American export ratio was 16.2, compared with 16.9 for the previous six months. This slight decline was less than that during the half year immediately before the new rates came into effect.

Turning attention now to the ratio of America's foreign purchases to imports throughout the world, we find a similar trend. In 1913 only 8.3 per cent of the world imports were absorbed in the United States; from 1921 to 1925, 12.5 per cent; in 1928, 11.7 per cent. Although the figures for the recent years are not exactly comparable, as they do not include the lesser commercial nations, they indicate that our imports were in excess in the first part of 1929 and that our proportion has since been declining. In the first half year under the new tariff our share was 11.1 per cent, compared with 12.6 per cent for the last half year under the old law. It is interesting to note that the percentage of all imports absorbed by the United States fell from 14.1 to 12.6 during the year before the Smoot-Hawley act took effect.

These calculations represent value and not physical quantity. Obviously, a country which chiefly exports raw materials will appear to have lost its relative position because of the drastic reduction in the prices of such products. Since prices of finished manufactures have been maintained more firmly, the countries of Western Europe, which manufacture many luxuries and specialties, assume a relatively more significant place in world commerce. America's share of international commerce appears to have shrunk partly because agricultural produce and raw materials still bulk large in our foreign shipments. During the last four years agricultural crops have constituted 36 per cent of our exports and semi-manufactures an additional 14 per cent. Low prices of such commodities as cotton and copper have contributed largely to fixing the ratio of American foreign trade at a slightly smaller figure.

One conclusion from a study of America's share of international commerce is inevitable, and that is that nothing calamitous has happened. Though trade overseas and across border lines has fallen off throughout the world, our portion of world exports remains about the same as in normal years before the depression. Our share of imports is slightly lower, as Congress intended it should be. The Smoot-Hawley tariff has proved to be a shock absorber against world-wide dumping.

To estimate our loss of trade with the losses of all other countries is only one way of calculating the effect of the tariff law. The relationship between domestic production and foreign commerce is even more significant. Some people who wish to attribute as much disaster as possible to the tariff talk as if foreign trade were one of our greatest industries, but it is not an industry at all. International commerce is merely an extension of domestic trade. Most industries produce primarily for the domestic market and sell their surplus abroad. International trade is thus subject to the laws of supply and demand and cannot be measured precisely from the height of customs barriers. An honest analysis must, therefore, discount the effect of domestic business on foreign trade before attributing the shrinkage to tariff changes.

How has business within the United States fared since the depression began? The most reliable data available show that industrial production began to decline about the middle of 1929 and continued with some variations until the first months of 1931. A reliable commercial index, which is based on production as well as distribution, shows a falling off of 40 per cent from the abnormal high peak of industrial activity two years ago. The extent of that decline is almost equally divided between the last two fiscal years, measuring 22 per cent from June, 1929, to June, 1930, and about 23 per cent from that time to the beginning of the Summer of 1931.

Another index of industrial production prepared by the Federal Reserve Board shows a decrease of 20 per cent during approximately the twelve months in which the 1930 tariff rates have been in effect. The index number for that year is 88, as compared with 110 for the previous year and 100 for 1923–25. Charts prepared by the Department of Commerce likewise show a decline of 20 per cent in wholesale prices during the last year, based on a combined index of 550 commodities and price quotations.

When domestic industry and business demonstrate such symptoms of maladjustment a similar condition may be expected in foreign trade. That is exactly what the records indicate. In the first quarter after the Smoot-Hawley bill became law exports fell off 19 per cent in quantity; in the second quarter, 22 per cent, and in the third quarter (from January to March, 1931), 24 per cent, each quarter being compared with the corresponding period of the previous year.

Imports held up much better in spite of the higher duties. In the first quarter under the Smoot-Hawley act the ebb of imports was quite pronounced. Shipments were 23 per cent lower than in the previous corresponding quarter. That can be accounted for by the rush in the last days of the Fordney-McCumber act to ship in large quantities of goods on which the duty was to be raised. In the next quarter imports were only 13 per cent lower. A decline of 16 per cent is registered for the third quarter.

This tendency for imports to hold their place better than exports is seen throughout the calendar year of 1930. While exports diminished 19 per cent in volume, the quantity of imports shrunk only 15 per cent as compared with 1929. Does this mean that the countries with which we deal have adopted more effectively restrictive tariffs than ours or that the Smoot-Hawley act affords inadequate protection for American enterprise? Many nations have certainly raised their customs duties far above those of the United States, but that has not been the primary factor in determining our ratio of imports and exports.

Purchasing power is undoubtedly the most important influence. Americans live much further above the margin of want than do the people of any other country. Wage scales were maintained here much longer and to a greater extent than in other countries. In time of depression, as in prosperity, the American people have more money to spend than their neighbors. The United States offers the world a better market than the world offers us.

Another factor is the decline in commodity prices. The unit value of exports for the first quarter of 1931 was 17 per cent below that of 1930, but the value of imports fell 25 per cent. Three-quarters of our purchases from abroad consist of raw materials, food-stuffs and semi-manufactures. Prices of those commodities have shrunk to a fraction of what they were when the depression began. Rubber, raw silk and wool, for example, are worth about 45 per cent less than a year ago. The world demand for such commodities has been curtailed, but they still flow into the most available market. Since the United States absorbs more imports than any other country except possibly Great Britain, and since 67 per cent of those imports come in without paying duty, it is not surprising that the volume of our foreign purchases has fallen off less than either exports or domestic production.

The unmistakable conclusion is that the decline in American business abroad is on a par with that in domestic industry. The proportion of our national output that is being exported has not diminished. Roughly calculated, both domestic industry and foreign commerce are a little more than 20 per cent below the level of last year. Equally evident is it that foreign interests have improved their position in the American market. Importers have about a 5 per cent advantage over domestic producers so far as the volume of goods moved in the last year is concerned.

The public often fails to understand this conclusion because it is confused by a maze of figures representing the dollar value of trade. In times like the present, statistics based on prices are extremely misleading. Changes in commodity prices in various countries upset almost any comparison of the dollar value of our trade. Indices worked out by the Department of Commerce show that since the depression began agricultural prices have decreased 37.6 per cent, food prices 29.4 per cent, and other commodity prices, mostly of manufacturers, 21.6 per cent. A combined index for the United States places prices 27.2 per cent lower than the apex in 1929. Similar indices show a decline of 25.8 in Canada, 25.3 in the United Kingdom, 21.2 in France, 19.1 in Germany and 32.7 in Italy. In some countries the articles entering into international trade have maintained relatively stable prices. On the other hand, the bottom seems to have fallen out of prices for many raw materials.

Although shipments of copper abroad during the first three months of 1931 were 20 per cent lower in value, 41 per cent more copper was actually exported than in the corresponding period of 1930. Coffee became a leading import in the same period. Measured in dollar value it was worth 33 per cent less than the five-year average, but in actual quantity it amounted to 21 per cent more than the five-year average. The price of unmanufactured cotton fell lower than it has been since 1914. The United States exported 841,000,000 pounds in three months, 3 per cent less than during corresponding months of 1930, but the return to farmers in actual money was 40 per cent less. Such fluctuations in price make comparisons of total values very dubious.

Americans are inclined to lose sight of the relationship between this country's capacity to supply human wants and its sales abroad. Exports are more easily measured than goods which pass into domestic consumption. Hence we marvel at the rise of our foreign trade without stopping to ask if its relative importance has grown. Enormous figures dazzle us; achievements in foreign commerce are paraded before us; the effects of tariffs are distorted and our business with foreign nations comes to be regarded as more important than ever before. The United States has undoubtedly assumed a more imposing rôle in world commerce. The gains in our percentage of world trade have already been noted, while no one can fail to be impressed by the growth in both volume and total value of our trade with foreign countries in the last quarter century. But in appraising these gains let us not forget the extent to which American industry and the American market also have developed.

At the beginning of the century the United States was selling 12.8 per cent of all its output abroad. When the World War broke out the percentage stood at 9.7. The demands from the belligerent nations in the subsequent five years resulted in the shipment abroad of 15.7 per cent of all American output by 1919.

Since that time the American market has been absorbing a greater portion of what we produce. In 1929, when our foreign commerce reached its highest point in history, only 9.8 per cent of movable goods produced was exported.

How then can it be said that the United States is more dependent than formerly upon foreign trade? The most striking feature of America's rise to the position of foremost industrial nation in the world is the creation of our immense domestic market. American inventive genius, American capital and labor and agriculture have been utilized to such an extent that the United States is becoming increasingly self-sufficient. Foreign trade is relatively a less significant factor in our economic life than it was before the days of quantity production. One authority has calculated that 96 per cent of our industrial production is absorbed in the United States. With such an opulent market of our own, and such diversified resources as we find within our confines, the United States is economically the most self-contained nation on earth. Yet the exports which spill over the edges of our vast home market exceed those of any other country.

The greatest free trade area in the world is the forty-eight States which comprise the American Union. Because of that every commercial nation clamors for the admittance of its products without duty. Obviously the United States could temporarily extend its import trade by lowering tariff barriers; and if other governments could be induced to do likewise, some gains might be made in exports. But would that possibility justify us in sharing our $50,000,000,000 domestic market to a greater extent with foreign producers in the hope of increasing our $5,000,000,000 market abroad?

Another unanswerable question confronts the economists who would have the United States turn toward a free trade policy. How could American buying power be sustained and preserved if the industries which create that buying power through high wages and dividends were submerged under foreign competition? Formerly it was argued that the United States would divert its energies to those industries for which it is especially adapted. But even with the preservation of all industries under the protective system millions of men are out of work. What would happen if part of our enterprises succumbed to foreign competition? Jobs are now far more important than cheap goods. Production has become so easy that the problem is to find work for the masses, to enable our people to supply their own wants, so far as is practical, and to maintain living standards commensurate with their productive capacity.

How the tariff is operating is indicated by a consideration of free and dutiable imports. More than two-thirds of our imports are not in any way affected by our protective policy, so that, if the tariff is responsible for the upset in our foreign business, it ought to be confined to dutiable commodities. But what do we find? In 1930 the variation between the shrinkage of free and dutiable imports was so slight as to be negligible. That comparison is, of course, unsatisfactory because the new duties were applied during only half the year. Matching the first nine months under the Smoot-Hawley act with the corresponding period one year earlier, we find a falling off of 35 per cent in the free column and 43 per cent in the dutiable column. But again we are handicapped by having to deal with values rather than quantities. Most of our free imports are raw materials, the prices of which have been dropping for at least a year. Nevertheless, there has been a considerable demand for such imports because most of them are not produced in the United States. We must have rubber, raw silk, coffee, &c., whether there is a depression or not.

After allowing for price changes part of the declines in dutiable imports may be attributed to the 1930 tariff act, which was devised to give a slightly higher margin of protection to American industry and to reserve so far as possible the agricultural market for our own farmers.

American industry as a whole does not enjoy greater protection than it did before the Smoot-Hawley act was passed. This does not mean that the new tariff has been ineffective, but that competition has increased. The quest for new markets by foreign countries to supplement failing markets at home has been frantic and persistent. Goods that in normal times would not have come in over the tariff wall have in this congestion of trade been dumped upon the American market. The tariff increases were thus not sufficient to give American enterprise a greater hold on the domestic market. The act of 1930 merely served to save industry from far worse consequences if duties had not been revised. In drafting the new tariff Congress did not entirely anticipate the intensified struggle for markets resulting from the world-wide economic derangement.

Congress was far more generous to farmers than to other producers. Ad valorem rates or their equivalent on agricultural raw materials rose from 38.1 per cent under the 1922 tariff to 48.92 under the 1930 tariff. Products manufactured from agricultural materials were allowed an increase from 36.15 to 48.87 per cent by way of compensation for the higher rates on raw materials. But industrial rates in which there was no compensatory element were raised only from 31.02 to 34.31. The Smoot-Hawley act was pre-eminently agricultural.

The value of protective duties to agriculture is frequently underestimated. Yet 90 per cent of all American crops come directly into competition with similar foreign products. In recent years the American market has been absorbing enormous quantities of foodstuffs from abroad, while our own farmers have been in distress because the tariff was not high enough to equalize costs of production. In the last year before the Smoot-Hawley act became effective our agricultural imports were valued at about $300,000,000 more than our agricultural exports. In the first nine months under the new tariff exports were worth more than imports, and at the close of the fiscal year, June 30, 1931, American farmers were close to a favorable trade balance for the first time in many years. This improved position is due to the tariff. The Department of Agriculture has prepared a table showing the relative volume of imports received during the first eleven months under the Smoot-Hawley act as compared with the same months of the previous year. It includes 44 chief commodities and groups of commodities, comprising 87 per cent of all agricultural imports. Free imports gained slightly in physical volume under the new tariff, indicating greater pressure from foreign countries upon our market, as a result of the depression. But agricultural imports that are dutiable decreased nearly 12 per cent. This difference may be regarded as further protection to agriculture.

The bottom has fallen out of agricultural prices because of fewer demands throughout the world. Excess production has brought distress to cotton and wheat growers. Although no tariff can remedy that, our protective system has saved our farmers from a deluge of foreign crops produced at lower costs by farmers with lower standards of living than ours.

In general, however, tariffs modify the world demand for goods in a rather minor degree. It is often said that countries against which the United States has raised its protective barriers are as a result refusing to buy American goods. But there is more theory than fact in the assertion. Other peoples buy our commodities not because of any policy adopted by Congress but because they need them. So long as we produce what the world wants and is able to buy we shall have markets regardless of tariff policies.

The trend of our foreign commerce since the depression began illustrates how little our customs duties actually interfere with our export trade. Most American tariffs are levied against the industrial products of Europe. In 1930 only 42.4 per cent of our imports from Europe were duty free. From the world as a whole 67 per cent were free. If it were true that the slump in our exports has been caused by retaliations against the Smoot-Hawley act, Europe should be taking less of what we sell abroad. But this is not so. In 1930 the value of our exports to Europe decreased 21 per cent as compared with 31 per cent for the rest of the world. Nearly 48 per cent of our foreign shipments went to Europe last year. In 1929, when no cause existed for retaliation against a new American tariff, Europe took only 44.7 per cent of our exports.

South American trade offers a remarkable contrast. Nearly 84 per cent of everything we import from South America comes in free, and the ratio of free and dutiable goods remains almost the same under the new tariff law. In 1929 South America took 10.3 per cent of our exports; in 1930, 8.8 per cent. Similar results may be noted in Asia, which sends 80 per cent of its imports to the United States free, in Oceania, with 69 per cent free and in Canada and Newfoundland, with about 70 per cent free.

Such comparisons are valuable only in that they illustrate how little influence a nation's import duties have on its export trade. European customers bought a larger percentage of our products because their purchasing power was better maintained.

Prices of their finished products were more stable than the prices of raw materials and foodstuffs which determine the purchasing power of nonindustrial regions.

In view of the world-wide economic and political upheavals it is remarkable that our commercial intercourse with other nations has not been more seriously interrupted. Today every nation is struggling to turn international trade to its own advantage. The United States must participate in this competition, using every aid that the tariff can give, or be overwhelmed by it. Yet when costs of production have been equalized and the domestic market protected, the exchange of goods with other nations continues. Neither the tariff nor any other force has destroyed or can destroy our international trade.

To sum up, the United States has not lost its relative position in world trade; the percentage of our total production exported has not changed; the volume of imports compared with domestic production has increased somewhat since the new tariff act became law; nations which live under the shadow of our tariff wall have purchased more from us since the depression than those countries that are only remotely affected by our protective policy, and, finally, our enormous extension of productive power has been made possible not by selling greater portions of the output abroad, but by intensive cultivation of the home market.

How can we escape the conclusion that the tariff has been a stabilizing influence? In the scramble of all nations to dispose of surpluses it has saved American producers from a deluge of cheap foreign goods. It has served to maintain the balance between domestic and international trade. A flow of imports equal to that of 1929 at a time when American enterprise was prostrate would have been a greater calamity than the temporary decline in our foreign trade.

The United States has demonstrated that foreign trade can be developed without opening the domestic market to unrestricted exploitation. Much of our trade will continue to be independent of all customs duties. No country will allow foreigners to supply those wants which can just as well be supplied by labor at home. There is no prospect of abandonment of the protective systems which now reach throughout the world. In the future, therefore, we can look for continuous development of international commerce, but it will flow chiefly in non-competitive channels or over tariff walls that tend to equalize costs of production.

Franklin D. Roosevelt, National Radio Address, 'Forgotten Man', 8 April 1932, from Albany, New York, Franklin Delano Roosevelt Presidential Library.

Although I understand that I am talking under the auspices of the Democratic National Committee, I do not want to limit myself to politics. I do not want to feel that I am addressing an audience of Democrats, nor that I speak merely as a Democrat myself. The present condition for our national affairs is too serious to be viewed through partisan eyes for partisan purposes.

Fifteen years ago my public duty called me to an active part in a great national emergency – the World War. Success then was due to a leadership whose vision carried beyond the timorous and futile gesture of sending a tiny army of 150,000 trained soldiers and the regular Navy to the aid of our Allies.

The generalship of that moment conceived of a whole nation mobilized for war, economic, industrial, social and military resources gathered into a vast unit, capable of and actually in the process of throwing into the scales ten million men equipped with physical needs and sustained by the realization that behind them were the united efforts of 110 million human beings. It was a great plan because it was build from bottom to top and not from top to bottom.

In my calm judgment, the nation faces today a more grave emergency than in 1917.

It is said that Napoleon lost the Battle of Waterloo because he forgot his infantry. He staked too much upon the more spectacular but less substantial cavalry.

The present Administration in Washington provides a close parallel. It has either forgotten or it does not want to remember the infantry of our economic army.

These unhappy times call for the building of plans that rest upon the forgotten, the unorganized but the indispensable units of economic power, for plans like those of 1917 that build from the bottom up and not from the top down, that put their faith once more in the forgotten man at the bottom of the economic pyramid.

Obviously, these few minutes tonight permit no opportunity to lay down the ten or a dozen closely related objectives of a plan to meet our present emergency, but I can draw a few essentials, a beginning, in fact, of a planned program.

It is the habit of the unthinking to turn in times like this to the illusions of economic magic. People suggest that a huge expenditure of public funds by the Federal Government and by State and local governments will completely solve the unemployment problem. But it is clear that even if we could raise many billions of dollars and find definitely useful public works to spend these billions on, even all that money would not give employment to the seven million or ten million people who are out of work.

Let us admit frankly that it would be only a stopgap. A real economic cure must go to the killing of bacteria in the system rather than to the treatment of external symptoms.

How much do the shallow thinkers realize, for example, that approximately one-half of our population, fifty or sixty million people, earn their living by farming or in small towns where existence immediately depends on farms. They have today lost their purchasing power. Why? They are receiving for farm products less than the cost to them of growing these farm products.

The result of this loss of purchasing power is that many other millions of people engaged in industry in the cities cannot sell industrial products to the farming half of the nation. This brings home to every city worker that his own employment is directly tied up with the farmer's dollar. No nation can long continue half bankrupt. Main Street, Broadway, the mills, the mines will close if half of the buyers are broke.

I cannot escape the conclusion that one of the essentials of a national program of restoration must be to restore purchasing power to the farming half of the country. Without this the wheels of railroads and of factories will not turn.

Closely associated with this first objective is the problem of keeping the home-owner and the farm-owner where he is, without being, dispossessed through the foreclosure of his mortgage.

His relationship to the great banks of Chicago and New York is pretty remote. The two billion dollar fund which President Hoover and the Congress have put at the disposal at the big banks, the railroads and the corporations of the nation is not for him.

His is a relationship to his little local bank or local loan company. It is a sad fact that even though the local lender in many cases does not want to evict the farmer or homeowner by foreclosure proceedings, he is forced to do so in order to keep his bank or company solvent. Here should be an objective of government itself, to provide at least as much assistance to the little fellow as it is now giving to the large banks and corporations. That is another example of building from the bottom up.

One other objective closely related to the problem of selling American products is to provide a tariff policy based upon economic common sense rather than upon political – hot air – pull.

This country during the past few years, culminating with the Hawley-Smoot Tariff of 1929, has compelled the world to build tariff fences so high that world trade is decreasing to the vanishing point. The value of goods internationally exchanged is today less than half of what it was three or four years ago.

Every man and woman who gives any thought to the subject knows that if our factories run even 80 per cent of capability they will turn out more products than we as a nation can possibly use ourselves.

The answer is that if they are to run on 80 per cent of capacity we must sell some goods abroad. How can we do that if the outside nations cannot pay us in cash – and we know by sad experience that they cannot do that. The only way they can pay us is in their own goods or raw materials, but this foolish tariff of ours makes that impossible.

What we must do is this: To revise our tariff on the basis of a reciprocal exchange of goods, allowing other nations to buy and to pay for our goods by sending us such of their goods as will not seriously throw any of our industries out of balance, and, incidentally, making impossible in this county the continuance of pure monopolies which cause us to pay excessive prices for many of the necessities of life.

Such objectives as these three – restoring farmers' buying power, relief to the small banks and homeowners and a reconstructed tariff policy – these are only a part of ten or dozen vital factors.

But they seem to be beyond the concern of a National Administration which can think in terms only of the top of the social and economic structure. They have sought temporary relief from the top down rather than permanent relief from the bottom up. They have totally failed to plan ahead in a comprehensive way. They have waited until something has cracked and then at the last moment have sought to prevent total collapse.

It is high time to get back to fundamentals. It is high time to admit with courage that we are in the midst of an emergency at least equal to that of war. Let us mobilize to meet it.

Herbert Hoover, Campaign Speech before a Crowd of 20,000 at Butler University, Indianapolis, Indiana, 28 October 1932, Herbert Hoover Presidential Library.

My fellow citizens, my friends in Indianapolis, and may I also include Senator Watson, for I wish to add that he must be your next Senator--we require his services in Washington:

Now, my fellow citizens, my major purpose tonight is to discuss those long-view policies by which we not only cement recovery but also by which we secure over the years the enlarged comfort and the steady progress of the American people. I propose to contrast them with the ideas which have been developed by the Democratic House of Representatives, the Democratic platform, and the Democratic candidate in the course of this campaign.

[...]

I would like also to reiterate the statement which I recently made at Detroit, that the most important issue before the American people right now is to overcome this crisis, that we may secure a restoration of normal jobs to our unemployed, recovery of our agricultural prices and of our business, and that we may extend generous help in the meantime to tide our people over until these fundamental restorations are established.

I pointed out on that occasion that the battle has now changed from a successful defense of our country from disaster and chaos to forward marching attack on a hundred fronts through a score of instrumentalities and weapons toward recovery. Since that time I have had further positive evidence showing that the measures and policies that we have set in motion are driving the forces of depression into further retreat with constantly increasing rapidity. If there shall be no change in the strategy of this battle, if there shall be no delay and hesitation, we shall have the restoration of men and women to their normal jobs and we shall have that lift to agriculture from its anxieties and its losses.

But before I begin the major discussion of the evening, I wish to take a moment of your time to revert to those methods and policies for protection and recovery from this depression in the light of certain recent misstatements of the Democratic candidate in respect to them.

I presume the Governor of New York will announce that I am acting upon the defensive if I shall expose the self-interested inexactitude which he has broadcasted to the American people. I am equally prepared to defend, attack, or expound. I shall not be deterred from my purpose to lay before the people of the United States the truth as to the issues which they confront, and I shall do it with a sense of responsibility of one who has carried out and must carry into effect these issues.

I wish to call your attention to the fact that the Governor of New York in a speech on October 25 stated:

'This crash came in October 1929. The President had at his disposal all of the instrumentalities of the Government. From that day until December 31, 1931, he did absolutely nothing to remedy the situation. Not only did he do nothing, but he took the position that Congress could do nothing.'

That is the end of the quotation, and it is a charge which extends over the first 2 years and 2 months of this depression. It seems almost incredible that a man, a candidate for the Presidency of the United States, would broadcast such a violation of the truth. The front pages of every newspaper in the United States for the whole of those 2 years proclaimed the untruth of that statement. And I need remind you but of a few acts of the administration to demonstrate what I say.

The Governor dismisses the agreements brought about between the leaders of industry and labor under my assistance less than 1 month after the crash by which wages of literally millions of men and women were, for the first time in 15 depressions of a century, held without reduction until after profits had ceased and the cost of living had decreased.

He ignores the fact that today real wages in the United States are higher than at any other depression period, higher in purchasing power than in any other country in the world. And above all, he dismisses the healing effect of that great agreement by which this country has been kept free from industrial strife and class conflicts.

He would suppress from the American people the knowledge of the undertaking brought about within 2 months after the crash amongst the industries of the United States to divide the existing work in such fashion as to give millions of families some measure of income instead of discharging a large portion of them into destitution, as had always been the case in previous depressions and was the case abroad. He ignores the fact that these agreements have held until this day for the staggering unemployment.

[...]

I have stated that my major purpose this evening is to speak upon some of the continuing policies of this administration and the Republican Party in contrast with the policies of our opponents.

Many of these continuing policies are dealt with in our platform. I dealt with some of them in my acceptance speech. Some have developed in the course of this campaign. Having had the responsibility of this office for 30 years, my views upon most public questions are already set out in many cases in the public record and by definite public action. I do not have to engage in promises in respect to them. I may point to performance.

The opposition has shown its true purposes by its legislation in the last session of the Democratic House of Representatives, through their platform, and through the statements or evasions of their candidate.

Of these subjects I may first refer to the tariff.

In a recent speech, in discussing the agricultural tariffs, I pointed out the specific disaster to our farms from the Democratic proposal to reduce the protective tariff. I pointed out that the Democratic Party had, in 1913, not been content with merely lowering the tariff, but had put a large part of the farm products on the free list. I pointed out that the Republican Party had passed an emergency farm tariff bill in 1921, as soon as they had a majority in the Congress, and that a Democratic President had vetoed it. I pointed out that the Democratic minority in Congress, in 1921, had voted against the revival of the emergency farm tariff, and that the Republican majority had passed it, and a Republican President had signed it. I pointed out that the Democratic minority had voted against an increase in agricultural tariffs in the Republican tariff act of 1922. I pointed out that most of the Democratic Members of Congress voted against the bill carrying the increases in tariffs on agricultural products in the special session of Congress which I called in 1929 for that purpose on which occasion we passed the Hawley-Smoot bill.

In the light of this historic attitude it is but natural that our opponents express their bitter opposition to the Republican tariff. They have habitually voted against these tariffs. And now they propose in their platform a 'competitive tariff for revenue,' and they denounce the Smoot-Haw. ley bill which is mainly devoted to the increase of farm tariffs. The Democratic candidate from the day of his nomination iterated and reiterated that he proposed to reduce the tariff. He stated that it was an unwarranted increase in the tariff.

During the first 7 weeks of this campaign he not only adopted the historic position of his party, but he constantly repeats their platform, and has reinforced it by repeated statements, as for instance:

'I support the competitive tariff for revenue.'

'The tariff law of 1932 was a drastic revision of the tariff upward in spite of the fact that the existing tariff levels were already high enough to protect American industries.'

'We sit on the high wall of the Hawley-Smoot tariff.'

'I condemn the Hawley-Smoot tariff.'

'A wicked and exorbitant tariff.'

'Sealed by the highest tariff in the history of the world.'

'Our policy declares for lowered tariffs.'

'A ghastly jest of the tariff.'

Mr. Roosevelt and his party knew that the major increases in the Hawley-Smoot act were farm tariffs when that platform was drawn, and he knew it was in effect when he made the statements that I have quoted. The evidence is complete that he and they intend to reduce the farm tariffs.

During the past 3 weeks I have reiterated this plain and evident purpose of their party and their candidate. Unquestionably my exposition has given their candidate great anxiety, because on the 25th of this month some 6 or 7 days ago, just 21 days after my first statement on the subject he announced another new deal. I call this a new shuffle. He now announces within 2 weeks of the election that he does not propose to reduce tariffs on farm products.

This is the most startling shift in position by a Presidential candidate: in the midst of a political campaign in all recent political history. What do you think Grover Cleveland or Samuel Tilden or Woodrow Wilson would have said to such a shift as that? Does the candidate realize that he has overnight thrown overboard the great historic position of his party? That he has rewritten the Democratic platform? Does he realize that he must withdraw large parts of the speeches in which he has denounced this Hawley-Smoot bill as the origin of all the world's calamity?

I have the privilege of informing him that 66 percent of all the duties collected on all of the imports into the United States are directly on imports of agricultural origin and the reduction of which would affect American farmers.

Are we to take it that all the diatribes we have heard from the Democratic orators throughout this campaign are in respect to only one-third of the American tariffs? For just 7 days ago the Democratic candidate said, 'The Hawley-Smoot tariff law carried the decline in world trade, and what amounted to a world calamity became a general international calamity.' Since that time he must have concluded that the farm tariffs have done the world no harm.

You will further remember that under the tariff act two-thirds of our imports are free of duty, and now he excludes two-thirds of the remaining one-third that are dutiable. Does the Democratic Party now pretend that this terrible world calamity which we have encountered was caused by the tariffs on one-ninth of the imports into the United States? And further, do they know--and they do know--that of this one-ninth of the imports of non-agricultural commodities less than one-half of them were increased by the Hawley-Smoot tariff bill?

Now to continue our mathematical explorations a little further, I'm wondering if they pretend that this calamity was caused by increase of tariffs on one-eighteenth of the imports of the United States? And I may pursue this mathematical course still further. Do they recognize that the whole of our imports, that is, the imports of the United States, constitute less than 12 percent of the imports of the world all taken together, and thus, in this revised view, the increased duties on one-eighteenth of one-twelfth or less than one-half of 1 percent of the world's import trade brought about this gigantic calamity by which 30 nations failed or gone to revolution.

Should not the Democratic candidate now at last search in the aftermath of the World War for the origins of our difficulties and stop this nonsense?

I wish to extend this discussion a little further. It is desirable that the Governor may explain himself some further on other tariff questions. Does he include the reduction of the tariff on cotton textiles, so largely manufactured in the South? I have included but a part of the textile duties in the agricultural tariffs – the tariffs on agricultural products-inasmuch as only a part of the raw cotton is dutiable. And I wonder whether he proposes to close up the Southern cotton mills?

In view of this new light of maintaining tariffs, I wonder if he has considered the grievous position that the oil industry might be in the States of California, Oklahoma, Texas, and Kansas, if they are left out? Has he considered the copper industry in the States of Arizona, Montana, Michigan, and Utah? Has he considered the tariffs on metal and other products which affect the welfare of the whole of the people of New England, New York, Pennsylvania, California, New Jersey, Ohio, Indiana, Illinois, West Virginia, and other States? Has he considered the tariff on pottery and chemicals and its effect upon New Jersey, Ohio, Indiana, Illinois, New York, Pennsylvania, West Virginia, California, and a lot of other States? And will he consider the tariffs on lumber and their effect on Oregon, Washington, California, and Wisconsin? If we are going to retreat from a reduction of the tariff those people ought to have some word of comfort also.

Perhaps if he would give the same consideration as to the effect of reducing the tariff for these other people, he will come to the same conclusion as that which he has been forced to come by this debate in respect to agriculture. Now, if political exigencies have forced this temporary conversion on agricultural products, how far is the Governor authorized to change at will the traditional policies and the platform of the Democratic Party? How far can he guarantee to bring with him the Democratic Members of the House and the Senate who voted against the bills carrying the increases in agricultural tariffs, and how about the men who wrote that plank in the Democratic platform? Now do you who are farmers believe in eleventh-hour conversion? Do you consider that your livelihood is safe in the hands of the traditional and the present enemy of the protective tariff?

Perhaps the Governor and the whole Democratic Party will now withdraw and apologize for the defamation to which I have been subjected for the past 2 years because I called a special session of the Congress and secured an increase in agricultural tariffs.

Now I am, myself, taking heart over this debate. If it could be continued long enough, I believe we could drive him from every solitary position he has taken in this campaign. They are equally untenable. But even on the tariff, he perhaps remembers the dreadful experience of the chameleon on the Scotch plaid. And I can illustrate this to you.

As to the balance of the protective tariffs, unless this late conversion extends further than agriculture, he proposes to reduce them in the face of the fact that during the last 12 months there has been a violent change in the economy of the entire world through the depreciation of currencies in some 30 European nations and thus a lowering of their standards of living and the creation of still greater differences between the costs of production in the United States and abroad.

Now, the Republican Party is squarely for the protective tariff. I refuse to put the American workers and farmers into further unemployment and misery by any such action as the unrepented principles of their Members of the Democratic Congress and their platform.

The Governor's new shuffle, however, requires that he give some further assurances to our farmers in order to make it consistent. The Democratic House of Representatives and their allies in the Senate passed a bill directing me to call an international conference for the purpose of reducing tariffs. The Governor has supported this in his program. That means that we should surrender to foreigners the determination of a policy which we have zealously held under American control for nearly 150 years, ever since the first protective tariff was enacted under George Washington's administration. This would, in that manner, place the fate of American workers and American farmers in the hands of foreign nations, and I vetoed the bill.

But the point that I wish to make now is that the Governor should give to the farmers that if he calls this conference which he has assured he will do, that he will exempt agricultural tariffs from the discussion therein.

Further than this the Democratic Party and their candidate propose to enter upon reciprocal tariffs. That idea is not entirely new in our history, although it is a violation of what has now become a firmly fixed principle of uniform and equal treatment of all nations without preferences, concessions, or discriminations. It is just such concessions and discriminations that are producing today a large part of the frictions over tariffs in Europe. I suppose our Democratic friends blame these European tariff wars on the Hawley-Smoot bill.

Though reciprocal tariffs are a violation of well-established American principles, this Nation has fallen from grace at times and attempted to do this very thing. At one time 22 such treaties were negotiated for this purpose. Congress refused to confirm 16 of them; 2 of the remaining failed of confirmation by other governments; and 4 others were so immaterial as to be forgotten. On another occasion Congress conferred on the Executive a limited authority to make treaties of this character. Twenty-two of them were agreed upon, all of which were repealed by tariff acts. Now this demonstrates just one thing: that in an intelligent democracy you cannot surrender the welfare of one industry or one locality in order to gain something for another.

But there is an overriding objection to a reciprocal tariff upon which the Governor's new shuffle requires that he give these further assurances to the farmers. The vast majority of the wishes of foreign countries about our tariffs is to get us to reduce our farm tariffs so that they may enter our agricultural market. The only concessions that we could grant through reciprocal tariffs of any great importance would be at the cost of our farmers. Since the Governor has assured the Nation of a policy of reciprocal tariffs, he should give an assurance to the farmers that the farm tariffs will not be included and that he will abandon the whole idea of reciprocal tariffs in relation to agriculture. This, of course, takes away the whole foundation of the trading value in reciprocal tariffs. And we may as well abandon the further discussion of that in this campaign.

In all this discussion about reducing tariffs it should be remembered that if any one of the rates or schedules in our tariff is too high, it has been open to our opponents during the whole of the last session of the House of Representatives to pass a simple resolution and thereby secure its review by the Tariff Commission. Did they do that? They did not.

The establishment of the Tariff Commission with this authority destroyed one of the campaign methods of the Democratic Party, and that was to conduct their campaigns by exhibiting kettles and pans to the housewives of the Nation and explaining what unjust cost was imposed upon them by the tariff. Now that maneuver is no longer effective, with the bipartisan Tariff Commission open to give remedy to the housewives of the United States.

The Democrats propose, in fact, passed a bill in the last session in the lower House, to destroy the authority of the bipartisan Tariff Commission by which it may change the tariff so as to correct inequities or to alter the schedules to meet the changing tides of an economic world. Thus, they propose to return to the old logrolling, the old orgies of greed, viciousness, and stagnation of business during general congressional action in review of the tariff.

The increased authority to the bipartisan Tariff Commission to make changes in the tariff with the approval of the President was brought about at my insistence, and with the sterling courage of your Senator, 2 years ago. That was the greatest reform in tariff legislation in half a century. And it originated from Theodore Roosevelt.

No better example of the vital importance of the flexible tariff exists than today, when we are in the crisis of men and women being thrown out of employment due to depreciated currencies abroad and of low-priced farm products moving over our borders. The commission is today reexamining the new differences in the cost of production at home and abroad that action may be taken to restore men and women to their jobs.

Sound public policy maintains the necessity of this Commission and its authorities. The Democratic policy is to destroy it, but perhaps the Governor of New York will offer us a new deal in this matter, also.

Now, related to the tariff, the Democratic candidate proposes to place the payment of the war debts owed to us by foreign countries squarely on the shoulders of the American workman and the American farmer by lowering the tariffs for this special purpose. He would let down the bars to the American market for foreign commodities to the extent necessary that foreign nations may collect from the profits of their manufactures the money with which to pay these debts. Will he now exclude the 66 percent of dutiable imports, which are farm products, from this proposal?

My own view in opposition to cancellation of the war debts is a matter of public record through many public statements and messages to Congress. I have proposed that if opportunity offers we should use the foreign debts, payment by payment, to expand foreign markets for our labor and our own farmers. That is not cancellation and that is the reverse of the announced policy of the Democratic candidate.

At no point in this campaign have our opponents stated clearly and definitely their position on immigration. I have looked for it. I may have overlooked it. If I have I apologize. I have stated that I favor rigidly restricted immigration. I endeavored to secure from the Congress the return of the quota bases from the national origins to the base previously given. I have recommended that a more humane provision should be made for bringing in the near relatives of our citizens. I shall persist in these matters.

I have limited immigration by administrative order during the depression in order to relieve us of unemployment or, alternatively, to save the jobs of our people who are now at work. Two years prior to that order going into effect slightly under half a million immigrants came into the United States. Since it went into effect, more have gone out of the United States than have come in. The distressed people with lowered standards of living that would have come in would have been a far greater addition to our unemployed than even this amount. The Democratic candidate, incidentally, overlooked that little item in stating that the Republican administration had done nothing in the first 2 years and 2 months of this depression.

[...]

My countrymen, I repeat to you, the fundamental issue of this campaign, the decision that will fix the national direction for a hundred years to come, is whether we shall go on in fidelity to American traditions or whether we shall turn to innovations, the spirit of which is disclosed to us by many sinister revelations and veiled promises.

My friends, I wish to make my position clear. I propose to go on in the faith and loyalty to the traditions of our race. I propose to build upon the foundations which our fathers have laid over this last 150 years.

'Trade Agreements or Free Trade?', *Review of the River Plate* (Buenos Aires, Argentina), 29 July 1934, translated by UK Embassy, Buenos Aires, PRO, BT 11/824.

Encl. in Buenos Aires

Despatch No. 282 'E'

July 27th 1934.

Buenos Aires.

20 July, 1934.

'REVIEW OF THE RIVER PLATE'

Trade Agreements or Free Trade?

Not altogether reassuring to those who would see trade in general expend to something like its old volume are the reports giving the general tenor of the conversations between Mr. Cordell Hull, the U.S. Secretary of State, and Dr. Espil, Argentina's Ambassador at Washington. That the United States are desirous of negotiating a commercial treaty with Argentina, but that under existing circumstances it was advisable to postpone all talk until next autumn, without fixing a date, looks very much as if the protectionist interests 'up North' were politically far too powerful to risk their being exasperated by any concrete agreement with Argentina which would enable this republic to pay for her purchases of American manufactures by shipments of her surplus produce. And one cannot help feeling that Mr. Cordell Hull is altogether too much an affable all-things-to-all-men type of politician to be dependable – when it comes to signing on the dotted line. His idealism at the World Economic Conference, like his enthusiasm over a commercial agreement of mutual benefit between the U.S.A. and Argentina, is evidently a sincere expression of his opinion as a man, but it seems, just as evident that he is merely used to throw dust in the eyes of those countries whose aims and aspirations in practical business happen to clash with the material profits of the United States. Therefore the only thing open to Argentina to do is to cut down, as far as she can, all official permits for dollar remittances, retaining as much export paper as she can get hold of in order to use it for the settlement of debt services in New York. Let America sell her goods here on the open market rate; unless and until her exporters to this country find it to their advantage to bring pressure to bear at Washington in favour of the Argentine producer. Only by thus acting will it be possible to bring home to both sides the basic principles of Free Trade which Mr. Cordell Hull professes to support. Free Trade will come to its own little by little, and trade agreements are a means to that desirable end. Meanwhile Argentina will do well to remember that fine words butter no parsnips, and, comparing her sales accounts in the different countries who are her customers, help the trade of those who help her revenue; in a word, 'Buy from those who buy from us.'

THE OTTAWA ECONOMIC CONFERENCE, 1931–2

In the interwar period, the world economy lacked a hegemon to stabilize the international economic system. As Charles Kindleberger has argued, 'the United States was able, but unwilling; Britain was willing but unable'.[1] Throughout the 1920s Britain had – with the notable exception of the failure to repeal the wartime McKenna duties on luxuries – maintained a policy of economic openness even under Conservative governments. The economic distraction of the First World War meant that the United States and Japan had the opportunity to enter and exploit traditional British markets in South America and China. While Britain's trade position in the interwar years improved compared to its pre-war performance with countries such as France and Russia, its trade deficit with the United States swelled by nearly 80 per cent, going from an annual average of approximately £71 million before the war to a one of £127 million in the years after the war.[2] Winston Churchill's endorsement of the City and Bank of London's preferences for returning the pound to the gold standard at the pre-war parity of $4.86 per pound helped the financial sector but decimated industry. At the pre-war parity, Britain experienced an overvalued exchange rate, uncompetitive exports and heightened unemployment.[3]

Previous imperial economic conferences in the 1920s had seen the Dominions press Britain to introduce preferential tariffs on non-Empire foodstuffs, but British governments had always refused. However, the increase in European tariffs in the late 1920s and the United States' Smoot-Hawley tariff of 1930 emboldened Conservative tariff reformers in the United Kingdom to step up their efforts at creating a system of imperial preference. The fall of the Labour government in autumn 1931 and the creation of the National government dominated by the Conservatives gave imperial preference a fresh start. While the National government failed to keep the pound on gold, its massive electoral triumph in October 1931 led to 556 of the 615 MPs in the House of Commons – 473 of whom were Conservatives – supporting the National government. The Labour opposition could muster only 46 MPs. While Ramsey MacDonald remained as Prime Minister after the October election, the free trade supporter Philip Snowden was replaced by Neville Chamberlain, son of Joseph Chamberlain, the political godfather of imperial preference. Although pledged to support the National government, the Liberal Party split into two factions within the government and a third, small group based around Lloyd George and his family in opposition. The 'official' Liberal Party of 33 MPs under the leadership of Herbert Samuel remained committed to free trade and ultimately left the National government in the wake of the Ottawa Agreement, as did Snowden. A group of 35 National Liberal MPs under the leadership of Sir John Simon remained within the National government and supported imperial preference after 1932.

As the political support for free trade collapsed in the House of Commons and government, the intellectual case was also experiencing serious erosion. By the middle of 1931, John Maynard Keynes was advocating a revenue tariff to shore up public finances, stimulate domestic demand and allow the pound's adherence to gold to be 'relentlessly defended'.[4] Within a matter of months, economic events replaced concern for the gold standard with concerns about stabilizing and consolidating imperial trade patterns. The September 1931 devaluation of sterling was seen as providing an immediate fillip to British exporters and import competers alike. The sudden devaluation of sterling by approximately 30 per cent against the dollar and other gold bloc countries gave British goods a competitive advantage and created the domestic price equivalent of a tariff on all gold bloc goods. As most of the Empire either used sterling or linked their currencies to the pound, the intra-Empire effects of devaluation were limited. The consequences were mainly felt on trade in those countries such as France and the United States that remained on gold or devalued by less than the pound, such as Germany. Many countries, including Canada, implemented additional tariffs against British goods in order to compensate for the 'artificially' low production costs of British manufactures.

The National government's passage of the Import Duties Act imposed a 10 per cent revenue tariff on goods, including raw materials and foodstuffs, entering the United Kingdom but delayed its imposition on Dominion and Empire goods until after the Ottawa Conference, where it was hoped preferential rates could be negotiated. These encouraged negotiations, but pressured Dominions to make concessions.[5] In introducing the Import Duties Act, Neville Chamberlain told the House of Commons that the bill would help fulfil his father's vision of imperial preference and a consolidated economic empire.[6]

The British Cabinet was of the opinion that the most substantial concession they could offer the Dominions was the creation of some form of Dominion wheat quota alongside agricultural tariffs. At previous economic conferences, Canada and Australia had pushed for wheat tariffs, but this smacked too closely to a return to the Corn Laws and a tax on bread for British policymakers to agree. However, a policy of quotas rather than tariffs might have the same results – guaranteeing Dominion grain producers a share of the British market – without the imposition of a government levy, although British resistance to food duties had evaporated by

1932.[7] This policy, British officials anticipated, would be especially attractive to Canada and Australia in the run-up to the Ottawa Conference.

Canadian Prime Minister Richard Bennett did little preparatory work for the Conference, and British officials were divided over whether this lack of preparation was due to bureaucratic incompetence, political stalemate or a calculated strategy on Bennett's part to avoid pre-committing Canada to tariff concessions to Britain. The Canadians did not send out a final agenda for the Conference until 7 July 1932, barely two weeks before the Conference was due to convene – and after several delegations had already set sail from the Antipodes and South Africa.[8] Although the Canadians were dilatory in their preparations, British ministries implemented a series of studies and innovations to generate potential British tariff and quota offers and seek out possible areas where the Dominions could make concessions. One of the innovations of the British negotiators was the creation of a panel of 'industrial advisors' in a range of industries. These representatives of industry had an informal role in advising British policymakers on the needs of British business, the desirability of certain concessions and the likely response of industry.[9]

Once in Ottawa, although the Canadians were interested in discussing trade and monetary issues, British negotiators were successful in stifling the discussion of monetary issues at the Conference and kept the focus of the agenda on trade concessions. British ambitions for an imperial secretariat based in London were likewise quickly sidelined by the sovereignty-conscious Dominions. The trade talks themselves quickly moved from multilateral talks to a series of bilateral discussions between the delegations from the United Kingdom, the Dominions and India. British proposals for a wheat quota met with a cool response from both Bennett and the Australians. The Australians repeatedly threatened to leave the conference – with the implied threat that the absence of a trade agreement might lead them to default on their debts to British bondholders – unless their demands for support for their meat and wheat industries were met. Faced with a potential breakdown in the Conference if they did not give way to Australian 'blackmail' on meat, the British delegation sought advice from Prime Minister MacDonald in London. He was characteristically noncommittal and the Conservative delegates Stanley Baldwin – Deputy Prime Minister and Lord President of the Council – and Neville Chamberlain – Chancellor of the Exchequer – were able to convince their more reluctant Liberal colleagues to accept a meat quota to salvage an agreement.[10] The British further agreed to impose additional duties on non-Empire products and maintain the 10 per cent tariffs of the Import Duties Act on third parties for at least five years.

In exchange for its range of concessions on meat, wheat and other raw materials, Britain received extended preferential tariff treatment from the Canadians, Australians and Indians on manufactures. New Zealand already imported almost all its finished goods from Britain and had low import duties across the board, so it had little to offer the mother country. Australia and Canada both agreed to accept the general principle of giving British goods equal footing with 'domestic production', although some disagreement remained about how to compensate for the depreciation of the pound and what levy to charge in order to equalize different wage rates. The Dominions and India all agreed to raise their tariffs on third parties while widening the margins of their preferential rates for British goods.

The Ottawa Conference had substantial political consequences at both the domestic and international level. Politically, divisions over implementing the Ottawa Agreements led to a decisive split in the Liberal Party, leading to its complete political marginalization. Internationally, the Ottawa Agreements had a mixed effect on British trading relations as they accelerated the international movement away from open markets and the consolidation of the world into separate trading blocs. Some countries, such as those Scandinavian countries traditionally oriented towards the British market, quickly sought preferential trading agreements with Britain for themselves. Britain's economic relations with other nations were further undermined. Imperial preference remained a sticking point in trade relations with the United States for years to come. American dissatisfaction was so intense that during the Second World War the United States insisted that Britain agree to dismantle the imperial preference arrangements agreed at Ottawa as part of the Lend-Lease agreements.[11]

Notes
1. C. Kindleberger, *The World in Depression, 1929–1939* (1973; Berkeley, CA: University of California Press, 1986).
2. Figures cited in F. Capie, *Depression and Protection: Britain Between the Wars* (London: George Allen & Unwin, 1983), p. 23.
3. D. E. Moggridge, *British Monetary Policy, 1924–1931: The Norman Conquest of $4.86* (Cambridge: Cambridge University Press, 1972).
4. *New Republic*, 8 April 1931, pp. 196–7. Keynes had, of course, famously opposed returning to the gold standard at the pre-war parity. See also R. Skidelsky, *John Maynard Keynes: The Economist as Saviour, 1920–1937* (London: Macmillan, 1992), pp. 360–87.
5. I. M. Drummond, *Imperial Economic Policy, 1917–1939: Studies in Expansion and Protection* (London: George Allen & Unwin, 1974), pp. 180–1.
6. A. Howe, *Free Trade and Liberal England, 1846–1946* (Oxford: Clarendon Press, 1997), p. 283.
7. See Report of the Committee on the Proposed Imperial Economic Conference at Ottawa, 23 November 1931, below, pp. 329–36, on pp. 331, 335.
8. Drummond, *Imperial Economic Policy*, pp. 208–10.
9. See Minutes of the Fourth Meeting at the Board of Trade with Industrial Advisors Prior to the Ottawa Imperial Economic Conference, 3 June 1932, below, pp. 346–8.
10. See Secret Note by the United Kingdom Delegation on the Canadian Tariff Proposals, 8 August 1932, below, pp. 356–9.
11. Capie, *Depression and Protection*, p. 31.

THE OTTAWA IMPERIAL ECONOMIC CONFERENCE, 1931–2

Report of the Committee on the Proposed Imperial Economic Conference At Ottawa, 23 November 1931, PRO DO 35/236/12.

COPY NO. 28
CABINET.
COMMITTEE ON THE PROPOSED IMPERIAL
ECONOMIC CONFERENCE AT OTTAWA.

REPORT.

1. At their Meeting on November 3rd, 1931 (Cabinet 73 (31) Conclusion 3) the Cabinet agreed in principle that as soon as the Government had been re-constituted, a Cabinet Committee should be set up which should include the following Ministers –

The Chancellor of the Exchequer

The Secretary of State for Dominion Affairs

The President of the Board of Trade

The Minister of Agriculture and Fisheries to examine all matters relating to the Ottawa Conference and to make recommendations to the Cabinet as to the policy of His Majesty's Government in the United Kingdom at the Conference; the Committee to have authority to invite the attendance of other Ministers adhoc as required.

3. The Committee have considered a Memorandum (Paper O.C. (31) 2 – Appendix I) submitted to them by the Secretary of State for Dominion Affairs relative to the main problems likely to arise in the course of his forthcoming mission to the Dominions and subsequently at the Ottawa Conference itself.

4. The Committee are of opinion that the failure of the Ottawa Conference to reach agreement on the large questions of policy remitted to it would be a fatal blow to Imperial interests, and that it is accordingly imperative that every effort should be made beforehand to ensure the success of the Conference. The mission of the Secretary of State for Dominion Affairs to the Dominions is designed to secure the largest possible measure of agreement in advance of the Conference, and it is certain that when visiting each Dominion he will be asked what the United Kingdom are prepared to do. It is essential, therefore, that before leaving England he should be fully aware of the policy which the Government intend to pursue on the various matters raised in his Memorandum.

5. With regard to one of these matters, namely a Dominion Wheat Quota, the Minister of Agriculture and Fisheries has circulated to the Committee a Note prepared in his Department (on the basis of investigations which took place during the period of Office of the Labour Government) with regard to a possible quota for Dominion wheat and wheat flour. In his covering Memorandum to this Note, the Minister observed –

'It should be borne in mind that the general principles of a quota policy, whether for Home or Dominion wheat, have not yet been considered by the Cabinet. I propose in the near future to circulate a document to the Cabinet on the subject asking for authority, if the general principles of a quota scheme are approved, to discuss the practical administrative details of a home scheme with the industries concerned, whose co-operation is essential to success. While, therefore, the Ottawa Committee will wish to give early consideration to the possibilit of a quota for Dominion wheat and wheat flour, it is important that detailed investigation by this Committee should follow and not precede the decision by the Cabinet and the subsequent discussion with the industries referred to above.'

6. The Cabinet are reminded that the Canadian and Australian representatives who; at the opening of the 1930 Imperial Conference, had advocated Tariffs and had regarded the Quota Scheme with disfavour, changed their view of the Quota during the Conference, and ended with an inclination to support such a scheme. On the other hand, at its termination the Conference was informed that the United Kingdom Government had put forward the scheme for consideration, but must not be regarded as being committed to it without further examination. At no stage during the discussions had any guarantee of price formed part of the Wheat Quota Scheme. The Dominion representatives never, indeed, asked for a guaranteed price. The discussions all centered on what the Quota should be, and the nature of the machinery that would be required to work it.

7. The Committee[1] are of opinion that, subject to the decision to be reached by the Cabinet on the proposale of the Minister of Agriculture and Fisheries (see paragraph 5 above) the reply to the question raised in paragraph 13 (1) of the Memorandum of the Secretary of State for Dominion Affairs should be (1) that the United Kingdom Government are now prepared to offer a Dominion Wheat Quota, and (2) that in the event of the Secretary of State for Dominion Affairs being authorised to offer a Dominion Wheat Quota, that quota should be without any guarantee of price.

8. In paragraph 5 and subsequent paragraph of his Memorandum, the Secretary of State for Dominion Affairs asked for the guidance of the Cabinet as to the line which he should take when he was asked (as he would be) what course the United Kingdom Government proposed to take as to United Kingdom tariffs and whether he should proceed on the assumption that preferential tariffs on articles of food (with or without specified exemptions, e.g. wheat) are now permissible in principle as a basis for discussion with the Dominions (see paragraph 18 (ii) of the Secretary of State's Memorandum). The Committee are agreed that the Government's mandate does not rule out such tariffs, and that the answer to this question should accordingly be in the affirmative.

9. In order to avoid delay the Committee have invited the Interdepartmental Committee to make a preliminary survey of articles appearing most suitable for possible tariff concessions to the Dominions, and to report thereon to the Committee not later than 3rd December next. The Committee will include recommendations on this subject in their next Report to the Cabinet.

10. On the assumption that the Cabinet agree in principle that concessions by the United Kingdom by way of quotas or preferential tariffs on any articles of food are admissible as a basis for discussion with the Dominions, it is necessary to examine the three important questions summarised in paragraph 13 (iii) (iv) and (v) of the Secretary of State's Memorandum. These questions can most conveniently be considered together.

11. The first question is whether such concessions are to be granted voluntarily by the United Kingdom, or only in return for specified concessions on the part of the Dominions concerned, or partly voluntarily and partly as a result of a quid pro quo. The second question is whether the principle hitherto invariably observed by the United Kingdom (though not by the Dominions) is to be maintained, first every United Kingdom concession must be extended to the whole Empire without discrimination. The third

---

1 Note. The President of the Board of Trade reserves his opinion on the question of a Dominion Wheat Quota until he has had an opportunity of considering the documents which have been circulated to the Committee on the subject.

question is whether a concession for which one part of the Empire would be prepared to make a corresponding concession, is to be withheld from the whole Empire (including that part) until all other parts to which the concession would also be valuable have also agreed to make corresponding concessions.

12. With regard to these questions, the attention of the Cabinet is specially drawn to the arguments in favour of maintaining the present system of voluntary concessions applicable to the Empire as a whole set out in paper E.E. (B) (30) 44, a copy of which is annexed to the Secretary of State's Memorandum. The Cabinet will realise the political and economic dangers involved in the alternative policy of discrimination between different parts of the Empire. In this connection it will be remembered that the discrimination by Canada in favour of Australia as against New Zealand produce in the recent Canadian-Australian Trade Agreement has given rise to considerable feeling between Canada and New Zealand.

13. On the other hand, it has been represented to the Committee that, having regard to the very diverse needs of the different Dominions, it is difficult to see how the problem could be satisfactorily solved on the lines. suggested in the Memorandum and its annex, namely that the concessions to be made by the United Kingdom should, as in the past, be on a purely voluntary basis, and should extend without discrimination to the whole Empire. In this connection it must not be overlooked that in the past the policy of the generous gesture has not produced any very striking results.

14. Moreover, it would certainly be much easier for the Ministers of a particular Dominion to defend (as against their own manufacturing interests) tariff concessions on imported United Kingdom goods, if they could show that in return they got some special advantage from the United Kingdom with regard to their own products. If, however, that Dominion could obtain the advantage automatically and without giving any specific quid pro quo it was difficult to see what answer could be made to the Dominion manufacturing interests, who would certainly be opposed to any such concessions unless it were shown that the long range benefits thereby secured out weighed the immediate disadvantage to themselves. Precisely the same considerations applied at home, and it would be much easier to defend concessions in the cases of the imported products of a particular Dominion if it could be shown that in return our manufacturers were receiving corresponding advantages in that Dominion. The Government would be open to serious criticism here if they made substantial concessions and obtained nothing definite in return, especially in view of the fact that the concessions to the Dominions must almost necessarily have reference to taxation of food stuffs.

15. The Committee submit the following conclusions on these questions to the Cabinet –

The Committee agree that discussions must be conducted in the first instance with each Dominion on the following basis:-

(1) That concessions by the United Kingdom should be balanced by an adequate preference to the United Kingdom on the part of the Dominion concerned.

(2) That it should be explained to each Dominion in turn that it was proposed to offer the concession made by the United Kingdom with regard to any article to other Dominions (if interested in the article) but only in exchange for a corresponding adequate preference.

(3) That in the event of failure to secure a corresponding adequate preference from a Dominion desiring to receive the United Kingdom concession, abandonment of the concession in respect of that Dominion would be the first result, but in that case the whole circumstances would have to be reviewed again, and conceivably the original arrangement might have to be abandoned or modified.

The Committee further agree that the results of all the discussions in accordance with the above procedure should be reviewed by the Ottawa Conference, and if it were found that the reciprocal mutual concessions were generally satisfactory, those concessions should be consolidated into a single multilateral recommendation by the Conference.

16. In paragraph 12 of his Memorandum (Appendix I), the Secretary of State for Dominion Affairs said that he assumed that for the purpose of his visit to the Dominions he could proceed to discuss matters with the respective Prime Ministers on the basis that

'(a) we hope to obtain further tariff concessions from the Dominions:

(b) we rule out any idea of Import Boards and Bulk Purchase:

(c) we are in favour of furthering a scheme of industrial co-operation on the lines suggested in the Report (Paper O.C. (30) 28) submitted to the previous Cabinet Committee.'

17. In order to facilitate the attainment of (a) above the Board of Trade have prepared schedules of commodities in respect of which new or increased Customs tariff preferences in each of the Dominions would be of assistance to the export trade of the United Kingdom. These schedules are in course of examination by the trade associations concerned, and the President of the Board of Trade proposes to circulate to the Committee at a very early date the various schedules together with memoranda dealing with the volume and general direction of the trade of the Dominions, the nature of their Customs tariffs and the broad effects of recent changes therein and certain other trade features which merit special mention. [...]

19. As regards (b) of paragraph 16 above, it will be recalled that the possibility of the United Kingdom offering economic advantages to the Dominions based on Import Boards and Bulk Purchase was discussed by the Imperial Conference of 1930, but that arrangements of this kind were found on subsequent examination to be impracticable.

The Committee agree with this conclusion, and accordingly recommend that any idea of Import Boards and Bulk Purchase should be ruled out from consideration.

20. As regards (c) of paragraph 16 above, the Committee attach for the information of the Cabinet, the Inter-Departmental Committee's Report on Inter-Imperial Industrial Co-operation (Appendix II). The Committee favour the furtherance of a scheme of industrial co-operation on the lines suggested in this Report.

21. The Secretary of State for the Colonies has reminded the Committee that there are large areas in the Colonial Empire over which no preference for British goods can, for various reasons, be given; for example, we are precluded by international agreement from making any such arrangement as regards the Congo Basin for a period of at least five years. Nigeria will have to give a year's notice before according any preference and in that case account would also have to be taken of possible French colonial retaliation. Many other Colonies are in such a depressed financial condition that they cannot risk the loss of revenue involved in granting increased or additional preferences beyond those at present accorded; on the other hand they may be able to give such preferences when trade revives. Some of the Colonies are already in receipt of Treasury grants; others will be driven to seek Treasury assistance when their balances are exhausted, unless their trade materially improves.

22. In these circumstances the Secretary of State for the Colonies asked for a decision on the following two questions of principle:–
    (1) that it should be open to him to ask for preferences on commodities imported into the United Kingdom from the Colonies; and
    (2) that the granting of any such request should not necessarily be dependent upon the grant of reciprocal concessions by the Colonies concerned.

23. The Committee agreed that an regards (2) above, the position of the Colonies is essentially different from that of the Dominions and that it would be impracticable, therefore, to insist on any arrangements with the Colonies being upon a strictly reciprocal basis.

    The Committee recommend to the Cabinet –
    (1) That the Secretary of State for the Colonies should be at liberty to make suggestions to the Chancellor of the Exchequer with regard to preferences on commodities imported into the United Kingdom from the

Colonies whether those commodities are now subject to Customs Duties or not.

(2) That the acceptance of any suggestion under (1) above should not necessarily be made dependent upon the grant of reciprocal concessions by the Colonies concerned.

24. The Conclusions and Recommendations of the Committee may be summarised as follows:-

Dominion Wheat Quota (paragraph 7).

>(a)(i) Subject to the decision to be reached by the Cabinet on the proposals of the Minister of Agriculture and Fisheries (see paragraph 5 of this Report) the United Kingdom Government are now prepared to offer a Dominion Wheat Quota.
>
>>(ii) In the event of the Secretary of State for Dominion Affairs being authorised to offer a Dominion Wheat Quota, that quota should be without any guarantee of price.

Preferential Tariffs in the United Kingdom. (paragraph 8 & 9)

>(b) (i) The Government's mandate does not rule out preferential tariffs, and accordingly the Secretary of State for Dominion Affairs should proceed on the assumption that preferential tariffs on articles of food (with or without specified exemptions, e.g. wheat) are now permissible in principle as a basis for discussion with the Dominions.
>
>>(ii) The Committee's recommendations as to the articles which appear to be most suitable for possible tariff concessions to the Dominions will be embodied in a later Report to the Cabinet.

Tariff Discussions with the Dominions (paragraph 15.).

>(c) (i) Discussions must be conducted in the first instance with each Dominion on the following basis.
>
>>(1) That concessions by the United Kingdom should be balanced by an adequate preference to the United Kingdom on the part of the Dominion concerned.
>>
>>(2) That it should be explained to each Dominion in turn that it was proposed to offer the concession made by the United Kingdom with regard to any article to other Dominions (if interested in the article) but only in exchange for a corresponding adequate preference.
>>
>>(3) That in the event of failure to secure a corresponding adequate preference from a Dominion desiring to receive the United Kingdom concession, abandonment of the concession in respect of that Dominion would be the first result, but in that case the whole circumstances would have to be reviewed again, and conceivably the original arrangement might have to be abandoned or modified.

(c) (ii) The results of all the discussions in accordance with the above procedure should be reviewed by the Ottawa Conference, and if it were found that the reciprocal mutual concessions were generally satisfactory, those concessions should be consolidated into a single multilateral recommendation by the Conference.

Tariff Concessions from the Dominions (paragraphs 16 – 18).

(d) It is hoped to obtain further tariff concessions from the Dominions. The Committee's recommendations regarding commodities on which new or increased customs tariff preferences in each of the Dominions would be of assistance to the export trade of the United Kingdom, will be comprised in a further report to be submitted by the Committee to the Cabinet in due course.

Import Boards and Bulk Purchase (paragraph 19).

(e) Any idea of Import Boards and Bulk Purchase should be ruled out from consideration.

Industrial Co-operation (paragraph 20).

(f) Approval should be given for the furtherance of a scheme of Inter-Imperial industrial co-operation on the lines suggested in the Report [...] of the Inter-Departmental Committee.

Colonies and Protectorates Tariff Preferences (paragraph 23).

(g) (i) The Secretary of State for the Colonies should be at liberty to make suggestions to the Chancellor of the Exchequer with regard to preferences on commodities imported into the United Kingdom from the Colonies, whether those commodities are now subject to customs duties or not.

(ii) The acceptance of any suggestion under (i) above should not necessarily to made dependent upon the grant of reciprocal concessions by the Colonies concerned.

Signed on behalf of the Committee.
J. H. THOMAS.
Chairman.

'Dominion Industries', *The Times*, 18 December 1931, p. 13.

DOMINION INDUSTRIES

Mr. Bennett had no sooner arrived in Ottawa than he hastened to inform the Canadian public of the preparations that are being made for the Imperial Economic Conference. Arrangements, he said, had been made for a preliminary survey of their fiscal and economic position by all the Dominions; committees would be set up to explore different problems; there would be continuous consultative exchanges; and, when agreements manifestly could not be made offhand, every effort would be made to work out satisfactory compromises. He hoped that when the Conference met the governing principles of an Imperial cooperative policy would have been determined and the broad scope already defined of the agreements they hoped to reach. Mr. Thomas on his part had set out a few days earlier the steps which the British Government were taking to further the success of the Conference. The Cabinet Committee of which he was chairman was meeting regularly to determine questions of policy, and was assisted by an inter-departmental committee which was collecting and co-ordinating all the information necessary for a fair examination of the problems. In addition he had invited every Dominion to choose or to send representatives to collaborate in that work, and he had offered them the services of work, and he had offered them the services of the British Trade Commissioner in every Dominion to assist in similar work at home. On the day when Mr. Thomas made his speech it was announced that the British Preparatory Committee for the Imperial Conference of 1930 – which included representatives of the Association of British Chambers of Commerce, the Federation of British Industries, and the Chamber of Shipping of the United Kingdom – had been reconstituted under the title of the British Committee on Empire Trade in order to consider representations to be made to the British Government with a view to the Ottawa Conference. And it is expected that before long similar preparatory committees will be formed in the Dominions, and that these committees will get into touch with one another and with the committee in London in order to exchange views and information, establish agreements, and clear up misunderstandings.

The necessity for all this preparatory work and for a full and frank interchange of views before the Conference meets is shown by the comments of some of the Dominion newspapers on Mr. Thomas's statement. Mr. Thomas had announced that, subject to a satisfactory arrangement being made and to a real and genuine *quid pro quo*, the Government were prepared to offer the Dominions a guaranteed quota of wheat. The announcement was welcomed in Canada and Australia, the two wheat-exporting Dominions, and Mr. Bennett lost no time after his return to Canada in expressing his gratification. But in some of the newspaper comments there seemed a note of alarm, as if the reference to a *quid pro quo* contained a threat against the interests of the secondary industries in the Dominions. The Melbourne *Age*, for instance, said that Mr. Thomas's statement should bring home to the electors the necessity of choosing a Government composed of 'genuine Australians definitely pledged to protection, whose first loyalty will be to Australian secondary industries.' The Montreal *Star* went so far as to accuse Mr. Thomas of envisaging the Empire as an organization in which all the manufacturing is to be done in Great Britain while the Dominions continue to be the reservoir of cheap food and raw materials. It is quite clear that, if the British Government held any such antiquated views of the economic relationship between Great Britain and the Dominions, then there would be no use in holding a Conference at all, for it would be impossible to arrive at any agreement with the Dominions on those lines. But no such views are held in this country in any quarter that counts. The right of the Dominions to develop and extend their secondary industries is recognized without reserve, just as the right of Great Britain to maintain and develop her agricultural production is recognized in the Dominions. No one in the Dominions will object to the first place in the British market being reserved for the British farmer, and in the same way no one in Great Britain objects to the first place in the Dominion market being reserved for the Dominion manufacturers. But that does not rule out the possibility of mutually beneficial arrangements. Great Britain cannot grow all she needs – though she hopes to be able to grow a larger proportion of it. The Dominions cannot manufacture all they need – though they hope to manufacture an increasing quantity and an increasing variety. Our mutual interests dictate that we should open our markets as widely as possible to their productions and that they should open theirs as widely as possible to ours, while giving every reasonable consideration to our need to encourage our farming industries and to their need to encourage their manufacturing industries. The extent to which we can help one another will depend very largely on what is regarded as reasonable on one side and the other. On that point there will be wide differences of opinion, but it is not one on which we can dictate to them or they to us. It is here precisely that there is room for mutual accommodations and concessions – for the 'genuine *quid pro quo*' of which Mr. Thomas spoke and the 'satisfactory compromises' to which Mr. Bennett referred.

These mutual accommodations may be difficult to arrange. There is no use in ignoring the difficulty; but there is equally no use in exaggerating it; and indeed it will largely disappear if all parties recognize from the beginning that they have common interests which should rule out any narrow huckstering spirit in the negotiations. At the Conference the representatives of each Government will represent primarily, no doubt, the interests for which that Government is the trustee. But it would be fatal to take a narrow view of these interests. Among the chief interests of Great Britain is the prosperity of the Dominions, and this is true even from the lowest, most materialist, point of view, for they constitute the best and the most promising market for her industries. It is equally true that the prosperity of Great Britain is a vital interest of all the Dominions, if for no other reason than that the British market is all-important for their primary producers. The Conference in fact is an opportunity, not for higgling and bargain-making between trade competitors, but for mutual helpfulness between partners whose fortunes are tied up with one another. And if the Conference is approached in that spirit the apprehensions expressed by the Melbourne *Age* and the Montreal *Star* will easily be shown to be without foundation. It is true that there was at one time widespread in this country a half resentful regret that the Dominions had ceased to devote themselves exclusively to the production of food and raw materials. But that attitude is now altogether out of date. It is recognized that the development of secondary industries was necessary in the Dominions if they were to lead a full national life. Such criticism as is still heard – and it is a criticism heard just as often in the Dominions themselves as in Great Britain – is that eagerness to develop has sometimes led to the placing of heavy handicaps on industries which were economically sound in order to foster others for which conditions were not yet ripe and which could only be maintained at a loss to the whole community. That, however, is in every case the business of each particular Dominion. So far as British industries are concerned it is recognized that, given the proper cooperative spirit, the more complete development of the Dominions should result in a greater, not a smaller, demand for goods produced in Great Britain, though naturally there will be a change in the type of goods demanded. There is therefore no desire in this country to hinder the development of the Dominion industries. On the contrary, there is a growing desire to cooperate in that development; and one of the main objects of those who are preparing for the Ottawa Conference must be to work out plans by which the industries in Great Britain and in the Dominions can enter into effective partnership with one another to their mutual advantage and to that of the whole Empire.

'Memorandum of a Conversation with the [Canadian] Prime Minister on Friday, March 11th, Concerning Agenda for the Imperial Conference', 14 March 1931, PRO, PREM 1/112, no. 15.

MEMORANDUM OF A CONVERSATION WITH THE PRIME MINISTER ON FRIDAY MARCH 11th, CONCERNING AGENDA FOR THE IMPERIAL CONFERENCE.

On receipt of the Secretary of State's telegram Number 34 of the 11th March forwarding an enquiry from the Governor-General of New Zealand with regard to the agenda for the forthcoming Imperial Economic Conference, I asked the Prime Minister to see me and he was good enough to give me an interview on the same afternoon at the House of Commons.

2. As I have already reported in my telegram Number 38 of the 12th March, he talked freely about his ideas concerning the agenda and the Conference generally, but they are still rather in the air and no decisions have yet been taken by the Cabinet. Mr. Bennett's provisional conception of the Conference is that in the circumstances of this year the agenda should be narrowed down to two main headings, trade and currency. As regards the former, he has especially in mind the issues which may be regarded as having a direct and immediate influence on trade rather than those such as research, etc., which, however important in themselves, are less likely to be productive of immediate results. He considers that the three principal matters to be dealt with under the heading of trade should be tariffs; inter-imperial rationalisation, both industrial and in relation to raw products and the development of the Colonies; and propaganda such as the work of the Empire Marketing Board. Practical, concrete business in fact should be the note. Later on in our talk the Prime Minister once more emphasized that he and his government were not yet committed to these suggestions, but he authorised my communicating them to the Secretary of State and said that he would be glad to hear how they commended themselves to His Majesty's Government in the United Kingdom.

3. As our talk had started from New Zealand's enquiry, the Prime Minister broke off at on early stage in the conversation to refer to the New Zealand agreement. He read me part of a telegram which he had sent to the Prime Minister of New Zealand in the endeavour to persuade that government to agree to defer further action on the New Zealand-Canada agreement until after the Conference, or alternatively, if they could not accede to this post-

ponement, to agree that the arrangement when brought into force should be regarded as provisional and liable to modification, if necessary, as a result of the Conference.
4. With regard to the question of tariffs, it was obvious, as the action in respect of the New Zealand agreement indicates, that the Prime Minister would prefer to go into the Conference with as free a hand as possible. He referred to his endeavour in 1930 to secure recognition of the 'principle of preference' and appeared not altogether convinced that even now this principle was fully established in the United Kingdom – in the sense, I suppose, that he does not yet regard the United Kingdom as being permanently committed to a substantial general tariff with preference for the Empire. Affirmation, therefore, of the principle will probably be proposed, but he was not very clear about how that affirmation should be defined. On the one hand his language seemed to suggest that he would like to see a sort of parity of preference between the different self-governing members of the Commonwealth, but on the other hand he is conscious (a) that existing agreements such as that between Canada and Australia may be troublesome in this connection, whence no doubt his desire to postpone signature of the agreement with New Zealand; and (b) that preferences have to be negotiated in detail with results which, as circumstances vary in each case, may interfere with parity. He was at some pains to defend his doctrine of an imperial system based on one's own country first and the Empire second as against the outer world, and quoted with approval a recent speech in which Lord Hailsham had developed the same thesis from the standpoint of the United Kingdom. He illustrated his case by contending that Sir Wilfred Laurier had made a capital error in 1897 in neglecting this principle and giving Great Britain tariff preference for nothing. Obviously, there was a good deal that might have been said on this latter point, but as I wanted to get all the light I could on the Conference of 1932, it seemed prudent to avoid debate on what are now matters of history.
5. The Prime Minister talked a good deal about the Colonies. The subject has been much in his mind since his visit to London and a conversation he had there with Sir Philip Cunliffe-Lister, which he has mentioned to me more than once. The question of the Colonies has also had a good deal of prominence in the last few days owing to speeches by Mr. Churchill during his recent visit. When addressing the members of the two Houses of Parliament at a luncheon given by the Prime Minister, Mr. Churchill devoted a good part of his time to this theme and especially urged that Canada should continue her good work of helping the development of the West Indies. The Prime Minister would like to bring the Colonies into a general scheme of preferences, either through tariffs or by rationalising devices which would secure to

them markets for their raw materials. He rather regretted, he said, that they could not be more fully represented at the Conference, a point with which Mr. Churchill had also been concerned. He welcomed the separate representation of Southern Rhodesia and had been thinking whether it might not also be possible to have the West Indies directly represented. I suggested that this might be rather awkward as appearing to favour one group of Colonies against the rest, and that there was also the practical difficulty that the larger West Indian Colonies were not very good at working together and would probably each want their own representative. I told him that I was sure the secretary of state for the Colonies would be fully posted on colonial needs and on any concessions which the Colonies themselves might be able to make. I understood in fact that special enquiries were already being made on these points. I do not think that the Prime Minister is likely seriously to pursue the question of separate representation for the West Indies.

6. As he was expressing so special a concern for the interests of the Colonies, I felt that it was an apposite moment for referring to the unhappy case of canned pineapples from Malaya which have been heavily penalised as part of Canada's bargain with Australia (see my despatch Number 34 of the 25th February). The Prime Minister was rather apologetic on this subject. I ventured to suggest that while one must fully recognise the difficulty of bringing third parties into negotiations of the kind, it would be only fair to a Colony, when a proposition was brought forward by which its interests were likely to be affected, that some consultation should take place through this office or with the Colony direct. The Prime Minister agreed that this was reasonable.

7. As regards industrial rationalisation, the Prime Minister said he attached great importance to it, but he was not very specific in detail as to how it should be approached. His conception, however, of how trade preferences should be given, i.e. in respect of classes or sub-classes of goods which are not made in Canada, in fact involves the rationalising principle, especially as he has put it up to the Canadian manufacturers to furnish the necessary information and proposals. He told me incidentally that reports had so far been received only from two groups of Canadian manufacturers, viz. chemicals and electrical goods. He was very candid as to the difficulties arising from the selfishness of outlook of some of the manufacturing firms, which he said had been brought home to him in connection with his tariff policy.

8. As he had opened up this subject, I took the opportunity of telling him that the question had been raised whether representatives of the British steel and woollen industries might not usefully get into contact with Canadian manufacturers with a view to arriving at agreements which might facilitate the granting of tariff preferences (see my telegrams Numbers 32 and 39 of the 2nd and 12th March respectively). The Prime Minister welcomed this idea.

9. It is perhaps worth mentioning in connection with the rationalisation issue, though I forgot to refer to the point when talking with the Prime Minister, that I have had some talk recently with Dr. Tory, President of the National Research Council, with reference to his plans for making Canada self-contained in the testing of all kinds of materials and apparatus and in standardisation generally. A note of my discussion with him has been sent by Mr. Field to the D.O.T.
10. Mr. Bennett also spoke of the possibility of applying the principle of rationalisation in respect of the marketing of empire foodstuffs and raw materials – e.g. the dividing up of a market between different sources of supply, as in the case of the market for butter in Canada, where his government were endeavouring to arrange some sort of allocation system with the aid or tariff agreements between the Canadian producers and those of Australia and New Zealand.
11. The Prime Minister said he hoped that through concentrating on a small number of crucial questions the Conference might finish its labours in a shorter time than usual. He was planning to take the delegates a trip across Canada after the Conference was over.

(sd.) W. H. CLARK.

OTTAWA.

March 14th, 1932.

Letter from the High Commissioner for the United Kingdom in Ottawa to Sir Edward Harding (Under Secretary of State for Dominions), 17 March 1932, PRO, PREM 1/112, no. 5.

Office of the High Commissioner for the United Kingdom, Earnacliffe, Ottawa.

17th March, 1932.

My dear Harding,

I have sent by despatch a full report of my talk with the Prime Minister in regard to the agenda for the Conference. Quite outside of official circles there is a good deal of anxiety in Canada about the Government's delays in getting a move on. One aspect of that was illustrated to me at a men's dinner the other night at Government House by Senator Smeator. White, the owner of the 'Montreal Gazette', talking postprandially with perhaps a little less than his usual caution. He said that he had no doubt that we on our side, both the government end of it and the British business men, would come fully prepared for the Conference, and, indeed, were fully prepared already, while Canada was still unprepared and we should have it all our own way accordingly. This thought accounts for a rather hesitant tone in recent articles about the Conference in the Gazette and it is a point of view which is shared, I fancy, by a good many business men in Canada. His Excellency, for instance, told me that when he was dining a few nights ago at Montreal with Beatty, the latter said he was much disturbed at the delays and had done his best to impress upon Bennett the need for getting a move on. His Excellency himself takes such opportunities as he can to egg him on, but nothing much has been done as yet. Bennett himself told me the other day that he had approached Sir Joseph Flavelle and asked him whether he would take the chairmanship of a sort of business men's advisory committee but Flavelle refused on the ground that his time was fully taken up with the Transportation Commission. I understand also that no Cabinet Committee has as yet been appointed. The fact is that Bennett's lack of confidence in his own ministers is deep-seated and things don't seem to have been improved, as I hoped might have been the case, by the appointment of Rhodes as Finance Minister. So I doubt if much will happen till Bennett has time to deal with the whole question himself, but luckily when he does take hold he is a very quick worker.

By the way, I had a chance at a dinner last night of putting a point to him which I have wanted to for some time. You have doubtless realised that the mainspring of his tariff policy has been not so much the desire to protect industries as to protect the Canadian exchange. Hence the ferocity with which the customs people have been encouraged within the last few months to exercise their various arbitrary powers. Talking last night I accounted on his having achieved his aim, in that the trade figures for the year ending with the end of February show quite a substantial balance on Canada's side as against the heavy unfavourable balance for the preceding year. He was gratified, and spoke with unexpected candour of the sacrifices and injury to trade which it had involved. I said that I hoped he would now be able to relax his restrictive policy and he declared that he proposed to do so. I hope that we may see some results.

Yours ever,

(sgd) W. H. CLARK.

Minutes of the Fourth Meeting at the Board of Trade with Industrial Advisors [Motor Trade Representatives] Prior to the Ottawa Imperial Economic Conference, 3 June 1932, PRO, CAB 21/364.

OTTAWA IMPERIAL ECONOMIC CONFERENCE.

Fourth Meeting with Industrial Advisers.
Place: Board of Trade.
Date: 3rd June, 1932.
Present:-
Sir Horace Wilson (in the Chair)
Sir Gilbert Vyle
Lord Weir
Sir Alan Anderson
Mr. Citrine
Mr. Bromley
Mr. Dunwoody
Mr. Moir Mackenzie
Mr. Milne Bailey
Mr. Browett   Board of Trade.
Mr. Wiseman   Dominions Office.
Mr. Braddock   Department of Overseas Trade.
Mr. Griffiths   Board of Trade.
Mr. Hale   „ „ „
Motor Trade Representatives.
Mr. P.F. Bennett   (J. Lucas & Sons).
Mr. Blake   (Morris Motors Ltd.)
Mr. Graham (Dunlop Rubber Co.)
Mr. Nixon   (Leyland Motors)
Mr. W.E. Rootes   (Humber – Hillman).
Col. Hacking   (S.M.M.T.).

Sir Horace Wilson explained the position of the Industrial Advisers, and referring to the Schedules, said that it was desired to ascertain from a number of important industries – cotton, wool, iron and steel, hosiery, machinery and motors – what were the major points at which those industries desired to aim.

On behalf of the Motor Trade, it was stated that the industry placed first the question of Empire content. They were in favour of a content of 75% British labour and materials, and considered that chassis, engine, gear box and axles should each separately have such a content in order to qualify for preference. This was claimed to be a practicable rule. It was however stated that the industry were most anxious not to find themselves in a less favourable position in the home market than that which they now enjoyed under the Mackenna duties. The home market was of far greater importance than any other, and the industry would be unwilling to sacrifice any of the existing protection in that market for an improved position in regard to Empire content. It was stated that opinion in Canada was favourable to an increased Empire content, which would increase the amount of work assigned to Canadian factories by the American firms which control them. Opposition to increased content came from the American controlling interests. New Zealand already required a 75% content from Canadian cars in order to qualify for preference.

At the same time it was made clear that the industry would not regard the question of Canadian competition as solved by the adoption of the higher content proposed. To some extent the interests of the Canadian and United Kingdom industries went in step, and the adoption of the 75% content would, it was thought, mean more work for the industries in both countries; but the trade representatives evidently feared that Canadian costs might still be lower than ours. Questioned as to the reason for this, they said that the Canadian factories only produced the most successful models of the American firms with which they were affiliated, and enjoyed the advantage of all the research and experiment done by those firms. The United Kingdom industry was gaining ground every day, but the effort to expand its markets involved considerable expenditure in order to attack the previously dominating position of American firms, and we were not therefore in a position to give anything away. For this reason a position in which Canadian cars could compete with United Kingdom cars on equal terms in Empire markets would, even with a 75% content, be regarded with some anxiety.

Sir Horace Wilson explained that the whole question of Empire content was under examination by the Imperial Economic Committee and was a most complex problem. A 75% content might suit us for motors, but not for other exports – e.g. cotton.

The motor trade representatives then said that they would like to see customs duties on motors throughout the Empire assessed on a basis of weight instead of on an ad valorem basis. It was stated that the weight basis was administratively simpler than the ad valorem basis and was general on the continent. They would be quite prepared to see it adopted here. A further memorandum is being prepared by the S.M.M.T. following a previous meeting with Lord Weir.

(At this point Sir Horace Wilson had to leave tho meeting, and Sir Gilbert Vyle took the chair).

Reference was made to the unfortunate history of the attempt to manufacture motor bodies in Australia. The plant had been much too big for the market, which was not sufficiently large to support a plant of this kind, and the only result of the prohibitive duty which had been placed on bodies (with a preference which owing to the height of the tariff was purely theoretical) was to drive the industry into American hands to the grave detriment of the United Kingdom industry. Mr. Blake stated that costs in this plant were over three times those of his own plant, and even on the higher class bodies the excess costs over those in the United Kingdom was said to be 100%. Detailed information on the subject was asked for. It was stated that under a reasonable allocation of function between the United Kingdom and Australian industries, Australia should let in skeleton bodies free, and the bodies might then be fitted in Australia.

Mr. Bennett, speaking on behalf of himself and Mr. Graham, said the United Kingdom industry would accept as reasonable the claim that Australia should make her own tyres and batteries. These were replacement demands, and the market was sufficient to maintain an economic industry.

'Imperial Preference', *Economist* (4 June 1932), pp. 1228–9.

IMPERIAL PREFERENCE.

LESS than two months hence the representatives of Great Britain, India and the self-governing Dominions will be assembling for the Imperial Economic Conference at Ottawa. There has been a tendency among many whose views on the general question of Protection and Free Trade are not unlike our own to belittle the Ottawa Conference and to minimise its importance. We do not take this view, but on the contrary regard it as highly important, seeing that while it may bring advantages to British trade, unwise arrangements might do very real harm. It is also critical, for it is our first essay in tariff negotiation, and the nature of the agreements, if any, that are arrived at may well influence the possibility of effective action in the wider field of tariffs generally. Concessions to our exporting industries would be bought at too high a price if they prevented us from taking a firm stand for the mutual reduction of the barriers throughout the world that are not merely paralysing trade but are making impossible the restoration of the free movement of capital. On the other hand, the common ties which unite the countries of the Empire and the exceptional interest that each unit has in the prosperity of the others should create a favourable spirit of accommodation. The Empire has a great opportunity of setting an example of mutual concession and farsightedness. We have here an opportunity of showing to the world that there are some countries, at all events, which appreciate the truth that countries must buy freely if they wish to sell freely, and that a wise seller will try to promote the prosperity of his customers.

We shall have occasion hereafter to examine the economic position of the several Dominions, the chief characteristics of our mutual trade, and the possibility of bringing about by agreement adjustments and preferences in the various tariffs of the Empire. The final views of the Dominion Governments will not emerge until the Conference itself, but their Ministers have been sufficiently outspoken in the past few months to justify a reasoned guess as to what their policies will be. Before we consider, however, the different parts of the Empire separately and in detail, and before we offer any definitive comment upon this country's line of policy at Ottawa, it seems necessary to lay down a few general principles which must guide us in all our considerations of Imperial preference.

Tariff preferences are designed, whether in return for corresponding fiscal advantages or for wider reasons, to divert trade from one channel into another. In general, this must tend to the reduction of the world's wealth, since it would be most unlikely that artificial devices would be needed to secure the most advantageous division of economic effort. But if the grant of preferences implies, in the sum, a reduction of tariffs, then the uneconomic diversion of trade may very well be outweighed by the promotion of trade within the limited area. If, to take an extreme and unlikely instance, France and Germany were to enter into a complete customs union, then despite their continued tariffs against other countries the event would almost certainly enhance the general wealth of the world. That is a consideration of leading importance for us at Ottawa. Its implication is – and the same conclusion could be reached upon much more specific grounds – that Dominion tariffs must be reduced and not merely increased against third parties – as has so often been the case in the past. Moreover, the reduction must be substantial if it is to make good any of the restrictive effects upon trade generally that have been caused both by our own tariff and by the serious increases that have lately been made in those of the Dominions.

Leaving aside the question whether substantial reductions are at all likely, the British delegates must clearly consider carefully what effects are likely to be produced by any particular tariff that may be maintained by Great Britain for the sake of Imperial preference. Obviously if at present the Empire supplies us with only a small proportion of our imports of some commodity, to impose a tax on the foreign product would mean a considerable burden upon British consumers and, if its preferential intention were successful, a peculiarly uneconomic diversion of trade. In such cases, any preferential arrangement would be a very one-sided bargain unless a very large reduction of Dominion tariff barriers to British goods were offered in exchange. On the other hand, if the Empire already supplied us with a large proportion of our needs, the diversion and the burden would be correspondingly slight – but so would be the possible advantage accruing to the Dominions and Colonies. Of our imports of mutton, for instance, over two-thirds comes from the Empire, so that even if some preferential arrangement involving the removal of mutton from the free list were to halve our imports from foreign countries, no Empire producer could count upon increasing its sales to Great Britain by more than one-quarter of their present amount. Other commodities in this category are frozen beef, tea, cocoa, apples, tinned pineapples, asbestos, rubber, ground-nuts and palm kernels, while in the former group – products of which the Empire supplies only a small proportion of our needs – are included maize, oil cake, tinned meats, bacon and ham, eggs, fish, most classes of fruit and vegetables, condensed milk, tobacco, soft woods, hemp, and cotton.

The division between the two categories is, of course, more or less arbitrary, and there is really a continuous range from those articles of which the Dominions and Colonies supply all but an insignificant fraction of our imports (live poultry, for instance, of which 93 per cent. of the imports come from the Irish Free State) to those where the position is reversed (such as condensed milk, of which nearly 95 per cent. of our imports come from foreign countries). It is, incidentally, necessary to be sure that the classification in the trade returns really covers a homogeneous group. It would be misleading, for example, to take as the basis of a fiscal argument the bare fact that 86 per cent. of our imports of cheese in 1930 came from the Empire, since the foreign cheeses were most of them special varieties, and it is ridiculous to suppose that Camembert competes merely on the scale of prices with Canadian cheddar. The question of alternative products is also important. Soya beans, for instance, are now produced almost entirely outside the Empire, whereas the production of ground-nuts in India and tropical Africa actually exceeds the total demand by Empire markets; but these products, along with palm kernels, may in many uses be directly substituted for each other, and the value and disadvantages of Imperial preference must be considered in that light. It is obvious, therefore, that the economic effect of Imperial preference cannot in most cases be discussed in general terms. Each proposal has to be examined on its merits, bearing in mind the proposition with which this discussion opened, that the net result, properly calculated, must be a reduction of tariff barriers.

But there is one general class of products about which definite conclusions can be established in advance, namely, those of which the Empire is a net exporter; that is to say, those of which the normal exportable surplus of the Dominions and Colonies exceeds the normal demand of Great Britain and other Empire countries. This category includes three extremely important items – wheat, wool and jute. The conclusion that logically follows is that no preferential expedient, whether tariff advantage or import quota, can assist the Empire producers either to market a greater quantity of their product, or to obtain a better price for it, unless competition is somehow dismissed from the industries concerned. Consider wheat as an example. It is true that Great Britain imports large quantities of wheat from the Argentine and other foreign sources. But even if we were prepared to face all the far-reaching effects both to ourselves and to other countries and endeavour to buy exclusively from the overseas Empire, Canada and Australia would still have to sell part of their crop to foreign countries. Moreover, no matter how high the duties imposed by Great Britain on foreign wheat, the Dominions would have to accept the world price for their whole crop so long as competitive conditions prevailed within the Dominions or between them. Indeed, it is possible that the world price might actually be driven down by the concentration of non-British competition in neutral markets. A compulsory or otherwise complete Wheat Pool in Canada might succeed in holding the British consumer up to ransom, but even then co-operation with a similar organisation in Australia would be necessary in order to eliminate competition between the two Dominions. A preference on products of this character could never do much good, and it might do considerable harm.

The field of possible advantage by Imperial preferences is thus strictly limited. It is still more restricted by the determination of the Dominions to maintain their secondary manufacturing industries at all costs. There is very real danger that in their ardour for Imperial preference for its own sake, and their determination to bring back some spoils from Ottawa, the British delegates may be led to impose fresh and serious restrictions upon our own trade either without any returns from the Dominions or in exchange for a still further enhancement of the latter's duties on foreign goods – a step which would still further put out of balance the productive forces of the world and make the present confusion of world trade worse confounded.

Notes on the Cotton Delegation in a Letter from the High Commissioner for the United Kingdom in Ottawa to G. G. Whiskard (Dominions Office), 15 June 1932, PRO, CAB 21/367.

OFFICE OF THE HIGH COMMISSIONER
FOR THE UNITED KINGDOM,
KARNSCLIFFE,
OTTAWA.
June 15th, 1932.

My dear Whiskard,

I spent a long and rather sultry day yesterday with the British cotton trade delegation. They arrived at my office at 12 o'clock and we did not part company until six. In the intervening hours I had a lunch for them at Earnscliffe, to which Stevens came (the Minister for Trade and Commerce), and they had a long talk with him afterwards. I then took them to see the Prime Minister – it is characteristic of arrangements here that the Prime Minister generally receives his deputations separately from his colleagues. Then we had a further talk about policy over tea at the Chateau Laurier and finally they departed to catch their train to Montreal. Field will be reporting on the details, and I will only touch in this letter on points which are of general interest as throwing light on Conference prospects.

2. They found themselves up against a complete brick wall during their five or six days at Montreal. It is possible that they did not exercise supreme tact in their dealings with the Canadians, but on the whole I am convinced that the Canadian textile representatives did not mean business. They encouraged them to come because they felt it would be bad policy to appear ungracious about it, but they used to the full the fact that the Lancashire people only proposed to stay in Canada for a week.

3. Stevens gave a clever little address in reply to Grey's statement of the position, but he rather gave things away by letting drop that he had been on the telephone to Daniels, the President of the Dominion Textile Company. He held out no hope of any let-up in the present protectionist treatment of cotton goods; in fact he said at one moment that obviously, so far as the cotton trade was concerned, they would have to look for expansion to other parts of the Empire. At the same time he showed himself not averse to fuller investigation of the question of relative costs of production and threw out a suggestion that if they stayed on for another week the Government might possibly send down one of their tariff experts to share in the discussions, but

safeguarded himself by saying that he had not consulted the Prime Minister and did not know whether he would approve.

4. As a matter of fact, the Prime Minister did not approve. The Lancashire people were keen about the point and I brought it up myself two or three times during our talk with the Prime Minister, but each time he put it aside. He treated the delegates to one of his best displays. He has just been away for a short holiday and has come back full of life and was obviously determined to charm and give them of his best. The thing was extraordinarily well done, and the delegates quite genuinely enjoyed it, but they are a hard-headed crowd and were not to be side-tracked by his flow of talk. The one thing that did emerge was that he wanted them to stay, and while they were in the room rang up Daniels and said as much as he could before us about the resumption of discussions. He also, as he told me subsequently, rang him up again later and I gather put it across him pretty hard, as much to our amusement Daniels has contributed this morning an interview in the 'Montreal Gazette' in which he practically denies any divergences of opinion between the two delegations and continues cheerfully about the conference going on.

5. There are a considerable division of opinion in the delegation when we discussed matters afterwards as to whether they should go or stay. I was quite definite that it would be a great strategic blunder for them to go, and put it to them that if they really wanted to get back on their Canadian friends the best way to do it was to stay and carry on. They stipulated, however, that a Canadian official should be sent down to participate with Field as his opposite number. I put this to the Prime Minister later in the evening and he was very obviously reluctant. It is very significant that he telephoned this morning to say that he had decided to send a man and was despatching him at once.

6. It is clear that the Prime Minister was willing to go a considerable way in order to avoid creating trouble and pre-conference publicity about Canadian stickiness. His earlier reluctance to send an official down was also in its way rather significant. His objection to me was that if he did it, it would be bringing the Government in and the Government would be, or might be asked to take some decision. I pointed out to him that after all that was precisely what the Government was being asked to do in regard to the tariff schedule and surely it was useful that they should get the fullest information before doing it. We always come up against this same reluctance on his part to deal with concrete instances in connection with tariff policy. Whatever happens in the second week of this particular conference. I am sure it has been a useful thing that these Lancashire people should have come out. It has, at any rate, cleared the air as regards one industry, even though

it is not likely to secure them any very valuable concessions. They are, by the way, entirely philosophical on that point themselves and don't seem to have expected any great results, but seem to have felt that it was worth their while to come in order to clear up the situation.

Yours sincerely,

(Sd) W. H. Clark.

Secret Note by the United Kingdom Delegation on the Canadian Tariff Proposals, 8 August 1932, PRO, CAB 21/363.

IMPERIAL ECONOMIC CONFERENCE, OTTAWA, 1932.

THE CANADIAN TARIFF PROPOSALS

Note by the United Kingdom Delegation.

SECRET

1. As was promised at the meeting on the 4th August last, the United Kingdom delegation have caused the detailed proposals for alterations in the Canadian tariff then submitted to be examined and analysed with great care. The result of that examination has been a great disappointment to the United Kingdom delegation, a disappointment which they believe will be shared by the Canadian delegation when they realise what the effect of these proposals will be. At the previous meeting with the United Kingdom delegation Mr. Bennett divided the import of goods into Canada into two classes – viz. (i) goods of a kind produced in Canada, and (ii) goods of a kind not produced in Canada.

2. With regard to the former class, Mr. Bennett then stated that the Canadian Government was prepared to deal with these on the principle that the tariff should be so arranged as to put the United Kingdom manufacturer into the position of a 'domestic competitor'; that is to say that the tariff should be so adjusted as to countervail any advantages in the cost of production which were enjoyed by the United Kingdom manufacturer, as against an efficient Canadian manufacturer, but so as not to give any further protection to the Canadian manufacturer beyond what was necessary to effect that countervailing.

3. With regard to the second class, Mr. Bennett stated that he was willing so to adjust the tariff as to ensure that with reasonable efficiency the United Kingdom manufacturer could have a monopoly of the market, as against any foreign competitors. The United Kingdom delegation had understood that the proposals submitted to them on Thursday last were designed to give effect to these two principles. In addition, it was stated at the meeting that the Advisers of the Canadian Government calculated that the proposals ensured a trade of some $55,000,000 a year to the United Kingdom, and that with reasonable enterprise that trade might easily be increased to

something like $80,000,000. The examination of the details of the proposals does not justify these anticipations.

4. The United Kingdom delegation have been quite unable to detect in the proposals either of the two principles enunciated above. The total imports into Canada of goods affected by the proposals amounted only to $155,000,000 out of total Canadian imports in 1930-31 of $907,000,000, or only 17 per cent. The field covered by the proposals, with only a few exceptions, is confined to the second of the two classes referred to by Mr. Bennett, viz. the trade in goods not produced in Canada. After the most careful analysis and estimate possible on the materials available, it is concluded that the utmost which United Kingdom manufacturers could hope to gain from the adjustment would be $10,000,000 instead of $55,000,000 or $80,000,000.

5. To take only a few specific items – in the iron and steel trade the net result of the proposals as submitted would be to reduce United Kingdom imports by something over $200,000[1]; in the case of coal an increase of 6d. a ton, or something less than 2 per cent. on the average f.c.b. value, is not likely to be effective in producing any substantial diversion of trade; imports of this commodity alone account for no less than $22,000,000 annually.

6. Such industries as engineering, machinery, and equipment, electrical apparatus other than telegraph and telephone apparatus, tin plates, ready made clothing, boots and shoes, ropes cordage and twine, biscuits and confectionery, artificial silks, hosiery, carpets, curtains, blankets etc. do not appear in the list at all.

7. In the case of cotton piece goods the only change proposed, apart from velveteens, is in respect of several fine tissues made of yarns of over 100 counts; in the case of woollen goods modifications are proposed only for grey cloth of 4 ozs. or less per square yard, and woollen and worsted fabrics of 18 ozs. or more per square yard. No reduction whatever is offered in the extremely high duties on the general range of cotton piece goods or on the valuable middle ranges of woollen goods, or in any of the ranges of the other groups of woollen commodities the Canadian delegation will be aware of the effect of the present specific rates of duty on cotton and woollen goods, which render trade impossible.

8. In this connection attention may be directed to the case of silk hosiery: Canada has increased her sales to the United Kingdom of real silk hose from 1,566 dozens in the first six months of 1931 to 11,184 dozens in the first six months of 1932, while Canada maintains against the United Kingdom manufacturer of hosiery, duties, which, with landing charges, aggregate 100%.

---

1   It is understood that, the significance of the proposals in regard to iron and steel having been realised, fresh proposals are now under consideration by the Canadian Delegation.

9. As regards jute, while some concession is proposed for bleached goods, there is no suggestion of any modification of the duties on the much larger class of unbleached jute goods.
10. In these circumstances the United Kingdom delegation are driven to the conclusion that the Canadian proposals are quite inadequate to effect the Imperial purposes of the Conference expressed by the Prime Minister of Canada.
11. The Canadian delegation will realise that the concessions which are being asked for by the various Dominion delegations are concessions in matters which vitally affect the life of the great masses of the population of the United Kingdom. They will be closely scrutinised and bitterly assailed. The only justification for making any concessions of such a character must be the adoption of broad principles of Imperial trade which will lay a foundation for the great stability and closer association of the Empire and which will offer increasing prospects of markets for the products of United Kingdom factories and, therefore, for the employment of her people.
12. The United Kingdom delegation had seen in the propositions enunciated by Mr. Bennett basic principles which might satisfy these conditions. They had hoped that in any agreement entered into between Canada and the United Kingdom, broad principles which were to govern the trade relations of Canada and the United Kingdom over a period of years might be laid down, and means might be established for attaining the basis proposed by him, if necessary by progressive stages: and they had expected that immediate adjustments of the Canadian tariff might be put forward which should give effect to those principles as far as possible and which should provide some means of re-adjustment in accordance with those principles in the future.
13. There were certain other suggestions on matters of principle which might well have been incorporated in such an agreement: the United Kingdom Delegation would refer particularly to the suggestion made by Mr. Bennett for preferential treatment in the matter of drawback in respect of certain goods produced in the Empire and imported for use in manufacture in Canada.
14. Similar considerations apply to the question of anti-dumping duties. The United Kingdom Delegation had learned, with interest, from the Canadian delegation, of the provisions as to dumping duties in the Treaties existing between Canada and Australia and Canada and New Zealand respectively. They had hoped that consideration might be given to the possibility of an understanding between Canada and the United Kingdom that there should be unconditional exemption of the goods of either country from anti-dumping or similar special duties in the trade between the two countries.

The United Kingdom delegation have caused to be prepared a schedule of changes in the Canadian tariff which, as nearly as they can judge, will give effect to the principles enunciated by Mr. Bennett. They will be glad to submit that schedule for examination and for discussion between the expert advisers of the two delegations if the Canadian delegation so desire. They regret very much to be unable to regard the present proposals of the Canadian delegation as adequate and they will be very glad to cause their own advisers to give any explanations which may be desired on matters of detail and to have a further meeting with the Canadian delegation in order to discuss the matter in its broader aspects if the Canadian delegation agree with them in thinking that such a meeting is desirable.

Parliament Buildings,

Ottawa.

8th August, 1932.

Memorandum by Industrial Advisors Representing the British Trades Union Congress on the Imperial Economic Conference, 8 August 1932, PRO, CAB 21/364.

CONFIDENTIAL.
IMPERIAL ECONOMIC CONFERENCE, OTTAWA, 1932.
MEMORANDUM BY INDUSTRIAL ADVISERS REPRESENTING THE BRITISH TRADES UNION CONGRESS.

1. Now that the Conference has reached a stage in its deliberations when it is possible to see the direction in which policy is tending, we think it desirable, and indeed necessary, to place on record our views on the present position of the discussions.
2. At the outset we wish to express our grave dissatisfaction and apprehension regarding the general policy of the Conference. Prior to the opening of the Conference the Trades Union Congress, jointly with the Federation of British Industries, published a statement indicating the general considerations that ought to influence the minds of all concerned in the discussions.
3. In our view, the primary need was that the Conference should be regarded as a step towards the recovery of world trade and world prosperity, that the nations of the Commonwealth should point the way to saner policies on the part of all countries, and that it would be fatal to approach the discussions in a narrow spirit, with objectives limited to huckstering over preferences for this and that commodity.
4. It appears to us that already those larger aims have been dropped, and that the narrow bargaining spirit we regarded as fatal dominates the proceedings. As far as we are able to judge, the Conference has lost sight of the world situation, and of the urgent need of all nations to-day to reduce the restrictions that are strangling international trade, to establish saner monetary policies, and in future to plan wisely the economic life of the Commonwealth and of the world.
5. The discussions of the Conference have not so far touched the problem of increasing the buying power of the people generally. On the contrary, the air has been full of proposals for tariffs and quotas which would reduce the standard of life of the people by forcing increases in the cost-of-living wholly disproportionate to any advantage that might accrue to the sellers of goods. At the same time, no stops appear even to be under serious con-

sideration whereby the rise in wholesale prices that is so urgently needed by primary producers everywhere may be brought about.
6. In short, the Conference has apparently failed so far to rise to the level of the great constructive effort we visualised, and has degenerated quickly into a series of petty bargaining talks on specific items, a course which, whether it terminates in agreements or not, cannot be of any real value in lifting the world out of its present chaos. For the great objective of restoring trade and re-establishing prosperity, it substitutes the futile aim of diverting trade from one blocked-up channel to another, and any embargo on trade between Great Britain and Russia could only accentuate this evil.
7. We are happy to say that we cannot blame the British Delegation for this failure, except perhaps to the extent to which they have been less resolute in pressing their own point of view. We believe Mr. Baldwin and most of his colleagues have been and are fully alive to the importance of the considerations we have urged, and we only regret that they have not carried their view with some of the Dominion representatives who seem scarcely to be aware of world forces and world problems.
8. Even at this stage we hope it is not too late for the Conference to be given a now orientation that will make it a notable success and an inspiration to the rest of the world. If it fails, and it will be accounted a failure if the result is nothing more than a series of tariff bargains that add to the restrictions on international commerce, the reaction among the workers in all lands will be profound. Organised Labour will offer the most strenuous opposition to the perpetuation of such economic insanity and chaos. We therefore desire, before it is too late, to urge that the entire policy of the Conference should be reconsidered with the larger consideration we have mentioned in mind.

JOHN BROMLEY.

WALTER M. CITRINE.

8th August, 1932.

J. G. Coates (Leader of the New Zealand Reform Party) to Stanley Baldwin, 8 August 1932, PRO, CAB 21/365.

IMPERIAL ECONOMIC CONFERENCE, 1932
NEW ZEALAND DELEGATION
OTTAWA, CANADA.

8th August, 1932.

Dear Mr. Baldwin,

Referring to the interview which you and your colleagues were kind enough to accord to Mr. Downie Stewart and myself, we have as requested given consideration to the suggestion of a possible limitation of Empire supplies of meat. I appreciate the expression of your opinion as to the necessity of restricting supplies in order to protect the interests of the Home and Dominion farmer.

It is difficult for us however to consider the proposal as one that should form part of the national policy of New Zealand, as our whole effort for fifty years past has been to steadily develop the meat export trade to the United Kingdom. We regard restriction of foreign supplies as being based primarily on the principle of Imperial Preference whereas restriction on Dominion output is based on the idea that it will raise the price-level. But if the object of the Conference is to increase Empire trade and the development of the Dominions this can hardly be accomplished by restricting Empire production.

In view of the fact that the considerations applicable to a restriction of foreign imports are much more forcible than those applicable to a Dominion quota, we would be very grateful if you could indicate (1) whether you would be willing to consider that imposition of a foreign quota by itself; (2) in any case, to what extent would you be prepared to restrict foreign supplies.

Our reason for asking these questions is that they will have an important bearing on our reply to your proposal. It does appear to us that a reasonable curtailment of present foreign imports will be sufficient to improve wholesale prices. In this connection we beg to draw your attention to the fact that foreign imports of meat into the United Kingdom are now 76% as compared with Empire supplies of 24%. It seems to us that there is ample margin here for a reduction of foreign supplies, without raising the question of restricting Dominion supplies, at any rate until the effect of foreign reductions has been tried out.

I have already set out the New Zealand view on the meat question, which differs from that of some of the Dominions, and I enclose a copy of this for closer consideration.

In the meantime I should be glad if you could let me know your views on the above questions, and I will hold myself at your disposal at any time if you wish to see me.

Yours respectfully

(Sgd) J.G. Coates.

The Rt. Hon. Stanley Baldwin, M.P.,

UNITED KINGDOM DELEGATION.

Most Secret Report of a (UK) Delegation Meeting at Ottawa on the Australian and New Zealand Negotiation and a Duty on Meat, 15 August 1932, PRO CAB 21/363.

Prime Minister

The enclosed most secret note of a Delegation Meeting at Ottawa is a very human document.

It shows the straights to which the Delegation were reduced and their anxiety not to put you and the National Government in a fix.

M.P. A. Hankey
MOST SECRET.
THE AUSTRALIAN AND NEW ZEALAND
NEGOTIATIONS AND A DUTY ON MEAT.

Note by the Secretary of the Discussions at the Meeting of United Kingdom Delegates held in the 'Tudor' Room, Chateau Laurier, on Monday, August 15th, 1932 at 10.45 p.m.

(See O. (U.K.) (32) 54th Conclusions Minute 4).

The United Kingdom Delegates discussed the situation which had arisen vis à vis the Australian and New Zealand Delegations as a result of those Delegations having been informed that the United Kingdom Delegation was not prepared to entertain the proposal that a duty should be imposed on imports of foreign meat into the United Kingdom.

The Australian Delegates, on hearing this decision, had stated that, so far as they were concerned, the Conference was at an end, all offers must be regarded as withdrawn, and it would be necessary to start again de novo and examine inter alia the question of the maintenance of the Australian preferences to the United Kingdom and of the United Kingdom preferences to Australia.

The New Zealand Delegates had intimated that it was impossible for them to return to New Zealand and inform their people that they must restrict production.

The Meeting was informed by the Chancellor of the Exchequer and the Secretary of State for War, who had throughout been in close consultation with Mr. Bruce and Mr. Coates, that they did not think that either Australia or New Zealand would accept a restriction scheme pure and simple, and that they would both insist on duty on the foreign product being embodied in any arrangement that might be reached.

THE LORD PRESIDENT OF THE COUNCIL said that it would be a perfect tragedy if the Conference was to break down on a matter, namely duty on meat, that could not possibly do any good.

THE CHANCELLOR OF THE EXCHEQUER said that he, personally, hoped that another effort would be made to reach agreement with the Australian and New Zealand Delegations.

THE SECRETARY OF STATE FOR WAR said that he did not think that Australia would agree to a restrictive scheme by itself, or, for that matter, that New Zealand would agree to such a proposal.

THE LORD PRESIDENT OF THE COUNCIL said that the question was whether it was worth while for the United Kingdom to agree to ¾d or 1d. duty on foreign meat in order to keep Australia and New Zealand in the Conference.

THE SECRETARY OF STATE FOR WAR reminded his colleagues that on the previous day they had decided, whether rightly or wrongly was immaterial, that they would not agree to a duty on imports of foreign meat. This decision had been communicated to the Australian and New Zealand Delegations, and their reply had been that they could not contemplate a restrictive scheme by itself, and that so long as the United Kingdom Delegation adopted the attitude that no duty on imported foreign meat could be conceded, there could be no agreement with those Delegations.

THE CHANCELLOR OF THE EXCHEQUER observed that Mr. Bruce had stated that, in his opinion, the position had been made very much more difficult and embarrassing by the publication of his (Mr. Chamberlain's) speech on the Report of the Monetary Committee.

THE SECRETARY OF STATE FOR DOMINION AFFAIRS said that the correspondent of the 'Daily News' had informed him that a copy of Mr. Chamberlain's speech had been handed to him by a Canadian Minister, and that he had not felt that he was under any obligation not to publish it.

THE SECRETARY OF STATE FOR THE COLONIES said that if there was now a breakdown of the Conference, the Australians would go back and there would be a default in Australia with all the consequences which such a default must entail.

THE MINISTER OF AGRICULTURE AND FISHERIES said that both Mr. Bruce and Mr. Coates wanted ¾d on mutton and 1d. on lamb, and would no doubt agree that there should be a time limit for the duration of the duty. They argued that if a World Conference on Meat was held next year as proposed, the Conference was bound to be subjected to political influences. He was disposed to think that both Australia and New Zealand would, in the last resort and with some pressure, accept a duty on mutton and lamb limited to one year plus the World Conference, and they might be persuaded to abandon their demand for a duty on beef. There was no doubt that their ultimate aim was a very severe restriction of foreign imports. Mr. Coates seemed to think that New Zealand had more to fear from a change of Government in the United Kingdom if there was a restriction scheme than if there was a duty on meat.

It was pointed out that this showed how very little Mr. Coates appreciated the political situation in England. A restriction scheme was very much more likely to survive a change of Government than any meat duty.

THE SECRETARY OF STATE FOR DOMINION AFFAIRS said that he was very unhappy indeed as to the latest developments in the situation. He was less committed than any of the Delegates in regard to this matter. He believed that the failure of this Conference would be a disaster of the greatest magnitude, not only to the Empire but to the whole World. He had come to the conclusion, however, after giving the matter the fullest consideration, that it was impossible to proceed on the present lines. He paid a very warm tribute to Mr. Chamberlain and Lord Hailsham for the manner in which they had conducted the negotiations with the most splendid loyalty to their colleagues, and in face of every possible kind of insult and discourtesy. He (Mr. Thomas) declined any longer to be blackmailed. No-one had suffered more from Mr. Bennett than he had, and he was prepared to sink all personal feelings, but he could not shut out from his mind the thought that in the whole of this matter the real source of trouble and friction was Mr. Bennett himself. The position in which he found himself was an extremely cruel one. The United Kingdom Delegation had been giving way to the demands of the Dominions in every possible direction, and the point had now been reached when it was only possible to defend the concessions which we had made by an appeal to sentiment, and by urging that we must not look to the immediate future for any return, but that we were sowing the seeds of a great harvest which our posterity would gather in. The United Kingdom Delegates had now reached the stage when they were being held up to blackmail and ransom. The limits of all possible concession were long past, and while he would not for one moment stand in the way of anything which his colleagues might decide to do, and would carry on until the Delegation returned to England without giving any indication whatever of any change, he must make his position quite clear, namely that he could not assent to the proposal that the decision of the previous day not to impose a tax on meat, should be reversed.

THE PRESIDENT OF THE BOARD OF TRADE said that he agreed generally with the views of the Secretary of State for Dominion Affairs. He also would not stand in the way of anything which his colleagues might wish to do. He would not indeed stand in the way of duty on meat, but he did not believe that to agree to impose such a duty would settle anything. Supposing that the Secretary of State and himself stood aside, how would this help matters.

THE SECRETARY OF STATE FOR WAR said that it was quite impossible to contemplate any action which the Delegation as a whole did not agree to.

THE SECRETARY OF STATE FOR DOMINION AFFAIRS repeated that he, at all events, would not stand in the way of his colleagues.

THE LORD PRESIDENT OF THE COUNCIL remarked that the new development made it all the more important that an agreement should be reached with Mr. Bennett.

THE SECRETARY OF STATE FOR WAR indicated the arrangements for the following day which seemed to point to Mr. Bennett thinking that an agreement would be made with him.

THE PRESIDENT OF THE BOARD OF TRADE enquired whether, even if we gave Australia and New Zealand what they asked for in respect of meat, was it likely that they would be satisfied.

THE SECRETARY OF STATE FOR WAR believed that if faced with the alternative of a breakdown of the Conference or a restrictive scheme and a duty of ¾d on mutton and 1d. on lamb until such time as a permanent agreement was made, Australia and New Zealand would accept the latter. It was obvious that the duty would not help them. Supposing that a restrictive scheme was put into operation in respect of bacon, and we agreed to a duty on mutton and lamb, he (Lord Hailsham) believed that within a year Australia and New Zealand would be clamouring for the abandonment of the duty and the application to mutton and lamb of restrictive arrangements.

THE PRESIDENT OF THE BOARD OF TRADE said that if we offered Australia and New Zealand a duty on mutton and lamb, with or without a restrictive scheme, we were going to offer them a policy in which we did not believe and which moreover would compel us to face most grave political and other trouble at home. He would be very reluctant indeed to concur in a policy which he knew from the outset was a wrong policy.

THE SECRETARY OF STATE FOR WAR doubted whether there would, in fact, be serious trouble at home, in as much as he did not believe that the duty would cause any material increase of price.

THE PRESIDENT OF THE BOARD OF TRADE said that he was not so much thinking of trouble due to economic considerations, but to difficulties for the National Government involving probably the sacrifice of all that great permanent policy for which the National Government stood. He also must make it clear that he shared the views of the Secretary of State for Dominion Affairs with regard to the manner in which the Dominions were attempting to extort concessions from the United Kingdom.

THE MINISTER OF AGRICULTURE AND FISHERIES observed that if we failed to get any agreement at Ottawa it would mean chaos in our own home market, to which Mr. Runciman replied that he could not see how the imposition of a duty would help in that respect.

THE CHANCELLOR OF THE EXCHEQUER said that he felt that his own position was one of extraordinary difficulty. He had only proposed the imposition of a duty on meat as a very last resort. He expressed his great gratitude to those of his colleagues who were not members of the Conservative Party for the manner in which they had acceded to the wishes of their colleagues up to the present, and he felt that he could not possibly ask them to go further than they had already gone. He confessed, however, that the idea that the Conference should break down filled him with despair. The effect on the Party would be very serious indeed. The whole course of world affairs would be set back. While there was no excuse for the way in which the United Kingdom Delegation had been treated, he thought that it was an intolerable position that Australia should be allowed to go out of the Conference on this issue. He did not believe that Mr. Bruce had misused his position. Throughout he had been studiously moderate and had tried, within his limitations, to be reasonable.

THE LORD PRESIDENT OF THE COUNCIL enquired what view the Prime Minister would probably take of the position.

THE SECRETARY OF STATE FOR DOMINION AFFAIRS said that the Prime Minister would certainly be influenced by whatever he (Mr. Thomas) had to say, and that if the Prime Minister asked his opinion, he would feel it his duty to state it with the most complete frankness. He would prefer to sleep over the matter, and in any case he would take very good care not to make the position more difficult for the Prime Minister. Only that day in his message to the King, the Secretary of State said that he had again emphasised the complete unanimity among the United Kingdom Delegates. He again stated, with considerable emotion, that he would make no difficulty whatever and would not embarrass his colleagues in any way or in any shape or form.

THE SECRETARY OF STATE FOR WAR enquired whether it would be any use for the Chancellor of the Exchequer and the President of the Board of Trade to meet Mr. Bruce. Mr. Runciman would be able to represent the views of the Delegation from a somewhat different angle.

THE LORD PRESIDENT OF THE COUNCIL asked the President of the Board of Trade to say whether, if there was a chance of saving the Conference by agreeing to a duty on meat, he thought that the United Kingdom Delegates should agree to the imposition of such a duty.

THE PRESIDENT OF THE BOARD OF TRADE said that it was impossible to make a balance sheet, and if one could be made we could not defend our concessions on a £.S.D. basis.

In reply to the Lord President's question, Mr. Runciman said that he would like to sleep over the matter before giving a final answer, but his present inclination would be to reject the proposal. Moreover he was most anxious to protect the Prime Minister whose whole present position and future would be placed in jeopardy by a wrong decision. If he was asked now for a decision it would have to be a negative one.

THE LORD PRESIDENT OF THE COUNCIL enquired whether the Secretary of State for Dominion Affairs would speak with the Prime Minister.

THE CHANCELLOR OF THE EXCHEQUER agreed that the United Kingdom Delegates ought to know what the Prime Minister thought before reaching a final decision.

THE SECRETARY OF STATE FOR DOMINION AFFAIRS agreed to arrange to speak to the Prime Minister at 7 a.m. on the morning of August 16th. to report the result of the conversation to the Meeting of the United Kingdom Delegates to be held at 10 a.m. on that day.

Chateau Laurier,

Ottawa.

15th August, 1932.

Selections from the Ottawa Agreement, August 1932, PRO, DO 35/242/6.

VI. – SUMMARY

The conclusions of the Conference may be summarized as follows:–

(a) Resolutions and Statements Regarding the Promotion of Trade within the Commonwealth

With regard to the determination of the percentage of Empire Content necessary to secure preferential tariff treatment, the Conference draws the attention of the several Governments of the Commonwealth to the importance of this subject, and recommends that each of the Governments of the Commonwealth should investigate, as rapidly as possible, the standard of Empire Content which should be required by them for the import under preferential rates of the different classes of goods, bearing in mind the following principles:

(a) That though it must rest with each Government to decide what standard it will require, a greater degree of uniformity throughout the Commonwealth is desirable;

(b) The standard required should not be such as to defeat or frustrate the intention of the preferential rate of duty conceded to any class of goods.

With regard to the question of export bounties and anti-dumping duties within the Commonwealth, the Conference adopted the following resolution:

This Conference, recognizing that export bounties and exchange depreciation adversely affect the value of tariff preferences within the Commonwealth, expresses the hope that with a rise in the level of commodity prices and with stabilized exchanges such bounties and the special duties which have been adopted as a means of adjusting the situation so created, may be withdrawn.

With regard to the conclusion of certain Agreements for the extension of mutual trade by means of reciprocal preferential tariffs, the Conference adopted the following resolution:

The nations of the British Commonwealth having entered into certain Agreements with one another for the extension of mutual trade by means of reciprocal preferential tariffs, this Conference takes note of these Agreements and records its conviction:

That by the lowering or removal of barriers among themselves provided for in these Agreements the flow of trade between the various countries of the Empire will be facilitated, and that by the consequent increase of purchasing power of their peoples the trade of the world will also be stimulated and increased;

Further, that this Conference regards the conclusion of these Agreements as a step forward which should in the future lead to further progress in the same direction and which will utilise protective duties to ensure that the resources and industries of the Empire are developed on sound economic lines.

The Agreements referred to are annexed hereto and the Conference commends them to the Governments of the several parts of the Empire.

(b) Resolutions Regarding Customs Administration

The Conference recommends that the aims to be kept in view should be:
(i) The avoidance of uncertainty as to the amount of duty which would be payable on the arrival of goods in the importing country;
(ii) The reduction of friction and delay to a minimum;
(iii) The provision of facilities for the expeditious and effective settlement of disputes relating to all matters affecting the application of the Customs Tariff; and that any measures which Customs Administrations might take to safeguard themselves against evasion should be consistent with these principles.

(c) Statement Regarding Commercial Relations with Foreign Countries

The Conference considered two broad groups of questions affecting the commercial relations of the several members of the Commonwealth with foreign countries.

In the first place, the Conference discussed the general question of the relationship between intra-Commonwealth preferences and the most-favoured-nation clause in commercial treaties with foreign powers. Each Government will determine its particular policy in dealing with this matter, but the representatives of the various Governments on the Committee stated that it was their policy that no treaty obligations into which they might enter in the future should be allowed to interfere with any mutual preferences which Governments of the Commonwealth might decide to accord to each other, and that they would free themselves from existing treaties, if any, which might so interfere. They would, in fact, take all the steps necessary to implement and safe-guard whatever preferences might be so granted.

In the second place, attention was drawn to recent tendencies in foreign countries to conclude regional agreements between themselves for the mutual accord of preferences which were designed as being exclusive, and not to be extended to countries which were not parties to, or did not adhere to the agreements. On this point, there was a general agreement that foreign countries which had existing treaty obligations to grant most-favoured-nation treatment to the products of particular parts of the Commonwealth could not be allowed to override such obligations by regional agreements of the character in question. Particular reference was made in this connection to the question of the Danubian States in regard to which preferential treatment was in contemplation for the cereal exports of the States concerned, – exports which constitute a substantial proportion of the world's exports of the cereals in question. The Conference were, however, informed that in the discussion which took place at Lausanne on the matter, the rights of third countries had, at the instance of the United Kingdom, been expressly reserved.

The Conference recognized that the fact that rights are accorded by most-favoured-nation treatment does not preclude a foreign country from seeking the consent of the various Governments of the British Commonwealth to the waiver of their rights in particular cases, and that these Governments must be guided by consideration of their individual interests in deciding whether or not to meet the wishes of the foreign country concerned, so long, however, as the general principle that rights of this kind cannot be arbitrarily withdrawn is fully and carefully preserved.

The Conference would, however, recommend that where two or more Commonwealth Governments share a common interest in any proposal for the waiver of particular treaty rights, they should consult together with a view to arriving, in so far as possible, at a common policy.

(c) Resolutions and Statements Regarding Methods of Economic Co-operation

(i) General Resolutions

This Conference, having discussed the question of Economic Consultation and Co-operation within the Commonwealth, and having considered the annexed report prepared for it on the constitution and functions of existing agencies operating in these fields:

Recommends that a committee should be appointed forthwith, consisting of not more than two representatives of each of the participating Governments, to consider the means of facilitating economic consultation and co-operation between the several Governments of the Commonwealth, including a survey of the functions, organization and financial bases of the agencies specified in the annexed report, and an examination of what alterations or modifications, if any, in the existing machinery for such co-operation within the Commonwealth are desirable.

The Conference further recommends that it shall be an instruction to the Committee to elect their own Chairman from among their members, and to report to the several Governments represented thereon not later than the 31st May next, with a view to the consideration of their report by the several Governments not later than September, 1933.

The Conference was given to understand by the representatives of the United Kingdom that, in order that the necessary time might be available for the preparation and consideration of the report of the Committee concerning the existing and future machinery for economic co-operation within the Commonwealth, the Government of the United Kingdom would continue to furnish any funds which may be required to finance essential work of the Empire Marketing Board down to the end of September, 1933. The Conference records its deep appreciation of the action of the United Kingdom in this respect.

With regard to the above recommendations reservations were made by Mr. Havenga, for the Union of South Africa, and by Mr. Lemass, for the Irish Free State, respectively, in the following terms:–

(Mr. Havenga). 'While not wishing to object to the acceptance of the report of the Committee on Methods of Economic Co-operation, I desire, in order to remove any ground for misapprehension, to record the following reservations on behalf of the Union of South Africa:

'1. While not generally adverse to the institution of *ad hoc* bodies for economic investigation and preparation, the Union Government will not associate itself with any scheme for the erection of any organization in the nature of a permanent secretariat or preparatory committee to Commonwealth Conferences, whether economic or otherwise.

2. That portion of the report which introduces the draft resolutions relating to the appointment of a Committee to consider the means of facilitating economic consultation and co-operation, must not be read in the sense that the Union Government is committed in principle to give financial support to Commonwealth Economic Organizations.'

(Mr. Lemass). 'I do not object to the adoption of this report and the accompanying resolutions, but I wish it to be made perfectly clear in the published records of the Conference that the Government of the Irish Free State are not prepared to contemplate the setting up of an Imperial Economic Secretariat or of any similar organ of centralization.'

VII – PROMOTION OF TRADE WITHIN THE COMMONWEALTH

A – Report of Committee

The meeting of Heads of Delegations, held on July 22nd, set up a Committee on the Promotion of Trade within the Commonwealth to consider the following matters on the provisional agenda of the Conference:

'Examination of aspects of general trade and tariff policy and administration affecting Empire trade, including, *inter alia*, the following subjects:
  (a) Recognition of the principle of reciprocal tariff preferences within the Commonwealth;
  (b) General application of existing and future tariff preferences within the Commonwealth;
  (c) Extension to other parts of the Commonwealth of tariff advantages accorded foreign countries;
  (d) Determination of percentage of 'Empire Content' necessary to secure preferential tariff treatment;
  (e) Export bounties and anti-dumping duties within the Commonwealth.'

The Committee beg to submit the following report:

1. *Negotiation of Trade Agreements*

At its first meeting, the Committee decided that the formulation of any proposals which might be submitted to the Delegation of the United Kingdom would be assisted by the constitution of five groups made up of representatives of those Dominions which were interested in: (1) dairy products (including poultry and eggs); (2) meat (including live cattle and pig products); (3) fruit and vegetables; (4) cereals (including flour); (5) metals and minerals. A sixth group on tobacco was formed later on.

These groups held numerous meetings and their activities were of great assistance in connection with the bilateral negotiations between the United Kingdom and certain of the Dominions. The results of their studies in respect to each group of commodities were co-ordinated by an informal committee. Inasmuch as the groups and the co-ordinating committee were not constituted as regular sub-committees of the Committee on Trade Promotion, no report was made by them to the Committee. The conclusions which they reached, however, were made available by them for the use of the interested Delegations.

2. *General Matters before the Committee*

The Committee have carefully considered the general questions placed on their agenda concerning general trade and tariff policy and administration as affecting trade within the Commonwealth. Many of these questions were also discussed in the course of the bilateral negotiations.

In considering the determination of the percentage of Empire Content necessary to secure preferential tariff treatment, the Committee have briefly examined the statement submitted by His Majesty's Government in Canada summarizing the various regulations at present in force within the Commonwealth governing the percentage of Empire Content necessary to qualify for tariff preferences and the report of the Imperial Economic Committee on 'The Definition of Empire Goods.' The question was further examined by a subcommittee under the chairmanship of The Right Hon. Walter Runciman.

The Committee suggest that the Conference should draw the attention of the several Governments of the Commonwealth to the importance of this subject, and should recommend each of the Governments of the Commonwealth to investigate, as rapidly as possible, the standard of Empire Content which should be required by them for the import under preferential rates of the different classes of goods, bearing in mind the following principles:

(a) That though it must rest with each Government to decide what standard it will require, a greater degree of uniformity throughout the Commonwealth is desirable;

(b) The standard required should not be such as to defeat or frustrate the intention of the preferential rate of duty conceded to any class of goods.

On the question of export bounties and anti-dumping duties within the Commonwealth, the Committee recommend for the consideration of the Conference the following resolution:

This Conference, recognizing that export bounties and exchange depreciation adversely affect the value of tariff preferences within the Commonwealth, expresses the hope that with a rise in the level of commodity prices and with stabilized exchanges such bounties and the special duties which have been adopted as a means of adjusting the situation so created, may be withdrawn.

At an early stage in its deliberations the Committee was informed that negotiations were in progress between the various delegations for the conclusion of trade agreements, and accordingly a drafting committee, under the Chairmanship of the Right Hon. Neville Chamberlain, was appointed to prepare a resolution to record and present the bilateral trade agreements so negotiated during the Conference. The Drafting Committee presented the following resolution which is recommended by the Committee to the Conference for consideration:

The nations of the British Commonwealth having entered into certain Agreements with one another for the extension of mutual trade by means of reciprocal preferential tariffs, this Conference takes note of these Agreements and records its conviction:

That by the lowering or removal of barriers among themselves provided for in those Agreements the flow of trade between the various countries of the Empire will be facilitated, and that by the consequent increase of purchasing power of their peoples the trade of the world will also be stimulated and increased;

Further, that this Conference regards the conclusion of these Agreements as a step forward which should in the future lead to further progress in the same direction and which will utilize protective duties to ensure that the resources and industries of the Empire are developed on sound economic lines.

The Agreements referred to are annexed hereto and the Conference commends them to the Governments of the several parts of the Empire.

B – Conference Conclusions

The Conference approved the above report, adopted the statements and resolutions contained therein, and commended them to the several Governments for their consideration.

VIII – CUSTOMS ADMINISTRATION

A – Report of Committee

The Committee submitted the following statement for the consideration of the Conference:

The Committee on Customs Administration is of the opinion that the aims to be kept in view should be:–

I. The avoidance of uncertainty as to the amount of duty which would be payable on the arrival of goods in the importing country:

II. The reduction of friction and delay to a minimum;

III. The provision of facilities for the expeditious and effective settlement of disputes relating to all matters affecting the application of the Customs Tariff.

It is also agreed that any measures which Customs Administrations may take to safeguard themselves against evasion should be consistent with these principles.

B – Conference Conclusions

The Conference approved the above Report and adopted the statement contained therein and commended them to the several Governments for their consideration.

IX. – COMMERCIAL RELATIONS WITH FOREIGN COUNTRIES

A – Report of Committee

At a meeting of the Heads of Delegations held on the 22nd of July a Committee was constituted to consider commercial relations with foreign countries as included in the provisional agenda in the following terms:–
'(a) Relation of inter-Imperial preferences to concessions to foreign countries;
(b) Interpretation of most-favoured-nation clause, particularly with reference to the development of regional preferences and of systems of import quotas.'

REPORT

The Committee considered two broad groups of questions affecting the commercial relations of the several members of the Commonwealth with foreign countries.

In the first place, the Committee discussed the general question of the relationship between intra-Commonwealth preferences and the most-favoured-nation clause in commercial treaties with foreign powers. Each Government will determine its particular policy in dealing with this matter, but the representatives of the various Governments on the Committee stated that it was their policy that no treaty obligations into which they might enter in the future should be allowed to interfere with any mutual preferences which Governments of the Commonwealth might decide to accord to each other, and that they would free themselves from existing treaties, if any, which might so interfere. They would, in fact, take all the steps necessary to implement and safeguard whatever preferences might be so granted.

In the second place, attention was drawn to recent tendencies in foreign countries to conclude regional agreements between themselves for the mutual accord of preferences which were designed as being exclusive, and not to be extended to countries which were not parties to, or did not adhere to the agreements. On this point, there was a general agreement that foreign countries which had existing treaty obligations to grant most-favoured-nation treatment to the products of particular parts of the Commonwealth could not be allowed to override such obligations by regional agreements of the character in question. Particular reference was made in this connection to the question of the Danubian States in regard to which preferential treatment was in contemplation for the cereal exports of the States concerned, – exports which constitute a substantial proportion of the world's exports of the cereals in question. The Committee were, however, informed that in the discussion which took place at Lausanne on the matter, the rights of third countries had, at the instance of the United Kingdom, been expressly reserved.

The Committee recognized that the fact that rights are accorded by most-favoured-nation treatment does not preclude a foreign country from seeking the consent of the various Governments of the British Commonwealth to the waiver of their rights in particular cases, and that these Governments must be guided by consideration of their individual interests in deciding whether or not to meet the wishes of the foreign country concerned, so long, however, as the general principal that rights of this kind cannot be arbitrarily withdrawn is fully and carefully preserved.

The Committee would, however, recommend that where two or more Commonwealth Governments share a common interest in any proposal for the waiver of particular treaty rights, they should consult together with a view to arriving, in so far as possible, at a common policy.

B – Conference Conclusions

The Conference approved the Report of the Committee and adopted the statement set forth in the Report appended thereto and commended them to the several Governments for their consideration.

'Textile Industry Reserves Opinion', *Montreal Gazette*, 23 August 1932.

TEXTILE INDUSTRY RESERVES OPINION
Suspend Judgment of Conference Till Revised Schedules Are Known
PROBE IS NOT FEARED
Industry Not Worried If Investigation Is Properly Carried Out, Statement Says

The Canadian Government's undertaking in review duties before the tariff board, as the result of the Imperial Conference, can give the Canadian textile industry no cause for apprehension, the Canadian cotton manufacturers declared yesterday in an official statement.

At the same time the proviso is made that such an investigation must be carried out with a comprehensive understanding of all the factors involved. Textile distribution costs in Canada must be considered. Also, the nature of competition offered by imported merchandise must be looked into, because it is said, British textile interests have been exporting into Canada at below United Kingdom production costs.

Final judgment, however, is reserved by the manufacturers pending publication of the full list of textile tariff revisions. The statement follows in part:

'Textiles occupied a prominence in the conference discussions out of all proportion of their importance in relation to opportunity for further expansion of trade between Canada and the United Kingdom, Commencing with the conference held in Montreal in June between representatives of the Canadian and Lancashire cotton industries, a continuous barrage of propaganda was maintained in an attempt to discredit the Canadian textile manufacturing Industry and prejudice Canadian public opinion on the subject of the importance at the Canadian market to British textile interests and the entry of British textiles into this market. Throughout the discussions at Ottawa the representatives of the cotton and wool industries of the United Kingdom maintained a very close contact with the official British delegation and a powerful section of the British press maintained that the success of the conferences would depend upon the measure of further tariff concessions granted to imports from Great Britain by the Canadian Government. It is obvious that the free trade interests of the United Kingdom centred their campaign upon textiles as representing a 'protected' industry in Canada, and as the basis of the broad international trading policy for Great Britain sponsored by these interests. The Canadian Government has not acceded to the British demand that the board should have mandatory powers. It would appear that first Canada has retained her national prerogative in this connection, and it remains now in determine by what measures the heard will undertake to investigation the efficiency of the Canadian textiles manufacturing industries and the extent and nature of the competition of British goods in this market. The domestic textile industries have no reason to fear such an investigation, provided it is carried out with a comprehensive understanding of all the factors that are involved. The cost of distribution of textiles in Canada must be surveyed as well as the nature of competition offered by imported merchandise. It is a well known fact that British textile manufacturers and merchants have been exporting large quantities of goods to Canada in recent years at prices below the fair market value and below the cost of production in United Kingdom. The basis of retail or consumer textile price levels in Canada must also be investigated to determine the stabilizing effect of primary domestic production on market conditions in this country, if all these factors are taken under consideration without prejudice of low-tariff influences the Canadian textile industry has no reason for apprehension as to the favorable outcome of such an inquiry. The main objection or criticism lies in the unsatisfactory trade conditions incidental to such an investigation.'

'Premier Disappointed: Taschereau Says Little Done For Lumber Industry', *Montreal Gazette*, 23 August 1932.

PREMIER DISAPPOINTED

Taschereau Says Little Done For Lumber Industry

Quebec, August 22 – To the Quebec lumber industry the results of the Imperial Economic Conference are 'far from satisfactory,' declared Premier L. A. Taschereau of Quebec in a statement today. 'What we in this province have been primarily interested in while the conference has been in progress is the lumber question. I must admit that as far as I see it, and I feel the opinion will be shared by the Quebec lumber industry, the result has been far from satisfactory. I am willing to admit that Premier R.B. Bennett and his colleagues did what they could, but they did not carry their point,' Premier Taschereau stated.

They were unable to agree as to the terms upon which Soviet lumber should enter Britain and the result has been that the decision rests alone in the hands of the British Government. It has been made clear by the British delegates that nothing can be accomplished regarding a possible embargo on Russian lumber for at least six months, when the existing British-Soviet trade agreement will expire.

'No doubt the Ottawa Government did its best, but we must take the facts as given out from the conference and they certainly indicate that with regard to the lumber question in which this province is most vitally interested, not much was accomplished.

I am afraid that the lumbermen of this province will not be pleased with the results. The great drawback which they face is the uncertainty in which they are placed. They want to know how they stand, especially with regard to this winter's output.

They also want to know what means the imperial Government intends to adopt to restrict the entry of Russian lumber into Britain. This we have not been told.

I don't want to criticise the Canadian Government. I suppose it obtained what it could with regard to this important question, but I do not think there is any room for the partisan press to crow over the existing uncertain situation with regard to the lumber industry of the Dominion.

As far as the other questions dealt with by the conference are concerned, I must frankly confess that I am not qualified to express an opinion. It needs an expert on the question of tariffs to understand exactly what they mean to Canada and Great Britain,' Premier Taschereau said.

'Ottawa Reactions', *Sydney Morning Herald*, 24 August 1932.

Sydney Morning Herald
OTTAWA REACTIONS.

Current criticisms of the Ottawa Conference agreements afford striking illustration of the difficulties which the conference itself found. There are the Labour extremists of this country who allege that the Federal Government has of 'malice prepense' ruined Australian manufacturing Industries and brought no benefit to our farmers; and the Labour extremists of Britain who declare that the whole performance is barren and nebulous. These critics must be suspected of having largely prepared their comments on the result before the conference had assembled. There are also some Country party spokesmen who assert, in effect, that the Federal Government has refused to reduce the Australian tariff, and consequently could not obtain sufficient benefits from Britain. Both these views betray crude ignorance of the powers of the Commonwealth Government, or any other, to bind itself to action which the community behind it would never accept. There is another very lively interest to be considered besides that of Australian secondary industries, which, where essential and economically efficient, are still assured of necessary protection. That is the interest in the British home market of British agricultural producers. The leading agricultural activity in Britain is the livestock industry, worth (first and last) some £200,000,000 a year, and it relies largely upon cheap oats, barley, and wheat for stock-feeding purposes. Those dominion producers and others who talk glibly about demanding protective duties on meat from Britain do not begin to appreciate the opposition (voicing demand for upkeep of prices) from the foremost and expanding primary industry of Britain's own people. The cry in Britain for cheap grain arises not solely from bread requirements, but also by reason of the importance of grainstuffs in animal husbandry.

Other critics of Ottawa raise their voices from both Britain and foreign quarters. In Britain, apart from the alertly watchful farmers, intent upon protecting their market prices (and therefore preferring a quota of imports to any taxation), the Liberal section of the Cabinet and the Liberal newspapers dare not approve of the inauguration of a system of regulated Empire trade. Their antagonism to what British representatives have done arises from the fact that they cannot approve of it without abandoning the article of political belief which mainly distinguishes them from the Conservatives. Inevitably the comment now runs that if Liberal Ministers can still remain in the National Cabinet then they have ceased to be Liberals. The dilemma is unfortunate for them, but they must have foreseen the day when finally they would have to make their choice. The form of attack is taking the line that the British Government has now thrown away its chance of preaching freer trade at the coming world conference. The obvious answer is that made recently when the import duties were imposed – that Britain has been for years preaching freer trade to the world, while the world has remained unmoved, and seems attentive only to obligation to make some bargain about the matter. American decrying of the Ottawa results is natural, but will mislead none of those concerned in the conference. There are few more significant signs than the determined refusal of party leaders in the United States to discuss the coming world economic conference at all until after the presidential elections.

As for our own agreement with Britain at Ottawa, the full detail of it has yet to be known, though from the published statements it should, all things considered, be regarded as a highly satisfactory achievement. There are two secrets still kept. One is 'the 'formula representing the absolute maximum of restriction by Britain upon foreign meat imports without causing a dislocation of the market.' This is being withheld in order to prevent any rushing of foreign supplies to Britain. The other is the 'undisclosed formula under which Britain will receive increased preferences in Australia on a wide range of commodities.' The Government will not wait for a report from the Tariff Board before adjusting British preference margins in accordance with this formula. Inadvertently Mr. Bruce's statement of the agreement on this point was misprinted by the 'Herald' on Monday, and the word 'not' was dropped. Minor adjustments, therefore, will be made over practically the whole tariff schedule, either immediately Parliament meets or as soon as the Minister for Customs returns. Thereafter, in accordance with both the treaty and the Government's election policy, the Tariff Board will revise the tariff generally. The undertaking at Ottawa does not represent the discovery there for the first time that the Australian Customs tariff must be recast, 'Scientific revision' for the stimulation of efficiency in our industries, and specifically for the expansion of export trade and the encouragement of reciprocal agreements within the Empire, was clearly laid down as the Ministerial parties joint policy for the elections last December. Upon that policy the Ottawa treaty formula for British preference has been superimposed.

'The Riddle of Ottawa', *Adelaide Advertiser*, 24 August 1932.

THE RIDDLE OF OTTAWA

There is a conspicuous lack of agreement between those students of political economy who, from Dan to Beersheba, have been peering so eagerly into the future, in the hope of finding out in advance how the agreements reached at the Ottawa Conference will influence the course of world trade. There can be little dispute about the excellence of the intentions of the politicians and permanent officials who framed these agreements. They were acutely conscious of the danger inherent in every attempt arbitrarily to control the vast economic forces that have got so much out of hand in the past two or three years. They realised the folly of any scheme designed to benefit the British Commonwealth at the cost of the world at large; and may be credited with having done their best to frame an Empire policy tending to stimulate international trade over the widest possible area. To what extent they have succeeded, it is still difficult to guess. Even among opinions which should at least be impartial, some are flatly contradictory. The Berlin newspaper 'Vossiche Zeltung.' for example, says that 'the Ottawa Conference has for the first time successfully interrupted the tendency to spilt the international market into atoms.' Certain French newspapers, on the other hand, true to their disinclination to agree with anybody about anything, speak resentfully of the erection of 'a Customs barrier isolating the Empire from the rest of the world.' One organ of Parisian opinion goes so far as to say that England plans a vast colonial economic zollverein, which, if it is successful, must force the other nations to band together in self defence, and so destroy the League of Nations. If Ottawa has at least weakened some of the barriers of economic nationalism, can it be equally true that the agreements by which this great good has been accomplished, are calculated further to obstruct world trade?

A possible answer to the question is supplied by the New York 'Times.' It can hardly be denied that, in the words of this notable American newspaper, the agreements reached at Ottawa – which have as their basis the exchange of tariff preferences between the members of a group of protectionist countries for a term of five years – are 'one further step by Britain away from her historic policy of Free Trade.' And 'It may prove that, although she has done something to bind the Empire together, losses elsewhere will overbalance this gain.' Speculations of this kind go to the root of the long-continued and violent contention on the fiscal question which, in normal times, is the distinguishing feature of British politics. Has Britain most to gain from Free Trade or Protection? The 'Manchester Guardian,' still adhering to its traditional Cobdenism, declares that 'the Ottawa agreements will be looked back upon as one of the most disastrous episodes in

British economic policy, not merely because of their one-sidedness, but mainly, perhaps, because of their effect in preventing a general reduction of tariffs.' This is a point of view which must be thought to have some validity for Australia also. At what general level the tariff wall will stand in this country, after the promises made at Ottawa have been redeemed, it is difficult to estimate; but, whether or not the Ottawa scheme takes us any nearer to the now equally distant and desirable goal of a 'scientific tariff,' it is clearly designed to ensure a virtual halt for five years.

In itself, this is not a particularly pleasant prospect. Even those Australians with the most tolerant views about Protection, had come to regard as almost inevitable a necessarily slow but continuous reformative effort directed to the entire remodelling of our tariff system on rational lines. As a result of Ottawa, we are invited to expect, for the most part, 'minor adjustments' exactly consonant with 'existing policy.' Just what this means, no one who is not sworn to secrecy is in a position to say. The Tariff Board, it seems, is to be restored to that important place in the fiscal system which it was originally intended to occupy. But we cannot yet foresee the consequences of its being empowered to declare, without the risk of being subsequently over-ridden by interested politicians – as seems to have been promised by Mr. Bruce at Ottawa – what ought to be the maximum protection afforded to Australian manufactures against their British rivals. The agreement stipulates that the duties imposed on imports shall not be such as to deny British firms 'a full opportunity of reasonable competition, on the basis of the relative costs of economic, efficient production, provided that, in the application of this principle, special consideration may be given to industries not fully established.' Why Mr. Bruce should have had so much difficulty, as related in our columns today, in substituting 'may' for 'shall' in this last proviso, and why the British delegates were eager that it should be obligatory upon Australia to give special consideration to what have been sardonically described as our 'backyard industries.' is one of the minor mysteries of the negotiations. Time may be expected to clarify much that is now obscure; nor are our manufacturers alone in their eagerness to see the dark passages of the agreement made plain. Wheat-growers, for example, are sadly perplexed about the preferential duty intended for their benefit. If that part of the Australian crop exported to Britain is to yield a price above world parity, what pool, or what merchant, is to be permitted to enter this desirable market, or, if the proceeds of the promised British duty are to be equally divided, on what principle, and by what agency, is the rule of equity to be preserved? This difficulty has doubtless been foreseen, and, in any event, an attempt will have to be made to overcome it; but how?

'The Harvest of Ottawa', *Economist* (27 August 1932), p. 379.

THE HARVEST OF OTTAWA.

IT may, or may not, be unfair to accuse the statesmen lately assembled at Ottawa of the intention deliberately to mystify the public as to the fruits of their negotiations. Whether hasty drafting be pleaded in defence, or whether the British delegation, conscious of their initial optimistic declarations, felt uncomfortably aware, as they surveyed the concrete results of Imperial affection, that 'there's beggary in the love that can be reckoned,' the fact remains that the Ottawa agreements, summarised on a later page of our present issue, yield a significantly 'dusty answer' to those who seek for certainties in the shape of solid economic advantage. There is so much in the way of ambiguous phraseology, so much detail to be filled in where glaring gaps obtrude, that it is still impossible finally to appraise the harvest reaped at this lime-lit conference. Yet this may be said: the draft agreements, incomplete as they are, reveal sufficient indications of the trend of the concerted policy to warrant the conclusion that, from the standpoint of particular British interests and that of the world advantage alike, much more has been lost than has been gained.

Let us endeavour, without partiality or fiscal prejudice, to see what can be set down on the credit side of the Ottawa ledger. It is to the good, admittedly, that the educative experience of this Conference has exploded finally the futile delusions of the Empire Free Trade campaign; that, notwithstanding heated weeks of haggling and log-rolling, an accord of sorts has been patched up whereon the conception of Imperial economic unity may still, however precariously, repose; and that, above all, Great Britain has not been forced completely to abandon her ability to maintain at least the position of being, potentially, a low-tariff country. For these mercies we are duly grateful; but, when all is said, there is little enough comfort to be derived from such negative blessings. Positively – and this is the real test – the Conference, as we see it, has failed utterly to realise its only worthwhile objective – the expansion, as opposed to the mere diversion, of trade.

On the barren question, which side – Britain or the Dominions – has 'won,' we do not propose to dwell unduly. Until we know precisely what Dominion duties are to be altered in our favour, it is difficult to assess the value of even the limited 'concessions,' which we have apparently been promised. Given perpetuance of restrictive tariffs, it is something that our industrialists should have the right to a hearing before Dominion tariff boards. Indeed, if the tariff boards act impartially and their recommendations are adopted by Dominion parliaments, we may find that a check is to some extent imposed on the upward march of tariffs against British goods. At the same time, the agreed principle of compensatory tariffs (with 'infant industry' reservations) is in itself a denial of the only sound conception of specialised international exchanges of goods; and we have still to be convinced that the proclaimed 'opening' of the Dominion markets to British manufactures will have more than a trivial effect on employment in this country. Yet, as a price for these doubtful gains, we have assumed a fiscal burden, and surrendered our own negotiating power, for a lengthy period and to a far from negligible extent. We are pledged, over the wide range of our existing tariff, to maintain for five years a 10 per cent. preference in the Dominions' favour, with the single reservation that in the case of dairy produce our domestic agriculturists, after three years, may be granted fiscal shelter even against Empire producers. Our diminishing free list is further curtailed by the imposition of duties on foreign wheat, copper, linseed and one special type of maize. On a number of commodities our existing duties are to be raised in order to give greater Imperial preference. In the case of meat and (subject to the Pig Commission's findings) bacon, we are committed to the pernicious folly of import quotas, combined with approval of producers' cartellisation at the exporting end.

Thus, irresistibly generous or naively 'had for a mug,' the British Government has gone some way to turn this country fatally into a high-price, high-cost island, in return for promises whose implementation is questionable and whose value, at best, is far from substantial. It has had, on any showing, the worst of the bargain. But this is not the gravamen of the real count against Ottawa. Weighty though the objections may be against the perpetuation and extension, to which we are committed, of our present sweeping tariff, the British Government can still plead successfully that, with certain exceptions, it is free to negotiate reciprocal arrangements with foreign countries on the basis, at any rate, of mutual 10 per cent. duties, thus establishing a minimum standard of fiscal decency. Equally, it can argue that, save for the almost prohibitive proposed copper duty and the tariff on linseed, its new excursions into preferences may not seriously affect British costs. For example, the wheat duty, unless Canada establishes a cast-iron selling pool (and the preference is conditional on sales at the 'world price'), will probably hurt the British consumer as little as it benefits the Canadian producer; and the proportion of 'flat white' maize in our total maize imports is inconsiderable. In these instances and, it may prove – when the 'programme' is published – in the case of meat also, the practical results may turn out to be less harmful (and equally less profitable to any vested Dominion interest) than the essentially vicious principle set up. Where the real failure of Ottawa lies is in the total absence of any vindication of the truth that economic progress is to be sought in the general lowering of tariff barriers. Nowhere in the agreements – and our judgment is confirmed by Mr Bennett's loudly Protectionist exultation – do we detect any evidence that the Dominions have modified in essentials their adherence to the policy of high protective tariffs. Where 'general' tariffs are to be altered, they are actually to be raised.

This said, there is little to be added. When silence falls on the nauseating symphony of Imperial wind-instruments braying 'triumphal success,' the Ottawa agreements stand as the limited achievement in £. s. d. bargains realisable by Great Britain in negotiation with an Empire resolutely determined to protect its own manufacturing industries. They involve, on the one hand, the likelihood of some damage both to our own interests as a food and raw material importing country and to those of our important foreign customers whose goods, to some extent, are to be excluded from this market. On the other hand, though the relatively restricted scope of the agreements may comfort those who feared that Ottawa might seek to create an Empire ringed universally by an impenetrable tariff wall against the outer world, the mere fact that Great Britain has refused, for the most part, to impose, for preferential purposes, inordinate duties, is scant solace to those who hoped that the Conference might justify Mr Baldwin's promise that it would give a lead to 'freer trade' throughout a tariff-ridden world. Stripped of their equivocal verbiage – the British right to sales at 'world prices,' the Dominions' right to 'reasonable' protection, the agreement to prohibit imports frustrating 'by State action' the proposed preferences – all of which is likely to involve acrimonious controversy hereafter, the Ottawa agreements in substance are narrow and sterile. As a prelude to the World Economic Conference (at Ottawa the bond of sentiment was surely a factor not to be paralleled at Geneva) they are a bitter disappointment. For, if the verdict may be summarised in a sentence, the only visible result of Ottawa is that the Empire has, in part, been humbugged and, in part, so far as concerns Britain's power to pursue policies of fiscal sanity, ham-strung.

'An Ottawa Impression', *Economist* (3 September 1932), pp. 421–2.

AN OTTAWA IMPRESSION.
(BY OUR SPECIAL CORRESPONDENT.)

OTTAWA, August 22.

THE tumult and the shouting dies. Armed with red coats and large revolvers, Royal Canadian Mounted Policemen, whose want both of mounts and of Stetson hats must have been a great disappointment to some of Ottawa's visitors, still guard a remnant of delegates. But the Château Laurier, for a month achoke with Ministers, secretaries, experts, lobbyists and newspaper men, has reverted in a few hours to its usual summer rôle of momentary home for commercial travellers and American tourists. Ottawa has that 'morning after' feeling, sick with a surfeit of too much official and unofficial entertainment and of reflected glory from a multitude of the Empire's great men assembled in one of the smaller of its cities.

Of the feelings of the departing great one can only guess the gist. That the British delegates were glad to be quit of Ottawa, despite their official expressions of gratitude and regret, and despite the unstinted hospitality with which they were treated by Government and private citizens alike, their mien on departure bore eloquent testimony. The weather, though too hot for some of them, had been fine; it was the Conference that had been stormy, and the thunders not of Jove but of Dominion statesmen that had drawn the lines of care and weariness on their foreheads. The most enthusiastic Imperialists among them return the most disillusioned and disheartened, while the more sceptical, never having expected much, are not disappointed, but instead profess an enlargement of their hopes. Whatever diversion of trade the Ottawa Conference proves to have caused, it has been but a faltering step towards the ambition of Imperial economic unity which Mr Chamberlain has inherited from his father, 'whose almost inspired vision,' declared Mr Bennett at the closing session, 'made possible to-day the realisation of his hopes.' The sting, perhaps, was in the 'almost'; at least it is certain that Mr Joseph Chamberlain must have turned many times in his grave as the haggling arguments proceeded here, sometimes between Messrs. Chamberlain and Bennett their worthy selves.

The leading financial paper of Canada appears this week (having gone to press before the Conference concluded) with the headline 'Conference Amazed at Britain's Refusal to Put Empire First.' The exchange of the like politenesses between the press of the Dominions and the Mother Country has, of course, been one of the more entertaining, if less fortunate, features of the Conference, but one can say with fairness that, on the contrary, the Conference was nearly wrecked on the Canadian Government's determination to stick to 'Canada First.' There was a moment, halfway through the Conference, when it seemed that Mr Bennett would have to face the failure of the Conference to achieve any agreement between Canada and the United Kingdom (with all the political consequences which such an exposure of his responsibility would have meant for him and his party) or, if he chose, to split his Cabinet and party by plunging for a policy of lower tariffs, and seeking his support rather in the West and among the farmers than in the East among the industrial elements of the country. But the show-down was never forced, and in the end a compromise emerged, in which, while Canada conceded some immediate advantages and a principle whose working out may or may not prove satisfactory to British industry, she did not go far enough to justify the grant of more than a portion of Mr Bennett's original demands. The timber industry, for instance, wanted a tariff of 20 per cent., and at least a quota on Russian imports; what it got was a guarantee of the continuance of the actual 10 per cent. preference and a generally worded undertaking to deal with frustration of the preference through State action on the part of any foreign country, if and when it occurs. The most curious item in the agreement, from the political point of view, is the duty of 2s. a quarter to be imposed on foreign wheat imported in Great Britain, with the proviso that the duty will be repealed if Empire supplies are not made available at world prices. Representatives of the grain producers of Canada were almost unanimous in their agreement with those of Australia that neither preference nor quota could really help an industry dependent on foreign countries for markets, even if Great Britain were to buy the whole of her requirements within the Empire; presumably, then, all that the preference can do, in the eyes of the wheat farmers themselves, is to secure an uneconomic diversion of trade and render competition with foreign producers all the more keen in non-British markets. Yet up it bobs in the Ottawa agreements, apparently for one reason alone, that Mr. Bennett dared not go back to the farmers of the Western prairies and confess that his long-boasted plans for the amelioration of their lot had come to nothing because, on examination, they had been shown to be worthless.

There were those who hoped, a few weeks ago, that the Canadian Prime Minister would take for himself the rôle of the Man Who Made the Ottawa Conference. An autocrat by nature, he has on occasion in the past taken bold steps in the face of opposition from within his own camp, and he was capable, if any Conservative leader was, of playing Sir Robert Peel in Canada's political drama. But the hopeful were disappointed. Tribute must be paid to the navigational skill with which Mr Bennett negotiated the straits between the outright failure of the Conference and the resignation of part of his Cabinet, but his was the course of compromise rather than of courage. Moreover, the compromise was achieved, not by splitting the difference, but by blurring it. To what lobbying, to what quarrels between Dominion and Mother Country, have we not to look forward over the clause relating to State action in frustration of preferences, intended as it is by the two parties to the agreement to mean quite different things? What prospect is there that Messrs. Cahan and Ryckman and their fellow high-protectionists in the Canadian Cabinet will be content to let the new Tariff Board operate with genuine independence or even be manned with any but those of their own opinion? And what variety of practical interpretations could not be placed on the phrases' industries which are reasonably assured of sound opportunities for success,' 'full opportunity of reasonable competition,' 'relative cost of economical and efficient production,' 'industries not fully established,' which appear in the compromise-beaten formula on which British industry is to rely for the future of its markets in Canada? Perhaps even the expression 'protection by tariffs' is susceptible of *double entendre*. Those who recall that Imperial sentiment and blood ties did not prevent the trade agreement between the New Zealand Government and Mr Mackenzie King's Administration, later denounced by Mr Bennett, from heralding a two years' tariff war between the two Dominions are inclined to wonder whether the cement with which, our tariff enthusiasts assure us, the Ottawa Conference has bound the members of the British Commonwealth in ever faster union will not prove after all to be dynamite.

In the topical discussions over food taxes, dumping, tariff boards, quotas, preferences and so forth it tends to be forgotten that the greatest innovation that the Ottawa Conference has wrought is the commitment of the United Kingdom, through inter-Governmental agreements having the form of treaties, to maintain specific rates of duty for a period of years. We have treaties, it is true, pledging us to much more serious obligations, with which no one would quarrel on the point of political principle; but in foreign policy proper we have managed to maintain a great measure of continuity between successive Governments, partly because these affairs touch only remotely and hypothetically on the daily lives of the people. We have, too, a large number of commercial treaties with foreign countries; but they are couched in general terms and do not pledge us to tax ourselves in any specific manner. Even the undertaking of Mr Baldwin's first Government in 1923 to impose certain duties for the sake of the corresponding Empire preferences was conditioned by the reservation of budgetary liberty. That birthright, the freedom of every Parliament to tax the people it represents as it pleases, we have sold for a mess of promises. That is not a very apt way of encouraging a hesitant Opposition to place their faith in the Imperial ideal.

It would have been entertaining and valuable to have organised simultaneously an Imperial Economic Conference at which the Parliamentary Oppositions and not the Governments of the several members of the British Commonwealth would have been represented. It is not obvious what line the rump of the Labour Parties of Australia and New Zealand would have taken, though presumably Mr Scullin might have assumed the part of Mr Bennett as the confirmed protectionist reluctant even at the point of threats to reduce local tariffs. With Mr Cosgrave in Mr O'Kelly's chair, of course, the whole face of the relations (which publicly were non-existent) between the two Mother Countries would have been changed. The Nationalist Opposition in India was actually represented, but in that country there is always a powerful opposition to the Left of every Parliamentary party, and, in spite of their satisfaction both at their bargain and at their treatment as spokesmen of an equal nation, the Indian delegation doubtless go home to face bitter opposition from conscientious objectors to Imperial preference. General Smuts might have gone a little further in granting tariff concessions to the United Kingdom, but it would have been in the monetary deliberations that his substitution for Mr Havenga would have given South Africa's defence of the gold standard at least moral support for his own natural conservatism. What Mr Mackenzie King could have done would have depended on whether the starting point was the present or the previous Canadian budget, for in no public pronouncement before the Conference did the leader of the Opposition pledge the Liberal Party definitely to go beyond the Dunning schedule, to which, it is stated in some rather optimistic quarters, the Canadian tariff will approximate after the specific changes are carried out and the Tariff Board has had its say. As for the Opposition in Great Britain, what is its Imperial economic policy? Let us hope that there will be a positive answer, for these are not days in which purely negative criticism will restore the world, the Commonwealth included, to economic sanity.

COPYRIGHTS AND PERMISSIONS

R. Giffen, 'Commercial Union between the UK and its Colonies' (BT memo, 1891), PRO, CAB 37/29/7. Reproduced with permission from the National Archives (Kew, Surrey).

R. Giffen, 'The Relative Growth of Free Trade and Protection,' 25 May 1892, Gladstone Papers, BL, Add. MS 44258 fol. 282. Reproduced with permission from the British Library, London.

Memorandum on Terminating the Belgian and German Commercial Treaties, 10 June 1897, PRO, CAB 37/44/26. Reproduced with permission from the National Archives (Kew, Surrey).

'Commercial Diplomacy 1860–1902', PRO, T 172/945. Reproduced with permission from the National Archives (Kew, Surrey).

J. A Hobson, *The Fruits of American Protection* (London: Cassell,1907), pp. 9–11. Copyright © estate of J. A. Hobson.

'Tariff Reform in Canada', *Nation*, 20 August 1910, pp. 725–6. Copyright © W. G. Foyle Ltd., reproduced with permission.

Foreign Office Note of Invitation from the French Ambassador for British Government to Participate in an Economic Conference in Paris, 10 February 1916; Foreign Minister Edward Grey's Memorandum on British Participation in Paris Economic Conference, 11 February 1916, PRO, CAB 37/142/29. Reproduced with permission from the National Archives (Kew, Surrey).

Confidential Correspondence between Edward Grey and Sir Francis Villiers, British Ambassador to Belgium, 6 March 1916 and 5 April 1916; Considered Views of Interdepartmental Committee to Consider Dependence of the British Empire on the United States, October 1916; Confidential Cabinet Report of the Foreign Office on the Interdepartmental Committee to Consider the Dependence of the British Empire on the United States, 31 October 1916, PRO, CAB

37/158/3. Reproduced with permission from the National Archives (Kew, Surrey).

J. A. Hobson, 'The New Protectionism', *War and Peace*, 3:31 (April 1916), pp. 104–5. Copyright © estate of J. A. Hobson.

Commercial Correspondence between Edward Grey and Sir Francis Villiers, British Ambassador to Belgium, 27 June 1916, PRO, CAB 37/150. Reproduced with permission from the National Archives (Kew, Surrey).

Report on the American Press's Response to the Paris Conference, June 1916, PRO, CAB 37/152. Reproduced with permission from the National Archives (Kew, Surrey).

Confidential Telegram from Sir Conyngham Greene (British Ambassador to Japan) to Edward Grey (Foreign Minister) regarding Japanese Participation in the Paris Economic Conference, 27 June 1916, PRO, CAB 37/154/7. Reproduced with permission from the National Archives (Kew, Surrey).

A. Stanley, 'Economic Desiderata in the Terms of Peace', February 1917; Secret Report on Economic and Non-Territorial Desiderata, Committee on Terms of Peace, Imperial War Cabinet, April 1917; Memorandum by the Board of Trade on Economic Considerations Affecting the Terms of Peace, November 1918, PRO, CAB 29/1.

Reed Smoot, 'Our Tariff and the Depression', *Current History*, 35:2 (November 1931), pp. 173–81. Copyright © estate of Reed Smoot.

'Trade Agreements or Free Trade?', *Review of the River Plate* (Buenos Aires, Argentina), 29 July 1934, translated by UK Embassy, Buenos Aires, PRO, BT 11/824. Reproduced with permission from the National Archives (Kew, Surrey).

Report of the Committee on the Proposed Imperial Economic Conference at Ottawa, 23 November 1931, PRO, DO 35/236/12. Reproduced with permission from the National Archives (Kew, Surrey).

'Memorandum of a Conversation with the [Canadian] Prime Minister on Friday, March 11th, Concerning Agenda for the Imperial Conference', 14 March 1931; Letter from the High Commissioner for the United Kingdom in Ottawa to Sir Edward Harding (Under Secretary of State for Dominions), 17 March 1932, PRO, PREM 1/112, nos. 5, 15. Reproduced with permission from the National Archives (Kew, Surrey).

Minutes of the Fourth Meeting at the Board of Trade with Industrial Advisors [Motor Trade Representatives] Prior to the Ottawa Imperial Economic Conference, 3 June 1932; Memorandum by Industrial Advisors Representing the British Trades Union Congress on the Imperial Economic Conference, 8 August 1932, PRO, CAB 21/364. Reproduced with permission from the National Archives (Kew, Surrey).

Notes on the Cotton Delegation in a Letter from the High Commissioner for the United Kingdom in Ottawa to G. G. Whiskard (Dominions Office), 15 June 1932, PRO, CAB 21/367. Reproduced with permission from the National Archives (Kew, Surrey).

Secret Note by the United Kingdom Delegation on the Canadian Tariff Proposals, 8 August 1932; Most Secret Report of a (UK) Delegation Meeting at Ottawa on the Australian and New Zealand Negotiation and a Duty on Meat, 15 August 1932, PRO, CAB 21/363. Reproduced with permission from the National Archives (Kew, Surrey).

J. G. Coates (Leader of the New Zealand Reform Party) to Stanley Baldwin, 8 August 1932, PRO, CAB 21/365. Reproduced with permission from the National Archives (Kew, Surrey).

Selections from the Ottawa Agreement, August 1932, PRO, DO 35/242/6. Reproduced with permission from the National Archives (Kew, Surrey).

'The Riddle of Ottawa', *Adelaide Advertiser*, 24 August 1932. Copyright © The Advertiser, reproduced with permission.

For Product Safety Concerns and Information please contact our EU representative GPSR@taylorandfrancis.com Taylor & Francis Verlag GmbH, Kaufingerstraße 24, 80331 München, Germany

Printed and bound by CPI Group (UK) Ltd, Croydon, CR0 4YY
08/05/2025
01864526-0004